Advance Praise for

Lights, Camera, Campaign!

"Placing political advertising in the broader context of traditional media and pop culture, this wide-ranging and creative set of readings fills a gap in the literature. Its breezy style and current examples will engage students, luring them into its more sophisticated substance."

Steve Frantzich,
Professor, Department of Political Science, U.S. Naval Academy

"David A. Schultz's edited collection of essays is an indispensable resource for scholars interested in campaign advertising. Dr. Schultz has assembled an impressive assortment of scholars, all of whom offer significant and timely observations about campaign advertising in the new millennium. The authors address stalwart topics, including the use of media consultants, the effects of negative advertisements, and the impact of network news election projections. But the book really shines when it addresses novel topics including the rise of Spanish-language campaign advertisements, the increasing importance of late-night talk shows in presidential campaigns, and how American campaign advertising compares to that in Canada. All in all, the book is a fascinating look at the world of campaign advertising, and one that deserves a broad audience."

Anthony J. Nownes,
Associate Professor of Political Science, University of Tennessee

Lights, Camera, Campaign!

Popular Politics
& Governance
In America

Steven E. Schier
General Editor

Vol. 11

PETER LANG
New York • Washington, D.C./Baltimore • Bern
Frankfurt am Main • Berlin • Brussels • Vienna • Oxford

LIGHTS, CAMERA, CAMPAIGN!

Media, Politics, and Political Advertising

Edited by David A. Schultz

PETER LANG
New York • Washington, D.C./Baltimore • Bern
Frankfurt am Main • Berlin • Brussels • Vienna • Oxford

Library of Congress Cataloging-in-Publication Data

Lights, camera, campaign!: media, politics, and political advertising /
edited by David A. Schultz.
p. cm. — (Popular politics and governance in America ; vol. 11)
Includes bibliographical references (p.) and index.
1. Advertising, Political—United States. 2. Television in politics—United
States. 3. Political campaigns—United States. I. Schultz, David A. (David
Andrew). II. Series: Popular politics & governance in America ; v. 11.
JF2112.A4L54 2004   324.7'3'0973—dc22   2004005492
ISBN 0-8204-6831-2
ISSN 1529-241X

Bibliographic information published by **Die Deutsche Bibliothek**.
Die Deutsche Bibliothek lists this publication in the "Deutsche
Nationalbibliografie"; detailed bibliographic data is available
on the Internet at http://dnb.ddb.de/.

Cover design by Dutton & Sherman Design

The paper in this book meets the guidelines for permanence and durability
of the Committee on Production Guidelines for Book Longevity
of the Council of Library Resources.

Printed in the United States of America

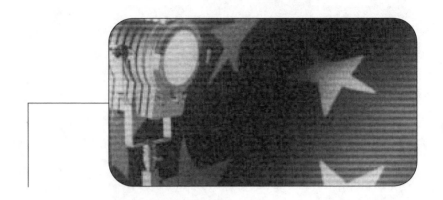

Table of Contents

Note to the Reader

Please visit the web site for *Lights, Camera, Campaign! Media, Politics, and Political Advertising.* At this site are many of the political commercials and ads that are discussed in this book.

The web site is located at http://davidschultz.efoliomn2.com. Click on the tab with the title of the book *Lights, Camera, Campaign! Media, Politics, and Political Advertising.* When it asks for the user, enter "student" and then enter "campaign" for the password.

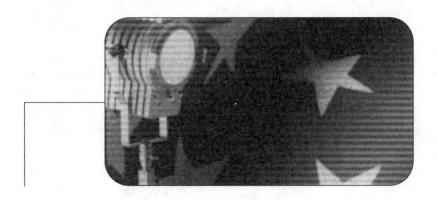

Introduction
Selling Candidates and Soap

David A. Schultz

Political advertising is a ubiquitous feature of contemporary American campaigns and elections. While it is hard for many to remember a time when political ads on television did not dominate campaigns and elections, it was not always the case that campaigns and candidates were made for television events. Using political ads as a primary vehicle or tool in elections is a relatively recent phenomenon.

Campaigning has always been a part of elections and also the primary way candidates run for office. When many think of what they would most like to see in campaigns, perhaps images of the Lincoln-Douglas debates come to mind. Such a vision depicts candidates locked in face-to-face debate with one another, articulating their position on the issues. This image of campaigning also depicts candidates as engaging the public, shaking their hands, going door to door, or meeting the voters in various town forums. While such campaigning may still exist today at the local level in some communities—or perhaps even in places like the Iowa caucuses or the New Hampshire primaries for the presidential race—for the most part the days when the public gets face time with candidates belong to a halcyon past. Contrary to the Simon and Garfunkel line in their song "Mrs. Robinson," we no longer go to the candidate debate on a Sunday afternoon.

Candidates come to voters today predominately through political ads on television. Political advertising can make or break a candidate. Ads that define candidates, attack opponents, and relay messages that set tones or that otherwise define critical issues are central to campaigns and elections at the national and state level. They are also increasingly becoming even more important at the local level in many communities.

The use of paid advertising to communicate with the public is a relatively recent phenomenon. Perhaps it started in 1952 when Rossier Reeves teamed up with Dwight Eisenhower to do a series of political ads depicting average voters asking the candidate questions as part of a larger campaign called "Eisenhower Answers America." Yet from these humble origins what has changed the nature of running for office is television.

Television and running for office are particularly suited for one another. Television's need to tell a story, to personalize lives, to define good versus evil—or David versus Goliath—is great drama that sells advertising and generates revenue. Television is all about name recognition: It is about using niche marketing, demographics, and survey data to create images that are appealing and will capture market shares and sell products (Hamilton 2004). And television has been hugely successful in what it has done. Today many more people recognize Mr. Clean, Ronald McDonald, the Tidy Bowl Man, Mr. Whipple, Betty Crocker, Tony the Tiger, and the Pillsbury Doughboy than recognize their neighbors or public officials. Lines from commercials such as "I can't believe I ate the whole thing," "You deserve a break today," "Where's the beef?" and "I'd like to teach the world to sing" are staples of American pop culture, recognizable and familiar across generations. Television is the great democratic force, reaching into every living room in America.

Similarly, campaigns are perfectly suited for television. Campaigns have traditionally been about telling stories, defining good versus bad, us versus them, and the underdog versus the favorite. Candidates seek name recognition, access to voters and also want to tailor their message to the variegated constituencies that make up their electorate. Campaigns seek catchy phrases and images to identify candidates, hoping that buzz words or themes such as "Morning in America" or other similar slogans will resonate with voters. For the most part, the similarity in themes or scripts with both running a successful campaign and producing good television are remarkable, making television a natural home for candidates to sell themselves to the American public.

But the sheer size of the United States, both in population and geography, or within many states for that matter, renders personal campaigns impractical. It would be impossible to meet all the voters, speak with them personally, or attend enough town forums to reach everyone. But even if candidates could, the reality is that most Americans do not go to debates, attend town forums, or show up at political stump speeches. Instead, the average voter can best be reached in her living room, through her television, in much the same way that McDonald's, Coke, and other advertisers reach their customers. Politics is thus in competition with the rest of popular culture for the attention of the American voter. It is a noisy, crowded competition, necessitating that candidates often ape themes from pop culture in order to cut through the crowd.

Politics today occurs through television and political advertising more often than it does in any other fashion. It is from television that voters often learn much about candidates. While the public may deny the impact or efficacy of political ads, there is no question that hundreds of millions of dollars are spent on these ads and that voters literally see hundreds if not thousands of these ads during an election season. The irony is that many voters are receiving important information and images about candidates, issues, and political parties from the very ads that are often disparaged.

Indications of the scope of political advertising come in many ways. The Alliance for Better Campaigns, a Washington-based non-partisan organization that monitors the broadcast industry and television coverage of politics, reported that in 1982, sale of political ads brought in a little over $200 million in ad revenue (Alliance 2000). By 2000, local television stations took in over $1 billion from the sale of political ads. Even after adjusting for inflation, this is still a fourfold increase in ad revenue. In the first seven months of 2000, the top 75 media markets took in over $211 million from political ads. Put into perspective, of the estimated $4 billion spent in total on national, state and local campaigns in 2000, 25% of that money was spent on political ads.

Projections are that $1.6 billion will be spent on political advertising in 2004, up from the $1.2 billion spent in 2002 (McConnell 2004). As of the 2004 Iowa caucuses, $3.8 million had been spent on political ads, with presidential candidates Howard Dean and John Kerry each spending in excess of $2 million in Iowa alone. All told, political ads for the 2004 Iowa caucuses averaged to more than $90 per caucus voter (Wisconsin Advertising Project 2004).

If dollar amounts alone were not enough of an indication of how omnipresent political advertising on television has become, counting the actual number of ads should paint a clearer picture. In the top 75 media markets in 2000, nearly 287,000 political ads were run—the equivalent of 99 solid days of political advertising (Alliance 2000). Through December 31, 2003, almost 11,000 ads had been run in the Des Moines, Iowa, market, and by some estimates, as the January 19, 2004 Iowa caucuses got close, one could see up to 150 political ads per day on television (McConnell).

Finally, proof that political ads are a ubiquitous presence in campaigns lies in the fact that ads stand out and are remembered by viewers—as citizens—as surely as are ads by car companies, hamburger joints, and beer companies. Among the classics there is the famous "Daisy" ad from the 1964 presidential race where President Johnson had a little girl counting flower petals, only to have the commercial fade to a nuclear bomb detonation. This ad successfully used the fear of war to dissuade voters from voting for Barry Goldwater. In 1984, President Reagan's "Bear in the Woods" ad exploited fear of the Soviet Union, while his "Morning in America" depicted an optimistic American looking towards the future. In 1988, the "Willie Horton" ad exploited fear of crime and racism to depict Democrat Michael Dukakis as weak on crime, and more recently, ads in the 2000 New Hampshire presidential primary by a friend of George Bush derailed John McCain's campaign. These are just some of the ads that have been considered as memorable uses of television to craft images and affect voter perceptions.

The sheer number of ads, how much campaigns spend on advertising, and how much money television stations rake in from candidates all point to the new reality of campaigns and elections—they are in fact made-for-television events. No matter what the public or its critics may think, two facts stand out: (1) lots of time and money is spent on political ads, and (2) political strategists and candidates assume the money and time spent on these ads are worth it.

Every election cycle brings with it a new crop of political ads. Some stand out; some become classics, and some are dogs. This book seeks to ask and answer a simple question: What impact do political ads have on campaigns and elections? It explores the many facets of political advertising and television, seeking to assess the trends, issues, and forces that shape political ads and, in turn, what impact these ads have on voters, campaigns, and candidates. Through case studies, interviews, and analysis of specific campaigns and ads—predominately in the United States and to a lesser extent in Canada—the book seeks to develop a better understanding of how ads are constructed, why some work, why some fail, and what it is about political ads that allows them to make or break a campaign.

Of course, this is not the first book written on political communication or political advertising. Among recent books that have explored various aspects of political advertising and television are Diamond and Bates' *The Spot: The Rise of Political Advertising on Television* (1988), Jamieson and Waldman's *The Press Effect: Politicians, Journalists, and the Stories That Shape the Political World* (2003), and Thurber, Nelson, and Dulio's *Crowded Airwaves: Campaign Advertising in Elections* (2000). Similarly, Vanderbilt University's Television News Archive (*http://tvnews.vanderbilt.edu/*), the Julian P. Kanter Political Commercial Archive at the University of Oklahoma (*http://www.presidentsusa.net/ads.html*), and the University of Wisconsin Advertising Project (*http://polisci.wisc.edu/tvadvertising/*) have committed considerable resources to understanding television news and political advertising. The Pew Center for the People & the Press (*http://people-press.org/*) and the Annenberg School of Communication at the University of Southern California (*http://ascweb.usc.edu/home.php*) are major forces in the examination of the relationship among television, the media, and politics.

This book goes beyond traditional notions of exploring political advertising. It places political ads in the broader context of the media, politics, and popular culture. It not only looks at how political ads, along with traditional news, are used to affect voters, but it also broadens the discussion even further, looking at new trends in campaigns on television. For example, it looks at the rise of Spanish-language advertising as well as the rise of late-night television and talk shows as new phenomena in advertising. In many ways, the book looks at political ads as competing with traditional commercial ads and entertainment venues for audience attention and then asks what the implications are of this rivalry.

In Chapter 1, Arthur Sanders draws an analogy between political ads and the production of commercial ads. Opening with the now-omnipresent Verizon Wireless "Can you hear me now?" line, Sanders details what makes for a successful political ad, finding parallels between selling candidates and cell phones. A good political ad does four things: it provides drama, plays on familiar themes, focuses on people and not policy, and makes a simple appeal to the viewer. In addition, good ads must fit within the context of a campaign and must also contrast candidates as a choice between good and evil. Often times political ads can piggyback on successful commercial ads or themes (think of, for example, Walter Mondale stealing the

"Where's the beef?" line from a then-popular Wendy's commercial to attack Gary Hart as lacking substance during the 1984 presidential primaries). Yet while political ads share much in common with their commercial cousins, they also differ in one critical aspect: Commercial ads generally do not try to attack competitors in order to depress consumption. Instead, they seek to steal market share. Political ads, however, can benefit equally from stealing voters and by attacking candidates and seeking to discourage voters from showing up and voting for others.

Stephen Medvic examines the role of media consultants in Chapter 2. He notes how these consultants, along with pollsters, have become a mainstay of campaigns and elections. Their job is to develop effective communications strategies for candidates and to prime voters while at the same time combating voter fatigue and cynicism. With so many political ads being run, one choice of developing a good communications strategy is simply to run more—and louder—ads. Yet other strategies are revealed in this chapter, including how wedge issues and attack ads are developed and how to fashion spots that voters will watch and remember, especially when they are competing for attention from other venues.

Chapter 3 presents Christopher Dolan's examination of one of the "most hated phenomena in political advertising": negative or attack ads. He performs a careful dissection of political ads, seeking first to define what is meant by a negative ad, and then offers a defense of them as legitimate tools for making policy differences clear. Dolan concludes by indicating that negative ads are often fair and effective campaign tools and, despite their criticism, often work and fulfill an important role in elections.

Geoffrey Peterson turns in Chapter 4 to another issue that often receives attention: the reporting of early election results. Many criticized the networks for early—and what turned out to be incorrect—reporting of the results in Florida in 2000 (much in the same way television was criticized for calling Ronald Reagan's victory in 1980 over President Carter while West Coast polls were still open). The concern is not only whether early reporting of East Coast returns has an impact on presidential voting in California and elsewhere out west but whether it has an impact on local races out west. Fashioning a novel research design and experiment, the conclusion is that there is evidence to suspect that the reporting of early returns does, in fact, affect voters and local races. Clearly such results raise important public policy questions that pit fair elections against the First Amendment.

In Chapter 5, Christopher Cooper and H. Gibbs Knotts turn to the use of attack ads in gubernatorial campaigns. Their interest is to learn more about how and when these ads are used and why candidates go for a negative approach. Examining the 2000 races, they found Republicans were more likely to go negative than Democrats, that most negative ads appeared in August and September and peak in October, and that candidates in competitive races are more likely to go negative than those who are not in such races.

Brendan Doherty and Melissa Anderson review the rise of Spanish-language ads in Chapter 6. With the increase in the number of Latinos and Hispanics in the United States and in anticipation of these groups becoming a political force in elections, the authors look at how Bush, Gore and the major political parties used Spanish-language ads in the 2000 race. Different patterns in terms of geographic and temporal use of campaign resources distinguished how these ads were employed, while Republicans displayed a greater tendency to structure these ads to reach out to Latino voters. Yet curiously, neither Bush nor Gore seemed to address issues in these Spanish ads that mirrored survey results of what Latinos considered priorities.

Chapter 7 by Amy Jasperson details one of the more interesting and bizarre races and events in recent American politics—the plane crash and death of Senator Paul Wellstone, the coverage of his memorial service, and the impact this had on the public. Through extensive interviews, Jasperson charts the changing media campaign in the final days before the election, concluding that Wellstone's memorial service and the media's coverage of it had a major impact on Norm Coleman's eventual win over Walter Mondale, who had replaced Wellstone after his death.

Timothy Vercellotti's examination in Chapter 8 of the 2002 Elizabeth Dole–Erskine Bowles senate race in North Carolina looks at how political ads were used to package and depict candidates. Dole, having high name recognition, successfully used ads to describe who she was. More importantly, because of Bowles' low name recognition, her campaign was able to tie Bowles to Clinton and Monica Lewinsky. This chapter shows how political ads are not only important tools for describing oneself but also for describing an opponent, especially when the opponent is a relative unknown. Ads can therefore be labeling tools but are only effective in specific circumstances.

In Chapter 9, David Schultz looks at the rising importance of late-night talk shows in presidential and national campaigns. He ties their use to the merger of politics and entertainment, using Jesse Ventura as the prototypical example of a new type of candidate—the *politainer*—who is both entertainer and politician. Politainment is a new phenomenon in American politics. The success of Hillary Clinton in 2000, after appearing on the *Late Show with David Letterman,* and Arnold Schwarzenegger's successful launch of his 2003 gubernatorial bid on the *Tonight Show with Jay Leno,* are just two signs that late-night talk shows—through their jokes, candidate appearances, and audience market share—impact campaigns and elections.

Chapter 10 is an in-depth case study by David Schecter of the 2003 California gubernatorial recall of Gray Davis and the campaign of Arnold Schwarzenegger. If ever a campaign were media driven, this was it. Most voters in California received their political information from the mass media and political ads, and television and the celebrity status of the candidates clearly drove much of the coverage.

In Chapter 11, Paul Nesbitt-Larking and Jonathan Rose offer a contrast to American campaigns by comparing political ads in the United States to those in Canada. They see campaign ads as rooted in specific political cultures and practices, with Canadian ads bearing unique cultural and symbolic themes that distinguish them from those used in the United States. Despite how similar Canada and the United States are, the authors conclude that the border makes a difference in terms of themes and in regulatory practices toward political ads.

Finally, David King and David Morehouse ask in Chapter 12 whether too much money is being spent on political ads. They use the 2000 Gore race as a case study, exploring the impact his trip down the Mississippi River had on his campaign and support in the states and areas that border the river. They conclude that the personal visits from Gore certainly made a difference and speculate on what might have occurred had Gore taken other trips down the Ohio River and in Florida. Their chapter questions whether simply pumping more and more money into political ads is a wise strategy and whether it might not make sense to think about reallocation of some of the ad budget toward get-out-the-vote efforts or personal visits.

The various chapters in this book show how political ads increasingly are driven by specialized media consultants and pollsters, who see them as important tools to define images of their candidates and opponents. These ads, including negative ones, are culturally tied to specific campaigns, often stressing themes and images that resonate with voters in the same way that commercial ads resonate with consumers. In fact, as politics becomes even more entertainment driven, the techniques of commercial and political ads are becoming indistinguishable.

This book—and the accompanying web site, which contains many of the political ads mentioned in the following chapters—provides a multiplicity of perspectives on the relationship among the media, politics, and popular culture.

REFERENCES

Alliance for Better Campaigns. 2000. "Profiteering on Democracy: The Broadcast Industry and Big-Money Politics." Washington, DC. *http://www.bettercampaigns.org/reports/display.php?ReportID=* 5 (site lasted visited on January 22, 2004).

Diamond, Edwin, and Stephen Bates. 1988. *The Spot: The Rise of Political Advertising on Television*. Cambridge, MA: MIT Press.

Hamilton, James T. 2004. *All the News That's Fit to Sell: How the Market Transforms Information into News*. Princeton, NJ: Princeton University Press.

Jamieson, Kathleen Hall, and Paul Waldman. 2003. *The Press Effect: Politicians, Journalists, and the Stories That Shape the Political World*. New York: Oxford University Press.

McConnell, Bill. 2004. "Awaiting the '04 Windfall." *Broadcast & Cable*. January 22.

Thurber, James A., Candice J. Nelson, and David A. Dulio. 2000. *Crowded Airwaves: Campaign Advertising in Elections*. Washington, DC: Brookings Institution Press.

Wisconsin Advertising Project. 2004. "Candidates Airing Twice as Many TV Ads in Iowa than New Hampshire." Press release, January 14.

1

Creating Effective Political Ads

Arthur Sanders

"Can You Hear Me Now?"

The single line spoken over and over again by Verizon Wireless's "Test Man" is instantly recognizable to most TV viewers. In fact, reading that line likely caused you to picture Test Man, the clean-cut, efficient, white male with glasses, who has now appeared in over 50 different ads and has infiltrated popular culture as a target of satire on programs such as *Saturday Night Live*. While it is hard to make exact attributions between corporate success and specific advertising campaigns, Verizon, the number one wireless service before this campaign began, has maintained that position seeing, for example, a 14% increase in subscribers in the second quarter of 2003.[1] The continuing use of Test Man also reflects the success of this advertising campaign.

The elements that go into a successful ad are, in many ways, quite simple—whether those ads are meant to sell products or political candidates. In spite of that, it is often more difficult to create successful ads than that simplicity would suggest. This chapter examines what makes for effective advertising, the strategic environment facing any advertiser, and pays particular attention to the similarities and differences in the environments facing political and product ads. It also examines how the interaction of that environment with the ads produced can lead to the success or failure of particular ads. Recognizing how advertisers make appeals and the underlying strategies and concerns that go into effective ads can make viewers better consumers of both products and political candidates.

The Logic of Television Advertising

The logic of television is quite simple. The most important factor for anyone making a television program or ad is the need to get people to watch.[2] For regular programming, this means figuring out ways to entice viewers to become regular watchers of a particular program, as a steady audience is one that the networks can sell to advertisers. For the makers of advertisements, this means creating ads that will attract the attention of people during the breaks in the programs they are watching—something that has become increasingly difficult over the years as technology has opened up many more options for people. In the 1950s, Milton Berle and Lucille Ball could count on an audience share in the seventies or higher. By the mid-1980s, Bill Cosby's top-rated show was watched by just over half of the viewing audience. And now, twenty years later, an audience share of 20 is considered outstanding. The proliferation of cable television stations, VCR and DVD technology, and remote control devices make it very easy for viewers to turn to something else if they do not like what they are watching. Both programmers and advertisers now face enormous pressure to create products that will keep people tuned in to their television sets without switching over to watch some other program or ad. For advertisers, this pressure is compounded by the sheer number of ads that people watch. When the commercial break comes, there is a series of ads, one after the other. Producers not only need to make people keep watching, they also need to create something that stands out enough for the audience to remember the message. Test Man worked because he became a visible symbol of Verizon's willingness to "work for you." Unfortunately for advertisers, most of what we watch is soon forgotten. The goal is to create an advertisement that will remain with people.[3] This simple rule—attract an audience—leads to a number of more specific "rules" that govern the creation of effective political advertisements. What follows is a brief discussion of four rules for making effective political (or product) ads.

First, ads need to grab our attention, so rule number one is that the best ads are dramatic ones. That does not mean they are dramatic in the sense that all ads must be exciting and filled with tension. Rather, they need to be dramatic in the sense that they need to tell a good TV story.[4] Good visuals, catchy music, memorable slogans, and compelling images all make for better television ads. But the visuals, music, slogans, and images by themselves are not enough. The best television ads will also tell a little story that keeps the viewer interested and provides a lasting memory. We see Test Man in all kinds of environments, checking to see that the Verizon network is available. The dramatic tension is in the story and is more implied than stated. The audience recognizes the problem: cell phone networks with dead spots and bad reception. Test Man is relentless in his efforts to insure that Verizon is working to solve this problem. Given time constraints—telling such a story in 30 seconds—ads will often need to rely on familiar patterns so that viewers can quickly process the message. Test Man's simple phrase, "Can You Hear Me Now?" encapsulates the larger problem quickly and clearly. In the same way, the 1984 Reagan campaign ended almost every ad with the phrase "President Reagan: Leadership That's Working."

Another way to reach an audience quickly is, as Nelson and Boynton discuss, the use of common genres that allow viewers with limited knowledge of the details of politics (or products) to understand the message.[5] In the 1992 presidential campaign, George Bush ran a commercial with a bleak black-and-white landscape including the image of a vulture, ominous music, and a litany of the failures of then-Governor Clinton in his home state of Arkansas. Democrats ran ads focusing on what they saw as the devastation of the environment in Texas, particularly the air in Houston, to attack George W. Bush in the 2000 campaign. Ads such as these use the genre of horror, carrying a message through the words spoken, music and background noise, and images portrayed to create a mood and theme that viewers can easily absorb. The story is one of horror—the horror that will result if we elect *that person* to office. Thus, effective ads draw on common themes, phrases and storylines (which is rule number two), coupled with dramatic images and sounds, to create a memorable and compelling message. In the process, the ads attempt to link the specifics of the campaign with broader feelings and associations that may be in the minds of viewers. These ads may possibly distort campaign specifics, as these underlying associations and feelings may be only tangentially related to the issues in question in the ad—just as checking to see if a cell phone network is available is not the same thing as investing money to fill in those "bad" spots. There are, of course, many familiar genres available besides horror. We can have uplifting tales of heroes who will save us; thoughtful family men and women who will bring our values to government; and hardworking, successful people, such as Test Man, who will help to create a better America—or at least a better wireless network! But while the potential number of stories that can be told is theoretically limitless, the need for familiar themes that people can grasp in just thirty seconds, and the nature of TV audiences, means that some approaches and themes are more prevalent than others. This leads to a third rule of political advertising: people are better than policy.

Television as a medium tends to emphasize individual people.[6] Viewers find it easier to relate to characters than to more abstract principles. They can empathize with or despise the people they see, and candidates rely much more heavily on ads about people than ads that stress their issue positions. Richard Joslyn, for example, in a small sample of ads from a variety of campaigns, found that the personal quality of the candidates was the most common content of ads, with specific issue positions being the least common appeal.[7] Darrell West found similar results in his broader look at presidential campaign ads, noting that ads were "more likely to emphasize personal qualities (32%) and domestic performance (30%) than specific domestic or foreign policy appeals (25%)."[8] Thus, viewers see many ads that introduce us to the candidate and his or her family. In thirty seconds it is much easier to tell us a story about people than more complex problems. Test Man is hard working and relentless, so viewers are asked to assume that whatever complexities go into creating an effective wireless network will be solved by his efforts. Similarly, political ads find it easier to make appeals where the candidate is a hero (or the opponent is a villain), someone the viewer can relate to and like (or be put off by and dislike), than it is to present a defense of a detailed policy position.

This reliance on personal appeals over issues in political ads is reinforced by the fact that voters who rely most heavily on issue appeals or on partisanship are less likely to be the targets of political ads. The strongest partisans already know which candidate they are likely to support. Similarly, voters who have strong feelings about particular policy issues are likely to seek out candidate positions on those issues and make their decisions accordingly. Ads are less likely to persuade these people. It is those viewers who Michael Robinson termed the "inadvertent audience" who are targeted.[9] These are citizens who are not paying a lot of attention to the campaign. They are watching the news to find out what the weather is going to be or are tuned into a program they enjoy when a political ad pops up on the screen. Personal image is much more likely to grab their attention, and thus we get campaigns that focus on such appeals.

Finally, the fourth rule for effective political ads: simple is better than complex. Thirty seconds is not enough time to discuss the details of policy, and even if it were, viewers are not likely to engage in such discussions. The ads roll by on the screen, one after the other. The first three rules provide ways to grab the attention of the audience, but if the message is too complicated, the ads will not linger in memory. This can best be seen in the way that policy is, in fact, dealt with. When policy is discussed, it tends to be at a very broad, simplistic level. Candidates discuss what is wrong with what we are doing and how they will make it better. But the appeal will be a simple one. Just as Test Man gives us the message that Verizon will work hard to give us the best network possible, in political ads the simple policy message is that the candidate, if elected, will provide a better economy, a stronger defense, or more effective schools, or a better health care system. Details are best left out of the discussion.[10]

Thus, the need for audience attention leads to four rules for making effective ads: good ads need (1) drama, (2) familiar themes or storylines, (3) a focus on people rather than policy, and (4) to make simple, not complex appeals. Before we take a closer look at how the political and media environment can shape the success or failure of ads that follow these rules, there are two other issues regarding political ads that we need to examine more closely—the problem of credibility and the issue of negativity.

Making Political Ads Credible

All ads face a credibility barrier. Viewers know that these are ads designed to sell something (be it a product or a candidate), and thus, they tend to have their defenses up. People think that they can get past the hype and that they are not easily persuaded. The realities may be different, but viewers are on the alert.[11] They will take the messages with a grain of salt. An effective ad, then, must break through this barrier of distrust.

This problem is exacerbated in political advertising because of the low level of trust that the public has in political structures and government. This decline in trust has been well documented. Joseph Capella and Kathleen Jamieson, for example, note that the percentage of the public who think that the government would "generally do the right thing" declined from 60% in 1964 to 10% in 1994.[12] Since 1994 there have been increases in trust. The American National Election Series has found, for example, an increase from a low of 21% trust in 1994 back up to 44% in 2000.[13] But these levels are still far below those that were routinely found in the 1950s and early 1960s. Viewers expect that our political leaders may not always be telling us the truth, so when they advertise, viewers are skeptical.

Those creating political ads, then, need to overcome this barrier and make an advertisement that people will believe. There are a number of ways to do this which we commonly see used. One is to rely on "objective sources." Political ads will often cite newspaper articles or list the actual votes in Congress or the state legislature, which they project as supporting the claim they are making. Documentation lends credence to the claim. Note that while product ads must have evidence to support the claims that are made, political ads, at least those made by candidates, do not. According to FCC (Federal Communications Commission) regulations, candidate ads cannot be refused because of "false claims." (Ads by political parties, interest groups, or other noncandidate organizations have no such protection, and in those cases stations can demand documentation before running an ad. But ads from the candidates' own committees cannot be refused. The only requirements are that the ad clearly state who is paying for it and, for the first time beginning in the 2004 election cycle as a result of the new campaign finance laws, that the candidate has personally approved the message. If those requirements are met, the station must run it.) But the issue of credibility leads candidates to attempt to document as many of the charges and claims they make as is possible.

Secondly, campaign ads rely on trusted spokespeople to make claims for the candidate. Political endorsements are not particularly effective in this regard because viewers assume that a politician endorsing another politician is simply "politics as usual" and not, therefore, credible. (Why should a viewer make much of the fact that Republican Senator Charles Grassley supports the Republican challenger Greg Ganske in Ganske's race against Democratic incumbent Tom Harkin? Such ads, which did run, are unlikely to persuade very many voters.) But ads that can rely on "ordinary people" to make claims are much more likely to be believed. It was not hard to find a citizen from Arkansas who did not like Bill Clinton or a citizen from Texas who was unhappy with George W. Bush when those men served as governors of those states. The opponents of those men found it useful to find such citizens and have them raise concerns in the ads that they ran. From the perspective of viewers, such ordinary citizens are more credible sources than other politicians.

Similarly, celebrity and newspaper endorsements can often be credible, particularly if the celebrity or the newspaper has a reputation or image of fairness. And, again, effective TV ads can make use of this. Finally, the candidate himself, looking directly into the camera with no "smoke and mirrors," can be credible as well. The first ads of the 2004 presidential campaign from former Vermont governor Howard Dean and North Carolina senator John Edwards relied on this technique. The key is to convince viewers that this ad is not really an ad pushing a product/candidate. Rather, it is a story, claim, or concern that the viewer needs to take seriously. Credibility of source is crucial to achieving this goal.

The Attractiveness of Negative Advertising

One final pattern that needs discussion and which results from the factors discussed above is the attractiveness of negative ads—ads that attack the candidate's opponent. It is relatively easy to capture people's attention with dramatic, simple portrayals of one's opponent. Negative ads make for good television. They focus viewers' attention more quickly and effectively than broader, positive claims. And the message that "you cannot trust my opponent" is a familiar one that resonates with the predispositions people have about politicians, making it easy for people to relate to, understand and remember.[14] Thus, candidates find such ads to be effective.

This is particularly true of the candidate who is behind in the polls. If one's opponent is winning, a candidate's job is to get some of the opponent's weaker supporters to rethink their position. A negative ad is a good way to do so. Marcus, Neuman, and MacKuen have found, for example, that the emotional appeal of a threat leads people to reconsider their standing decisions. In contrast, people who are satisfied or feeling positive are much more likely to rely on the standing decisions or familiar patterns of evaluation that are stored in memory.[15] Candidates and their consultants have learned that such ads are effective, at least by this standard, and their use has been increasing over time. Roderick Hart, for example, found that what he labeled "reactive ads" (ads that involve sustained attacks on the opposition or responses to such charges) increased steadily from 11% of ads in 1960 to 43% in 1996.[16] So candidates find such advertising an effective way to cause people to rethink their views of the relative attractiveness of the candidates and may even encourage those who feel threatened to vote.[17]

There is, however, a dark side to negative ads. Such ads turn voters off, strengthening their general cynicism toward the political world and make it less likely that they will vote at all.[18] As Marcus, Neuman, and MacKuen argue, then, there is no single effect of negative ads. It can both stimulate interest and turnout among those who feel threatened (while also causing them to rethink their standing decisions), and increase cynicism and alienate those who conclude it is politics as usual.[19] But note that the way in which these two contradictory effects work will more often than not, make negative ads attractive.

In this regard, it is useful to compare product ads with political ads, as this is one way in which the environment for political ads is very different from that for product ads. Both product ads and political ads want to grab attention and prove the superiority of their product/candidate when compared with the opposition. But there is an important difference. When products advertise, there are two different ways to increase profits (the goal of the ads). One way is to increase the share of the market. Verizon can increase profits by getting more cell phone users to use Verizon and fewer to use U.S. Cellular, but the profit level of Verizon also depends on the size of the market. If Verizon runs ads attacking U.S. Cellular as unreliable and U.S. Cellular runs ads attacking Verizon as unreliable, some users may decide that neither of these companies are reliable and go back to using traditional phones instead. That is why, to use a different example, after an airline crash, the competition does not run ads with pictures of the mangled plane saying, "Fly us. This won't happen." Even if some passengers, after checking safety records (fear makes us reexamine standing decisions), do change and market share goes up, in the long run, ads like that will only help Amtrak and Greyhound as some will rethink not which airline to fly but whether to fly at all.

Candidate ads, on the other hand, are only concerned with market share and then only with market share on a particular day. The candidate needs to have more votes than all of his or her opponents on election day. It does not matter if the size of the market (turnout) is 55% of the electorate or 15% of the electorate. And the longer view (what this means to people's views of the system over time) is also not important. From the perspective of the candidate, then, when you advertise negatively you may (1) stimulate some supporters to come to the polls through fear of the opposition and (2) cause some weakly committed supporters of the opposition or undecided voters to rethink their views and support the candidate running the negative ad. On the other hand, if the candidate is blamed for too much negativity, some of his or her supporters may become disenchanted and stay away from the polls. They are unlikely to switch to support for the opposition because they are not threatened by the candidate running the negative ads, just disenchanted by the candidate's tactics and the political system that it represents.

Without threat, they are unlikely to rethink their relative vote preference. So while turnout may be depressed by this reaction, the potential for positive (in terms of campaign outcomes) responses along the first two reactions will usually lead to a decision to run negative ads. At some point, the cumulative effect of negative ads may lead the disincentives to outweigh the incentives, but that point is impossible to know ahead of time, and so a candidate, especially one who is losing, will almost inevitably find that the risk is worth it. In spite of the long-term harm they may do to the system, negative ads will tend to be, from a candidate's perspective, effective political appeals.

Making Effective Political Ads: Some Examples

What goes into making effective political ads, then, is relatively simple. Candidates and consultants need to follow the four rules outlined above. Ads should be: (1) dramatic, (2) rely on familiar themes or storylines, (3) focus on people rather than policy, and (4) make simple, not complex appeals. And they need to do so in ways that viewers find credible. Negative attacks on one's opponent can easily fit these criteria, but too many negative ads can backfire, so candidates cannot simply attack. They must also create ads that show their character or positions in a positive light. But while this sounds very simple, in the real world of politics, it is, in fact, quite difficult because ads must be created in the context of an ongoing campaign and a skeptical public. Candidates have their message to get out there, but so does the opposition, and so does the media. And citizens/viewers have their own perspectives and predispositions as well. I want to conclude with a discussion of four ads from the 2002 elections in the state of Iowa; two from the senatorial campaign, two from the gubernatorial campaign. Each of these ads follows the four rules above, but only three ended up being credible, and only two were successful. Looking at these ads can illustrate the barriers that must be overcome to create a memorable and effective political ad.

Watch Out. The Governor Is Leading Us to Ruin

Ads have different goals, and so an effective ad is one that accomplishes the task it is designed to accomplish. No single ad is created with the notion that "this ad will win the election for us." Rather, ads are part of an overall strategy designed to bring campaign victory. The goal is not to create healthy democratic dialogue and debate but rather to shift the views and impressions that people have about the candidates in a direction that favors the candidate creating the ad.[20] For a challenger, as noted above, one key is to convince the public that they need new leadership. Problems with the incumbent need to be highlighted. If things are okay, why change? One way to make such an appeal is to highlight the failures of the incumbent, and the first ad we shall examine was designed with this goal in mind.

In the 2002 Iowa gubernatorial race, Republican challenger Doug Gross was running against Democratic incumbent Tom Vilsack. Iowa, like most states in 2002, was in financial difficulty. A financial surplus had turned into a deficit. Governor Vilsack, of course, blamed national economic conditions and made the point that Iowa was in much better shape than many other states. But challenger Gross wanted to pin the blame on the governor. The challenger's internal polling data early in the campaign showed that he was leading the governor, but the lead seemed more generic, based on unhappiness with the state of the state. Thus, the campaign felt that they should reinforce these notions that people had that things were not going well and that it was "the governor's fault."[21]

The commercial called "Truck" begins with the announcer telling us that when former Republican Governor Terry Brandsted left office, there was a billion-dollar surplus, but now there was a billion-dollar deficit. We hear this information as we see a man who looks like the governor—he has the same build, and we are never able to see his face—happily throwing two bags of money (a billion a bag?) into a truck labeled the "Vilsack Spending Company." As the announcer asks where the money went, the truck drives by a school with, presumably, students and teachers standing empty-handed outside (not for education), a factory with, presumably, workers standing empty-handed outside (not for jobs), and what looks like the downtown of a small town presumably in Iowa (not in our small towns). We then get an image of a confused-looking cow (not for agricultural growth either!) and the truck driving on down the highway (there goes the money!) as the announcer says "Two billion dollars. Gone. Where did all our money go?"

This ad works on a number of levels. It tells a little dramatic story. "We seem to have lost $2 billion." It is a simple story with a simple answer. The governor wasted our money. The ad, in fact, never says this. That is left for the viewer, but the implication is clear. It fits our pattern of thinking about government.[22] In fact, one might argue that there may even be an implication that Vilsack is stealing (driving off) with the money, which also would fit our images of the "politician as crook." But the tone of the ad—light, not horror—makes waste, not theft, the more likely implication. (It is the wasteful Democrats up to their old tricks, squandering, not stealing, the public trust. But it is still something that must be corrected.) The cow with the funny look on its face, the sound effects (the truck horn, music), the movement of the man who is supposed to be the governor (including the way he carries and then throws the money into the truck), and the announcer's tone of voice all contribute to the lighthearted tone of the ad, and do so in a way that makes the ad interesting, enjoyable, and memorable. It raises important questions about the competence of the governor to manage the public trust. The ad, thus, has a dramatic, simple, familiar story. It attacks a person. It is about the governor and his incompetence. It is not about the policies that failed or the structural difficulties facing the state. And even if the particular details are not entirely clear (the governor's office disputed the billion-dollar deficit claim), the story of government waste is a very credible one. And the ad, then, was able to focus public attention on this issue in a way that should have put Governor Vilsack on the defensive as it highlighted his personal failures, not a comparison of who had a better plan to solve these problems.

But in the end, this ad did not work. Shortly after it ran, the Gross campaign found that their lead had disappeared. The ad was memorable and seemed to be on target. It had all the elements of an effective ad, but it proved to be an example of negativity gone too far. The ad was run early in the campaign, before the Gross campaign had established with voters why he was the kind of person who could make a good governor. And, in fact, the Vilsack campaign was already running ads (one of which we will examine below) painting the challenger as someone who did not have the personal qualities needed to be an effective governor. The immediate response ad of the governor's campaign to this ad was an ad with the governor speaking directly into the camera, describing his efforts to deal with the problems of the state. The contrast of a hard-working governor willing to deal with problems in a serious way and a challenger who simply made fun of the governor caused the ad to backfire on Doug Gross. It reinforced an image that he was developing as someone who was not the right person to lead the state. This ad then failed, not because it was poorly conceived or poorly done but rather because of the context within which it was run. Had the Gross campaign first sent out a message that made clear that Doug Gross was the kind of person who could make a good governor or had the governor's campaign not been so effective at raising questions about the personal qualities of the challenger, the intended message of this ad (we cannot trust the governor) might have come through more clearly. Instead, the tone of the ad led to viewers questioning whether the person making the ad was up to the task at hand.

The Challenger as Threat: He Will Stoop to Any Level

For Governor Vilsack, given the fiscal problems of the state, the optimal strategy was to make electing Doug Gross more of a threat than sticking with familiar Governor Vilsack. This, however, can be a difficult thing to do with advertising, especially when running against a challenger who has not held elective office. Candidates with prior political experience will, almost inevitably, have records that can be exploited. It is rare to find someone who did not cast a vote (perhaps on an amendment or procedural motion) that cannot be cited as evidence of their failure to look out for the best interests of the nation. Ads making such claims are common. The citation of the vote lends needed credibility to the charge. In the New York presidential primary in 2000, for example, John McCain was attacked in an advertisement for voting against providing breast cancer research funding to a New York Hospital. McCain opposed this funding because it was added as an amendment without going through normal appropriations channels, not because he opposed breast cancer research. But the ad, with its "objective citation" of the amendment in question, put the senator on the defensive.

Doug Gross, Vilsack's challenger, had no such political voting record. He had served on the staffs of two Republican governors, but he had never held elective office. Having an attack from the governor or some other prominent Democrat would simply be dismissed as politics as usual, lacking the credibility to make the charges stick. But the governor's campaign found a perfect spokesperson to make the claim that Doug Gross was a mean-spirited person who was more concerned with the special interests than ordinary Iowans. The particular ad in question dealt with a major issue in Iowa: large corporate farming interests wanting to set up large hog lots. The issue raised two concerns: protecting smaller family farms from large corporations and the environmental problems that can occur in trying to deal with hog manure (containing such manure without having runoff into rivers and streams and odor are the largest problems in this area). Doug Gross's law firm represented Iowa Select, the largest Iowa-based hog producer in a battle this corporation had when they established a large hog lot in Hamilton County, a battle that was settled out of court in 1997. Doug Gross was one of the attorneys involved in the negotiations with local residents. The ad itself is quite simple. It shows Rebecca Cole, one of the local citizens who had been a party to the lawsuit against Iowa Select, discussing her version of what happened in the interactions between Doug Gross and local residents. Ms. Cole had actually come forward to the Vilsack campaign. She had seen some of the ads that the Gross campaign was running portraying the candidate as a small town success.[23] This caused her to feel outraged, and she volunteered to tell her version of Doug Gross.

She paints him as a mean-spirited lawyer who was willing to do anything to help his large corporate client. "He is for big business and big business only," she says, also noting that "the odor is awful," the "flies are terrible" and "he [Gross] knows hogs stink." It was, clearly, a battle of good (the local community) versus bad (the big corporate hog producers), and Doug Gross was the representative of evil—and the implication is that he liked doing it.

This depiction of Doug Gross was credible to people because the source was credible, an ordinary Iowan who said Mr. Gross had treated her badly. She comes across as credible, and, in fact, the ad was not scripted. The Vilsack campaign came to her house and asked her to talk about her experiences. The ad simply shows her talking with strategic cuts to pictures of hogs and unflattering pictures of Doug Gross. The ad also fits the kinds of stereotypes we have of lawyers (think of all of those jokes by Jay Leno or David Letterman about "dirty, rotten lawyers") and of greedy corporate interests. Furthermore, the immediate reaction of the Brown, Winnick, Graves, Gross, Baskerville and Schoenbaum law firm (the firm where Mr. Gross works), which was to threaten Ms. Cole with legal action for violating a non-disclosure agreement that was part of the final settlement with the people in the community, only served to reinforce the image the ad was trying to create.[24] Even if the law was on the side of the firm in its complaint (they never did take legal action against her so we do not know), "justice" was on the side of the woman who was "only telling the truth about what happened."[25]

Thus, this ad succeeds by telling a compelling, dramatic, simple, familiar story (big bad interests beating up on poor innocent citizens and their environment, all for money). It tells the story in a way that focuses on the people involved—Doug Gross versus the ordinary citizens of Hamilton County, Iowa. And it finds a perfect credible source for delivering this message, a woman whose credibility was enhanced by the law firm's hostile reaction to the ad. The governor may be wasting Iowa's money, but at least he was not a mean-spirited lawyer who would be, as the ad concludes, "the wrong choice for our communities."

Can Tom Harkin Be Trusted? A Charge That Did Not Stick

In marked contrast to the Vilsack ad attacking Doug Gross, the Greg Ganske campaign, and the National Republican Senatorial Committee (NRSC), ran an ad that attempted to attack Senator Tom Harkin which back-fired. The contrast with the Vilsack ad is instructive in showing the impor-tance of source credibility in shaping the effectiveness of a political ad.

The ad in question was designed to raise questions about Democratic incumbent Senator Tom Harkin. Harkin was a three-term incumbent, but one who was always, or so it seemed, quite vulnerable. He has one of the most liberal records in the United States Senate, and he is not afraid to take strong, colorful and visible stands. (For example, he called the impeachment case against President Clinton a "pile of dung."[26] And he once drank ethanol on the floor of the Senate to demonstrate its safety.) Unlike Iowa's other senator, Republican Charles Grassley, who is widely regarded as a "good solid Iowan" and has not faced a strong challenge in years, Harkin is divisive. Iowa Republicans have an almost visceral dislike of him. At a meeting of the Iowa Caucus of Political Scientists, one week before the 2002 election, Republican official Steve Roberts noted that if Harkin won, he would begin raising money the very next day for the "very important pur-pose of getting Tom Harkin out of the Senate."[27]

But Harkin has never been an easy target. He defeated Republican incum-bent Senator Roger Jepsen in his first race for the Senate in 1984. In his three subsequent elections Iowa Republicans recruited sitting members of Congress to run against him: Tom Tauke in 1990, Jim Ross Lightfoot in 1996, and, in this election, Dr. Greg Ganske. Ganske, like the others, was not able to succeed, but as in the past, he seemed like a strong challenger. He needed to weaken Harkin's appeal. The senator may not have won by large mar-gins, but enough Iowans liked him so that he was able to keep winning.

The National Republican Senatorial Committee attempted to weaken Harkin by raising doubts about his trustworthiness.[28] One of the reasons Harkin was controversial was (and is) his presumed willingness to speak his mind. This may enrage his opponents, but it also provides a level of sup-port from those who believe that Harkin will "stand up and tell the truth." So undermining that image of trust might go a long way toward getting some of Harkin's supporters to rethink their support. The ad attempts to under-mine trust on the issue of Social Security. An elderly woman walks slowly down a road and, while shaking her head slowly, recounts how the tax that Senator Harkin, as a member of the House of Representatives, voted for back in 1983 is hurting her Social Security income. She speaks slowly, and both her tone of voice and her look give off the sense that she is very disturbed. She used to trust the senator. "I trusted him for 30 years," she says, but when you look at his record, he has betrayed her, and all the other elderly Iowans who have been counting on him for support, and she says "I can't trust him anymore." The senator may say he is on the side of ordinary elderly Iowans, but look at what he is doing to them, supporting a tax that makes her life so difficult.

The ad is not really concerned with Social Security, the presumed policy focus of the discussion. Rather, it is about the senator and his trustworthiness or lack thereof. It tells a short, simple, dramatic story—Harkin the politician is not what he seems to be. He says he fights for us, but, like many, he does not. And it plays upon the public's notion that Democrats are more willing to raise taxes than Republicans. This would seem to be an effective strategy. Harkin's defense on substance would be that this particular tax had bipartisan support (Charles Grassley voted for it and President Reagan signed the bill) and that it strengthened the Social Security system. (In fact, it is hard to imagine that Dr. Ganske would not have voted for it had he been in the Congress at the time.) But such an approach still puts Harkin on the defensive with respect to his trustworthiness and commitment to Iowa's seniors.

Instead, however, the ad failed because it lost credibility. The NRSC made a concerted effort to go on the offensive on the Social Security issue in many races around the nation running ads similar to this one. Everywhere they did so, they managed to put their Democratic opponents on the defensive— everywhere except Iowa. As it happened, the elderly woman in the ad was an actress, not an Iowan. And this became the focus of the response to the ad. The local media, especially the *Des Moines Register*, and the Harkin campaign, attacked Ganske and the NRSC for their deception.[29] Tom Harkin had not, they said, betrayed the trust of this woman (or by implication, anyone else) because he never represented her. How could she be betrayed by him after 30 years of trust when he was not, as she seemed to claim, her senator? Instead of "Can we trust Harkin?" the message of the response to this ad became "Can we trust Ganske?" An ad that seemed to have all the elements of an effective ad—it told a simple, familiar, dramatic story that focused on a person, not the actual policy dispute, and did so in a way that seemed credible, relying on a vote that Harkin had, in fact, cast in a way that fit stereotypes of Democrats on the issue of taxes—did not succeed because the credibility of the person delivering the message disappeared. (The column by Rekha Basu which brought this to light concluded with a quote from Bill Allison of the Center for Public Integrity, stating that "If this were really a problem it shouldn't be difficult to find someone who would say that legitimately."[30]) Had the NRSC taken the time to find an ordinary elderly woman from Iowa willing to express the same sentiments as those in the ad, the resulting ad might have succeeded in putting Senator Harkin on the defensive. But they did not, and the ad blew up in their faces. The NRSC did, in fact, subsequently make an ad with three elderly Iowans making, essentially, the same claim, but by then, it was too late. This potential issue had been lost.

Harkin and Cloning: Avoiding the Deluge

Finally, I want to take a brief look at an ad that was remarkably successful at applying the rules of good ad making in a credible format. This ad was a defense of Senator Harkin's position on the issue of cloning.

The ad had a relatively limited objective. It was designed to head off what might have been an effective attack on the senator. Congressperson Ganske ran an ad that attempted to put Senator Harkin on the defensive over the issue of cloning. That particular ad showed a statement Senator Harkin had made where he said he "welcomed" advances in human cloning technology. The ad did not make clear that Harkin was referring to the use of cloning for medical treatment, not cloning for creating human life. It borrowed music from the TV program the *X-Files* and showed the senator in a very distorted light, creating the image of someone who was far from the mainstream on this issue, someone who could not be trusted. (Again, the use of an issue to make a point about the person.) Internal polling by the Harkin campaign indicated that this issue and the portrayal of the senator that it created could be damaging if this framing dominated discussion.[31]

Senator Harkin had long been active in legislative battles for funding for medical research and alternative medical treatments, and he had, as a result, a number of contacts he could rely on to help him in this area. He called on one of those contacts to make an ad for him, the actor Michael J. Fox.

The ad is very simple. It shows Michael J. Fox, visibly shaking from the effects of Parkinson's disease. He says that Harkin is "the leading supporter of biomedical research in the Senate" and that he supports stem cell research to find cures for life-threatening illnesses, noting at the same time that the senator opposes the use of cloning to create life. Fox concludes by asserting that Harkin's commitment in this area may save the life of "you or someone you love." In many ways, the ad is brilliant in its simplicity. It stars a beloved TV actor who, for older and middle-aged Iowans, grew up on the TV sitcom *Family Ties,* coming into their homes every week (as a conservative, no less; someone who would never have voted for a liberal like Tom Harkin!). Younger Iowans, too, knew him well from either the *Back to the Future* movies or, more often, from his role in the TV sitcom *Spin City* (a "good guy" at heart in a corrupt political world), a role he was forced to give up because of the progression of Parkinson's disease. Senator Harkin, the ad stated, was simply trying to help fight disease and help those we love including, by implication, Michael J. Fox. The senator was, by implication, compassionate and caring. Anyone on the other side of this issue was, again by implication, condemning Michael J. Fox and others we love to a cruel fate.

How could we not support such research? The ad was dramatic, compelling, and simple, telling a story about the good-hearted senator using a credible and beloved source. There was no negativity here, just a positive discussion of Senator Harkin's views on stem cell research and cloning. But the unstated implications of the message and what it implied about Congressman Ganske were devastating. No overt attack was necessary. The Ganske ad on cloning was pulled the day after this ad began running, and within a week, as the ad continued to run, Harkin's polling showed that his stand on the issue of cloning was preferred to that of Ganske.

Conclusions

In the end, then, we can draw a number of lessons about ads for political campaigns and for viewers of them. First, the elements of an effective ad are quite simple. The ads need (1) drama, (2) familiar themes or storylines, (3) focus on people rather than policy, and (4) make simple, not complex appeals, and they need these things done in a credible way. Second, ads need to fit within the context of the ongoing campaign. The Michael J. Fox ad was effective because it met a specific challenge that faced the Harkin campaign. The Doug Gross "Truck" ad had the potential to be effective because it focused on a topic that was of major concern to the voters of Iowa, but it failed because it delivered a negative message in a way that reinforced negative feelings about the person making the ad rather than about the subject of the ad.

Third, good ads tend to provide a contrast between the candidate and the "evil" competition. Sometimes this contrast is explicit (hence the prevalence of negative ads), while at other times, as in the Michael J. Fox ad (or the Verizon Test Man ads), it is only implied. And finally, much of the message of ads is sent by inference and implication, not explicitly. The thirty-second time frame is part of this, but the more important part is the way that familiar themes, genres, and images (visual, verbal, and aural) draw on our memories and understandings of the world to create rich and lasting impressions of the candidates and their opponents. For those who make these ads, the challenge is to do so in a way that is dramatic, interesting, credible, and different enough to stand out in a sea of ads (both political and product) and register with viewers. For citizens the challenge is to cut through the drama and images to get at what the ad is actually trying to say and to evaluate those claims with a certain distance and understanding.

The makers of these ads want us to react to these messages without extensive cognitive thinking. They want us to be drawn into the emotional appeal and accept the message as part of a broader sense of how politics works and, therefore, as a reason to support their candidate or to rethink our support of their opponent. A sense of what ad makers are trying to accomplish and the ways in which they try to accomplish their goals would, hopefully, improve the ability of citizens to take in these ads and evaluate their claims without being swept up too fully in the emotional, verbal, and aural world of the ad. Ironically, if citizens recognize a good ad for what it is, the ability of the ad to work is lessened. That does not mean that ads cannot still be effective. They can. But when citizens can recognize and dissect a good ad, then effectiveness will depend much more on the underlying appeals or claims the ad is making not the techniques used to make those claims. And that would be a healthy outcome for democratic electoral debate.

ENDNOTES

1. Emily Bryson York, "Verizon Keeps 'Test Man' on a Short Leash," *Advertising Age,* August 25, 2003, p. 7.

2. For a more extended discussion of the logic of television programming, see my *Prime Time Politics* (Glen Allen, VA: College Publishing, Inc., 2002), especially Chapter 2.

3. Doris Graber, in *Processing the News,* (New York: Longman, 1984), found that people will often remember the broad message from a newscast even after they have forgotten the details, and there is additional evidence from studies of information processing and memory that supports this as well. (For a good introduction to the study

of memory, see Daniel Schacter, *Searching for Memory* (New York: Basic Books, 1996.) But even recognizing this, ads must still leave a strong enough impression on people to get stored in memory even if only at the level of broad messages not specific details.

4. For a more detailed look at this aspect of creating effective ads, see John Nelson and G. R. Boynton, *Video Rhetorics* (Urbana, IL: University of Illinois Press, 1997) and the videotape that comes with the book.

5. See chapter two of Nelson and Boynton, *Video Rhetorics.*

6. For a more extended discussion of TV's preference for people over plots in prime time programming, see chapter two of my *Prime Time Politics,* especially pages 31–34.

7. Richard Joslyn, *Mass Media and Elections* (Reading, MA: Addison-Wesley, 1984), pp. 42–47.

8. Darrell West, *Air Wars,* Third Edition (Washington, DC: CQ Press, 2001), p. 48. Also see Tables 3–1 and 3–2 on pages 49 and 52. In creating these tables, West relies on Kathleen Hall Jamieson's *Packaging the Presidency,* Third Edition (New York: Oxford University Press, 1996), which is the best and most comprehensive history of presidential campaign advertising.

9. Michael Robinson, "Public Affairs Television and the Growth of Political Malaise," *The American Political Science Review,* 70 (1976): 409–432.

10. The discussion in West (*Air Wars*), noted above (see note 8) makes this distinction by distinguishing more common "policy performance" themes from less common specific policy themes.

11. For a good study of teenagers who deny the influence of ads but exhibit attitudes and behavior that belie those denials, see Roy Fox, *Harvesting Minds* (Westport, CT: Praeger, 1996).

12. *The Spiral of Cynicism: The Press and the Public Good* (New York: Oxford University Press, 1997), p. 18. They have an extended discussion of the decline in trust in Chapter 2.

13. The data from the American National Election Study can be found at their web site: www.umich.edu/~nes/nesguide/toptable/tab5a_1.htm

14. For example, Montague Kern and Marion Just found that negative ads in the 1990 North Carolina Senate election were particularly useful because they reinforced public cynicism. See "How Voters Construct Images of Political Candidates," in Pippa Norris, editor, *Politics and the Press: The News Media and Their Influences* (Boulder, CO: Lynne Rienner Publishers, 1997).

15. George Marcus, W. Russell Neuman, and Michael MacKuen, *Affective Intelligence and Political Judgement* (Chicago: University of Chicago Press, 2000).

16. *Campaign Talk: Why Elections Are Good for Us* (Princeton, NJ: Princeton University Press, 2000), p. 136.

17. Martin Wattenberg and Craig Brians, "Negative Campaign Advertising: Demobilizer or Mobilizer," *American Political Science Review,* 93 (1999): 891–900.

18. See, for example, Kim Kahn Fridkin, and Patrick Kenney, "Do Negative Campaigns Mobilize or Suppress Turnout? Clarifying the Relationship between Negativity and

Participation," *American Political Science Review,* 93: (1999): 877–889, and Stephen Ansolabehere and Shanto Iyengar, *Going Negative: How Political Advertisements Shrink and Polarize the Electorate* (New York: Free Press, 1995).

19. *Affective Intelligence and Political Judgement,* pp. 137–138.

20. In *The Winning Message* (New York: Cambridge University Press, 2002), Adam Simon describes how the dynamic of political campaigns works to minimize healthy democratic discourse. Political advertisements often fit into that dysfunctional dynamic.

21. Details from the campaign's perspective concerning this ad come from a telephone interview with Doug Gross, September 9, 2003.

22. According to the 2000 American National Election Study, 97% of the public think the government wastes money a lot (59%) or some (38%) of the time. These data can be found at: www.umich.edu/~nes/nesguide/toptable/tab5a_3.htm

23. Information about this advertisement comes from an interview with John Lapp, campaign manager for the Vilsack campaign, August 20, 2003.

24. The firm sent a letter to Rebecca Cole's lawyer asking her to stop the ad. See Thomas Beaumont, "Gross Critic in Vilsack Ad Told: Stop," *Des Moines Register,* July 3, 2002, p. 1A.

25. Anne Norton, in *Republic of Signs: Liberal Theory and American Popular Culture* (Chicago: University of Chicago Press, 1993), discusses how law and justice can, at times, come into conflict. In such a conflict, she argues, television always comes out in favor of justice. This ad benefits from that television bias. See Chapter 5 of her book for a more general discussion of this tension.

26. Cited in Michael Barone with Richard Cohen, *The Almanac of American Politics 2004* (Washington, DC: The National Journal, 2003), p. 629.

27. Steve Roberts, speaking at the Annual Meeting of the Iowa Conference of Political Scientists, Drake University, Des Moines, Iowa. November 2, 2002.

28. Details about this advertisement come from an interview with Chris LaCivata, National Political Director of the National Republican Senatorial Committee, August 20, 2003.

29. See Rekha Basu, "Poor Lady Lamenting Harkin's 1983 Vote Is from Central Casting," *Des Moines Register,* September 15, 2002, page 20.

30. Ibid.

31. The information from the Harkin campaign on this issue and this advertisement comes from an interview with Harkin's campaign manager, Jeff Link, on July 29, 2003.

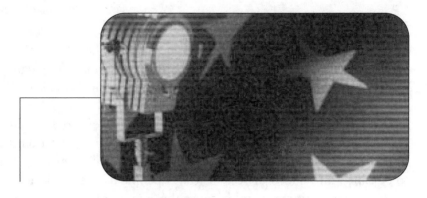

2

Developing "Paid Media" Strategies
Media Consultants and Political Advertising

Stephen K. Medvic

The development and dissemination of communication strategies in politi-cal campaigns require a delicate balance of art and science. Bringing these divergent perspectives together for a common purpose is a difficult endeavor and requires input from a variety of people involved in a campaign. However, one group of operatives—B Media Consultants—has developed both the cre-ative and analytical skills necessary to produce effective communication cam-paigns. Indeed, the centrality of media consultants—rivaled only by pollsters—to modern political campaigns and the mystery surrounding what they do have helped make legends of more than a few consultants. Though the talent of many media consultants is impressive, the mythology surrounding their abilities deserves a critical examination.[1]

Based in part on interviews with professional political consultants, this chapter addresses strategic communication and the role of professional media consultants in political campaigns.[2] First, I'll describe the communi-cation environment in which campaigns now operate. Potential voters are facing *information overload* as sources of information proliferate, while the fragmentation of audiences means that more and more people get informa-tion that is most relevant to their interests from niche media. The "noise" created by information overload coupled with the potential that fragmentation creates for targeting campaign messages makes the services of professional media consultants indispensable for any serious campaign. For several decades now, citizens have been growing increasingly cynical. This leads to a tendency to disregard any message that sounds like politics as usual. In addition, the glut of information with which voters are bombarded creates confusion and, consequently, a tendency to tune out all but the most essential information. Indeed, the efficacy of political advertising has begun to be called into question because fewer people use network television for news and entertainment and because those who do are equipped with the technological wherewithal to avoid commercials (e.g., remote controls, VCRs, and TiVo).

Finally, party and interest group advertising has increased so dramatically in recent years that it threatens to crowd out candidate messages and take control of the campaign agenda out of candidates' hands. The result is that candidates find themselves competing (in some sense) against not only their opponents but often their own parties or sympathetic interest groups as well. Of course, consultants are central to not only candidate but to party and interest group advertising as well.[3] Occasionally, one even finds the same consultant working for a number of candidates, a party committee or two, and some interest groups in a single election cycle (though rarely for more than one client per race).

Having reviewed the context in which campaign advertising takes place, I will then provide a general explanation of how campaigns develop communication strategies. It is the job of media consultants to develop strategies that will frame the campaign debate on their candidates' terms. While the specifics of any given strategy will differ from campaign to campaign, I will argue that campaigns, in general, "deliberately prime" voters by emphasizing messages (including policy positions and/or character traits, or issues and values) that work to their candidates' advantages (as revealed by public opinion polling). Tactically, media consultants must determine the media mix to be used (e.g., earned vs. paid; air [broadcast] vs. ground [mail]; television vs. radio; cable vs. network) as well as the content, tone, timing, and audience for the campaigns' ads. Furthermore, buying advertising time has become so complicated that some consulting firms specialize in that alone.

The chapter will conclude by briefly discussing the normative implications of consultant-driven political advertising strategies. On the one hand, deliberate priming suggests that, rather than manipulating voters by pushing less salient but highly emotional issues upon the electorate, campaigns actually respond to voter preferences (albeit in a selective way). Yet advertising contributes to the notion that campaigns talk past one another by emphasizing different sets of issues. Advertising is also perhaps the most ethically problematic aspect of political campaigning, and consultants are often responsible for the questionable practices. If nothing else, it is often said to "dumb down" the dialogue that would occur in the ideal campaign. Consultants, of course, disagree with much of the criticism. It is, therefore, important to understand exactly what it is that consultants are responsible for with regard to political advertising if we are to make an independent judgment about the health of our campaigns.

The Communication Environment

Today, campaigns take place amid the cacophony of commercial, entertainment, and public affairs communication. Technological innovation has made possible a glut of information that citizens have access to in a variety of venues. Economies of scale make it possible for the typical family to have televisions, radios, and computers stationed in nearly every room in the house. Hundreds of television channels and radio stations, made available by cable and satellite, offer round-the-clock opportunities to use programming that caters to narrow interests. Twenty-four-hour media coverage of current events exaggerates the importance of some stories in order to fill news holes and encourages entertainment value for the sake of capturing market share (see Delli Carpini and Williams 2001). Newspapers, magazines, and books add their share of information as do the postal service and telephone marketers. But nothing compares to the role of the Internet in the creation of what David Shenk (1997) calls "data smog," that is, "the noxious muck and druck of the information age" (p. 31). The Internet, of course, makes possible the World Wide Web, e-mail, as well as Internet Relay Chat (IRC) and messaging services.

The School of Information Management and Systems (SIMS) at the University of California at Berkeley has attempted to track the increase in information around the world. According to their data, "The world produces roughly 250 megabytes for every man, woman, and child on earth" (Lyman and Varian 2000). In terms of media usage (including television, radio, print sources, music, movies, video games and the Internet), SIMS estimates that, on average, Americans used 3,380 hours of media in 2000, or 9.26 hours per day (Lyman and Varian 2000). With regard to advertising, specifically, Shenk (1997) reports, "In 1971 the average American was targeted by at least 560 daily advertising messages. Twenty years later, that number had risen sixfold, to 3,000 messages per day" (p. 30). Undoubtedly, that number has risen further in the last decade. Thus, as consultants note, candidates are not only competing against their opponents, they are competing for attention with commercial advertisers. "Coca-Cola and Dell are the competition too," says media consultant John Franzen.[4]

At the same time that increasing amounts of information are being produced, society appears to be fragmenting. That is, there is an increase in "the polarization or differentiation among different regions or ethnic or ideological communities" (Neuman 2001, p. 304). In *Republic.com,* Cass Sunstein (2001) suggests that fragmentation may evolve into the "complete personalization of the system of communications" (p. 5). He describes a future where, "You need not come across topics and views that you have not sought out. Without any difficulty, you are able to see exactly what you want to see, no more and no less" (p. 3). Fragmentation itself is the result, at least in part, of new media outlets that cater to niche markets. Furthermore, many of these outlets, in an attempt to be interactive, allow users to join the fray and share their own views on the subject matter at hand. In so doing, they contribute not only to fragmentation but to the glut of information.

It is difficult, of course, to measure the effects of too much information. Nevertheless, Shenk (1997) reviews recent psychological research and suggests that a number of problems are the result of information overload. For our purposes, the most relevant of these are an increase in confusion over information as well as frustration with it, in addition to impaired judgments with a concomitant overconfidence in those judgments (pp. 37–38). In other words, people find information overwhelming, which leads to mistaken conclusions and yet a high degree of certainty in one's beliefs. We might also reasonably conclude that the daunting task of processing so much information forces people to avoid information altogether. How else to explain the fact that with as much information available as there is for politics, the lack of political knowledge is as extensive as it is?[5]

Yet citizens may not be given as much credit as they deserve. To begin with, media coverage of campaigns is extremely low, particularly at the local level and especially on television. A 2000 study of 75 television stations revealed that local news programs devoted an average of one minute fourteen seconds to "candidate centered discourse" during the last 30 days of the campaign (Kaplan and Hale 2001, p. 8). Of the stories that did cover campaigns, 53% focused on the presidential race, while only 19% focused on congressional or senatorial races, 10% on state races and 6% on local races. Furthermore, the story frames in presidential and congressional races were primarily strategic as opposed to being issue based (Kaplan and Hale 2001, p. 10). Thus, citizens cannot rely on television news if they hope to become informed voters.[6]

Furthermore, research in political psychology suggests that citizens are "cognitive misers." That is, they "do not actively seek out all available information in order to make some rational, value-maximizing decision; instead, they rely on cognitive heuristics and short-cuts based on prior experience to make all varieties of decisions, from the most mundane to the most earth-shaking" (Lau, Smith, and Fiske 1991, pp. 647–648). This behavior amounts to "low information rationality" according to Samuel Popkin (1994). In effect, rather than remain blissfully unaware of the political world around them, many citizens pay just enough attention and gather only the information required to make reasoned decisions, then discard the information once a judgment has been made.

Whether rational or not, the low levels of interest in (and knowledge of) politics result in limited exposure to political information. Indeed, the same technology that helps create increasing amounts of information also helps citizens avoid information. According to media consultant Ray Strother, the remote control was "devilish" enough to get information to people,[7] now VCRs allow people to watch their favorite shows from beginning to end without being forced to sit through ads and, more recently, TiVo provides programming that is literally commercial free. In other media, satellite radio offers ad-free listening, and caller-ID allows people to screen telephone numbers and avoid unsolicited calls, including political persuasion calls.

Complicating matters for the media consultant is the increase in voter cynicism over the last several decades (see Nye, Zelikow, and King 1997). There is a widespread belief that politicians will say anything to get elected and that political campaigns are more negative today than ever.[8] Thus, even if potential voters were to sit and watch political ads, it seems likely that they would view them as politics as usual unless the ad was particularly unique. Strother describes cynicism as one among many barriers or screens that get in the way of delivering information from candidates to voters. He maintains that these screens are "growing thicker and thicker and less porous," and we might assume that is particularly true with respect to cynical attitudes.[9]

Media consultants are acutely aware of the difficulties they face in reaching the electorate. Their response, says Ed Brookover, has simply been to "yell louder."[10] According to an estimate by Bradley Todd, three times more gross ratings points (or "points") are put behind ads today than were just 15 to 20 years ago. [11] Simply buying more time, however, will not necessarily reach more voters. John Franzen suggests that campaigns must not only run more ads but must produce more arresting ads in an effort to "intrude" upon those who have little interest in politics.[12] Nevertheless, "the cost of pushing a message over paid media is not only rising, but it is increasingly difficult to do at any cost," argues Dick Morris.[13]

Part of the difficulty in effectively using television advertising, which Peter Fenn calls the "nuclear weapon of advertising," is that viewers are avoiding mass programming.[14] So while campaigns feel compelled to buy more and more advertising time, the ads are thought to have diminishing effect. One apparent solution, according to Fenn, is to buy time on news programs, where relatively large audiences still congregate. The problem with this, however, is that the people watching television news tend to be less persuadable than other voters, and it is the voter with little interest in politics who is often the real target of campaign communications.[15]

Fragmentation, too, poses difficulties. Though one might think that targeting becomes easier with fragmentation, Todd maintains that it gets harder "as people scatter."[16] That's because it becomes difficult to find a vehicle of mass communication that can reach enough voters, with tailored messages, to make its use cost effective. One result of this difficulty is that direct mail is becoming more and more important in the communication arsenal of candidates.[17] Mail is relatively cheap and can be targeted with increasing precision. As direct mail consultant David Gold recently put it, "Campaigns are moving toward greater sophistication in targeting and database management. One example is the enhancement of voter files with census and other commercially available demographic information, creating the opportunity to find key clusters of voters across precinct lines" (Mitchell 2002, p. 57).

Consultants also point to other factors that complicate the process of communicating with voters. One that is becoming increasingly relevant is early voting.[18] Fourteen states now allow early voting and 25% of the voting-age population live in states that use the procedure (Hansen 2002, p. 164). In addition to early voting, 22 states have liberalized absentee voting; that is, no reason is required in order to be provided with an absentee ballot. Finally, Oregon voters now cast ballots in statewide elections entirely by mail. In all, 26 states, covering 44.5% of the voting-age population, have early voting and/or liberalized absentee voting (plus Oregon's mail system), making it quite easy to cast a ballot sometime before election day (Hansen 2002, p. 164). As one might imagine, this has enormous influence on a campaign's media operation. According to consultant Jay Smith, campaigns have to be on the air at least two to three weeks before early ballots are mailed. By forcing campaigns to start their advertising runs earlier, these balloting procedures have undoubtedly added to the costs of campaigning. For consultants, there is also the added burden of trying to determine when and how to deliver closing messages in a campaign with what amounts to a floating election day.[19]

As if all this weren't enough, voters are exhibiting less and less partisan loyalty.[20] This increase in independence means that candidates cannot rely exclusively on partisan appeals. Instead, candidate-centered messages are crafted in an attempt to reach the growing number of voters who "vote the person, not the party." Ultimately, the need to persuade swing voters, many of whom possess low levels of information, is what is driving the extensive use of mass-mediated communications.[21] And yet grassroots organizing for mobilization of one's base is making a comeback. The Republicans' 2002 effort, the "72 Hour Task Force," is but one example of the new emphasis (Nagourney 2002; Balz and Broder 2003). And some consultants see the trend continuing, with less importance placed on advertising, as voters demand a more personal approach from candidates. As Dick Morris (2003) argues, "the television habit which underlays media domination of politics has ebbed." Gone are the days of "plastic" candidates and "coat-over-the-shoulder" ads. Consultants increasingly believe that voters today want authenticity.[22] Consequently, successful campaigns of the future, Morris suggests, will "grow virally through Internet groups and constituency organizations."[23]

Finally, candidates are not the only political actors involved in the campaign process. The political parties and interest groups also have a stake in the outcome of elections. As a result, they too engage in communication with voters, including political advertising. In 2002, the parties and interest groups occasionally dominated the airwaves, in some cases spending more on advertising than the candidates themselves and setting the agenda for the campaign (see, for example, Medvic and Schousen 2003). The messages the parties and interest groups send, while not necessarily at odds with their preferred candidates, are not always on the same page. Thus, when the outside groups control the campaign, candidates find themselves competing nearly as much with their allies as with their opponents.[24]

The above description of the communication environment is one in which contemporary campaigns operate generally. Consultants are quick to note that the landscape surrounding a campaign depends upon the level at which the campaign is being conducted.[25] Obviously, the higher the office, the more information the voter has[26] and the more attention people pay to the race.[27] That has a dramatic effect on what political advertising is expected to accomplish in the campaign. In campaigns near the top of the ballot, according to Bradley Todd, ads are used to change the agenda of the campaign; farther down the ballot, "ads have to do all the work."[28] That is, in low information races, ads are expected to establish the issue agenda, create an image of the candidate(s), persuade voters, and mobilize support-ers.[29] In addition, the level of the race helps determine the relative impor-tance of framing and priming in the media strategy.[30] It is the broader process of developing those media strategies, and the tactics for implementing them, to which we now turn our attention.

Crafting and Implementing Media Strategies

Media strategy, according to John Franzen, is "not chess, it's checkers; it's very basic, though consultants like to pretend it's chess."[31] Though they may not all acknowledge the simplicity of the process, media consultants share a remarkable similarity in the way they approach the development of media strategies for candidates. Almost to a person, they say that the cam-paign's communication strategy begins with the candidate.[32] Answers to ques-tions about why the candidate is running, what issues matter to him/her, and generally "who the candidate is" as a person are used to initiate the process of crafting a message. Consultants argue that, contrary to popular belief, positive candidate images cannot be created out of whole cloth.[33] This is particularly true when a public perception of the candidate already exists. When the candidate is unknown, however, consultants have more latitude in developing an image. Still, they would argue that the image has to be rooted in reality and that the candidate has to be able to credibly por-tray the image.

The next step in working through a strategy is to assess the context within which the campaign is being waged.[34] That includes background informa-tion on the opponent (e.g., voting record, public statements, personal infor-mation); a district profile including voting history, demographics, and voter attitudes; and what Ray Strother calls the climate—any local, state, or national political factors that might be relevant to the race in question.[35]

One of the most important tasks at this stage in the campaign is to identify the voters whom the campaign will target. Who, in other words, is persuadable and whose support is weak and needs shoring up?[36] Though a lot
of effort will be put into the mobilization of sympathetic voters, the creation
of a message is geared primarily to so-called swing voters who are targeted
based on their potential receptiveness to campaign appeals.[37]

Once the campaign context has been established, consultants turn to
polling data to help develop the campaign message. While the role of pollsters in campaigns is beyond the scope of this chapter, it must be said that
they have become central to the strategic decision-making structure of
campaigns. The influence that a particular pollster has in a specific campaign is based on a number of factors including the star power of the pollster, the personalities and reputations of other consultants in the campaign
(perhaps especially the media consultant), and the trust the candidate has
in the various operatives involved. Nevertheless, as a general rule, Bradley
Todd suggests, "the longer the media campaign, the less important is the
pollster."[38]

Whether or not the pollster will be the chief strategist, most media consultants concede that a pollster will have been hired by a campaign before
they are brought on board.[39] Thus, benchmark poll results will be available to help determine the focus of the campaign message.[40] Consultants
stress that the polling does not determine the positions that candidates take
on issues, but only the areas of emphasis and, perhaps, the language to be
used in framing the issues.[41]

Often, the key differences between candidates are obvious even without a poll. A race in which a novice is challenging a twenty-year incumbent
will in all likelihood be framed as a contest between "new blood" (or an
outsider) and experience. Still, the benchmark can reveal factors that might
not immediately be apparent. In the 1997 race for Virginia governor, both
sides had polling suggesting that the candidate who pledged to cut the personal property tax (or "car tax") would have a "silver bullet" issue.
Republican Jim Gilmore seized the issue early in the campaign, using "No
Car Tax" as a slogan; the race was never close (see Wepman 1998).[42]

A more nuanced explanation of Gilmore's win is that, by making the
campaign about an issue that voters trust Republicans more than Democrats
to handle satisfactorily, Gilmore set the terms of debate according to his
strengths. This is an example of the *issue ownership* theory of partisan advantage (see Aldrich 1996), which consultants tend to accept as valid. It is generally recognized that each of the two major parties is perceived as better

at handling some issues than others. For instance, most voters believe that Republicans are better at handling crime, national defense, foreign policy and taxes; Democrats, on the other hand, are thought to perform better on the environment, education, Social Security and health care. As Byron Shafer and William Claggett (1995) explain, Democrats tend to have the advantage when elections turn on an economic/welfare principle (such as social welfare, social insurance and civil rights) and Republicans when the issues are cultural/national (including cultural values, civil liberties and foreign affairs). One goal of campaign strategy, therefore, is to emphasize issues upon which one has an advantage over the opponent. There is, in fact, empirical evidence that candidates and parties do just that (see Budge and Farlie 1983; Aldrich 1980; Jacobs and Shapiro 1994; and Simon 2002).[43]

Candidates do not, however, simply emphasize issues that generally play to their party's advantage. The issues must also be salient to the voters.[44] Rather than force an issue onto the agenda, it is much easier (and more responsive) to discuss issues that are top priorities for the public. This is why, for example, there are countless ads about education during campaigns; voters consistently name it as one of the most important issues facing the nation/state/district/city.[45] Consultants do, however, acknowledge that candidates can occasionally influence the public's sense of the importance of an issue, but they also believe that is far more difficult (and expensive) than using issues the public already deems important.[46]

In addition, consultants look for issues upon which there is a difference between the candidates.[47] Democratic media consultant Tad Devine illustrates the importance of the latter point by noting that the most important issue to voters in Massachusetts during the 1994 U.S. Senate race was child immunization. Neither candidate talked much about the issue, however, because there was no difference between them on it.[48]

The flip side of emphasizing issues that are salient to voters and on which your candidate has an advantage over the opponent is avoiding issues upon which the candidate is at a disadvantage. Though it may not meet the criteria for ideal campaign dialogue, consultants would prefer that candidates simply ignore issues that work against them. This is easier to do down ballot than in high-profile races, where candidates are forced to address all issues of concern to the voters.[49] In these situations, the most obvious being a presidential election, framing becomes central to the communications campaign.[50] Framing is "the process by which a communication source constructs and defines a social or political issue for its audience" (Nelson, Oxley and Clawson 1997, p. 221). One media consultant refers to framing as "playing defense" because it is a way to guard against negative repercussions of one's issue positions.[51]

For example, a hypothetical candidate who opposes the death penalty in a district that has majority support for capital punishment might make two arguments in response to a question about his/her opposition. First, he/she might say that the death penalty is cruel and unusual punishment or that it is a violation of human rights. Alternatively, he/she might make a limited government argument by suggesting that capital punishment gives the government too much power. The second "frame" is not likely to win the candidate any votes, but it may neutralize the issue enough to keep him/her in the race.[52]

But candidates do not always cede an issue to their opponents when they are disadvantaged by it. A perfect example is George W. Bush's emphasis on education in the 2000 election. Though most voters generally viewed Al Gore as better able to handle education, Bush refused to surrender and by talking about it throughout the campaign, narrowed the gap in opinion on that issue between him and Gore. This illustrates the point, made by consultant Tad Devine, that gaining credibility on an issue for which you begin at a disadvantage cannot be done "in one fell swoop but by reassuring voters by addressing it constantly."[53]

Regardless of the specific issues a candidate hopes to emphasize, the campaign needs a single theme. Though theme and message are often used interchangeably, typically the campaign's theme is the rationale for the candidacy while messages reinforce the theme to various audiences. As consultant Peter Fenn explains, the campaign theme is like the trunk of a tree while the messages are like branches.[54] The important point to remember, according to consultants, is that "theme" is not a word that should ever have an "s" on the end; there is only one theme" (Bradshaw 1995, p. 42). And the theme, quite simply, is a one-sentence answer to the question, "Why should your candidate be elected—to this office at this time?" (Bradshaw 1995, p. 42). In the end, despite frequent mention of "staying on message" and "message discipline," the most fundamental principle of campaign communication is "single theme-ism" (Medvic 2001, p. 21).

Thematic development takes a variety of forms. Devine, for instance, suggests creating two or three profiles of the candidate from which one will eventually be chosen based on polling. From that profile, a theme emerges based on the candidate's background (e.g., biography or achievements) or on issues.[55] Bill Greener, Ed Brookover, and Eddie Mahe, on the other hand, recommend defining a question for the voters for which your candidate is the affirmative answer.[56] Though the theme is expected to convey a lot about the candidate, it must also be "simple, uncluttered, easily understood, and credible."[57] It should also be positive, though Devine notes that "the most powerful positive campaign is one that helps your candidate and hurts your opponent at the same time."[58] For example, a theme centered on the integrity of a candidate whose opponent is perceived to be untrustworthy simultaneously helps the candidate and hurts the opponent even if the opponent's character is never directly disparaged.

In addition to a single theme, there will also be multiple messages in a campaign. One way of formulating some of the most fundamental messages is to complete a *message box* (see Figure 2.1).[59] This heuristic device simplifies what both candidates in a campaign will be saying about themselves and one another. Of course, although the consultants know what their candidate plans to say about him/herself and the opponent, what the opponent is shown to be saying is just speculation, based either on an educated guess or on polling results that suggest a fruitful line of attack for the opponent.

Once the consultants have devised theories about what themes and messages might match up well against the opponent, the theories are tested with more polling and focus groups (provided the campaign can afford it).[60] The result of these efforts is a refinement of the message and a clearer focus on two or three issues (or values, candidate traits, etc.) to emphasize.[61] Fairly early in the campaign, then, the message should be set and resources put behind reinforcing that message.

Ultimately, developing and disseminating a communication strategy is what I have elsewhere called a process of "deliberate priming" (Medvic 2001).[62] In short, campaigns attempt to prime voters with issues on which they have an advantage over their opponents. Underlying the theory of deliberate priming are assumptions about voters (i.e., that they have pre-established, but dynamic, mental frameworks for making sense of politics called schemas) and the communication process (i.e., that it occurs through

Figure 2.1: The Message Box

	Candidate A	Candidate B
What Candidate A says about	Candidate A (*For*)	Candidate B (*For*)
What Candidate B says about	Candidate A (*Against*)	Candidate B (*Against*)

Source: Powell, Larry, and Joseph Cowart. 2003. Political Campaign Communication: Inside and Out. Boston, MA: Allyn and Bacon, p. 38.

the use of signs, or words, pictures, symbols, etc. that stand for something else) that are beyond the scope of this chapter. Nevertheless, the process it describes is validated by conversations with consultants. Generally speaking, paid media strategies attempt to deliberately prime voters based on evidence from polls about which issues (or values, candidate traits, etc.) work best to promote one's candidacy.

This theory does, however, have one caveat. Though priming is central to nearly all campaigns, it is more or less central depending upon the level of the campaign. High-profile races (e.g., those for president, governor, U.S. Senate) must rely on a good deal of framing, in addition to priming, in order to neutralize the effect of issues that are salient to the public but that work against one's candidate; low-profile races (e.g., those for mayor, city council, state representative) rely heavily on organization and voter mobilization though priming is likely to help in those efforts.

While paid media strategies can be explained theoretically by the concept of deliberate priming, campaign ads are the concrete application of the theory. The translation of the strategy into advertising requires the use of a variety of campaign tactics that media consultants are uniquely qualified to implement. To simplify, there are at least five tactical considerations that consultants must address: the content, tone, and timing of the ads plus the audience to be targeted and the media mix to be used.[63]

Many media consultants argue that the effectiveness of campaign ads depends on the ability of the ads' emotional content to resonate with voters.[64] Emotional appeals have been an essential part of political advertising since Tony Schwartz began making commercials in the early 1960s (Diamond and Bates 1992, pp. 112–116). According to Schwartz (1973), successful advertising "seek[s] to strike a responsive chord in people, not get a message across" (p. 27). "The critical task," Schwartz maintained, "is to design our package of stimuli so that it resonates with information already stored within an individual and thereby induces the desired learning or behavioral effect" (p. 24).[65]

Increasingly, however, "media consultants have become conduits for the pollsters."[66] Where media handlers deal in emotions, pollsters are said to be linear and expect ads to provide rational arguments about issue positions.[67] As a result, media consultants find pollster-driven ads to be "laundry lists"[68] that lack "life, humor and fun."[69] In the end, it is still the media consultant who usually controls the content of the ads, including not only the substance but the audio and visual content as well.

The timing and tone of ads are also important tactical considerations. To begin with, campaigns must decide when to begin their advertising campaigns. The first ads for most campaigns are aired around Labor Day, though in competitive races it is increasingly common to see ads during the summer of an election year. In presidential elections, advertising starts even earlier, especially if one candidate is the incumbent. In 1996, for example, the Clinton campaign began running spots a year and a half before election day (Morris 1999, p. 192; see also Morris 1997, pp. 138–157).[70]

Campaigns also have to decide what the tone of their ad campaign will be—that is, they have to decide whether or not to run negative (or attack) ads (see Skaperdas and Grofman 1995). These are ads that focus solely on the shortcomings of the opponent (Jamieson, Waldman, and Sherr 2000). Most campaigns, of course, do run at least some ads that are not *advocacy,* or purely positive, ads. Non-advocacy ads include not only attack but *comparative* ads, where the two candidates are compared and contrasted.

In addition to determining the mix of advocacy, comparative and attack ads, the campaign must decide when to launch a particular type of ad. Ideally, according to Jay Smith, an ad campaign will begin with a positive definition of the sponsoring candidate, develop into a statement of what the candidate stands for, turn to a comparative look at the two candidates, and then end on a positive note.[71] Nevertheless, campaigns are going negative increasingly early in the process. Furthermore, more and more campaigns are running negative ads straight through to election day, though this practice is most often seen in ad campaigns sponsored by the parties and interest groups (see Brennan Center 2002, Ch. 6).

A final tactical concern that media consultants are expected to handle is targeting of the message. Decisions about whom to target, of course, are grounded in a campaign's strategy. Nevertheless, once targeted voters have been identified, the campaign must determine exactly how to reach those voters. This requires various decisions about the mix of media to be used. To what extent, for example, should the campaign rely on direct mail versus broadcast advertising? Direct mail allows for a level of targeting precision that television advertising cannot match. On the other hand, television operates in a wider sensory environment, providing consultants with more ways to strike the responsive chord in voters.

Consultants must also make decisions about the use of television versus radio and, once on television, cable versus broadcast (i.e., the networks). While radio can be very effective for certain purposes—particularly attack ads, since it is less intrusive than television given its lack of graphics—consultants who specialize in buying advertising time suggest using network television first, cable second, and radio third.[72] Radio, like direct mail, is a one-dimensional medium with respect to the senses, and its reach is shorter than network television's. And cable television, though cheaper than broadcast television, typically does not allow for fixed placement of ads; that is, an ad placed on cable will be aired anytime between 6 a.m. and midnight.[73]

There are many more aspects of the paid media campaigns that cannot be addressed in this chapter. It should be obvious, however, that developing and implementing a communications strategy for a campaign require professional assistance. Strategic decision making is as much art as it is science, and yet those with experience have developed informal theories that can be applied in a variety of campaign contexts. Whether or not consultants increase the odds of candidate success—or decrease the odds of making strategic mistakes—the perception certainly exists that their counsel is necessary in contemporary competitive elections. Whether or not their presence in campaigns is beneficial to democracy will be briefly taken up in the following section.

Normative Considerations

There are far too many normative issues regarding the role of media consultants in campaigns to fully address in this chapter. Nevertheless, the potential consequences of the processes described herein ought to be noted. Perhaps the most common criticism of consultants, and the campaigns they are at least partly responsible for, is that they are political puppeteers, controlling a candidate's every move and utterance. In some forms of the argument, consultants force *wedge issues* upon the electorate. Wedge issues may or may not be significant in terms of policy, but they have enormous symbolic and emotional content and are highly divisive. As such, so the argument goes, they are perfect subjects for political advertising. The result is heated, but substantively empty, campaigns. A modified version of the puppeteer argument holds that when consultants allow candidates to address substantively important issues, they force them to take positions that are popular regardless of what the candidate sincerely believes.

The theoretical explanation of consultant activity I provided earlier (i.e., deliberate priming) suggests that consultants are not puppeteers. Candidates are not only free to take sincere positions on issues, they are encouraged to do so. And far from pressing an agenda on the electorate, consultants prefer to work with issues that are already salient to the voters. Of course, they do so selectively, which may lead to a different set of normative concerns (see below). But the notion that consultants force allegedly irrelevant issues on voters is doubtful. As consultant Ray Strother maintains, "We follow, we don't lead."[74]

The charge that advertising "dumbs down" campaign discourse is, nevertheless, a serious one. Though the concept of wedge issues probably collapses upon close inspection (after all, the leading examples of wedge issues—abortion, race relations, gay rights, the death penalty, etc.—contain important policy questions), the sense that campaigns treat contentious issues in largely symbolic ways is well established and based on fairly good evidence (though see Hart 2000). The question, of course, is who is to blame for that trend? While the media point fingers at consultants (and voters at parties and candidates), many consultants imply that voters are at fault. To begin with, voters pay little attention to politics, especially when compared to various forms of entertainment. In 2000, for instance, more people watched the finale of *Survivor* in August (about 52 million) than watched the first presidential debate between Al Gore and George Bush (nearly 47 million; Jurkowitz 2000). Furthermore, voters do not appear to have very sophisticated demands for information. Detailed campaign information is out there, say the consultants, not only in newspapers and on programs like PBS's *News Hour with Jim Lehrer,* but increasingly on candidate Websites. However, few voters utilize those venues. The result is that "campaigns are a mirror of society."[75]

If consultants are not entirely to blame for the lack of substantive campaign dialogue, they may shoulder much of the responsibility for dishonest advertising. The problem is not that consultants deliberately lie in the ads they produce for their clients, though that does occur.[76] More often, what consultants see as truthful is not viewed as such by others. Because consultants apply a self-interest framework to campaigns, as opposed to a civic responsibility standard, they believe their duty is to their clients first and democracy second (though they would be quick to argue that by serving their candidates, they are serving democracy, much as a lawyer serves the legal system best when putting the interests of his/her client first (Nelson, Medvic and Dulio 2002).[77] The result is that consultants may be more likely than journalists or voters to view an ad as truthful when it is technically true but misleading.

For instance, ads often take legislative votes out of context. A candidate may have voted nine times for a particular measure but voted against it once as part of a larger package. An ad stating that the candidate voted against the measure is factual, but the implication is misleading. While ad content is often the result of a group effort within the campaign, media consultants occupy the most substantial role in that process. As a result, they should bear primary responsibility for the advertising they produce (though holding them accountable is much easier said than done given the lack of effective mechanisms in place to do so).

One last charge often leveled at consultants is that they contribute to the phenomenon of campaigns talking past one another. Ideally, campaigns should function like debates, where candidates express their issue positions on a comprehensive set of policy domains that are significant to voters (Kelley 1960). The theory outlined above and a number of empirical studies suggest that contemporary campaigns fall far short of the normative ideal. Rather than engage in dialogue, candidates largely ignore one another in an attempt to set a campaign agenda that will work to their advantage. Still, it is not entirely clear whether consultants are more likely to violate the normative ideal than are party operatives or the political directors of interest groups. We can say with certainty that consultants have not done much (if anything) to improve the conduct of campaigns. Whether they have made them measurably worse remains an open question.

REFERENCES

Aldrich, John. 1980. *Before the Conventions: Strategies and Choices in Presidential Nomination Campaigns.* Chicago: University of Chicago Press.

Aldrich, John. 1996. "Issue Ownership in Presidential Elections, with a 1980 Case Study," *American Journal of Political Science* 40: 825–850.

Balz, Dan, and David S. Broder. 2003. "Close Election Turns on Voter Turnout," *Washington Post,* 1 November.

Bradshaw, Joel. 1995. "Who Will Vote for You and Why: Designing Strategy and Theme." In *Campaigns and Elections American Style,* eds. James A. Thurber and Candice J. Nelson. Boulder: Westview Press.

Brennan Center. 2002. *Buying Time 2000: Television Advertising in the 2000 Federal Elections.* New York: Brennan Center for Justice at New York University School of Law.

Budge, Ian, and Dennis J. Farlie. 1983. *Explaining and Predicting Elections: Issues, Effects and Party Strategies in Twenty-three Democracies.* London: Allen and Unwin.

Delli Carpini, Michael X., and Scott Keeter. 1996. *What Americans Know About Politics and Why It Matters.* New Haven: Yale University Press.

Delli Carpini, Michael X., and Bruce A. Williams. 2001. "Let Us Infotain You: Politics in the New Media Environment." In *Mediated Politics: Communication in the*

Future of Democracy, eds. W. Lance Bennett and Robert M. Entman. New York: Cambridge University Press.

Diamond, Edwin, and Stephen Bates. 1992. *The Spot: The Rise of Political Advertising on Television,* 3d ed. Cambridge, MA: MIT Press.

Hansen, John Mark. 2002. "Task Force on the Federal Election System." In *To Assure Pride and Confidence in the Electoral Process: Report of the National Commission on Federal Election Reform.* Washington, DC: Brookings Institution Press.

Hart, Roderick P. 2000. *Campaign Talk: Why Elections Are Good for Us.* Princeton, NJ: Princeton University Press.

Heclo, Hugh. 2000. "Campaigning and Governing: " Conspectus." In *The Permanent Campaign and Its Future,* eds. Norman Ornstein and Thomas Mann. Washington, DC: American Enterprise Institute and The Brookings Institution.

Hsu, Spencer S. 1996. "John Warner Fires Consultant Who Altered Challenger's Photo in Ad," *Washington Post,* 11 October.

Jacobs, Lawrence R., and Robert Y. Shapiro. 1994. "Issues, Candidate Image, and Priming: The Use of Private Polls in Kennedy's 1960 Presidential Campaign." *American Political Science Review* 88: 527–540.

Jamieson, Kathleen Hall. 2000. *Everything You Think You Know About Politics, and Why You're Wrong.* New York: Basic Books.

Jamieson, Kathleen Hall, Paul Waldman, and Susan Sherr. 2000. "Eliminating the Negative? Categories of Analysis for Political Advertisements." In *Crowded Airwaves: Campaign Advertising in Elections,* eds. James A. Thurber, Candice J. Nelson, and David A. Dulio. Washington, DC: Brookings Institution Press.

Johnson, Dennis W. 2001. *No Place for Amateurs.* New York: Routledge.

Jurkowitz, Mark. 2000. "47 Million Viewers Tune in to Debate," *Boston Globe,* 5 October.

Kaplan, Martin and Matthew Hale. 2001. "Local TV Coverage of the 2000 General Election." The Norman Lear Center Campaign Media Monitoring Project, USC Annenberg School for Communication, http://www.learcenter.org/pdf/campaignnews.PDF.

Keith, Bruce E., David B. Magleby, Candice J. Nelson, Elizabeth Orr, Mark C. Westlye, and Raymond E. Wolfinger. 1992. *The Myth of the Independent Voter.* Berkeley: University of California Press.

Kelley, Stanley, Jr. 1960. *Political Campaigning: Problems in Creating an Informed Electorate.* Washington, DC: Brookings Institution.

Lau, Richard R., Richard A. Smith, and Susan T. Fiske. 1991. "Political Beliefs, Policy Interpretations, and Political Persuasion," *Journal of Politics,* 53: 644–675.

Lyman, Peter, and Hal R. Varian. 2000. "How Much Information." School of Information Management, University of California at Berkeley, http://www.sims.berkeley.edu/how-much-info.

Malbin, Michael J., Clyde Wilcox, Mark J. Rozell, and Richard Skinner. 2002. "New Interest Group Strategies: A Preview of Post McCain-Feingold Politics?" Washington, DC: Campaign Finance Institute.

Medvic, Stephen K. 2001. *Political Consultants in U.S. Congressional Elections.* Columbus: Ohio State University Press.

Medvic, Stephen K., and Matthew M. Schousen. 2003. "The Pennsylvania 17th and 6th Congressional District Races." In *The Last Hurrah: Soft Money and Issue Advocacy in the 2002 Congressional Elections,* eds. David B. Magleby and J. Quin Monson. Provo, Utah: Center for the Study of Elections and Democracy, Brigham Young University.

Miller, Dale E., and Stephen K. Medvic. 2002. "Campaign Ethics: Civic Responsibility or Self-Interest?" In *Shades of Gray: Perspectives on Campaign Ethics,* eds. Candice J. Nelson, David A. Dulio and Stephen K. Medvic. Washington, DC: Brookings Institution Press.

Mitchell, Amy K. 2002. "Direct Mail Q&A: Trends and Techniques," *Campaigns & Elections,* May.

Morris, Dick. 1997. *Behind the Oval Office.* New York: Random House.

Morris, Dick. 1999. *The New Prince.* Los Angeles: Renaissance Books.

Morris, Dick. 2003. "Dean Phenomenon Signals New Age in Politics." Original manuscript, received via e-mail, August 16. Published as "Dean's Internet Revolution," http://www.frontpagemag.com/Articles/ReadArticle.asp?ID=9252.

Nagourney, Adam. 2002. "TV's Tight Grip on Campaigns Is Weakening," *New York Times,* 5 September.

Nelson, Candice J., Stephen K. Medvic, and David A. Dulio. 2002. "Hired Guns or Gatekeepers of Democracy?" In *Shades of Gray: Perspectives on Campaign Ethics,* eds. Candice J. Nelson, David A. Dulio, and Stephen K. Medvic. Washington, DC: Brookings Institution Press.

Nelson, Thomas E., Zoe M. Oxley, and Rosalee A. Clawson. 1997. "Toward a Psychology of Framing Effects," *Political Behavior* 19: 221–46.

Neuman, W. Russell. 2001. "The Impact of the New Media." In *Mediated Politics: Communication in the Future of Democracy,* eds. W. Lance Bennett and Robert M. Entman. New York: Cambridge University Press.

Nye, Joseph S., Jr., Philip D. Zelikow, and David C. King. 1997. *Why People Don't Trust Government.* Cambridge, MA: Harvard University Press.

Patterson, Thomas E., and Robert D. McClure. 1976. *The Unseeing Eye: The Myth of Television Power in National Politics.* New York: Putnam.

Popkin, Samuel L. 1994. *The Reasoning Voter: Communication and Persuasion in Presidential Campaigns.* Chicago: University of Chicago Press.

Powell, Larry, and Joseph Cowart. 2003. *Political Campaign Communication: Inside and Out.* Boston, MA: Allyn and Bacon.

Schwartz, Tony. 1973. *The Responsive Chord.* Garden City, NY: Anchor Press/Doubleday.

Shafer, Byron E., and William J.M. Claggett. 1995. *The Two Majorities: The Issue Context of Modern American Politics.* Baltimore, MD: Johns Hopkins University Press.

Shenk, David. 1997. *Data Smog: Surviving the Information Glut.* New York: HarperEdge.

Simon, Adam F. 2002. *The Winning Message: Candidate Behavior, Campaign Discourse, and Democracy.* Cambridge: Cambridge University Press.

Skaperdas, Stergios, and Bernard Grofman. 1995. "Modeling Negative Campaigning." *American Political Science Review* 89: 49–61.

Sunstein, Cass. 2001. *Republic.com.* Princeton, NJ: Princeton University Press.

Wattenberg, Martin. 1996. *The Decline of American Political Parties, 1952–1994.* Cambridge, MA: Harvard University Press.

Wepman, Noah. 1998. "Gilmore vs. Beyer: How a Republican Won the Virginia Governorship with a Focused Message and Smart Issue Positioning." *Campaigns & Elections,* December/January.

LIST OF INTERVIEWS

Brookover, Ed, Republican media consultant, Greener & Hook, LLC, July 29, 2003 (Washington, DC).

Devine, Tad, Democratic media consultant, Shrum, Devine, & Donilon, Inc., July 30, 2003 (Washington, DC).

Fenn, Peter, Democratic media consultant, Fenn & King, August 5, 2003 (Washington, DC).

Franzen, John, Democratic media consultant, Franzen & Co., August 4, 2003 (Washington, DC).

Goldman, Dean, Democratic generalist, Goldman & Associates, May 23, 2000 (Norfolk, VA).

Greener, Bill, Republican media consultant, Greener & Hook, LLC, July 29, 2003 (Washington, DC).

Mahe, Eddie, Republican generalist, Mahe Company, June 13, 2000 (Washington, DC).

Manson, Marshall, Republican direct mail consultant, Persuasion, Inc., June 28, 2000 (Fredericksburg, VA).

Morris, Dick, political consultant, August 16, 2003 (e-mail correspondence).

Mullen, Erick, Democratic media consultant, Main Street Communications, July 14, 2000 (Washington, DC).

Roberts, Kyle, Republican media buying and placement consultant, Media Placement Technologies, July 29, 2003 (Alexandria, VA).

Smith, Jay, Republican media consultant, Smith & Harroff, Inc., July 24, 2003 (Alexandria, VA).

Strother, Ray, Democratic media consultant, Strother Duffy Strother, June 16, 2000 (Washington, DC).

Strother, Ray, Democratic media consultant, Strother Duffy Strother, August 4, 2003 (Washington, DC).

Todd, Bradley, Republican media consultant, Todd Castellanos, August 6, 2003 (Alexandria, VA).

ENDNOTES

1. As much as anything, Hollywood has contributed to this mythology. See, for example, *The Candidate* (1972), *Power* (1986), and *Wag the Dog* (1997).

2. For a complete list of consultant interviews, see List of Interviews.

3. Some, but not all, of what is described in this chapter holds true for issue and party/interest group campaigning though the focus of the chapter is on candidates and their campaigns.

4. Franzen interview; references to consultant interviews will be made in endnotes.

5. This could, of course, be explained by a simple lack of interest in politics (though even the lack of interest itself could be the result of voter confusion over political information). See Delli Carpini and Keeter (1996) on political knowledge, which turns out to be a bit more complicated than the conventional wisdom suggests.

6. Consultants sometimes imply that much of the reason for alarming rates of spending on television advertising is the lack of media coverage for their candidates. John Franzen, for example, suggested that even incumbents sometimes have to "purchase" their name recognition since they get so little coverage between elections (Franzen interview). In fact, for some time now, political scientists have believed that campaign ads have an educational component, perhaps surpassing that of television news (see Patterson and McClure 1976). Yet it is hard to imagine that campaigns would advertise less if the media covered politics more. As Dick Morris notes, "A free media has never been good at carrying messages" (Morris interview). That is, even if the news media informed voters, they wouldn't be reliable conduits of a campaign's persuasive efforts.

7. Strother 2003 interview.

8. Campaigns today probably are not, in fact, more negative (see Jamieson 2000, 49–53).

9. Strother 2003 interview.

10. Brookover interview.

11. Todd interview. Gross ratings points are a measure of how many people are likely to see a particular ad.

12. Franzen interview.

13. Morris interview.

14. Fenn interview.

15. Fenn interview.

16. Todd interview.

17. Strother 2003 interview; Brookover interview.

18. Smith interview.

19. Smith argues that this is yet another factor that makes direct mail an increasingly vital element of a campaign; Smith interview.

20. Brookover interview. For academic confirmation of this, see Wattenberg (1996); for a skeptical view, see Keith et al. (1992).

21. Greener interview.

22. Strother 2003 interview.

23. Morris interview.

24. Of course, 2002 was the final cycle before the Bipartisan Campaign Reform Act took effect. Assuming that the Supreme Court upholds the act (which is not a safe assumption), parties and interest groups will have a harder time dominating a race through advertising. Of course, parties will be able to spend unlimited hard dollars, and interest groups have a variety of options. For instance, they might continue to run advocacy ads prior to the 60-day window within which they would be prohibited from naming candidates. Or they might also decide to spend unlimited hard dollars. Alternatively, they might regroup as unincorporated associations and continue to buy exactly the same messages as [they] could under the old law (Malbin et al. 2002, p. 32). Finally, wealthy individuals will still be able to engage in independent expenditures.

25. Devine interview; Todd interview.

26. Greener interview; Brookover interview.

27. Franzen interview.

28. Todd interview.

29. Of course, at very low levels, messages rarely break through to voters; in these races, turnout becomes the key to victory (Manson interview).

30. Mullen interview; Manson interview.

31. Franzen interview.

32. Smith interview; Todd interview; Devine interview; Franzen interview; Fenn interview; Strother 2003 interview.

33. Franzen interview; Todd interview; Strother 2003 interview.

34. Strother 2003 interview; Smith interview.

35. Strother 2003 interview. The campaign budget is also an important aspect of the early planning process. Of course, the amount of money a candidate will have determines what the campaign will be able to do with respect to communication.

36. Fenn interview; Franzen interview; Todd interview.

37. Greener interview. There are two caveats that should be mentioned here. First, low-level elections are often determined exclusively by turnout (Manson interview). This does not mean that message is irrelevant in these races but that organizational considerations are usually more important. Second, in those races where the message is designed to attract swing voters, care must be taken not to alienate base voters with the message. To simplify the matter greatly, the more centrist the message, the less enthusiastic the base will be, and the less likely core supporters will be to show up on election day.

38. Todd interview.

39. Todd interview; Strother 2003 interview; Mullen interview.

40. A benchmark poll is an initial survey taken by the campaign to assess the political environment and develop a campaign strategy by obtaining a description of the atti-

tudes and beliefs of the voting population as a whole, and identifying any demographic or psychographic differences among those voters (Powell and Cowart 2003, 169).

41. Franzen interview.

42. Devine interview.

43. Mullen interview; Strother 2000 interview.

44. Fenn interview; Strother 2003 interview; Todd interview.

45. Franzen interview.

46. Smith interview; Strother 2003 interview.

47. Devine interview; Strother 2000 interview; Mahe interview.

48. Devine interview.

49. Mullen interview; Devine interview.

50. Strother 2003 interview; Mullen interview; Goldman interview; Manson interview.

51. Mullen interview.

52. There is, of course, the matter of whether or not the candidate *believes* the argument that he or she is making. Even though the issue position itself is sincerely held, the justification for it might not be. Whether or not a disingenuous rationale for a genuinely held position amounts to unethical campaigning may depend upon the standard you apply to campaign behavior (see Miller and Medvic 2002).

53. Devine interview.

54. Fenn interview.

55. Devine interview.

56. Greener interview; Brookover interview; Mahe interview.

57. Smith interview.

58. Devine interview.

59. Greener interview; Brookover interview; Todd interview.

60. Smith interview. Despite what seems like an enormous amount of polling, consultants point out that campaigns test messages far less than corporate clients, who test everything, including ad concepts, messages, storyboards and production (Fenn interview; Brookover interview).

61. Fenn interview; Franzen interview.

62. See also Budge and Farlie (1983) on saliency theory and Jacobs and Shapiro (1994) on intentional priming.

63. For a complete description of the process of implementing a communication campaign, see Johnson (2001, Ch. 6).

64. Strother 2003 interview; Franzen interview; Fenn interview.

65. For Schwartz (1973), one of the most effective ways to tap a person's storehouse of information is through auditory channels (see pp. 27–40).

66. Franzen interview.

67. Strother 2003 interview.

68. Fenn interview.

69. Franzen interview.

70. Most of the ads that were run during the summer of 1995 were actually sponsored by the Democratic National Committee and were ostensibly issue ads about legislative battles, particularly with respect to the budget. In fact, the ads both framed those legislative debates and laid the groundwork for the president's reelection campaign.

71. Smith interview.

72. Roberts interview.

73. Roberts interview.

74. Strother 2003 interview. This makes it possible, I suppose, to blame consultants for a lack of leadership in politics. But it seems unfair to expect consultants to find the perfect blend of leadership and responsiveness (a blend that is notoriously difficult to concoct). Besides, given a choice between those two options, I suspect most citizens would prefer a responsive politician to one who leads in a direction they oppose.

75. Todd interview.

76. A particularly egregious example occurred in the 1996 Virginia U.S. Senate race. The media consultant for incumbent Senator John Warner produced an ad in which he altered a photograph of Senator Charles Robb with President Clinton and former Virginia governor Douglas Wilder. The consultant replaced Robb's head in the picture with the head of Warner's opponent (presumably to associate him with liberals like Clinton and Wilder, who is black). Senator Warner fired the consultant the day after news of the doctored photograph broke (Hsu 1996).

77. The legal analogy fails to hold when one considers the many differences between a campaign and the legal system (see Miller and Medvic 2002, pp. 30–31 and Heclo 2000, 13). The most significant difference is that there is no judge in a campaign who can enforce the equivalent of rules of evidence.

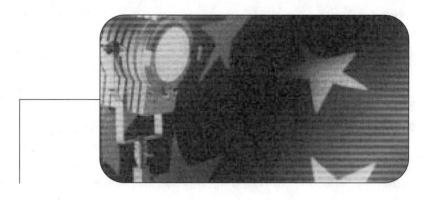

3

Two Cheers for Negative Ads

Christopher J. Dolan

> *Winning isn't everything, it's the only thing.*
> —*Vince Lombardi, Green Bay Packers*

I completely respect Vince Lombardi. He was one of the greatest coaches in football history not because he was nice or fair but because he was committed to one standard: complete and total victory. His players responded to his toughness, devotion to winning, and his clear-cut awareness of the difference between victory and defeat. Indeed, Lombardi was great not simply because the very thought of defeat was unacceptable, but because he was able instill this commitment into the hearts and minds of his players, who viewed the game of football as a struggle for ultimate victory.

The same is true for politics, particularly campaign politics, which is about winners and losers, victory and defeat, and communication between candidates and citizens. Negative ads and attack ads often bring out the worst in the candidates, given that the imagery in each of these very different advertising styles may be off-putting or even unethical. This chapter establishes the differences between certain types of campaign advertisements and details the strategic political use of negative and attacks advertisements in campaigns, contends that negative campaign tactics and attacks benefit the electoral process, identifies the thin line between attacks and lying, examines the use of attacks and negativity in the 2002 midterm elections, and analyzes whether or not the campaign system should incorporate reforms for decreasing the negative tone of campaigns and elections.

While candidate reliance on negative and aggressive campaigning is nothing new, the barbs have grown more nasty over the years. Are attack ads and negative campaigning really that detrimental to the electoral process? Are they reflections of the competitive nature of high stakes politics that is essential to citizen participation in the electoral process? Prevailing research demonstrates that despite warnings from political scientists, elected politicians, and journalists, negative campaigning and attack ads not only work to a great degree, they help to inform the voting public of the personal and political qualities of the candidates and their stands on the issues. It is time for political scientists and students of electoral politics to acknowledge their usefulness in campaigns for Congress and the presidency.

The Strategic Use of Political Advertisements

On the whole, political scientists tend to differentiate between three types of political advertisements. *Issue* or *contrast ads* illuminate the candidate's position on the issues or may highlight positive aspects of his or her campaign. *Negative ads* emphasize legitimate contrasts between the candidates on the issues, partisanship, or ideology in a highly critical yet justifiable fashion. For example, candidates may charge one another with being too liberal or conservative on the issues or too weak on certain policies. Attack ads are the product of deceptive and aggressive tactics that assail opponents on the issues or zero in on personal weaknesses and liabilities (Kolodny, Thurber, and Dulio 2000; Pfau and Kenski 1990).

The subject of this chapter is mainly concerned with negative and attack ads. It is believed that when a candidate highlights the negative aspects of his or her opponent or attacks them in a congressional or presidential campaign, the political effect is mostly negative. This is driven by the prevailing assumption that negative ads and attack ads are a powerful disincentive to vote and participate in the electoral process. It is also supported by the supposition that such ads are more easily remembered by citizens than more positive issue ads, and that attacks are always misleading and illegitimate (Elving 1996; Johnson-Cartee and Copeland 1991; Luntz 1988). This does not appear to be the case. Take President Reagan's 1984 ads against Democratic nominee Walter Mondale. The Republican ad in which Reagan's strength on foreign policy is compared to a bear, with the hint that Mondale would be weak in dealing with the Soviets, was much more memorable than the more touchy-feely "Morning Again in America" ad.

Citizens and even candidates often confuse negative ads with attack ads and use the terms interchangeably (Bode 1992; Bullock 1994; Elving 1996; Garramone 1984; West 1993). Attack ads focus in on personality and character flaws and use illegitimate means to contrast the candidates on the issues, whereas negative ads use justifiable tactics to establish these contrasts. Effective negative ads can actually educate the voters on the issues and provide them with clear choices on election day. According to William Mayer, "negative campaigning provides voters with a lot of valuable information that they definitely need to have when deciding how to cast their ballots" (Mayer 1996, p. 441). Even more, the use of negative ads in campaigns and elections has a significant public policy component. For Mayer, "the information and analysis embodied in negative campaigning are also valuable on their own terms, for they tell us something extremely relevant about the choices we are about to make" (Mayer 1996, p. 442).

With respect to negative ads, Robin Kolodny, James Thurber, and David Dulio conducted a survey of political consultants and found empirical evidence suggesting that negative ads do not degrade the electoral process or cause citizens to stay at home on election day. The researchers observe that the majority of negative ads contain relatively more accurate information about the candidates than issue ads, which tend to gloss over the issues and present rosy scenarios. While roughly 75% of consultants contend that attack ads and negative TV advertisements contribute to voter cynicism throughout the campaign season, they claim that conventional mass media and journalists and incumbent's poor policy performance in office does more to elevate levels of public apathy and disenchantment with the political process (Kolodny, Thurber, and Dulio 2000, p. 56).

Surprisingly, the use of attack ads, which employ controversial tactics to put forth misleading or false information to the voters, are usually lumped into the same category as negative ads that contain accurate information about a candidate and the issues. Roughly 94% of consultants held that making and issuing bogus statements about opponents clearly violate legitimate standards of campaigning and should not be confused with reasonable negative ads (Kolodny, Thurber, and Dulio 2000).

While they violate standards of legitimacy, cases of unethical and quasi-ethical attack ads are numerous throughout American history. The Declaration of Independence was nothing more than a long attack ad against the British monarch, King George III. The declaration's author and political consultant, Thomas Jefferson, accused the king of being a "tyrant, unfit to be the ruler of a free people." His litany against the ghastly king is relentless. For example, Jefferson describes the king in the following terms: "He has refused. He has dissolved. He has obstructed. He has abdicated. He has plundered." The Declaration of Independence set a nasty precedent for American campaigns and elections. Twenty-four years after Jefferson teed off on the king, in one of the first attacks in a presidential election, the Federalist-leaning *Connecticut Current* warned readers that if Thomas Jefferson defeated President John Adams, "murder, robbery, rape, adultery and incest will be openly taught and practiced" (quoted in Paletz 2002). Even Abraham Lincoln dabbled in attacks. In the 1854 Illinois U.S. Senate election, Lincoln accused Stephen Douglas of being "if not a dead lion at least a caged and toothless one." Douglas countered by calling Lincoln a "ghoul," "lunatic," and "traitor" (quoted in Paltez 2002).

In an aggressive 1948 campaign, summed up by the legendary phrase "Give 'em hell, Harry," President Harry S. Truman took to the rails to cross the country on a whistle stop campaign against Republican challenger Governor Thomas E. Dewey of New York. Throughout the campaign, Democrats combined legitimate negative campaign tactics with unethical verbal attacks on Dewey via highly dramatic public speeches. At the same time they were referring to the "Do Nothing Republican Congress," Democrats described the bland Dewey as looking like the "groom on the wedding cake." In order to protect his lead in the polls, Dewey responded by following an extremely cautious course. Rosser Reeves, the advertiser who would later create the 1952 "Eisenhower Answers America" presidential campaign theme, pleaded with Dewey to film some negative political commercials accusing Truman of being soft on Communism. While only roughly 500,000 homes had televisions, Reeves argued that careful ad placements in key districts could make the difference in a close race. Dewey, not expecting a close race, dismissed the idea. While Truman's election was a surprise, his combination of negative tactics with aggressive assaults on Dewey led to his comeback. Dewey's failure to respond proved that being warm and fuzzy does not translate into victory. However, the 1948 election was the last hurrah for a style of campaigning that would become increasingly rare in the television age.

Television has blurred the line between legitimate and illegitimate campaign tactics and has caused candidates to increasingly go on the offensive. The first case in which television was used to deflect attacks was in 1952 by Dwight Eisenhower's running mate Richard Nixon. In September of 1952, Nixon's spot on the Republican ticket as Eisenhower's vice president was threatened by unproved accusations of a secret fund set up by Nixon's business associates. In response to calls from fellow Republicans that he step down, Nixon broadcast a direct appeal in an informal speech airing after the popular Milton Berle Show. In what became known as the "Checkers" speech, Nixon detailed his family's finances and denied accepting gifts of any kind, except for a dog named Checkers, who was given to their daughter by a Texas fundraiser. As a result, Eisenhower and the Republican Party were swamped with telegrams urging that Nixon stay on the ticket. By playing the victim, Nixon brilliantly tugged at the electorate's heart strings and turned the attacks into a strategic win. In a related example, the 1960 televised debate between Vice President Nixon and Democratic candidate and U.S. Senator John Kennedy demonstrated that personal charm and charisma can be important variables in an election. The more physically attractive Kennedy was greatly helped in the first debate when he squared off against a tired and sick Nixon. While radio listeners felt Nixon had done better, TV viewers clearly favored JFK.

One of the first televised attack ads came four years earlier in the 1956 presidential election rematch between incumbent President Dwight Eisenhower and Democratic challenger Adlai Stevenson when Democrats again attacked Republican Vice President Richard Nixon. Playing on voters' fears about the health of Eisenhower, who had recently suffered a heart attack, Democrats produced a TV spot in which an announcer asked, "Nervous about Nixon? *President* Nixon?"

One of the most famous attack ads took place during the 1964 contest between Democratic President Lyndon Johnson and Republican Senator Barry Goldwater. Goldwater had the habit of making provocative "shoot-from-the-hip" remarks. Building on Goldwater's well-known hawkish views, the Democratic public relations firm of Doyle, Dane, and Bernbach (DDB) developed a devastating attack ad, which did not even identify the Republican candidate. The Democratic TV spot began with the camera on a little girl alone in a field counting, "One, two, three" as she picked petals off a daisy. She then looked up as the camera moved to her face and the screen went black. A man's voice was then heard counting, "Ten, nine, eight" and a nuclear weapon detonated. As the bomb blossomed into its mushroom shape, President Johnson spoke: "These are the stakes, to make a world in which all of God's children can live, or to go into the dark. We must either love each other, or we must die" (see Paletz 2002, 78). DDB's appeal was suited to a Johnson campaign that sought to remind voters of the administration's work fighting poverty and providing Medicare, while also capitalizing on fear of Republican opponent Barry Goldwater's views on nuclear weapons. Goldwater never recovered and Johnson was elected president.

Probably the most reviled, yet successful, attack ad was the 1988 Willie Horton ad, which was produced by current Fox News chief and Republican political consultant Roger Ailes for Vice President George Bush against Democratic opponent Massachusetts Governor Michael Dukakis. Although the ad was not officially produced by the Bush campaign, it described how Dukakis's support for "Democratic criminal justice weekend furloughs" for murderers resulted in a Maryland couple being held hostage by an escaped convict who raped and tortured his victims (Constitutional Rights Foundation 1996). The ad was factually correct in that Dukakis did support the furlough program, but the furlough program was installed by Dukakis's Republican predecessor Francis Sargent. The ad, which ran for roughly a month without a response from Democratic strategists, resonated with the voting public, which began finding credibility in Bush's theme that "America can't afford the risk" of a Dukakis presidency (Feder 1996; Paletz 2002). Other Republican ads against Dukakis proved equally as effective. For example, one ad showed Dukakis looking uncomfortable riding in a tank while a running list of the governor's opposition to key military programs appeared on the screen and was read to viewers. In effect, the attack ads defined the Dukakis campaign on the issues before the Massachusetts governor defined himself (Paletz 2002). Dukakis did run colorful and interesting attack ads against Republican vice-presidential nominee Dan Quayle, which played upon the public's lack of confidence in Bush's running mate, asking viewers if they had confidence in a potential Quayle presidency should Bush become ill. However, the ad was too little, too late in the campaign.

Along these same lines, during the 1990 U.S. Senate campaign in North Carolina, Republican strategist Alex Castellanos wrote and produced an ad effectively termed "Hands" for incumbent U.S. Senator Jesse Helms against challenger Harvey Gantt, whose support of affirmative action had been identified on surveys as an unpopular position. The controversial "Hands" ad featured a close-up shot of two hands, one white the other black, holding a letter and crumpling it as a narrator says, "You needed that job, but they had to give it to a minority." Helms surged ahead of Gantt and cruised to reelection.

According to Professor Kathleen Hall Jamieson, negative ads and attack ads do not, on the whole, taint campaign discourse. In fact, Jamieson notes that when used in combination with advocacy ads, negativity and attacks help voters distinguish between candidates (Jamieson 1992). The problem occurs when any ad—attack or negative—obviously misleads voters, especially those not dealing with issues or policy. False inferences, distorted records, half truths, or outright lies are what drive cynicism up and turn voters off. Jamieson refers to Clinton's use of visual techniques in the 1996 presidential election as a case in point. Democratic campaign strategists reinforced policy attacks on Republican U.S. Senator and challenger Bob Dole (R-KS) in black and white, with the goal of portraying Dole as too old and his policies as old fashioned (Jamieson, Waldman, and Scherr 1998). While Dole's age may have been a legitimate issue in the campaign, the insinuation that his age could produce antiquated policies was not.

This does not mean that purely negative ads are not problematic, especially because it is easy for the voters to misinterpret their messages. The most challenging negative ads are those that are factually accurate but seen by the viewer as out of context. Take, for example, the 1994 midterm congressional elections. One of the dirtiest and most expensive was the California U.S. Senate election between Democratic incumbent Dianne Feinstein and Republican challenger Michael Huffington (Brack 1994; Wolf 1994). After trading legitimate barbs on the issues, Huffington was called a hypocrite for ranting about illegal immigration while employing an illegal immigrant in his home while Feinstein was smeared as a "career politician who will say or do anything to stay in office" (Wolf 1994, p. 1A). Another example was the Virginia U.S. Senate race between incumbent and accused philanderer Democrat Charles Robb and accused liar and Republican challenger Oliver North. Republican ads asked, "Why can't Chuck Robb tell the truth?" while Democrats responded with "Vote your hopes, not your fears" (Wolf 1994, p. 1A). Widespread use of morphing technology, which produces a seamless transformation of one image into another, occurred in 1994 in televised ads. Democratic candidates were morphed into President Clinton and Republicans into Congressman Newt Gingrich (R-GA). However, morphing was more effectively utilized by Republican congressional candidates, who supplemented such technology with effective policy attacks. A generic ad run by the Republican National Committee attacking the "Clinton Congress" featured a woman claiming, "I just don't trust Bill Clinton" (Wolf 1994). A slew of Republican ads in the days before the November elections maintained that select House and Senate Democrats cast "the deciding vote" for President Clinton's deficit reduction measure, which included tax increases. Democrats countered by accusing Republican candidates of promoting a $2,000 cut in Social Security benefits to recipients. In reality, Republican ads on tax increases and Democratic ads on Social Security, while relatively accurate, were both out of context (Brack 1994; Elving 1996; Feder 1996; Wolf 1994). Vice President Al Gore, not Democratic congressional incumbents, cast the deciding vote in favor of the deficit reduction bill, and most Republicans, fearing a backlash from seniors, did not consent to most cuts in Social Security. Ethics aside, attacks on the White House were successful as Republicans assumed control of both the House and Senate and devastated Democrats in many gubernatorial elections.

Other researchers dismiss the adverse effects negative ads and attack ads have on the American political system as a whole. Lau, Sigelman, Heldman, and Babbitt contend the prevailing claims about the detrimental effects of such ads on voting and democracy are baseless (Lau et al. 1999). They also reject the popular notion that negativity is responsible for prevailing levels of public apathy and voter apathy. Quantitative analysis demonstrates that "the effects we observed for the 'unintended consequences' measures are too small in magnitude and too mixed in direction to provide empirical support for heated claims that negative ads are undermining public confidence and participation in the electoral process" (Lau et al. 1999, p. 859). While not concluding that the attack ads and negativity are directly linked with electoral success, the researchers affirm there is at present no significant support for the argument that such tactics harm the electorate.

John Theilmann and Allen Wilhite contend that there are actually two forms of campaigning that directly impact the electorate (Theilmann and Wilhite 1998). The first type examines the impact of negativity and attacks on voting and public opinion, while the second looks at incentives available for candidates to go on the attack. They contend that formal theory has a significant role to play in explaining the reasons why candidates decide to run negative ads and attack ads. According to the authors, "game-playing models appear to be a useful way to think about campaigns, and the decision to use positive or negative advertising" is a highly strategic one (Theilmann and Wilhite 1998, p. 1060). There is also a partisan variable at play here, as Republican candidates are more willing to utilize attack strategies and negative tactics than are Democrats. While Democrats are certainly willing to go on the offensive and use attack ads, their research suggests that in tight races, attacks seem to be more effective with voters and more frequently implemented by Republicans (Theilmann and Wilhite 1998).

On the whole, negative ads have proven to be highly successful when used strategically and effectively. If these ads are really that harmful to the citizenry, then we should stop and think about the alternative. Positive or issue ads that portray candidates in a glowing light ultimately downplay important differences, gloss over the substantive importance of the issues, and are more detrimental because they fail to inform the voters of necessary policy choices (Elving 1996; Finkel and Geer 1998). According to Professor Ken Goldstein, "we should not necessarily see negative ads as a harmful part of our electoral system. They are much more likely [than positive ads] to be about policy, to use supporting information and to be reliable" (Goldstein 2002). We therefore need to rethink the causal nexus between negative ads and public distrust of politicians and declining rates of voter turnout.

How Negativity and Attacks Benefit the Electoral Process

When examined in terms of effectiveness, one should realize that both negative ads and attack ads really work; this is the sole reason why candidates use them and why high-priced political consultants produce them. If the ads are accurate, the voters are more drawn to the candidates. Besides, according to most political consultants, negative ads and attack ads go through a more rigorous process before they are released to viewers than issue ads (Elving 1996; Luntz 1988; Sabato 1981; Theilmann and Wilhite 1997). Fred Steeper of Market Strategies Inc., who ran the Bush Sr. polling operation in 1988, claims that "attacks and negative ads are better researched than positive ads? Everyone knows that if you run a negative ad and are called on it, it will hurt your campaign" (quoted in Feder 1996, p. 21).

Regardless of the ad, they can be true or false, mostly true or mostly false, or sometimes true and sometimes false. In other words, if they come in the form of electronic ads they are open to interpretation by the viewer or the listener. If an attack is accurate and embarrassing, opponents will label it negative or claim to be the unfair victim of an attack. In reality, when a candidate says his or her record is being tarnished and distorted, she usually means voters should not be distracted by her stand on the issues or the ways in which she issued roll call votes and endorsed legislation (Mayer 1996). Take ads run by Republican candidates in the 1996 primaries. Bob Dole accused Steve Forbes of attacking him for being a Washington insider for over 35 years and for supporting a number of tax hikes. However, his

voting record in the U.S. Senate demonstrates he did vote for several pro-
posals to increase the income tax, and his over 35 years in Washington is
wholly impossible to dispute (Feder 1996). If a candidate fails to reveal the
truth or even to acknowledge it, opponents must make them accountable
and responsible (Kolodny, Thurber, and Dulio 2000).

According to conventional wisdom, voters are often annoyed and confused by negative and attack ads, especially when candidates twist and distort the issues and embroil themselves in the trivial elements of politics. Yes,
America's political environment has grown increasingly more negative and
the number of attacks has escalated; however, attacks and negativity are not
limited to paid campaign commercials. Conflict and entertainment are a powerful combination that attracts the attention of the viewing and voting public.

In fact, infotainment happens to be one of the primary reasons why candidates and consultants increasingly use negative messages. In *Going
Negative,* Stephen Ansolabehere and Shanto Iyengar argue that negative
attack ads are subverting democracy by polarizing the electorate and reducing voter turnout, particularly among nonpartisan, independent-minded
voters (Ansolabehere and Iyengar 1995). Advocates of heavier federal regulation of political campaigning are using this premise to support a reform
agenda that includes campaign-spending limits, greater federal censorship
of broadcast messages and even the elimination of paid political ads altogether (Brack 1994).

Unlike conventional political science examinations into political advertising that relied upon voter polls, Ansolabehere and Iyengar based their findings on controlled scientific experiments. Although there are many
methodological weaknesses in any ad-testing project and findings must always
be viewed with some skepticism, this one produced a number of interesting conclusions. Supporters of the reform agenda should carefully weigh two
of the authors' conclusions that contradict widely held misconceptions
about political commercials. First, voters get useful information from negative ads with strong and overt negative themes. *Going Negative* even
found that attack advertising is not "a pack of lies" and that "advertising
on the issues informs voters about the candidates' positions and makes it
more likely that voters will take their own preferences on the issues into
account when choosing between the candidates" (Ansolabehere and Iyengar
1995, p. 21).

Second, the authors concluded that attack ads are more persuasive than
manipulative, as they stimulate the electorate to at least talk about the candidates, the party system, and the issues. Exposure to advertising, they con-

cluded, is directly linked to political party affiliation and ideological dispo-
sition. "Individuals for whom the potential for manipulation is presumably
greatest—those lacking a sense of party affiliation—are, in fact, the least
likely to be persuaded by political advertising" (Ansolabehere and Iyengar
1995, p. 21).

As one observer claims, *Going Negative* also does not make an adequate
distinction between different types of overtly negative ads and attack ads
(Faucheux 1996). Negative ads can be informative and educate the voters
about the impact of opponents on policy and are carefully screened for accuracy. Attack ads can be dishonest, false, or just slanderous. To categorize
these ads together and pronounce one verdict on the entire pile without regard
to these critical differences is akin to falsely assuming that all politicians are
crooks or all journalists liberal.

In this atmosphere, blaming negative ads alone for widespread voter cynicism is a knee-jerk diagnosis. It is a simplistic way of explaining why
some citizens do not turn out to vote in congressional and presidential elections. Research has demonstrated that public disaffection with government and politics stems from the perception of the political system as
dishonest, self-serving, and inept, not from negative political ads (Finkel and
Geer 1998). Candidates who promise change in issue or even contrast ads
and fail to deliver ultimately create more voter alienation than do any
amount of negative ads, since they are raising the bar of public expectations
to the point where the public is guaranteed to be disappointed and cynical.
Citizens vote because they care about important issues or because they have
an affiliation with a political party, not because the candidates are not being
nice to one another on television. Therefore, to blame negative ads and attack
ads, which are run mostly during a campaign or election, for rising levels
of cynicism and apathy would be to ignore other potential negative forces,
such as electronic and print media, sitcoms, film, and literature. Should we
blame *Saturday Night Live,* Jay Leno, and David Letterman simply because
they poke fun at and negatively portray our elected leaders during and
between elections?

As research has shown, negative ads and attack ads do not appear as
causal forces that constrain voter turnout and citizen participation. Attacks
and negativity reinforce a public cynicism that already exists (Capella and
Taylor 1992; Finkel and Geer 1998; Martinez and Delegal 1990; Wattenberg
and Brians 1999). Moreover, attack ads may irritate the voters enough to
move them to the polls (Bullock 1994; Kamber 1997). Attack ads and negativity are healthy for campaigning if for no other reason than the need on

the part of voters for solid information so they can make choices among partisan alternatives (Kahn and Kenney 1998; Mayer 1996).

On a grander scale, Professor Robert Putnam contends that rising public cynicism and civic disengagement since the 1950s are due largely to the combined social impact of the automobile, suburbanization, residential mobility, career changes, fewer marriages, more divorces, rise of the service sector, decline of the manufacturing base and labor unions, fast food, and, of course, television (Putnam 1993 and 2001). To make the simple argument that attack ads and negative themes in contemporary presidential and congressional elections, which have been with us since July 4, 1776, contribute to an apathetic voting public is to ignore the social transformation of America since the late 1950s.

Candidates should not consent to media, academic, or even public demands to give up negative campaign tactics or even attacks simply because they are not nice. Besides, as the research cited here suggests, in the end, attack ads and campaign negativity do not contribute to lower voter turnout. Therefore, the real trick is to hit and weaken the opponent without hurting your own image and message. Remember, some of the most masterful and creatively designed attack lines in the history of campaign politics, to a certain extent, informed the voters. "There you go again!" Ronald Reagan chided the hapless President Jimmy Carter. "It's the Economy, Stupid," was used by Bill Clinton to irritate President George Bush. "I don't resent attacks. My family doesn't resent attacks. But Fala does resent attacks," FDR claimed, using his Scottish terrier to annoy and destroy his adversaries (Faucheux 1996). Before indicting all political attacks the way some now do and banning them from TV sets and radios the way some propose, consider what politics would be like without them: boring, bland, and unattractive.

Even attack ads, including the most vicious ones, do not delegitimize electoral politics. They are an essential component of a healthy electoral system that makes candidates accountable to the voters because they make politics interesting to the public as a whole. Issue ads can lie, distort, and mislead as openly as negative ones. The job of citizens is to make independent and informed judgments based on their own analysis and knowledge. It is not negativity that is the problem, as it is too easy for media pundits and political scientists to blame how the message is conveyed without blaming the message itself.

The Thin Line Between Attacks and Lying

Attacks and political lying can promote an image of strength for candidates. In a highly colorful manner, Democratic candidate Mike Freeman described his Republican opponent as a "A blow-dried bellhop to the rich" in the 1998 Minnesota gubernatorial election (McFeatters 1998). While he admitted to borrowing the colorful description from Ted Mondale, who was defeated in the Democratic primary, Freeman claimed he believed in campaigning in the style of "Minnesota nice" (McFeatters 1998). While Democrats succeeded in framing themselves as the party of the middle class, in the end it did not matter for Freeman or his Republican opponent, since independent candidate and former wrestler and actor Jesse Ventura was victorious. Similarly in Georgia, a Democratic candidate for governor was annoyed that his primary opponent voted against the Equal Rights Amendment in 1975 and opposed the state lottery in 1980 (McFeatters 1998). In doing so, Democrats positioned themselves alongside the prevailing wave of popularity surrounding the lottery program's ability to finance college tuition at Georgia state universities.

Being colorful is certainly not a tactic of late-twentieth-century campaign politics. In 1948 President Truman compared his opponent, Thomas E. Dewey, to Hitler, Mussolini, and Tojo. His crowds yelled "Give 'em hell, Harry," taking this as his feistiness (Feder 1996). Certainly Richard Nixon could creatively fight with brass knuckles. When he ran for the Senate against Helen Gahagan Douglas, one of his leaflets referred to "The Pink Lady" and was colored pink and listed her liberal voting record. The color pink implied she was a pale version of "red" Communists. Gahagan, married to actor Melvin Douglas, was a Hollywood leftist and not conspicuous for her opposition to communism. Nixon's leaflet was fair and accurate only if you think there's something "soft" about the relationship of left liberals to Communism (Paletz 2002).

Take for example Harry Truman's description of the charges against Alger Hiss as a "red herring," and Dean Acheson, after Hiss was convicted: "I will never turn my back on Alger Hiss." If he had said, "I won't kick a man when he's down," he would have gotten away with it, but he didn't. In fact, Acheson was a tough anti-Communist, and he deserves credit for NATO and the Marshall Plan, but the Republicans were playing hardball. Still, Joe McCarthy went too far when he spoke of "20 years of treason" and was unfair, if roguishly funny, when, at the Republican convention, he referred to "Alger, I mean Adlai, Stevenson" (Paletz 2002).

There is a difference between launching attacks and straight out lying. One of the great campaign liars in recent memory is former Vice President Al Gore, whose whoppers in the Democratic nomination phase of the 2000 presidential election were obvious but successful. In one of their New Hampshire debates, Bill Bradley accused Al Gore of lying. Bradley stated, "When someone says something that isn't true, it can be out of ignorance. But you, Al, know what is true and what isn't, and you are telling untruths." Quite brilliantly, Gore turned this around and projected himself as a victim of Bradley's negative campaigning: "Now, Bill, I have never accused you of lying, and I never will. I had hoped to keep our disagreements to a discussion of the issues." In effect, Gore "caught" Bradley attacking him by avoiding the question of his own lying (Hart 2000). For example, in Iowa the Gore campaign ran TV ads claiming that Bradley had opposed flood relief for Iowa farmers. In fact, Bradley had voted for it, while Gore, as vice president, had not cast a vote. Gore also lied when he said that he had "always" been a supporter of *Roe v. Wade* and abortion rights; he had opposed abortion when he was a congressman, and he had scored high on the right-to-life index. During his years in the House, he had an 84% positive record, according to the leading antiabortion estimate.

However, the continuation of Gore's whoppers into the general election demonstrated that lying can add to the strength of the opponent. While computer programmers at the Pentagon must have quietly chuckled when Gore claimed to have personally taken the lead in making the Internet available to the public, George W. Bush's chief spin doctors Karl Rove and Karen Hughes used it to define Gore as a distrustful and dishonest candidate who sees himself as "the father of the Internet." Other examples of Gore's lying strengthened the image of Bush as the candidate who would reestablish honesty, trust, and respect in the Oval Office. When Gore claimed that the young Harvard couple in *Love Story* was based on Tipper and him, its author Erich Segal emphatically denied it. In the first presidential debate, in order to look presidential, Gore claimed he was in Texas with FEMA Director James Lee Witt in managing federal relief to disaster victims. Rove and Hughes hammered Gore for lying, not only because Gore never went to Texas on such a trip, but because it was Governor George W. Bush who actually accompanied Witt. Gore spent more of his time trying to spin his whoppers and less time defining himself on the issues.

Accusing a candidate of lying may be construed as an assault on character, but if he or she is lying, it is perfectly legitimate to point it out, as Rove, Hughes, and Bush were ultimately successful in doing in 2000. Lincoln once

labeled the "Peace Democrats" as copperheads (poisonous snakes indige-
nous mainly to the southern United States). Indeed, for the preservation of
the Union, the northern Peace Democrats were dangerous. Union General
George McClellan ran against Lincoln as a Peace Democrat in 1864 and
might have won if Sherman had not obliterated and razed Atlanta by
November. For decades after the war, Republican candidates "waved the
bloody shirt" by accusing the Democrats of treason. Until 1948, the South
was solid territory for Democrats.

Negativity and Attacks at the Midpoint: Terrorism, War, and the 2002 Elections

In the run-up to the 2002 elections, new questions arose about whether
the tone of campaign advertisements would soften, given that the nation was
still reeling from the September 11 terrorist attacks on the World Trade
Center, the Pentagon, and the terrorist-caused crash in Western Pennsylvania.
Political ad experts held that September 11 and the worsening economy could
lead to never-before-seen uncertainties that might significantly alter campaign tactics (Booth and Balz 2002). In the months prior to November 2002,
the question was whether a kinder, gentler advertising climate would pre-
vail (Teinowitz 2001, p. 1).

For Republican incumbents and challengers, security was the preemi-
nent issue simply because a Republican president was in the White House
on September 11. According to Bush pollster Matthew Dowd, "Now we
have a new issue that we didn't have before Sept. 11, a dominant issue: homeland security and fighting terrorism. You can't avoid the elephant in the room.
We don't yet know if it will fill the landscape, but it will have to be dealt
with going forward" (quoted in DeFrank 2002, p. 23). Greg Stevens, who
handled Arizona Republican Senator John McCain's presidential race in
2000, stated "There is no question that the overarching theme of security
will be hugely important" (quoted in Fenn 2003, p. 22). It was clear that
Republican candidates were banking on the notion that national and homeland security issues would also limit Democratic attacks on the White
House, thereby weakening negative campaign efforts to link the economic
recession to President Bush (Seelye 2002).

While Democrats contended that security was an issue candidates
would discuss, they hoped it would not be the deciding issue on the minds
of voters. Instead, they suggested the deciding issue would likely be the economy and the federal budget deficit, issues they believed were fair game for

blaming the Bush White House (Postman and Pfleger 2003). Frank Greer, president of Greer, Margolis, Mitchell, Burns, & Associates, contended that his political consulting firm's polling shows voters are still concerned about issues that were there before September 11, including education and health care, but are now much more worried about the economy: "Democrats have a message on the economy—helping unemployed workers, raising the minimum wage—that will play strongly" (Teinowitz 2001, p. 1).

According to Mark Mellman, Democratic Party pollster and head of The Mellman Group, while there is concern about terrorism, there is not a lot of difference between the parties on security issues. Instead, the big question is not just the state of the economy, but which party will get blamed for the recession and the deficit. According to Mellman, "The bottom-line fact is this president was in very deep trouble before Sept. 11. The terrorist attacks improved Bush's standing, but now we're in reality, and the problems that bedeviled him before Sept. 11 are reasserting themselves" (Teinowitz 2001, p. 1). As the results of the midterm elections proved, Democrats failed to establish a nexus between Bush and America's economic woes or even attack him on economic issues (Postman and Pfleger 2003). They even contributed to their own demise in 2002, namely in the U.S. Senate race in Minnesota when Democrats transformed Senator Paul Wellstone's funeral into a national media event and campaign rally for the replacement candidate, former Vice President Walter Mondale, who was defeated by Republican Norm Coleman (Keen 2002).

While the effect of the issues remains open and the results of the election strengthened Republican congressional control, it was thought that political advertising would be headed for certain change in 2002, since that was the first major election since September 11. According to Professor Ken Goldstein of the University of Wisconsin, the closer November approached, the nastier the campaigns became. He describes Campaign 2002 in the following manner: "In July, more than 70% of ads were positive. By early November, that number had dwindled to fewer than 50%. A dramatic change developed in early September in the days before and immediately after the 9/11 anniversary, when more than 90% of the spots aired were positive. Just days after the anniversary, campaigns across the nation rapidly reverted to airing negative television" (Goldstein 2002). Furthermore, consistent with previous midterm elections, the closer the race, the nastier and more negative it became. In races deemed noncompetitive, roughly 70% of political advertisements were categorized as positive, whereas in competitive races, 51% of ads were positive (Goldstein 2002). Goldstein's research reveals some interesting numbers in congressional races where less than 50% of candidate or political party ads were positive (see Table 3.1).

Table 3.1: Top 10 Negative Races (Post-9/11)

State/ District	Positive Count	Negative & Contrast Count	% Positive Airings
NY -1	0	387	0
CA-18	59	803	6.84
IL-Gov	999	5713	14.88
NV-03	651	3127	17.23
AL-Gov	3306	14554	18.51
IN-02	1445	5933	19.59
NJ-Senate	1170	4453	20.81
NH-Senate	1793	6806	20.85
WI-Gov	1856	6765	21.53

Source: Ken Goldstein. "One Billion Dollars Spent on Political Television Advertising in 2002 Midterm Election." Final Report on the 2002 Election by the Wisconsin Advertising Project (December 5, 2002).

Nastiness reigned even after the November elections. In the run-off U.S. Senate election in Louisiana between incumbent Democrat Mary Landrieu and Republican challenger Suzanne Haik Terrell, each candidate ratcheted up the negativity and attacks. Louisiana's open primary system requires a winner to get at least 50% in the general election; otherwise, the top two finishers face a runoff. After Landrieu's 46%, Terrell came in second with 27%. She and her two major Republican challengers got more than half the votes on election day. With an almost fifty-fifty Democrat-Republican split, the stakes were high and negativity the norm (Randolph 2002). For example, in a television debate Terrell accused Landrieu, who supports abortion in certain circumstances, of losing her Catholic faith. Landrieu has said Terrell, the state elections commissioner, would be nothing more than a rubber stamp for Bush. "Every time Haik Terrell opens her mouth she supports Bush. The question is not who will support the Republican agenda the most, but who will support Louisiana," Landrieu spokesman Rick Masters maintained. And Landrieu effectively played the victim: "My attacks haven't been personal. I have been personally attacked, my faith, personally maligned. At least I have not attacked her children and her family." Terrell was put on the defensive as a result of Landrieu's ability to play the victim. (Randolph 2002, p. 1). In the end, Landrieu edged out Terrell to keep her seat, preventing the Republicans from ending 120 years of Democratic control of U.S. Senate seats from Louisiana.

Not only are high-stakes campaigns embroiled in negativity and saturated with attack ads, both the Democratic and Republican national committees are distributing more and more soft money to those state parties seen as most competitive. For example, in New Hampshire, the Republican Senatorial Campaign Committee sent $2.5 million to state Republicans, and the Democratic Senatorial Campaign Committee reported $1.9 million in soft money had been channeled to state Democrats. According to Steven Weiss of the Center for Responsive Politics, "Clearly you wouldn't expect that from a state the size of New Hampshire.... It shows that these elections are being closely watched by the national parties. The stakes are very high." (LeSage 2002, p. 23)

This has changed since the Bipartisan Campaign Reform Act of 2002 (BCRA) went into effect shortly after the November elections. While the act forbids political parties from raising or spending soft money, in 2002 congressional campaigns were determined to spend all their soft money before election day. In total, political parties, candidates, and interest groups spent about $1 billion on television advertising for the 2002 midterm congressional elections, racing to use up reserves of soon-to-be-banned campaign contributions. Spending on congressional races was close to $320 million, almost twice as much as in 1998, the last midterm elections. The $1 billion in advertising included just over $420 million spent on governors' races and the rest on local races and statewide referenda. In competitive Senate races since September 11, 2002 (one year after the terrorist attacks), Democratic candidates, interest groups, and the party spent more than their Republican counterparts, the report found. Again, televised and radio advertising grew increasingly negative as the campaign season moved on, especially in the most competitive races, the report found. The Democratic and Republican parties spent heavily after that; both parties spent $41 million on more than 65,000 ad spots (Goldstein 2002). Goldstein claims that money donated from specific groups, namely the United Seniors Association (pharmaceutical/business and industry), the AFL-CIO (labor union), and the Florida Education Association (education/teacher's union) funded most of the negative ads in highly competitive races (see Table 3.2).

Table 3.2: Top 10 Interest Group Spenders on Paid Television Ads

Interest Group	Cost (millions)	Count
United Seniors Association	8.7	15098
AFL-CIO	3.6	5616
Americans for Job Security	1.5	2125
Emily's List	1.3	1166
Sierra Club	1.2	1730
Florida Education Association	1.1	2669
Michigan Chamber of Commerce	0.69	855
Planned Parenthood	0.66	355
Club for Growth	0.56	1574
American Medical Association	0.55	1449

Source adapted from: Ken Goldstein. "One Billion Dollars Spent on Political Television Advertising in 2002 Midterm Election." Final Report on the 2002 Election by the Wisconsin Advertising Project (December 5, 2002).

Soft money is politically useful for the candidates, especially incumbents, because it allows them a certain degree of cover and protection in attacking opponents. Professor Michael Dupre of the New Hampshire Institute of Politics and St. Anselm's College contends that soft money supplies candidates with the protection of having interest groups go negative for them without doing it themselves. "They may make the snowball, but they want someone else to throw it. Soft money throws the snowball for them" (quoted in LeSage 2002, p. 23). Professor Andrew Smith, director of the University of New Hampshire's Survey Center, adds that because of the soft money–negative ad linkage, there were more political advertisements in 2002 than ever before. "There's so much negativity and money dumped into the race. Typically you don't see this volume until the last week (before the election). Since there are so many different political ads coming out, it makes it difficult for those lesser-known candidates who don't have a lot of money to get their message out" (quoted in LeSage 2002, p. 23).

Under the 2002 BCRA, interest groups such as the Chamber of Commerce or the United Auto Workers can run issue ads, but they will have a limited time frame in which they can do so. The new reform law also states that ads from outside groups are prohibited within 60 days of the general election and within 30 days of the primary. This restriction was challenged before the Supreme Court by a coalition of legislators in *McConnell v. Federal Election Commission*. However, on December 10, 2003, the Court upheld major portions of the BCRA. Specifically, the Court banned national office-holders or candidates from using soft money and upheld regulations on state parties that spend soft money on federal election activity. The Court also issued broad controls on the linkage between ads and soft money by prohibiting parties from transferring or soliciting soft money for politically active, tax-exempt groups, banning state candidates from spending soft money on public communications that promote or attack federal candidates, requiring that individuals disclose their spending on electioneering communications to the FEC, and issuing new Federal Communications Commission requirements for candidate disclosure, better known as the "stand by your ad" provision. The Court also defended the BCRA's definition of "electioneering communication" as a broadcast advertisement mentioning a federal candidate, targeted at their electorate, and aired within 30 days of a primary or 60 days of a general election (See *McConnell v. Federal Election Commission*, December 10, 2003).

Would the elimination of soft money mean we would witness less negative, more positive campaigns? The answer is no. The BCRA does not establish actual binding restrictions on the candidates themselves running negative ads and attack ads and sets no real limitations on the use of hard (regulated) money by corporations and unions in support of so-called issue-related ads. As stated by Smith, "there may be fewer ads (in the future), but the ads will not go away" (LeSage 2002, p. 23). Who's to say that regulated money from citizens and political action committees (PACs) will not fund negative political ads well into the future? The 2004 presidential and congressional elections are still open season for negative ads and attacks by both candidates and interest groups.

It was also thought that the outpouring of patriotism (Americans displaying flags on their cars, houses, or shirts) following the September 11 terrorist attacks would elevate voter turnout, yet turnout in the 2002 congressional primaries was a mere 17%—no better than four years before and only half that of three decades ago. Turnout on election day was 39.3%, significantly below what it once was, although this was a scant increase of 1.7% from the 37.6% who voted in 1998. It is likely that an estimated 78.7 million registered voters cast their ballots in the 2002 midterm with 121 million staying at home (Center for Voting and Democracy 2002). No doubt, ordinarily Americans share responsibility for their lapse in participation; it is always easier to leave the work of political participation to others.

Do We Really Need Reforms?

What, if anything, should we do about negative campaign tactics and attacks in our campaigns and elections? The incumbency advantage renders any real attempt at putting limits on attack advertisements on a specific level, and negative campaigning in general, almost impossible. As stated by Professor William Mayer, "Any move to limit negative campaigning, in short, would add just one more weapon to the already formidable arsenal with which incumbents manage to entrench themselves in office" (Mayer 1996, p. 452). Besides, in close races, attack ads allow incumbents to go on the offensive in order to pull away from challengers. Moreover, challengers must be able to rely on attack strategies if they are going to make campaigns competitive and in turn have a shot at dislodging the incumbent. This of course depends on the degree of success with which incumbents and challengers use negative campaign tactics and attack ads.

Take, for example, efforts by the Maine state legislature, which passed in 1996 a statewide Clean Elections Act that was originally passed as a referendum. The law was designed to limit the number of attack ads used by PACs and to decrease the incentives for candidates to use other negative campaign tactics, such as legitimate ads with contextual questions. On the whole, the legislation was intended to give candidates the option to run without incurring political debts to specific donors and to avoid making personal judgments of opponents (Porter 2002). Quite ironically, the law actually contributed to the harsh negative tone PACs injected into a number of state and local elections in November 2002, leading legislators to amend the legislation. In essence, although soft money contributions dropped, hard money and bundling tactics increased, resulting in an increase in the number of negative and attack ads.

On the issue of money and ads, the decision by the U.S. Supreme Court to uphold the BCRA may not be enough to head off a mad dash for large contributions from corporations, labor unions, and wealthy individuals as Democrats try to catch up with Republican fundraisers. The decision could render Maine's clean election measure, as well as other state efforts, null and void (Porter 2002). However, reaction on both sides of the campaign finance debate was muted because the complexity of the decision made it difficult to determine the full scope of its impact.

Democrats, in particular, are now at a disadvantage as a result of the soft money ban because they are not as proficient at raising more strictly regulated "hard money" as Republicans. In the 2002 election cycle, for example, the Republican National Committee raised $164 million in hard money and $114 million in soft money. The Democratic National Committee raised $67 million in hard money, $94 million in soft. Political analyst Charlie Cook contended that "The cold hard facts are that in the 2002 cycle, the Democratic committees raised almost as much 'soft,' now illegal-to-party-committees money as Republicans did. But the Republican committees raised almost twice as much hard money as the Democratic Party commit-tees. Although Democrats decried the influence of dirty soft money in pol-itics, they were more hooked on it than Republicans were. Democratic election lawyers warned their legislator-clients of the implications of these reform efforts" (Cook 2003, p. 1023).

The University of Virginia Project on Campaign Conduct proposed forc-ing the candidates into signing codes of conduct—no personal attacks on other candidates; no use of language or images that define other candidates based on race, sex, or personal characteristics; and no questioning another candidate's honesty, integrity, or patriotism. The project issued a survey report in July 1999, which reveled that "an overwhelming majority of respondents supported the idea of candidates adopting voluntary guidelines on campaign conduct such as a code of ethics (96% supported the idea) or limits on cam-paign spending (90%). Support for laws requiring candidates to adopt a code of ethics and limit spending was also around 90%" (Project on Campaign Conduct 1999, p. 2). The Project also believes that voters believe negative, attack-oriented campaigns are unethical, threaten the electoral process, decrease voter turnout, and produce leaders who are unethical (Project on Campaign Conduct 1999).

However, reports from the Annenberg Public Policy Center at the University of Pennsylvania concluded that negative ads sometimes have more substantive information about policy than personal "I'm-a-great-guy!" or "everything is great!" ads (see http://www.appcpenn.org/issueads/). Therefore, a code of conduct is not likely to be effective, since candidates, especially incumbents, who spend millions of dollars are too desperate in the waning hours of a campaign not to try a tactic that has been proven to work. As Vince Lombardi once said: "Winning isn't everything, it's the only thing." The bottom line seems to be that we're doomed to watch more attack ads in the future. In other words, instead of setting ourselves up by thinking that candidates will avoid negativity, we should devise better strategies for digesting the relevance of the messages and information provided in the attack ads. Forcing candidates to be warm and fuzzy is no practical solution to neg-ative political advertisements, which may or may not be problems in the first place.

Besides, being nice is inconsistent with prevailing mass media tactics that only encourage negativity. For example, the Advisory Committee on the Public Interest Obligations of Digital Television Broadcasters released a report in December 1998 recommending that TV stations air five minutes a night of "candidate-centered discourse" in the 30 nights preceding all elections. Such discourse allows candidates time to advance their policy positions and to define their positions on issues in the absence of an opponent. The committee found that candidate-centered discourse is largely ignored by mass media outlets and that broadcasters, who control the most widely used medium for political information, have permitted campaigns to be dominated by paid ads rather than free candidate discourse (Alliance for Better Campaigns and Annenberg Public Policy Center 2000).

More specifically, the amount of candidate-centered discourse provided by a typical local station during the height of primary season was just 39 seconds per night. The amount of candidate-centered discourse provided by ABC, NBC, and CBS during the month preceding multistate primaries on March 7, 2000, was an average of 36 seconds per night. As political fundraising continues to set records, the volume and cost of political advertising on television have also risen to record levels. In the first four months of 2000, stations in the nation's top 75 media markets (covering approximately 80% of the national population) aired 151,267 political ads at a cost of $114 million, according to research conducted by Power Television, an ad monitoring service, for the Alliance (Alliance for Better Campaigns and Annenberg Public Policy Center 2000). The numbers indicate that being nice simply does not pay as it becomes a disincentive for candidates to avoid airing attack ads and unprofitable for media outlets to turn down requests to run political advertisements.

Conclusion: Why We All Love
Negative Campaign Advertisements

This chapter has attempted to provide at least a tentative answer to the question of why negative political advertisements benefit candidates. We have witnessed here how negative ads and attacks also benefit the citizenry. Many political scientists have endeavored to show that the harshness of our campaigns threatens the processes by which we choose our leaders. They worry that bitterness and animosity turn our campaigns into political showmanship and make governing more tenuous. While there is some merit to this, it denies the very foundation upon which all of politics rest—

conflict and power. By expressing political animosities, negative advertising might, quite indirectly, be helpful.

Citizens are asked to perform many sacrifices in a constitutional republic, for example, paying taxes, fighting in wars, dealing with inept and incompetent political leaders on both sides of the aisle, and obeying laws and policies put forth by groups for the benefit of special interests at the expense of the public interest. Our constitutional republic has survived because citizens are, and have always been, willing to put up with the blatant and sometimes shameless expression of political ambition. This is the very reason why this is the best way for citizens and leaders to settle their disputes. Put simply, the ways in which we choose our leaders have worked because we have been able to channel our political conflict via messaging.

Why then is so much energy devoted to criticizing attack ads and negative campaign tactics? The answer is that political scientists and other observers misperceive them as causal variables on election day, when in fact, attacks and negativity merely reflect the contentious nature of politics since the founding of the nation. If Americans are really cynical about politics and detached from the political system, then we need to point to greater social and political trends in America that have contributed to rising public apathy, such as those highlighted by Professor Robert Putnam.

Consider the following two points. First, negative advertising helps to express resentment, whether it is directed at candidates and government from citizens and groups or from candidates to their opponents. Second, negative advertising reflects the divisions citizens have on the issues and public policy. By limiting the political use of attack ads in campaigns, candidates and citizens are forced to agree on the concepts and matters that drive their political interests.

Negative advertising brings political conflict into our homes, relationships and marriages, businesses, colleges and universities, and places of worship where political conflict exists in other forms. Such conflict helps us to express the realities of our own divisions. In the end, this should be seen as a good thing. Yes, the tension, zeal, sourness, and hostility of congressional and presidential campaigns are scary for some, but so is everything else in political and social life. This is the very reason why most constitutional republics have not stood the test of history. If we deny the existence of political disagreements and clashes or the means by which to express them peacefully through attacks and negativity, we deny citizens the very choices they need to make intelligent and informed decisions. In doing so, we further deny that politics are about conflict, struggle, and power—not peace, harmony, and joyfulness. In a convoluted way, negative advertising guarantees that popular sovereignty is alive and well and that our leaders in one way or another need us to justify governance.

REFERENCES

"Accentuate the Negative." Editorial. *Pittsburgh Post-Gazette* (November 5, 2002): A17.

Alliance for Better Campaigns and Annenberg Public Policy Center. "Broadcast Television & Campaign 2000." (2000): http://www.bettercampaigns.org/reports/display.php?ReportID=7

Ansolabehere, Stephen, and Shanto Iyengar. *Going Negative: How Political Advertisements Shrink and Polarize the Electorate.* New York: Free Press, 1995.

Bode, Ken. "Pull the Plug." *Quill* 80 (March 1992): 10–14.

Booth, William, and Dan Balz. "Many Voters Wary as Crucial Election Nears." *Washington Post* (October 29, 2002): A1.

Brack, Reginald K. "How to Clean Up Gutter Politics." *New York Times* (December 27, 1994): A21.

Bullock, David. "The Influence of Political Attack Advertising on Undecided Voters: An Experimental Study of Campaign Message Strategy." Ph.D. dissertation, University of Arizona, 1994.

Capella, Louis, and Ronald D. Taylor. "An Analysis of the Effectiveness of Negative Political Campaigning." *Business and Public Affairs* 18 (spring 1992): 10–17.

Center for Voting and Democracy. "Committee Report for the Study of the American Electorate: Post Election News Release." *2002 Voter Turnout Report* (November 8, 2002): http://www.fairvote.org/turnout/csae2002.htm.

Constitutional Rights Foundation. "Election Issues: TV Attack Ads and the Voters." Report of the *Bill of Rights in Action,* Vol. 13. (winter 1996): 1.

Cook, Charlie. "Democrats Will Be Crippled by Campaign Finance Reform; Unlikely to Take Back House." *National Journal* (February 5, 2003), 1023.

DeFrank, Thomas M. "Bush Sees Fate in Terror Fight." *New York Daily News* (September 8, 2002): 23.

Elving, Ronald D. "Accentuating the Negative: Contemporary Congressional Campaigns." *PS: Political Science and Politics* 29, no. 3 (September 1996): 440–446.

Fadley, Chuck. "As Vote Arrives, Lawyers Are Ready." *Miami Herald* (November 4, 2002): 1.

Faucheux, Ron. "Do Attack Ads Subvert the Political Process?; No." *News World Communications* (March 25, 1996): 23.

Feder, Don. "In Praise of Negative Campaign Ads." *Boston Herald* (February 19, 1996): 21.

Fenn, Peter. "Lessons Learned from the Last Election." *Campaigns and Elections* (February 2003): 22.

Finkel, Steven E., and John Geer. "A Spot Check: Casting Doubt on the Demobilizing Effect of Attack Advertising." *American Journal of Political Science* 42 (April 1998): 573–595.

Garramone, Gina M. "Voter Response to Negative Political Ads." *Journalism Quarterly* 61 (1984): 250–259.

Goldstein, Ken. "One Billion Dollars Spent on Political Television Advertising in 2002 Midterm Election." *Final Report on the 2002 Election by the Wisconsin Advertising Project* (December 5, 2002).

Hart, Jeffery. "Going Negative." *Dartmouth Review* (March 13, 2000).

Jamieson, Kathleen Hall. *Dirty Politics: Deception, Distraction, and Democracy.* New York: Oxford University Press, 1992.

Jamieson, Kathleen Hill, Paul Waldman, and Susan Scherr. "Eliminate the Negative? Defining and Refining Categories of Analysis for Political Advertisements." Paper Presented at the Conference on Political Advertising in Election Campaigns, Washington, DC, 1998.

Johnson-Cartee, Karen, and Gary A. Copeland. *Negative Political Advertising: Coming of Age.* Hillsdale, NJ: Lawrence Erlbaum Associates, 1991.

Kahn, Kim Fridkin. and Patrick J. Kenney. "Do Negative Campaigns Mobilize or Suppress Voter Turnout? Clarifying the Relationship between Negativity and Participation." *American Political Science Review* 93 (December 1998): 877–889.

Kamber, Victor. *Poison Politics: Are Negative Campaigns Destroying Democracy?* New York: Plenum, 1997.

Keen, Judy. "Make or Break Nine Weeks Awaits President." *USA Today* (August 29, 2002): 6A.

Kolodny, Robin, James A. Thurber, and David A. Dulio. "Producing Negative Ads: A Consultant Survey." *Campaigns and Elections* (August 2000): 56.

Lau, Richard R., Lee Sigelman, Caroline Heldman, and Paul Babbitt. "The Effects of Negative Political Advertisements: A Meta Analytic Assessment." *American Political Science Review* 93, no. 4 (December 1999): 851–875.

LeSage, Margot. "Is Soft Money Making Attack Ads Too Hard for New Hampshire?" *Eagle-Tribune* (October 6, 2002): 23.

Luntz, Frank I. *Candidates, Consultants, and Campaigns.* Oxford: Basil Blackwell, 1988.

Martinez, Michael D., and Tad Delegal. "The Irrelevance of Negative Campaigns to Political Trust: Experimental and Survey Results." *Political Communication and Persuasion* 7 (January/March 1990): 25–40.

Mayer, William G. "In Defense of Negative Campaigning." *Political Science Quarterly* 111, no. 3 (autumn 1996): 437–455.

McFeatters, Ann. "Political Attack Ads Unpopular, but They Work." *Chicago Sun-Times* (August 3, 1998): 27.

Paletz, David. *The Media and American Politics.* New York: Longman, 2002.

Pfau, Michael, and Henry C. Kenski. *Attack Politics: Strategy and Defense.* New York: Praeger, 1990.

Porter, Aaron. "Clean Elections Law Spawns Attack PACs." *The News at Ellsworth American.com* (October 28, 2002): 1.

Postman, David, and Katherine Pfleger. "Locke Speech May Help Tune Party's 2004 Pitch." *Seattle Times* (January 27, 2003): B1.

Project on Campaign Conduct. "Study Shows Voters Reject Unfair Campaign Attack Advertisements." *Thomas C. Sorensen Institute for Political Leadership at the University of Virginia* (July 6, 1999): http://www.virginia.edu/topnews/releases-/campaignads-july-6–1999.html.

Putnam, Robert D. *Making Democracy Work: Civic Traditions in Modern Italy.* Princeton, NJ: Princeton University Press, 1993.

———. *Bowling Alone: The Collapse and Revival of American Community.* New York: Touchtone Books, 2001.

Randolph, Ned. "Republicans Eye Further Gain in Louisiana Senate Race." *Macon Telegraph* (December 4, 2002): 1.

Sabato, Larry J. *The Rise of Political Consultants.* New York: Basic Books, 1981.

Seelye, Katharine. "The Next Campaign: Outcome Closes Some Doors for 2004." *New York Times* (November 7, 2002): 6B.

Teinowitz, Ira. "Will the Tone of Wartime Political Ads Have to Change?" *AdAge.Com* (November 26, 2001): 1, http://www.aef.com/channel.asp?ChannelID=6&DocID=1858&location=Hot%20Issues

Theilmann, John and Allen Wilhite. "Campaign Tactics: Positive Versus Negative Advertising." Paper presented at the Annual Meeting of the Public Choice Society, San Francisco, CA, 1997.

———. "Campaign Tactics and the Decision to Attack." *Journal of Politics,* 60, no. 4 (November 1998): 1050–1062.

Wattenberg, Martin P., and Craig L. Brians. "Negative Campaign Advertising: Demobilizer or Mobilizer?" *American Political Science Review* 93 (December 1999): 891–899.

West, Darrell M. *Air Wars: Television Advertising in Election Campaigns, 1952 to 1992.* Washington, DC: Congressional Quarterly, 1993.

Wolf, Richard. "Attack Ads Strike Chord with Voters." *USA Today* (November 1, 1994): 1A.

4

Can a Voter in New York Make a Candidate Lose in California?

An Experimental Test of the Release of Early Election Results on Voter Turnout

Geoffrey D. Peterson

Introduction

At 7:48 P.M. Eastern time, the major news networks made the first of several erroneous predictions. The results of their exit polling showed that Al Gore would win the state of Florida and the 2000 presidential election. While the battle over who the true winner of the state was would drag on for over a month, many political pundits and scholars raised serious questions regarding the release of the early election results. While there are certainly no clear answers at this point, the question is surely one that merits debate.

The focus of this controversy is what is often referred to as the West Coast effect. The West Coast effect is defined as the impact of the release of early election returns from the East Coast before the polls on the West Coast close. Potential voters on the West Coast gain access to new information about the developing election through the media, and this information changes their intended behavior. Access to the information may encourage or discourage voters from going to the polls, depending on which candidate they support and the content of the information they have received.

In essence, the debate surrounding the West Coast effect is a question regarding the introduction of information. There is little question that the introduction of new information can change political behavior. While the effect of the information can be moderated or exacerbated by outside forces, and the impact of the information may not be visible under certain circumstances, the new information remains a potential catalyst for behavioral change depending on the strength of the novelty. While it is difficult to find real-world situations in which the impact of new information can be accurately gauged, one is the West Coast effect.

The story surrounding the West Coast effect is an interesting one for both political science and political practitioners. If access to election-day information can alter voting behavior, it must be considered by political scientists attempting to explain and predict turnout in national elections. In addition, the West Coast effect has implications for students of the democratic process, the First Amendment, and the press. For practitioners of politics, this knowledge could, for example, alter which states are targeted in the last days of a presidential campaign. Since the early 1960s, politicians, political scientists, pollsters, and pundits have debated the potential impact of the West Coast effect. The debate over whether to limit media broadcasting of election results to minimize the West Coast effect in close elections resulted in hearings in the Senate Subcommittee on Communications in 1967, the House Committee on Energy and Commerce in 2001, and hearings by the Federal Communications Commission on several occasions.

Although widely debated, the issue itself is often viewed as esoteric and abstract by the general public. In order to put the controversy in more concrete terms, the issue is often framed in the form of a story about an individual voter.[1]

A mid-level manager is on her way home from work on election day in California. She had intended to vote all along, but her day had been busy and she had not found the time. As she begins the drive home, she turns on the radio in her car and hears that the presidential candidate she had intended to vote for has just conceded the election to his opponent on the basis of the early election returns from the East Coast. Realizing that she no longer has any hope whatsoever of altering the presidential election outcome, she decides not to vote and chooses to go home. When thousands of other members of her party choose to do so as well, several statewide elections are altered by the depressed turnout among supporters of the losing presidential candidate's party.

While apocryphal, this story presents the essential features of the West Coast effect. The introduction of new information to the electorate (the results of the East Coast voting) alters voting behavior on the West Coast. Since the presidential election outcome is already a foregone conclusion, the impact of decreased turnout is primarily felt among those running in state and subnational elections on the West Coast. Candidates for subnational elections may find themselves at the mercy of the presidential election outcomes, and they may well win or lose based on the result of the national election rather than the merits of their individual campaigns.

What Do We Know? The History and Literature Surrounding the West Coast Effect

The potential impact of reporting early election returns has been debated since the early 1960s. With the combination of sophisticated computer models and dramatic improvements in survey techniques, it became possible for the major news organizations to predict the election results with only a fraction of all of the votes in the state counted. When the networks announced they would release East Coast election predictions before the polls closed on the West Coast, politicians and pundits began to question the impact of this information on West Coast residents. Many predicted dramatic decreases in turnout, believing West Coast voters would choose to stay home in droves if they believed their votes could not alter the eventual outcome of the election. Others predicted a more modest impact, but the clear consensus was the information would cause turnout to decline.

The concern about the potential impact of these returns eventually became so great that the Senate Subcommittee on Communications held hearings in 1967 to discuss their potential impact.[2] Since there had been no systematic examination regarding the impact of this new technology, several political scientists set out to study the impact of the early returns on West Coast voting behavior in the 1964 presidential election.

The West Coast Effect and the Election of 1964

The outcome of the election of 1964 generated little controversy. When Senator Barry Goldwater won the Republican nomination, he immediately found himself trailing incumbent Democrat Lyndon Johnson by double digits. Over the months leading up to the election, Goldwater found himself consistently trailing Johnson by ever-widening margins, and the results of the election only confirmed the Johnson landslide the opinion polls had predicted for several months.

Three major surveys were conducted during and after the 1964 election to determine what impact, if any, the early election returns had on voting behavior on the West Coast (Fuchs, 1966; Mendelsohn, 1966; Lang & Lang,

1968). These studies provided the first objective measures of the West Coast effect. Both Mendelsohn and Fuchs used pre- and post-election surveys on the West Coast. Both authors attempted to contact voters a few days before and a few days after the election. Mendelsohn was interested primarily in voters who switched candidates after hearing the returns, but he found little evidence to support this possibility. Both authors concluded that turnout levels changed very little (if at all) due to access to the early results.

Substantial methodological problems in both studies raised serious questions about the validity of these conclusions. Fuchs's survey found that 92% of the persons surveyed in California reported voting in the 1964 election. While it is possible the survey process randomly selected a large number of actual voters, it is also true that these turnout numbers are dramatically higher than the overall turnout for the counties in which the respondents resided (Dubois, 1983). If the voters in Fuchs's survey were either deceptive or inaccurate in their answers to the voting questions on a regular basis, the inference that the returns had little impact must be called into question.[3]

In Mendelsohn's survey, the pool of potential respondents was chosen from the voter registration lists from the 1960 election in California. Since previous registration status is the single best predictor of likelihood to vote (Erikson, 1981), it should come as no surprise that Mendelsohn found little decrease in turnout. Previously registered voters are also more likely to be members of political parties and have stronger partisan leanings, both of which are factors that increase the likelihood of voting and decrease the likelihood of switching candidates. In using the 1960 registration lists, Mendelsohn also ignored all Californians who reached voting age between 1960 and 1964.

Finally, both authors ignore a central question surrounding the West Coast effect—the question of subnational election outcomes. Even if the release of East Coast returns lowers turnout on the West Coast, the impact would be minimal at both national and subnational levels if turnout decreases proportionally among both Democrats and Republicans.[4] It is when turnout decreases disproportionately for one of the two parties that the impact is felt on subnational elections. Both Fuchs and Mendelsohn spend little time examining this question, and their results are sparse and inconclusive.

The third study of the 1964 election was Lang and Lang's book *Voting and Nonvoting: Implications of Broadcasting Returns before Polls Are Closed* (1968). More far-reaching than the Fuchs or Mendelsohn studies, the Lang study was considered the definitive study of the West Coast effect for over a decade. Lang and Lang provided a lengthy discussion and analysis of the West Coast effect and concluded it was a creation of the media rather than fact.

However, Lang and Lang's results were inconclusive. The survey was limited to one community on the entire West Coast (in Oakland county), and the numbers surveyed (438) resulted in large margins of error for the survey. After eliminating those surveyed who voted before the returns were announced, Lang and Lang were left with slightly more than 100 individuals on whom to base their entire analysis.

There is another factor that may have dramatically biased the results of all three analyses. The election result for 1964 was, for most potential voters, a foregone conclusion. At no point during the presidential campaign did Goldwater get close to Johnson. As the election neared, poll after poll showed clearly that Johnson would win by a substantial margin. The logic behind the West Coast effect is that access to *new* information from the early election returns alters voting behavior. In the 1964 election, the returns from the East Coast provided West Coast voters with no new information. Polls had predicted for weeks that Johnson would win the election, and the early returns only confirmed these predictions. If Goldwater supporters decided not to vote based on the low probability their favored candidate would win the election, it is impossible to determine whether they made their decision based on the election day results or on the multitude of polls that provided the same information in the months prior to the election.

All three studies of the 1964 election assume that the decision whether or not to vote would be made on election day itself, but this assumption is seriously in error. If the pre-election polls induced West Coast voters to stay home before election day, the release of East Coast election returns that only verified their previous predictions should have had little impact on their final decisions. The election day returns are not new information for these potential voters, and it should come as no surprise that access to this information had little impact on the overall turnout levels. In fact, the only situation in which the East Coast returns would have provided *new* information would have been if Goldwater had won in states he was predicted to lose, thus providing West Coast citizens with unexpected information about the election in progress.

The particulars of the 1964 presidential campaign substantially invalidated all three studies. Since it is impossible to separate the effects of the pre-election polls and the election day returns, the causal connection is, if not completely disrupted, dangerously muddled. Even if the authors had avoided the other methodological problems present in their studies, the nature of the election they chose to study leaves the question of the West Coast effect open to further investigation.

The Second Wave: The Election of 1980

In the early 1980s, political scientists began to reexamine the West Coast effect in a new light. Between 1981 and 1983, five separate studies of the West Coast effect appeared in political science and public opinion journals assessing the effect of early election returns on West Coast voting behavior. While the elections of 1972 and 1976 generated little controversy regarding the release of early election returns, the election of 1980 proved to be a different story.

The election of 1980 is one in which the West Coast effect seems, on the surface, more likely to appear. Although Carter trailed in many of the polls leading up to election day, the difference between Carter and Reagan fell within the margin of error of many of the surveys, thus putting Carter and Reagan in a statistical dead heat (Delli Carpini, 1984; Jackson, 1983). Since pre-election polls told the voters the election would be close, the Reagan landslide on election day was unexpected. When the landslide began on the East Coast, there was widespread surprise among pundits (Epstein & Strom, 1981), and there was likely to be surprise among West Coast voters. In addition, incumbent President Carter conceded the election at 6:01 P.M. on the East Coast, which was 3:00 in the afternoon on the West Coast. If West Coast voters expected the election to be close, the early election returns and Carter's early concession speech were new and potentially important pieces of information.

If there was one clear problem in the earlier studies according to researchers in the early 1980s, it was the lack of a sufficient data pool from which to draw significant conclusions. To alleviate this problem, three of the five studies (Delli Carpini, 1984; Dubois, 1983; Epstein & Strom, 1981) used aggregate data rather than surveys, while the other (Jackson, 1983) used a much larger survey.

Three of the five studies use aggregate data to examine the election of 1980: Epstein and Strom (1981), Dubois (1983), and Delli Carpini (1984). In addition, all three studies calculate changes in aggregate turnout levels by comparing elections in which early returns were released before the polls closed (e.g., 1964, 1972) to elections in which the results were not released until after West Coast polls closed (e.g., 1968).

Although similar temporally and in basic methodology, the three studies differ in several details. Epstein and Strom (1981) use regional turnout data (West Coast, Pacific Northwest, Rocky Mountains states, etc.), arguing it is more accurate than the limited surveys used in previous research. Dubois (1983) uses state level turnout, claiming it is more accurate than the regional data of Epstein and Strom. Delli Carpini (1984) uses congressional districts, claiming a substantial improvement over the state-level data used by Dubois (1983). In each case, the change in level of analysis was justified as an improvement over previous research.

The results of the studies were inconclusive. Epstein and Strom found little impact on overall turnout. Dubois found a decrease in West Coast turnout but argued this was a unique effect of the 1980 election. Delli Carpini found a drop in turnout similar in magnitude to that of Dubois but in different areas of the West Coast. The end results are three studies that contradict each other. Although Delli Carpini and Dubois agree that turnout decreased, they disagree about what areas of the West Coast showed the decrease.

Although the differences in the results are troublesome, a far more prominent issue is ignored. Each of these studies fails to address the issue of information access. Although the level of analysis changes, the data are unable to discriminate between those voters who had access to the information and those who did not. Once again, the causal linkage is broken—without knowing which of the West Coast voters had access to the early election returns, it is impossible to make a causal statement about the effect of the early election returns.

Of all of the studies of the 1980 election, only the research of Jackson (1983) addresses the causal connection between information access and voter turnout. Jackson used questions from the University of Michigan's Presidential Election Study and from the Vote Validation Study by the Center for Political Studies. Combining these resources, Jackson was able to create a pool of 1,814 persons who were interviewed both before and after the election. Using logit regression analysis, Jackson found that the combination of access to early election returns and hearing Carter's concession speech reduced turnout between 6% and 12%. There was little evidence, however, that either party was disproportionally affected.

Although Jackson's survey solves the causal problems inherent in the other studies of the 1980 election, several methodological and statistical errors decrease confidence in the results. The methodological errors occur at two points in the analysis: the coding process and the case-selection process

(Epstein & Strom, 1984). One of several examples of these methodological errors is that Jackson assumes all polls closed at 8:00 P.M. local time,
an assumption that is incorrect for a majority of the states in the study.[5] The
case selection process in Jackson's analysis is also unclear and potentially
arbitrary. The final survey pool in his analysis included 1,123 respondents,
yet Jackson never explains why nearly 800 of those in the original survey
from the University of Michigan were excluded (Epstein & Strom, 1984).

Finally, there are some potential statistical errors that may weaken the
conclusions of Jackson's research. Jackson uses the results of the survey to
predict the likelihood an individual will vote and then uses these projections
to project turnout. Projections based on projections are potentially dangerous statistically. If there is error in the initial model, this error will be mag-
nified by the further projections. Although Jackson does not present the
overall standard error for the likelihood model, the errors for the individual probit coefficients are substantial.[6] If these errors are compounded in
the second prediction model, it becomes very difficult to determine the true
parameters of the variables he is attempting to predict.

The 2000 Election

After the controversies surrounding the 1980 election announcements,
debate over the impact of the early poll releases died down. While some
efforts were made to establish consistent poll closing times, these were met
with little interest. After the controversy in Florida, the level of interest rose
dramatically.

While the Florida recount was certainly the focus of media coverage after
the 2000 election, there was some debate regarding the release of early election returns. This debate centered on the fact that the Panhandle region of
Florida was in a different time zone than the rest of Florida. When Florida
was first declared for Gore at 7:48 P.M. Eastern time, the polls in the
Panhandle were still technically open for another twelve minutes. While scholars and pundits tend argue this had little or no impact on the eventual outcome of the election (Sobel & Lawson, 2002; Alterman, 2003), it nevertheless
brought the issue of early election results back into the political debate.

The Current State of the Research

Despite multiple surveys and aggregate analyses, the impact of early election returns remains surprisingly elusive. Some authors found declines in

turnout (Delli Carpini, 1984; Dubois, 1983; Jackson, 1983), while others found little or no effect (Epstein & Strom, 1984; Epstein & Strom, 1981; Fuchs, 1966; Mendelsohn, 1966). The differences in these conclusions appear to be independent of the election studied, the data used, or the statistical method employed.

In addition to the inconclusive results, there is a surprising failure on the part of several of these studies to address the *critical* underlying questions about the West Coast effect. Nearly all of the studies ignore the question of information access altogether, assuming (apparently) that all West Coast voters had access to the information. This is a serious misjudgment on the part of these authors. The access to the information is the causal link between the release of election returns and the decrease in turnout. If the researcher cannot control for which voters had access to the results and which did not, the causal link is broken, and the subsequent analysis is an exercise in futility.

Another dramatic shortcoming in most of the current literature is the failure to address the question of the impact of the West Coast effect on state and subnational elections. The controversy surrounding the West Coast effect has always been whether or not the returns have an impact on subnational elections. Concern about the impact on national turnout levels has rarely been raised as a major topic of debate. Measuring the impact on subnational elections is extremely difficult and time-consuming. Thus, examining the impact on the parties provides an acceptable substitute. If the early returns alter overall turnout without disproportionally impacting one party over another, the impact of the West Coast effect is nil. If the returns alter turnout more for one party than the other on the West Coast, subnational elections on the West Coast should be affected as well.

In either case, all of the research on the West Coast effect either ignores the question of subnational elections or gives it only cursory discussion. This is surprising, considering subnational elections are those most likely to be affected and those where the impact would be most pronounced. While this omission on the part of previous researchers is not fatal to the general line of research, it distorts the underlying questions of the West Coast effect.

Normative Implications of the West Coast Effect

The West Coast effect has the potential to be a substantial force in the electoral process. If access to the early election information changes turnout on the West Coast, it could change which party controls Congress, West

Coast state legislatures, or governors' offices. These possibilities raise serious questions about both the democratic process and the First Amendment.

On one side of the argument are the news media. Within the media, the right to a free press as defined by the Constitution is considered sacrosanct. If the information is available, the press has the right to release it to the public (Delli Carpini, 1984; Jackson, 1983). Some members of the media go so far as to argue they have an obligation to report the information. In either case, supporters of the press claim the West Coast effect is not a problem within their control. How people use the information provided by the media should not be a concern for journalists—the messenger should not be punished for the message.

On the other side of the argument are those who believe the early returns bias the results of elections. As Senator Jacob Javits pointedly discussed during the Senate's 1967 hearings on the West Coast effect, if the results of the East Coast elections encourage West Coast voters not to vote, it is an apparent violation of the principle of "one person, one vote." West Coast voters are being told, in effect, that their votes in the presidential election do not matter—the East Coast has already decided the election for them. Research has consistently shown that most citizens are primarily interested in the outcome of the presidential election, and their interest in subnational elections rarely equals that of the race for the White House. With their primary source of interest removed by the East Coast voters, West Coast voters may stay home rather than vote.

It is important to recognize that the impact of the West Coast effect does not have to be very large to alter the outcome of subnational elections. If only one percent of the supporters for a given candidate chose not to vote based on East Coast returns, the outcome of subnational elections could be altered. In districts with close elections, the West Coast effect could have been responsible for turning the election to the eventual winner. If the West Coast effect exists, it does not need to have an enormous impact in raw numbers to have a substantial effect on election outcomes.

One interesting irony of the West Coast effect is the paradoxical relationship between the media and the voters. All things being equal, it is easier for network pollsters to forecast the outcome of a blowout election than a close one—the results are more clear-cut, thus reducing the amount of error in the prediction. At the same time, blowout predictions are only informative for citizens if the blowout itself is unexpected, as in the election of 1980. If the blowout is expected, as in 1964 or 1972, the predictions provide only confirmatory evidence. If the election is too close to call on election day, the early election returns are far more valuable to the voters, yet accurate predictions are much more difficult to make when the results are close.

The West Coast effect remains, in many ways, an enigma in politics. Previous research has been inconclusive, and there has been little in the way of solid theoretical grounding. A central issue, the potential impact of early election information on subnational elections, has been largely ignored. The West Coast effect is largely unexplained despite its potential to have a significant impact on the process of governance. Given the controversy surrounding the 2000 presidential election, it is clearly an area in need of further study.

Information and Its Impact on Voting: The West Coast Effect

Can access to early election information alter voting behavior? While this question is still under debate, there is agreement that if the information does have an impact, it has the potential to alter both parts of the voting decision: whether or not to vote and which candidate to support. For this research, the focus will be on whether or not to vote. Although the question of vote choice is equally interesting, it serves little purpose to try to predict changes in vote choice if the probability of voting is unknown.

If the early election return information changes the probability of voting, which direction does it take? If a supporter of one party sees that the presidential candidate he supports has already won or lost the national election, he may choose to stay home. The vote would have a zero probability of affecting the outcome of the national election, so he chooses to save himself the time and effort associated with going to the polls. This is the argument most often used in the public debates surrounding the West Coast effect and the argument used to try to limit the ability of the news media to release early election results. This declining turnout argument assumes that many potential voters only go to the polls when they believe their vote can make a difference in the election outcome or that the benefits of voting in an election that has already been "decided" still outweigh the costs of voting.

It is also possible that early election return information raises the probability of voting by providing a very different picture of the election. If potential West Coast voters get access to the early East Coast returns and the East Coast totals are extremely close, the voters on the West Coast are allowed, in essence, to decide the outcome of the election. If East Coast voters tie, their votes are essentially meaningless when determining the outcome of the election, which gives the West Coast voters complete control over which candidate wins the election. If the West Coast voters comprehend this potential power, they have a stronger incentive to vote.

An Experimental Design to Test the West Coast Effect

The primary goal of experimental design is to eliminate confounding external influences on behavior by controlling the environment and individuals within the confines of the experimental setting. The amount of environmental background noise in any election can make the causal linkages extremely difficult to discern. While statistical methods have been developed to aid survey researchers in grappling with causality, even the most ardent survey statistician knows that advanced statistical techniques are no substitute for direct manipulation of the subjects and their environment. Through regulation over the environment and the randomization of subjects, experimental research gains a degree of control greater than any survey design could hope to achieve. Experimental designs allow researchers to test the causal impact of a single factor. Through careful measurement of behavior before and after this factor is introduced, it is possible to measure its effect with great accuracy. By removing exogenous factors from the pool of possible explanations for observed behaviors, the hypothesized causal linkages become more easily testable.

The central questions in the West Coast effect are whether access to early election returns can change voting behavior, and if so, does it change it in all elections or only in those too close to call? These questions will be answered using two separate experimental designs. In both cases, the answer revolves around changes in voting patterns over the course of the experiments.

Gauging changes in voting patterns requires both control and treatment measurements. The control measure determines the baseline voting patterns for the participants when none of them have access to the information. The treatment level provides a measure of voting change when the treatment—access to early election returns—is introduced. If consistent changes are observed among the participants who receive the information while those who do not receive the information show little or no change, one may infer the change in voting behavior is caused by the information.

First Experimental Design

In the first experimental design, the goal was to replicate elections in which the voters were unsure of the election outcome going into the day of the election. To best replicate the process of the West Coast effect, the participants in the experiment would need to be exposed to early election returns in some cases and not in others. In addition, they would need to believe that the results from the East Coast were close in some cases and not in others. To create a reasonable approximation of this process, the participants were randomly assigned to support a hypothetical candidate (either Orange or Green) in each simulated election. This support was varied from one election to the next.

In addition to supporting different candidates, the experiment needed to simulate the difference between those voters who had access to the early election returns and those who did not. To do this, the participants were randomly assigned to information groups. In each simulated election, those in the first information group received the results of the East Coast elections, while those in the second information group did not. All of the results from the East Coast voting were generated in advance of the experiment, but the participants were told that another group was voting in a nearby room just before the real participants were given the opportunity to vote.

In all of the elections in the experiment, there were equal numbers of participants assigned to both information groups (14), and equal numbers of participants supported each candidate (14), although which candidate was supported by each individual participant varied with each election. Each participant knew the number of supporters for each candidate in their group as well as the breakdown in the other group.

Since the candidates in the experiments are generic color names with no partisan identification, it would be unreasonable to expect the participants to vote without some other form of enticement. With no partisan affiliation or other methods of traditional political engagement available to motivate them, some other form of incentive is required. The most widely accepted substitute for personal political engagement in experimental research is avarice (Kinder & Palfrey, 1993; Davis & Holt, 1993; Kirk, 1982). Avarice may not be a perfect substitute for political engagement, but it is an important influence on the actual behavior of voters in the real world (Lewis-Beck, 1985). While substituting avarice for political engagement may not affect those few individuals who are willing to sacrifice their personal welfare for the good of society, it should be a suitable motivational substitute for a vast majority of the participants. To generate this avarice, the participants were told that if their preferred candidate won, they would receive $1, whereas if their preferred candidate lost, they would only receive $0.50. The participants were also assessed a voting cost of $0.10 to simulate the time and energy involved in voting.

The use of randomization mitigated any attempts by the participants to coordinate their activities as well as assuring anonymity among the participants. If the participants could accurately predict which candidate they would prefer before each election, it would be relatively easy for them to tacitly agree as a group that one candidate should consistently win every election. This would allow them to avoid most potential voting costs and ensure all participants receive the same payoffs at the end of the experiment.[7] Random assignment of participant preferences alleviated these effects by reducing the level of certainty for their predictions about preference distributions. While the average proportion of candidate support with two candidates was 50–50 across all participants, the use of random assignment meant that any individual participant is not guaranteed such a proportion. It is this possibility that encourages participants to remain within the experimental structure, allowing the causality tests to remain believable.

The overall experimental process consisted of four phases, each designed to test a different level of information access. Each phase consisted of six simulated elections. In each simulated election, random results were generated for the East Coast voters. These vote totals were combined with the actual votes by the experimental participants to determine an overall election winner.

Phase One. The first phase of the experiment was the control phase. Participants in the experiment were randomly assigned a candidate to support, but none of the participants was given any information about the East Coast results. The candidate who received the most votes of the combined totals from the fictitious East Coast voters and the participants won. Since none of the participants knew the results of the election until voting was completed, this phase essentially replicated a national voting process where early election returns are unavailable, such as the midterm elections for Congress.

Phase Two. The second phase of the experiment introduced information at the most basic level. During the second phase, all participants were provided with the results of the fictitious voting on the East Coast before voting. By providing the information to all participants, we established a baseline for how the participants acted with access to the information. Since all of the participants had access to the information, any change observed between the first and second phases was a result of the introduction of the information. This phase did not directly replicate any real-world situation rather it provided a transition from Phase One to Phase Three.

Phase Three. The third phase of the experiment introduced random access to information. During the third phase, half of the participants who supported the Orange candidate and half of the participants who supported the Green candidate received the results of the fictitious East Coast voting, while the other participants received no information. Who had access to the information was randomly assigned at the beginning of each election, guaranteeing that no one participant would always have access to the East Coast returns. This phase provided the most direct replication of the West Coast effect. During real-world presidential elections, not all residents of the West Coast hear the results of the early voting before they go to the polls. Random access to the information among the participants tested this access effect in the laboratory setting.

Phase Four. The fourth and final phase of the experiment repeated the first phase. In the fourth phase, the participants did not receive any information about the voting from the East Coast. The purpose of replicating the first phase was to measure the degree of learning that occurred over the course of the experiment. If the participants established a super-game pattern of alternating voting and nonvoting, the results of the voting in the fourth phase should be significantly different from the voting in the first phase.

Every effort was made to make each phase procedurally identical to the others. The forms were picked up in the same order each time, and all participants were provided with information sheets after the first group voted.

Second Experimental Design

The second experiment further tested the West Coast effect and the question of election closeness. Following the same basic processes established in the first experiment, the purpose of the second experiment was to determine if the West Coast effect occurs when the participants can be more confident in their expectations about the outcome in advance of the election itself.

To create a situation in which the outcome of the election could be predicted in advance, the distribution of the voters was altered from the first

experiment. Rather than having an equal number of participants supporting each candidate (14 for each), the voters were distributed to give one candidate a majority of the potential support in each election. In each election,
16 of the 28 participants supported one candidate (57%), while 12 of the
28 supported the other (43%). The candidate supported by the majority of
the participants was randomly determined for each election.

If the West Coast effect only exists when the information about the election is new or unusual, the only time the information should have any impact
in this design is when the minority candidate wins or ties in the vote totals
from the fictitious East Coast, which would be an unexpected outcome. In
any election in which the majority candidate wins the East Coast, the
information about that outcome is not new for the experimental participants
but merely confirms the expected outcome. Thus, when the majority candidate wins the East Coast, the introduction of the information should have
no significant effect on the behavior of the participants in the experiment.

With this design, it was possible to make comparisons both within and
among the phases. The changes in information levels among the phases provided intergroup controls for access to information. In addition, the use of
random assignment controlled, for any individual, the behavioral effects that
emerged in the course of the experiment.

First Experimental Run

All of the participants in the experiment were students in the business
college at the University of Iowa. After all of the instructions were read and
all questions answered, the participants were instructed to open their
experimental binders to the beginning of Phase One. The specific instructions for each phase were read out loud, and the participants were instructed
to proceed to the first election. The procedures followed the description of
the four phases listed above.

When all 24 of the elections were complete, the participants were
asked to complete the postexperimental questionnaire. While the participants filled out the questionnaire, they were asked to come to the front of
the room individually to compare the payoff total they had reached with
the total recorded by the experimenter. The participants were paid in cash
when the payoffs were verified. After the participants were paid and had
completed the questionnaire, they were free to leave.

Second Experimental Run

All of the participants in the second experiment were drawn from introductory political science courses at the University of Iowa. The pre-experimental processes repeated the first experiment in every respect. The design of the second experiment follows most of the structure of the first experiment, although the purpose was slightly different. As noted earlier, the goal of the second experiment was to determine whether or not the West Coast effect existed when the outcome of the election was more certain before voting commenced. This experiment was designed to replicate the circumstances of the Lang and Lang (1968) study of the 1964 election in which pre-election polling data allowed the voters to make accurate predictions about the election outcome before the actual ballot counting took place.

Hypothesis One: Access to early election returns will only alter voting behavior when the information either contradicts previous expectations about the election outcome or provides information about the election where none was previously available.

Within the experimental design, the participants will have believable information about the potential election outcomes. In the first experiment, the voters will know the result of the election is uncertain. They will know the breakdown of the overall preferences is 50/50 between the two candidates before each election begins. Access to information should always be valuable to the voters in the first experiment.

In the second experiment, the participants will know one candidate will always hold an outright majority of the preferences before the election begins. Access to the information should be most valuable when it contradicts the previous expectations, such as discovering the minority candidate is winning the election. Confirmation of those expectations should have little impact on voting.

Hypothesis Two: The impact of the information on turnout in participants will be causally related to the vote margin from the fictitious East Coast results.

If the West Coast effect alters voter calculus, it alters the probability portion of the equation. The information provided to the potential voter gives more information about the likelihood of casting the deciding ballot. If a participant in the second group learns the vote margin on the East Coast was zero (a tie), the participant should realize the outcome of the election will be determined by the voting among the experimental participants, thus increasing the probability of casting the deciding vote. Conversely, if the participant learns one candidate holds a large lead after the voting on the East Coast, the probability of his/her vote altering the outcome decreases, and that knowledge should be reflected in decreased turnout.

Hypothesis Three: Access to information will affect the supporters of both the winning and losing candidates equally.

Expected utility theory provides the basis for this hypothesis. Under expected utility theory, the direction of the information should not matter in determining its impact (Raiffa, 1968). If the participants find out one candidate won the voting on the East Coast by a large margin, the supporters of the winning candidate should abstain at a rate equal to the supporters of the losing candidate. The "winners" should not vote because their candidate has already won, thus any additional votes are unnecessary. The "losers" should not vote because the probability that the losing candidate will catch up is small. While turnout may decrease, it should do so proportionally for both groups.

Hypothesis Four: Access to early election returns will have a greater impact on the supporters of the losing candidate than on the supporters of the winning one.

Psychological research has shown that individuals are generally more sensitive to potential losses than to potential gains (Quattrone & Tversky, 1988). Supporters of the winning candidate should continue to vote even if the information is provided, perhaps out of a sense of unity or out of fear of a last-minute defeat. Supporters of the losing candidate should be much less likely to vote when information is present, seeing imminent defeat as the most likely outcome.

The experimental procedures outlined test two different questions surrounding the West Coast effect: (1) does the access to early election returns alter voting patterns, and (2) is the West Coast effect mitigated when the outcome of the election appears to be certain before the election begins? Through the use of carefully controlled experimental procedures, including the random assignment of participants between groups, it will be possible to directly examine the impact of the information on the voting behavior of the participants in the experiment.

Experimental Results

The West Coast Effect

The best test of the impact of information on voting behavior is in the third phase. In Phase Three, one-half of the participants were randomly chosen to receive the information while half did not. Figure 4.1 shows the differences in turnout between informed and uninformed participants. The average turnout for the informed participants was 31.2%, while it was 71.5% for the uninformed participants $(t = -4.68, p < 0.005)$.

Figure 4.1: Informed and Uninformed Turnout during Phase 3

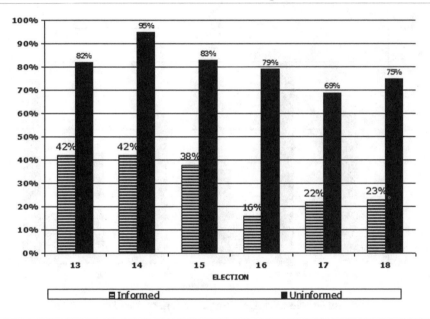

The results of the experiment demonstrate the influence of information on voting behavior. Informed participants were dramatically less likely to vote than uninformed participants across all of the simulated elections.

What about differential effects? Many pundits and theorists argue that voters who support the candidate that loses on the East Coast are less likely to vote than those who support the candidate who wins the East Coast. Others argue that supporters of the winning candidate may be less likely to vote, believing their preferred candidate has already won and that their additional votes are not needed.

Under expected utility theory, the direction of the information (your favored candidate is winning vs. your favored candidate is losing) should have no effect on the impact of the information. If prospect theory is correct, the negative information (your favored candidate is losing) should have a greater impact than the positive information (your favored candidate is winning). To examine this possibility, we need to look at the behavior of the informed participants. Since these participants know the results of the voting from the East Coast, they know whether or not the candidate they support won in the first round of voting. Figure 4.2 shows the differences between the winners and the losers in the third phase.

Figure 4.2: Comparison of Informed Voters by Results for Supported Candidate

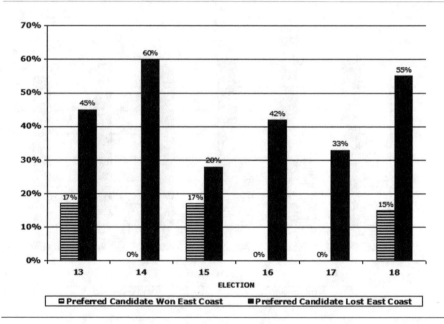

The data clearly support prospect theory over expected utility theory. In all of the elections, informed participants who supported the losing candidate voted at lower levels than those who supported the winning candidate ($t = -3.75$, $p < 0.033$). Informed turnout for the winning candidate was 43.8% and 8.3% for the losing candidate. In three of the six elections, not even one of the supporters of the losing candidate bothered to vote after receiving the results of the fictitious East Coast voting.

What is the overall impact of the information of turnout on the participants? Turnout for all uninformed participants in the second group was

57.9% across all phases, compared to 38.8% for all informed participants in Phases Two and Three ($t = -2.78$, $p > 0.009$). On average, access to information reduced turnout by 19.1% among the participants. In addition, if the favored candidate lost on the East Coast, mean turnout dropped to a paltry 8.3% among the informed participants who favored the losing candidate ($t = -5.28$, $p > 0.001$).

The results of the experiment demonstrate the strength of the West Coast effect in the laboratory setting. Participants who had access to the early election returns were significantly and consistently more likely to abstain than uninformed participants in the same election. The results clearly demonstrate the impact of the West Coast effect on the overall turnout levels within elections.

The results of the first experiment demonstrate that the West Coast effect exists. This experiment, however, only addresses part of the West Coast effect. In this experiment, all of the voters knew there were equal numbers of supporters for both candidates, making the overall election too close to call. While this has been the case in some recent presidential elections, most of the elections in the past thirty years have not been close. To test the impact of the presence of a clear frontrunner on the West Coast effect, a second experiment was run.

The Second Experiment: Introducing Clear Majorities

It may not be entirely surprising to find that information can alter turnout levels when an election is too close to call on election day. Voters who have a stake in the outcome of the election would find information about early results useful when deciding whether or not to vote. But is the same information as valuable to the voter when pre-election information shows one candidate has a large lead over the other?

The value of the information under these circumstances is dependent on what the information conveys. If the information provided to the West Coast voters confirms the majority candidate is winning, it is not new information but only information that verifies previously held expectations. While confirmatory information has some value, it is unlikely to cause voters to suddenly alter their behavior patterns. If the information provided shows the minority candidate is winning on the East Coast, then it is *new* information as it directly contradicts the voters' expectations. With this new information, supporters of the minority candidate may choose to participate, suddenly realizing their candidate has a chance to win the election.

Supporters of the majority candidate may abstain in greater numbers, believing they had mistakenly estimated the outcome of the election.

The second experiment was constructed so that one candidate always had the support of a majority of the potential voters, 16 of 28 (57%). If the arguments above are correct, information should have no impact on turnout when the majority candidate wins in the fictitious East Coast elections, yet it should have an impact when the minority candidate wins or ties on the East Coast.

As expected, the impact of information on turnout when the majority candidate wins in the first group is negligible. Compared to elections without information, turnout among the supporters of the majority candidate decreases slightly from 65% to 59% ($t = -1.05, p = 0.23$). Supporters of the minority candidate also turn out in slightly smaller numbers, dropping from an average of 37% to 25% per election, but the difference is insignificant ($t = -0.88, p = 0.43$).

When the minority candidate wins or ties on the East Coast and the participants know this, the impact on turnout is dramatic. Supporters of the minority candidate jump on the bandwagon to support their candidate in larger numbers, with average turnout increasing from 33% to 55% ($t = 2.15, p = 0.046$), while turnout from the supporters of the majority candidate plummets from 42% to 13% ($t = -1.97, p = 0.06$). This change in turnout is directly attributable to the presence of *new* information. When the information is not present, the minority candidate winning the East Coast has no impact on turnout ($t = 0.40, p = 0.66$). Figure 4.3 shows these differences.

Figure 4.3. Turnout by Information, Majority/Minority Status, and East Coast Winner

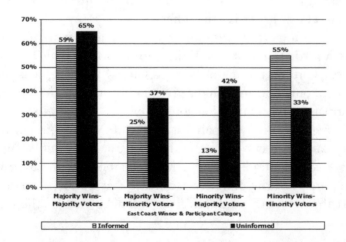

What about the impact on subnational elections? If the information provided to the second group only confirms the results of the pre-election information, the minority candidate in each in-group election should win approximately 33% of the elections.[8]

Table 4.1. Within-Group Elections for Group B

	Information Not Present	Information Present
Majority Win	5	8
Minority Win	1	10

Note: Pearson $Chi^2(1) = 2.74$ $p = 0.045$

Clearly the information makes a difference in the outcomes of the within-group elections. When the information is present, the minority candidate actually wins more subnational elections than the majority candidate wins. If the election outcome can be predicted by all participants with relative ease, why should access to information change the likelihood the minority candidate wins in the second group?

The reason is the change in turnout among the participants when the minority candidate wins the East Coast. In four of the ten cases where the minority candidate won among the participants, the minority candidate also won the fictitious East Coast voting. Take out those four cases, and the minority candidate won 33% of the elections—exactly the percentage predicted if the information had no effect. In other words, the minority candidate won more elections during the experiment than expected because knowing the minority candidate won on the East Coast was valuable information to the participants who supported the minority candidate. The minority supporters may have experienced a form of the bandwagon effect. Since their candidate won unexpectedly on the East Coast, they may have recognized they had a better chance of winning the overall election, thus making them more likely to vote.

The results of the second experiment add substantially to the understanding of the West Coast effect as well as explaining the discrepancies in the previous research. The one factor that determines if the information affects aggregate election outcomes is whether the information is new or not. When the outcome of the election is uncertain going into the election, access to the information substantially alters overall turnout and has a clear impact on within-group elections. When one candidate goes into the election with a lead in the polls, learning that candidate is winning the election has little impact on West Coast voters. Learning the majority candidate is losing the election provides new information and impacts the outcome of both the subnational and overall elections.

Conclusions and Implications

The evidence from these tests demonstrate that the West Coast effect can be re-created in a laboratory setting. The aggregate analyses repeatedly show the impact of information on turnout and the likelihood to vote. When participants had access to the information, they were generally less likely to vote than if they did not have the information. More specifically, the information showed a substantially greater impact on turnout when the access to the information allowed the participants to gain new information. When the information simply confirmed previous expectations (as in the second experiment), the impact on voter turnout was minimal.

It is this difference between *new* and *confirmatory* information that provides a convincing explanation for the wide variations in the level of impact of information in previous studies of the West Coast effect. If the studies were conducted during elections in which the information provided was primarily confirmatory (Lang and Lang, 1968, among others), it should come as no surprise that the authors found little or no evidence to indicate changes in voting behavior. If the elections were easily predictable from the pre-election polls, why should learning the polls were correct alter voting decisions?

For those studies that found evidence of the West Coast effect (Delli Carpini, 1984; Jackson, 1983; Dubois, 1983), the elections studied were ones in which there was still a reasonable chance that either candidate could win. All three studies examined the 1980 election that was still close according to the polls just before the election. For the potential voters in this election, the outcome was at least somewhat uncertain, making access to election information valuable to them.

In addition to demonstrating the circumstances under which access to information can alter voting behavior, the analyses set forth here directly address one of the questions long ignored by previous research: can an overall change in turnout actually alter the outcome of subnational elections? Although many previous authors have asserted this as being true, the results presented here provide clear statistical evidence that information can bias election outcomes at the subnational level. When information is present, minority candidates in the within-group elections are more likely to win than if the information is not available. This is true even when one candidate has a clear majority in the pre-election information.

Although this research began with a specific question about West Coast voters gaining access to East Coast information, the results of the experiments yield far more than an answer to a single question. In addition to answering a specific, policy-oriented question, the experiments provide substantial insight into the general questions about turnout. Through the process of testing the impact of the West Coast effect, it is possible to learn much about the general process by which individuals use information and what types of information are more valued.

The implications of this for public policy are many. When the media release the results of presidential elections to the general public before the polls close, voters on the West Coast are likely to be affected. If the presidential election is a landslide for one candidate, supporters of the opposing candidate on the West Coast will stay home in much larger numbers than if they had never received the information. It can be argued that the public has a right to know the results of the presidential election as soon as the information is available. While this may be true, it is imperative that the media, the public, and those in the government recognize the impact such releases have on turnout in the general public.

While the impact of early information access on turnout at the national level is clearly an issue worthy of concern, it is the impact of this information on the subnational elections that has been the focus of most of the public inquiry into the West Coast effect. The results of the experiments provide a glimpse of how this information alters subnational elections. The evidence is clear: when the information is available, candidates who are projected to win in subnational elections lose more often than when the information is not available. While these results are only preliminary, they raise serious issues about the rights of the media and the rights of voters.

It is this impact on subnational elections that should be of the greatest concern to all who are involved in politics, either as practitioners or as scholars. If subnational elections are altered by the early release of information in the real world at anywhere near the rate they were altered in the experimental models, serious questions must be raised about releasing early election information. Candidates for state and local offices across the West Coast may well find themselves at the mercy of voters they have never met and can never hope to influence. Democratic voters in New York may be responsible for the ouster of Republican incumbents in California, and the incumbents would be powerless to stop it from occurring. If this happens, one can argue that the release of the early election information deprives West Coast candidates of the right to be elected or defeated on their own merits. No matter how strong a candidate may be, if the East Coast election returns result in high levels of abstention, the candidate may well go down to defeat.

It has been over 30 years since television networks began to release early election returns to the public on election day. In that time, scholars and pundits have argued about the impact of this information on West Coast voters. Despite dozens of attempts by previous scholars, the evidence has remained inconclusive. The results of this research provide clear and convincing evidence of the existence of the West Coast effect. The evidence clearly shows that access to early election returns can decrease voter turnout and impact West Coast elections but only in situations in which the outcome of the national election is not a foregone conclusion prior to election day. Given this, society must seriously consider which is truly more important: freedom of the press or the principle of one person, one vote. The results of these tests demonstrate that we cannot have both.

ENDNOTES

1. This story is a combination of several examples discussed in the hearings of the 90th Senate collectively called the "Predictions of Election Results and Political Broadcasting," S1824–4 in 1967.

2. Among those called to testify was Prof. Warren Miller, who argued there was little significant impact on West Coast turnout.

3. This problem (over-reporting of turnout) has been found in most surveys in which vote validation (verifying the vote reports through the voter registrations lists) was not used.

4. In other words, if the West Coast effect decreases turnout proportionally for both parties, the state and local election outcomes do not change. Candidates who would win without the returns would still win with the returns present.

5. This error is particularly troublesome when one considers that several sources of data are easily available to provide accurate poll closing times.

6. In Jackson's defense, one must acknowledge that most statistical analyses of survey data produce substantial error coefficients, so this is not a problem unique to this survey. This should be interpreted as a caution to all researchers who use survey data in multiple projections.

7. This "super-game" effect is possible even if the participants can accurately predict the proportion of times they will support either candidate without predicting which

candidate they will support in any given election. For example, if the participants know with certainty they will support one candidate 50% of the time and the other candidate 50% of the time, they can tacitly agree to allow each candidate to win 50% of the elections, maximizing their overall payoffs.

8. There are a total of 63 possible election outcomes within each group. The majority candidate should win 55.5% of the within-group elections, the minority candidate should win 33.3%, and 11.1% should be ties.

REFERENCES

Alterman, E. (2003). *What Liberal Media? The Truth About Bias and the News.* New York: Basic Books.

Davis, D. D., & Holt, C. A. (1993). *Experimental Economics.* Princeton, NJ: Princeton University Press.

Delli Carpini, M. X. (1984). Scooping the voters? The consequence of the networks' early call of the 1980 presidential race. *Journal of Politics* 46, 66–85.

Downs, A. (1957). *An Economic Theory of Democracy.* New York: Harper & Row.

Dubois, P. L. (1983). Election night projections and voter turnout in the west. *American Politics Quarterly* 11, 349–363.

Epstein, L., & Strom, G. (1984). Survey research and election night projections. *Public Opinion* 7, 48–50.

Epstein, L. K., & Strom, G. (1981). Election night projections and West Coast turnout. *American Politics Quarterly,* 9, 479–491.

Erikson, R. S. (1981). Why do people vote? Because they are registered. *American Politics Quarterly,* 9, 259–276.

Fuchs, D. A. (1966). Election-day radio-television and voter turnout. *Public Opinion Quarterly* 30, 226–237.

Gigerenzer, G. (1984). External validity of laboratory experiments: the frequency-validity relationship. *The American Journal of Psychology* 97, 185–195.

Jackson, J. E. (1983). Election night reporting and voter turnout. *American Journal of Political Science* 27, 613–635.

Kinder, D. R., & Palfrey, T. R. (1993). On behalf of an experimental political science. In D. R. Kinder & T. R. Palfrey (Eds.), *Experimental Foundations of Political Science.* Ann Arbor: University of Michigan Press.

Kirk, R. E. (1982). *Experimental Design: Procedures for the Behavioral Sciences.* Pacific Grove, CA: Brooks/Cole.

Lang, K., & Lang, G. E. (1968). *Voting and Nonvoting: Implications of Broadcasting Returns Before Polls Are Closed.* Waltham, MA: Blaisdell.

Lewis-Beck, M.S. (1985). Pocketbook voting in U.S. national elections: Fact or artifact? *American Journal of Political Science* 29, 348–356.

McKelvey, R. D., & Ordeshook, P. C. (1986). Sequential elections with limited information: A formal analysis. *Social Choice and Welfare* 3, 199–211.

Mendelsohn, H. (1966). Election-day broadcasts and terminal voting decisions. *Public Opinion Quarterly* 30, 212–225.

Morton, R. B. (1991). Groups in rational choice turnout models. *American Journal of Political Science* 35, 758–776.

Palfrey, T., & Rosenthal, H. (1983). A strategic calculus of voting. *Public Choice* 41, 7–53.

Palfrey, T., & Rosenthal, H. (1985). Voter participation and strategic uncertainty. *American Political Science Review* 79, 62–78.

Quattrone, G. A., & Tversky, A. (1988). Contrasting rational and psychological analyses of political choice. *American Political Science Review* 82, 720–736.

Raiffa, H. (1968). *Decision Analysis: Introductory Lectures on Choices Under Uncertainty.* Reading, MA: Addison-Wesley.

Sobel, R. S., & R. A. Lawson (2002). The effects of early media projections on presidential voting in the Florida Panhandle. Typescript.

Traugott, M. W., & Tucker, C. (1984). Strategies for predicting whether a citizen will vote an estimation of electoral outcomes. *Public Opinion Quarterly* 48, 330–343.

Tuchman, S., & Coffin, T. E. (1971). The influence of election night television broadcasts in a close election. *Public Opinion Quarterly* 35, 315–326.

West, D. M. (1991). Polling effects in election campaigns. *Political Behavior* 13, 151–163.

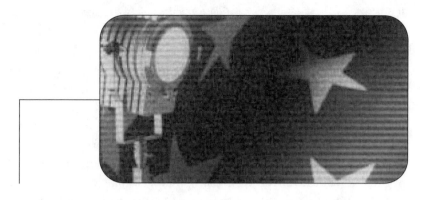

5

Packaging the Governor
Television Advertising in the 2000 Elections

Christopher A. Cooper
H. Gibbs Knotts

In recent years, political campaigns have evolved from relatively unprofessional events to high-tech, high-dollar affairs run by paid consultants (Johnson 2001). In many ways, the driving force behind these changes has been the rise of television campaign advertising. Scholars have debated candidates' decisions to "go negative" (Skaperdas and Grofman 1995) and the effects of advertising on citizen knowledge (Lang 1991), efficacy (Freedman and Goldstein 1999), and voter turnout (Ansolabehere and Iyengar 1995; Kahn and Kenney 1999a). In addition, the importance of televised advertising has been documented in presidential (Jamieson 1992), senatorial (Kahn and Kenney 1999b), and congressional (Herrnson 1998) campaigns but has largely been ignored in campaigns at the state level. Although campaigns for federal offices are important, by focusing predominantly on national elections, we have an incomplete understanding of campaign advertising in American politics.

In this chapter we examine the frequency and content of television campaign advertising in 8 of 11 gubernatorial campaigns during the 2000 election. We begin with a brief discussion of the importance of governors and argue that the content of gubernatorial campaigns deserves study. We then review the races covered in our analysis and discuss the advantages and limitations of our data. Based on Salmore and Salmore's (1996) contention that gubernatorial elections have become "presidentialized" we often present our results by comparing gubernatorial and presidential advertising. We conclude that gubernatorial advertising is expensive, policy oriented, and like presidential advertising, relies far more on positive than negative appeals to reach voters. Finally, when gubernatorial candidates do run negative advertisements, we find that Republicans are more likely to "go negative," that negative advertising increases as election day approaches, and that negative ads are more likely in competitive contests.

The State of U.S. Governors

Although governors were quite powerful before the American Revolution, the founders' fear of single-person rule meant that most early state constitutions were written to limit the authority of governors. As the nation matured and as state and local governments increased the services provided to citizens, gubernatorial power and stature have risen accordingly. As an example of their increasing appeal, governors have won six of the last seven presidential elections.

Existing scholarship on governors highlights the increasing experience these men and women bring to the statehouse (Rosenthal 1990). Despite the recent elections of Jesse "the Body" Ventura in Minnesota and Arnold Schwarzenegger in California, governors tend to be seasoned politicians. Gubernatorial candidates generally have experience as state legislators, members of Congress, or as members of the U.S. Senate. Once elected, incumbent governors are difficult to unseat and win re-election in 75% of cases (Jewell and Morehouse 2001).

As chief executives, all governors have ceremonial and symbolic power, but the specific powers of each governor vary from state to state. To compare gubernatorial power, Thad Beyle (1999) catalogued six factors: (1) the number of competing statewide political officials, (2) time in office, (3) budgetary discretion, (4) veto authority, (5) appointment power, and (6) the partisan makeup of the state legislature. These factors combine to form a commonly used scale of gubernatorial power, which suggests that governors wield the most power in Hawaii, Maryland, New Jersey, New York, Ohio, and Pennsylvania. The governors with the least institutional power include those in Alabama, Arkansas, New Hampshire, North Carolina, Rhode Island, and South Carolina. Regional differences are important as the South generally has less powerful governors but more powerful legislatures. Finally, gubernatorial power is a function of other intangible factors, such as the size of the state and the national media coverage of the state.

As gubernatorial power has increased, the race for governor has become more visible, more intense, and more costly (Salmore and Salmore 1996). For example, the average cost of gubernatorial elections increased from $2.7 million in 1980 to $14.7 million in 2002 (Beyle and Jenson 2003). Moreover, expensive gubernatorial campaigns are not unique to the largest states, as campaigns in medium-sized states have exceeded $20 million (Beyle 1999). Although professional campaigns require a variety of expenditures, including direct mail, salaries for campaign consultants, political polling, and travel, the largest proportion of money in gubernatorial elections is spent on campaign advertising. In the 2000 election, gubernatorial candidates spent approximately $31 million advertising in the 100 largest media markets in the country.[1] For example, in the 2000 North Carolina gubernatorial election, Mike Easley (D) spent over $8 million on television ad buys and Richard Vinroot (R) spent over $3 million (North Carolina State Board of Elections 2003).

The 2000 Gubernatorial Elections

Governors are important political officials and their election campaigns have become expensive and hotly contested events. To better understand the content, timing, and frequency of television gubernatorial advertisements, we focus on the 2000 gubernatorial elections. The 2000 election is best remembered as the controversial presidential contest where the Supreme Court ended the recount in Florida, making Texas Governor George W. Bush president, but there were also a number of important lower ballot elections.

As Table 5.1 indicates, the 2000 presidential election coincided with 11 gubernatorial contests. Despite losing the White House, Democrats won 8 of these 11 races. Overall, incumbents fared well, winning 5 of 6 elections. The only unsuccessful incumbent was West Virginia's Cecil Underwood (R), who lost a close election to former Congressman Bob Wise (D). Other close elections included Bob Holden's (D) defeat of Jim Talent (R) in Missouri and Judy Martz's (R) win over Mark O'Keefe (D) in Montana.

Across the United States, gubernatorial candidates spent nearly $100 million in 2000 (Beyle and Jensen 2003). The most expensive contest, at over $28 million, was the open seat in North Carolina, where Easley defeated Vinroot. Of course, $1 million in North Carolina will reach a larger pro-

Table 5.1 Gubernatorial Elections (2000)

State	Candidate	Vote %	Total Spending
Delaware	D-Ruth Ann Miner	60	1,338,012
	R-John Burris	40	1,469,433
Indiana	D-Frank O'Bannon,	56	9,657,956
	R-David McIntosh	42	8,263,035
	I-Andrew Horning	2	15,601
Missouri	D-Bob Holden	50	9,972,232
	R-Jim Talent	49	8,724,045
Montana	R-Judy Martz	51	964,784
	D-Mark O'Keefe	48	3,002,655
New Hampshire	D-Jeanne Shaheen,	49	1,159,296
	R-Gordon Humphrey	44	2,398,449
	I-Mary Brown	6	
North Carolina	D-Mike Easley	52	11,020,029
	R-Richard Vinroot	47	8,207,412
	I-Barbara Howe	1	
North Dakota	R-John Hoeven	55	1,123,818
	D-Heidi Heitkamp	45	1,176,637
Utah	R-Michael Levitt,	56	1,949,335
	D-William Orton	43	175,431
Vermont	D-Howard Dean,	51	946,444
	R-Ruth Dwyer	39	899,582
	I-Anthony Pollina	10	335,412
Washington	D-Gary Locke	59	3,783,521
	R-John Carlson	40	2,621,974
West Virginia	D-Bob Wise	50	2,814,667
	R-Cecil Underwood,	48	2,611,077
	I-Denise Giardina	2	36,149

Source: Compiled by the authors based on data from CNN.com (2003) and Beyle and Jensen (2003).

portion of the electorate than $1 million in California. Therefore, raw numbers do not tell the whole story, and the population of the state needs to be considered. In our sample, the cost per general election vote varied from $2.66 in Washington to $11.24 in Montana (Beyle and Jensen 2003).

The increasing responsibilities of governors and the high costs of campaigning make it important to examine gubernatorial television advertising in more detail. We outline a strategy for studying these issues in the next section.

The Research Strategy

The lack of data on candidate advertisements has limited our knowledge of gubernatorial elections. Without access to large numbers of television advertisements, researchers cannot determine whether gubernatorial candidates rely on positive or negative ads or whether they tend to concentrate ad buys early in a campaign or save money until a few days before the election. Fortunately a dataset has recently become available that allows us to analyze a large proportion of television advertisements. Political scientists at the University of Wisconsin, Madison, collected data on every political advertisement run in the 2000 election in the 100 largest media markets in the country. The 65,570 gubernatorial and 301,521 presidential ads were broadcast and captured via satellite. Next, research assistants coded each advertisement for factors including timing, content, tone, theme, and the show the ad ran on. The dataset also includes a complete storyboard that details the text of the ad and scenes from the ad.[2] Because we are ultimately interested in the impacts of political advertising, throughout the chapter we consider each time an ad ran rather than each unique ad. In other words, if a candidate creates one political advertisement but broadcasts the ad on 50 occasions, it would be included in our dataset 50 times.[3]

Researchers interested in political campaigns have never had access to a dataset this complete. These data allow researchers to analyze the content and frequency of political advertisements. However, no dataset is perfect, and we would be remiss if we did not point out the limitations of using these data. Of the 210 media markets in the United States, the dataset only includes broadcast information from the 100 largest media markets. If an ad ran only in small markets, it is not included. This particularly presents problems in small states where the dataset may include few if any media markets in that state. Because of these limitations, we have data for 8 of the 11 gubernatorial elections that took place in 2000—Delaware, Indiana,

Missouri, New Hampshire, North Carolina, Utah, Washington, and West Virginia. Further, the sample clearly overrepresents states like North Carolina which have a number of large media markets (Asheville, Charlotte, Greensboro, and Raleigh). Utah, with only one major media market (Salt Lake City), is underrepresented in our sample. Finally, the data are limited to a single presidential election year, meaning that our findings may not apply to gubernatorial advertising in nonpresidential years. These limitations notwithstanding, the dataset is unique in its coverage. Over 85% of the population lives within these 100 media markets. It is without a doubt the largest, most complete, and best resource available for studying political advertising (Ridout et al. 2003).

Table 5.2 lists the major characteristics of the states in our sample. The states are a representative cross-section and provide variation on many important variables. In our sample, elections in four states featured incumbent governors and four were open-seat contests. In addition, the 2000 general election gubernatorial contests were competitive in four states (decided by 5 percentage points or less) and noncompetitive in four states (decided by more than 5 percentage points). Finally, based on the index described earlier, gubernatorial power varies across the sample states. For example, Utah has a powerful governor, while others, like North Carolina, have weaker governors.

We now turn our attention to questions about the timing and content of gubernatorial television advertising. While the focus is always on governors, at times we analyze data on gubernatorial and presidential ads, allowing us to compare the advertising decisions of state and national executives.

The Basics of Gubernatorial Advertising

Television advertising for gubernatorial and presidential campaigns has many of the same characteristics. In both cases, candidates primarily rely on 30-second campaign spots. In our sample of the largest media markets, 96% of presidential ads and 95% of gubernatorial ads were 30 seconds in length. Just over 3% of presidential ads and about 2% of gubernatorial ads lasted 60 seconds. Costs were surprisingly similar between gubernatorial and presidential advertising. Gubernatorial ads varied in price from $19 to $17,700, with the average advertisement costing $474. For the 2000 presidential election, ads varied from $17 to $48,922, with an average cost of $682. Despite the different overall costs of gubernatorial and presidential campaigns, our findings suggest that similar amounts are spent on individual ads.

Table 5.2 Characteristics of the States in the Sample

State	Voting Age Population (2000)[1]	% Voter Turnout (2000)[2]	Institutional Power Index (1999)[3]	Number of Ads (2000)[4]
Delaware	582,000	60.7	3.3	699
Indiana	4,448,000	50.1	3.2	11,431
Missouri	4,105,000	59.6	3.5	10,938
New Hampshire	911,000	65.8	2.8	7,139
North Carolina	5,797,000	53.9	2.7	29,160
Utah	1,465,000	56.2	4.0	727
Washington	4,368,000	60.8	2.9	2,653
West Virginia	1,416,000	46.3	3.8	2,823

Sources:
1. *From the Federal Election Commission (2003).*
2. *Percent of voting-eligible population from McDonald (2002: 207-208).*
3. *From Beyle (1999). Scores range from a high of 4.1 to a low of 2.7.*
4. *Computed by the authors from Goldstein, Franz, and Ridout (2002).*

Recent debates over campaign finance highlight concerns over third party advertisements in political campaigns. For instance, campaign finance legislation calls for third parties to become more transparent in their funding of advertisements and to make it easier for citizens to determine sponsorship. In order to explore these issues, we determined whether gubernatorial candidates were likely to run their own ads or whether they relied on political parties or other groups to sponsor ads. Our data suggest that candidates themselves sponsored a large percentage of gubernatorial ads. Of all ads broadcasts, Republican gubernatorial candidates sponsored 31% and Democratic gubernatorial candidates sponsored 41%. The Republican and Democratic National Committees each sponsored only 1% of gubernatorial ads. Sponsorship of advertisements was much different at the presidential level. Based on our analysis of the presidential data, the Republican and Democratic National Committees sponsored 53% of presidential ads in 2000.

Next we turn to the timing of gubernatorial advertisements. Figure 5.1 displays the increasing magnitude of gubernatorial advertising between August 1, 2000, and November 6, 2000, the day before the general election. The graph shows a steady increase in the number of ads broadcast as the general election approached. The largest number of ads appeared on November 3, 2000, the Friday before the Tuesday election. Of all the gubernatorial ads in 2000, including primary election advertising, 11% were

Figure 5.1 Daily Gubernatorial Advertising (August 1, 2000-November 6, 2000)

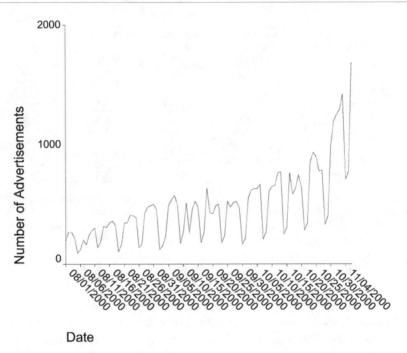

Date

Source: Computed by the authors from Goldstein, Franz, and Ridout (2002).

broadcast during the final week. It appears that gubernatorial candidates expend tremendous resources during the final push before election day. Our examination of the data on presidential elections demonstrates similar trends as the frequency of ads rises steadily as election day draws closer.

We also analyzed differences in the timing of ads between competitive and noncompetitive elections. We coded the eight gubernatorial elections as competitive and noncompetitive based on the margin of victory between the two major candidates. Between August 1 and November 6, we found that candidates made similar decisions on when to increase ad buys, regardless of whether they were in competitive or noncompetitive contests. For instance, in both election types the number of advertisements increased steadily as election day approached. The only exception was during the last two weeks of September, when the number of ads in noncompetitive elections actually decreased.

We now turn our attention to the time of day governors choose to advertise. As Figure 5.2 suggests, the largest percentage of gubernatorial advertising occurred in the early evening. Candidates advertised during local and national news broadcasts and in the period just before the prime time tel-

Figure 5.2 Timing of Gubernatorial Advertising

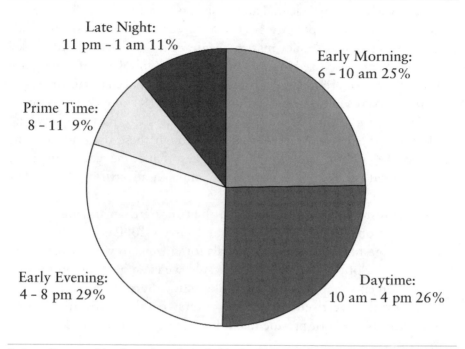

Source: Computed by the authors from Goldstein, Franz, and Ridout (2002)

evision lineup. Early morning was also a popular time for gubernatorial advertising. Like the early evening time slot, the early morning period included local and national news programs. Perhaps because of cost, gubernatorial candidates advertised less during the evening prime time television period. We found that presidential ads were broadcast at similar times during the day.

Based on the criteria discussed above, gubernatorial and presidential advertising share many of the same characteristics. In particular, the length, timing, and cost of advertisements are comparable. However, it should be the case that the content of ads is different in gubernatorial and presidential campaigns, as the president and the governor take on very different responsibilities in the federal system. We turn to the issue of content next.

The Content of Gubernatorial Advertising

Political commentators often decry the increasingly personal nature of electoral politics in the United States. To determine if personal appeals dominate discourse in gubernatorial ads, Table 5.3 compares the primary focus of gubernatorial and presidential advertising in 2000. About 59% of gubernatorial ads focused on policy matters compared to 64% of presidential ads focusing exclusively on policy matters. Many of the policy issues addressed by governors are discussed in more detail below. Only 10% of gubernatorial ads and 9% of presidential ads focused on personal characteristics. For example, in New Hampshire, Gordon Humphrey (R) noted that his opponent, incumbent Jeanne Shaheen (D), questioned the party loyalty and work ethic of Senator Mark Fernald. Although these data address the quality of the policy discourse, they do suggest that at the federal and state level, personal issues are less central to campaign advertising than policy issues.

Recent research has highlighted the ability of partisan and nonpartisan appeals to mobilize citizens (Gerber and Green 2000a; 2000b). These scholars suggest that third-party appeals for citizens to vote or otherwise take action are often successful. As a result, we examined the proportion of advertisements that urge voters to take action. Surprisingly, only 3% of gubernatorial advertisements urged voters to take a specific action. Comparatively, 11% of presidential advertisements encouraged voters to take action.

Conventional wisdom suggests that parties have become less important in American politics over the last 50 years. Whereas candidates once ran with the party, candidates now run candidate-centered campaigns. As a result,

Table 5.3 Primary Focus of Advertising (2000)

	Gubernatorial	Presidential
Policy Matters	38,138 -59%	192,521 -64%
Personal Characteristics	6,640 -10%	27,128 -9%
Both Policy and Personal	19,823 -31%	80,862 -27%
Total Ads	64,601	300,511

Source: Computed by the authors from Goldstein, Franz, and Ridout (2002).

very few ads mentioned the Republican or Democratic Party. Over 95% of gubernatorial ads and 96% of presidential ads did not mention a political party. Perhaps because of their broad constituency, gubernatorial and presidential candidates do not run with the party but rather focus on the individual.

Further evidence of candidate-centered campaigns can be found in the proportion of ads that mention the favored candidate. In gubernatorial ads, the favored candidate was mentioned in 90% of ads and appeared in 55% of ads. The candidate's opponent was mentioned in 42% of ads and an opponent's commercial was mentioned in 21% of ads. The favored candidate was mentioned in only 80% and appeared in just 40% of presidential ads. The candidate's opponent was mentioned in 46% of presidential ads and an opponent's commercial was mentioned in only 9%. In both cases, the focus appears to be on the candidate rather than the party.

Thus far we have learned that candidates tend to focus on individuals, but we do not know how they describe themselves and their opponents. Our findings suggest that most gubernatorial and presidential ads did not use adjectives to describe the favored candidate. The most common adjective in both types of ads was that the candidate was "tough" or a "fighter," with 9% of gubernatorial and 10% of presidential ads using these adjectives. In Washington, Governor Locke promoted his patient's bill of rights, promising to "fight back" if insurance companies interfered with the medical decisions of patients and doctors. Similarly, in his unsuccessful reelection campaign in West Virginia, Governor Underwood touted his prescription drug program for seniors saying "our seniors deserve leadership who will fight for us." The next most common candidate adjectives in gubernatorial ads were "proven tested experience" and "conservative." Based on the sample of presidential ads, the next most common adjectives were "committed" and "commonsense leadership."

Just over 68% of gubernatorial advertisements and 69% of presidential advertisements did not use adjectives to describe the candidate's opponent. The most common adjectives to describe gubernatorial opponents were "taxing" (or some version of liking taxes) and "dishonest/corrupt." A particularly heated exchange on taxes took place in 30-second television spots in the North Carolina governor's race. In one advertisement, Vinroot accused Easley of supporting higher taxes on phone bills and the Internet and noted that Easley "flatly refuses to sign the 'No Tax Increases' pledge." Easley countered with editorial comments from the *Greensboro News and Record* saying he "has never pushed a tax increase." In West Virginia, Wise

questioned the motives of his opponent, noting that he received special interest money from coal companies. The advertisement by Wise quoted a
judge saying that the transaction "smelled like dead and rotting carp." At
the presidential level, the most common opponent adjectives used were "dis-
honest/corrupt" and "friend of special interests."

Many commentators have expressed concern about candidates telling
the truth in political advertisements. As a result, candidates include supporting sources in their ads. These supporting sources take many forms but generally are included in either small type at the bottom of the screen or via a
voice-over that describes the source of the claim. In our sample, both presidential and gubernatorial candidates included supporting sources in a
high percentage of advertisements. Like the Easley spot mentioned above,
many candidates used supporting sources to boost the credibility of the advertisement. Over 74% of presidential ads and 67% of gubernatorial ads
mentioned supporting sources in the visuals or in the text of the ad.

Politicians have long used celebrities and other politicians in their
advertisements to add credibility and "star power" to their claims. For
instance, more than 40 years ago, John F. Kennedy enlisted former First Lady
Eleanor Roosevelt to endorse his candidacy. Our data suggest that this still
occurs, although perhaps not as often as one might expect. Compared to
presidential candidates, gubernatorial candidates were more likely to
include celebrities and other politicians in advertisements. Celebrities
appeared in over 10% of gubernatorial ads, and other politicians appeared
in over 4% of gubernatorial ads. Candidates in the closely contested North
Carolina gubernatorial election secured endorsements from two of the
state's most popular citizens. Legendary college basketball coach Dean
Smith endorsed Vinroot, a former player of his at the University of North
Carolina, calling him a "man of character and honesty." Easley countered
with an endorsement from television actor Andy Griffith, who proclaimed
"we deserve a governor who shares our values." Although not enough to
defeat Easley, Vinroot also broadcast an advertisement with an endorsement
from presidential candidate George W. Bush, who urged citizens to vote for
Vinroot saying that, "Richard Vinroot and I want better government, not
bigger government." At the presidential level, celebrities appeared in less
than 2% of ads, and other politicians appeared in less than 1% of ads.

Based on differences in duties of presidents and governors, it is not surprising that campaign themes differed between gubernatorial and presidential advertisements. As Table 5.4 suggests, education was the top campaign
theme of gubernatorial candidates in 2000, with 29% of all gubernatorial

Table 5.4. Top Five Campaign Themes in Gubernatorial
and Presidential Advertising (2000)

Gubernatorial	Presidential
1. Education (29%)	1. Health Care (19%)
2. Taxes (14%)	2. Education (16%)
3. Background (9%)	3. Social Security (16%)
4. Health Care (7%)	4. Taxes (9%)
5. Political Record (5%)	5. Background (8%)

Source: Computed by the authors from Goldstein, Franz, and Ridout (2002).

ads mentioning education. In a Missouri advertisement, Holden outlined his education plan discussing the importance of raising standards, requiring high school entrance exams, reducing class sizes, paying teachers for achieving national certification, and putting disruptive students in a class of their own. The issue of taxes was the second most popular campaign theme for gubernatorial candidates. In an Indiana advertisement, David McIntosh (R) presented his plan to reduce property taxes. According to McIntosh he would "slow the growth of government to match the rate of inflation, use the savings to cut property taxes by 25% over 4 years, freeze property tax rates for seniors at the new lower rates, and increase education funding without cutting other vital services." In addition to education and taxes, gubernatorial candidates emphasized background, health care, and the political records. The most common theme in presidential advertising was health care, followed by education, Social Security, taxes, and candidate's background.

One of the most interesting findings was related to the tone of gubernatorial advertising. Of all the broadcasts in our sample, 50% of ads promoted a particular candidate; 22% of ads contrasted the records of candidates, and 28% of ads attacked another candidate. An advertisement by Bob Holden (D) in Missouri provides a good example of a promotion advertisement. After praising the record of the late Governor Bob Carnahan, Holden outlined his education plan and concluded by noting that "education has to remain our top priority, and as Governor, I will never forget that." An example of a contrast ad appeared in North Carolina when police chief Harvey Cain drew comparisons between the crime records of Easley and Vinroot. In the Easley-sponsored advertisement, Cain notes, "It's Richard Vinroot that took a pay raise for himself and cut salaries of police officers." North Carolina also includes several good examples of attack advertisements. In an Easley spot, a live deer appears on screen followed by claims that Vinroot supports higher gasoline, car, and property taxes. The ad ends with the words "trust Vinroot on taxes and spending . . . that would be like the deer voting for the hunter." In Indiana, incumbent Frank O'Bannon (R) broadcast a negative ad about negative ads. He accused McIntosh of running misleading negative ads and then accused him of voting against drug-free schools, and voting to abolish the Department of Education twice, and to cut school lunches and college loans.

Figure 5.3 compares the tone of gubernatorial and presidential advertising. The tone of advertising was similar in both gubernatorial and presidential contests, with attack ads constituting 25% of total ads. Although similar, gubernatorial candidates had a slightly higher percentage of attack ads than did presidential candidates.

Not surprisingly, the content of gubernatorial and presidential advertisements differed. Gubernatorial ads focused more on the themes of education and taxes and tended to rely on endorsements from celebrities and other political figures. In addition, gubernatorial candidates and presidential candidates rely on negative advertisements at approximately the same

Figure 5.3 Tone of Gubernatorial & Presidential Advertising (2000)

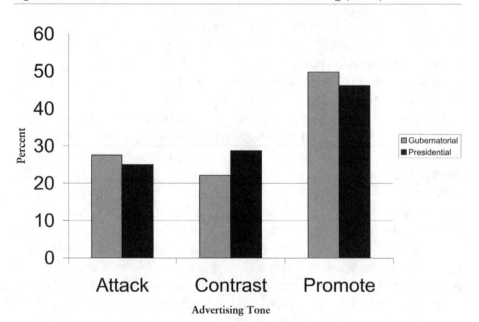

Source: Computed by the authors from Goldstein, Franz, and Ridout (2002).

rates. In the next section we look more closely at negative advertising and evaluate some of the factors that might affect the tone of gubernatorial television ads.

Factors Affecting the Tone of Gubernatorial Advertising

Given recent interest in negative advertising (Ansolobehere and Iyengar 1995; Kahn and Kenney 1999a; Lau et al. 1999; Wattenberg and Brians 1999), we explore explanations for negative advertising in gubernatorial elections. Figure 5.4 shows an increase in negative advertising during the period after August 1, 2000, displaying the percent of each day's advertisements that were attack ads. The percent of attack ads climbed to over 50% in September, and the biggest period of attack ads occurred in mid-October. For example, on October 14, 185 of the 249 gubernatorial ads were attack ads. Negative advertising decreased in late October and early November. Perhaps candidates wanted to present a more positive message as citizens

Figure 5.4 Gubernatorial Attack Ads (August 1, 2000-November 6, 2000)

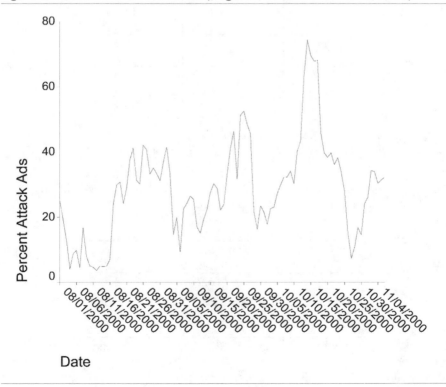

Source: Computed by the authors from Goldstein, Franz, and Ridout (2002).

prepared to enter the voting booth. Only 32% of the 1,683 gubernatorial ads broadcast the day before the election were attack ads.

Next, we test the hypothesis that the competitiveness of the general election affected the tone of political advertising. Table 5.5 demonstrates that after August 1, attack ads were more likely in competitive contests. Although 35% of advertisements in competitive elections were negative, only 19% of ads in noncompetitive races were negative. Based on the chi-square value, competitive and noncompetitive campaigns had statistically significant differences ($p < .00$) in advertising tone. Although there is a healthy debate on the subject, many believe that negative advertising, while often effective, may backfire on the candidate running the ad. As such, attack ads may constitute a risky strategy. Our data suggest that candidates in noncompetitive elections are least likely to take this risk.

Finally, we explored differences in the percentages of attack ads between

Table 5.5. Advertising Tone and Competitiveness in Gubernatorial Elections (August 1, 2000-November 6, 2000)

	Noncompetitive	Competitive
Attack	2,384	11,507
	-19%	-35%
Contrast	2,185	9,352
	-17%	-25%
Promote	8,276	12,463
	-64%	-37%
Total Ads	12,845	33,322

Note: chi-square = 2747.23, sig. at p < .00, two-tailed test
Source: Computed by the authors from Goldstein, Franz, and Ridout (2002).

Table 5.6. Tone of Advertising for Republican and Democratic Gubernatorial Candidates (August 1, 2000-November 6, 2000)

	Democratic	Republican
Attack	6,278	7,613
	-25%	-36%
Contrast	6,984	4,549
	-28%	-22%
Promote	11,973	8,737
	-54%	-42%
Total Ads	25,235	20,899

Note: chi-square = 773.17, sig. at p < .00, two-tailed test
Source: Computed by the authors from Goldstein, Franz, and Ridout (2002).

Republican and Democratic gubernatorial candidates. Table 5.6 illustrates that between August 1 and November 6, Republican candidates were more likely to broadcast attack ads than Democratic candidates. Approximately 35% of Republican ads were negative and only 22% of Democratic ads were negative, indicating a significant difference between partisanship and advertising tone. Ansolabehere and Iyengar (1995) found that Republicans are more susceptible to attack ads than Democrats. Perhaps Republican candidates sense this difference. In the end, our sample of eight races is too small to make any definitive conclusions, but our data suggest that timing, competitiveness, and partisanship influence the decision to go negative. Other scholars should investigate this phenomenon to determine whether this finding holds over many races or is merely an artifact of the 2000 election.

Conclusions

Scholars have devoted considerable attention to television advertising (particularly negative advertising) in congressional, senatorial, and presidential campaigns. Unfortunately, our knowledge of advertising for gubernatorial races is quite limited, even as the states and their chief executives are gaining power in the federal system. In this chapter we examined the content and timing of gubernatorial advertising in the 2000 election, utilizing a unique dataset of over 65,000 advertisements run in the country's 100 largest media markets. Though not perfect, these data allow us to provide a number of insights into gubernatorial advertising.

First, we found that televised advertising is an important part of gubernatorial campaigns. For instance, in the 2000 election gubernatorial candidates spent approximately $31 million advertising in the country's 100 largest media markets. These expenditures on television advertising represent a substantial portion of total campaign spending.

Second, we demonstrated that gubernatorial ads are much like presidential ads. For example, the production decisions are largely similar between the campaigns for the two offices. Candidates for governor and president were likely to run similar-length ads (30 seconds), at comparable times of day (generally early evening and during news programs), and at similar times of the year (increasing in frequency before election day). Despite these commonalities, we discovered some differences in the content of gubernatorial and presidential advertisements. For example, the most popular campaign themes for governors were education and taxes, while the most popular themes for presidents were health care, education, and Social Security.

Third, we examined the conditions under which candidates go negative. We found that Republicans run negative ads more often than Democrats and concluded that the proportion of negative ads is not consistent across the last few months of the campaign. For example, the frequency of negative advertising increased throughout August and September, peaked in mid-October, and decreased as election day approached. It also appears that candidates in competitive races ran a higher proportion of negative ads than candidates in noncompetitive elections.

Finally, our data provide good news for those concerned about an increasingly shrill and harsh style of campaign politics. Governors certainly broadcast negative ads, but these negative appeals did not make up the majority of the total advertisements. Further, based on our analysis of gubernatorial television advertising, policy issues were much more prevalent than personal issues.

Although this chapter catalogued and described advertising in gubernatorial campaigns, much work remains to be done. Scholars should continue to compare political advertising in campaigns for different levels of office. In addition, future studies should further investigate campaign strategies, particularly the decision to go negative. As televised advertising displaces retail politics in American campaigns and power continues to devolve from national to state governments, the study of state-level campaign advertisements will be increasingly important.

ENDNOTES

1. This amount is based on calculations from Goldstein, Franz, and Ridout (2002), explained in "The Research Strategy" section. The data were obtained from a joint project of the Brennan Center for Justice at New York University School of Law and Professor Kenneth Goldstein of the University of Wisconsin-Madison, and includes media tracking data from the Campaign Media Analysis Group in Washington, DC. The Brennan Center-Wisconsin project was sponsored by a grant from The Pew Charitable Trusts. The opinions expressed in this article are those of the authors and do not necessarily reflect the views of the Brennan Center, Professor Goldstein, or the Pew Charitable Trusts. Unless otherwise noted, all data come from this source.

2. For more details on the data, see Ridout et al. (2003).

3. This is the same decision made by Goldstein and Freedman (2002).

REFERENCES

Ansolabehere, Stephen, and Shanto Iyengar. 1995. *Going Negative: How Political Advertisements Shrink and Polarize the Electorate*. New York: Free Press.

Beyle, Thad. 1999. "The Governors." In Virginia Gray, Russell L. Hanson, and Herbert Jacob, eds. *Politics in the American States: A Comparative Analysis,* 7th edition. Washington, DC: CQ Press.

Beyle, Thad, and Jennifer Jensen. 2003. "Gubernatorial Campaign Expenditures Database." < http://www.unc.edu/%7Ebeyle/guber.html> Accessed on August 15, 2003.

CNN.com. 2003. "Governor Results Summary for All States." <http://www.cnn.com/ELECTION/2000> Accessed on August 15, 2003.

Federal Election Commission. 2003. "Voter Registration and Turnout 2000." <http://www.fec.gov/pages/2000turnout/reg&t000.htm> Accessed on August 15, 2003.

Freedman, Paul, and Kenneth M. Goldstein. 1999. "Measuring Media Exposure and the Effects of Negative Campaign Ads." *American Journal of Political Science* 42: 573–595.

Gerber, Alan S., and Donald P. Green. 2000a. "The Effect of a Nonpartisan Get-Out-the-Vote Drive: An Experimental Study of Leafletting." *Journal of Politics* 62: 846–757.

Gerber, Alan S., and Donald P. Green. 2000b. "The Effects of Canvassing, Direct Mail, and Telephone Contact on Voter Turnout: A Field Experiment." *American Political Science Review* 94: 653–663.

Goldstein, Kenneth, Michael Franz, and Travis Ridout. 2002. "Political Advertising in 2000." Combined File [dataset]. Final release. Madison, WI: The Department of Political Science at The University of Wisconsin-Madison and The Brennan Center for Justice at New York University.

Goldstein, Ken, and Paul Freedman. 2002. "Lessons Learned: Campaign Advertising in the 2000 Elections." *Political Communication* 19: 5–28.

Herrnson, Paul S. 1998. *Congressional Elections: Campaigning at Home and in Washington,* Second Edition. Washington, DC: CQ Press.

Jamieson, Kathleen Hall. 1992. *Packing the Presidency: A History and Criticism of Presidential Campaign Advertising.* New York: Oxford University Press.

Jewell, Malcolm E., and Sarah M. Morehouse. 2001. *Political Parties and Elections in American States,* 4th Edition. Washington, DC: CQ Press.

Johnson, Dennis W. 2001. *No Place for Amateurs.* New York: Routledge.

Kahn, Kim Fridkin, and Patrick J. Kenney. 1999a. "Do Negative Campaigns Mobilize or Suppress Turnout? Clarifying the Relationship between Negativity and Participation." *American Political Science Review* 93: 877–890.

———. 1999b. *The Spectacle of US Senate Campaigns.* Princeton, NJ: Princeton University Press.

Lang, Annie. 1991. "Emotion, Formal Features, and Memory for Televised Political Advertisements." In *Television and Political Advertising,* ed. Frank Biocca. Hillsdale, NJ: Lawrence Erlbaum, 221–244.

Lau, Richard R., Lee Sigelman, Caroline Heldman, and Paul Babbitt. 1999. "The Effects of Negative Political Advertisements: A Meta-Analytic Assessment." *American Political Science Review* 93: 851–876.

McDonald, Michael P. 2002. "The Turnout Rate among Eligible Voters in the States, 1980–2002." *State Politics and Policy Quarterly* 2: 199–212.

North Carolina State Board of Elections. 2003. "Campaign Finance Reports." <http://www.app.sboe.state.nc.us/> Accessed on August 10, 2003.

Ridout, Travis N., Michael Franz, Kenneth Goldstein, and Paul Freedman. 2003. "Measuring the Nature and Effects of Campaign Advertising." Unpublished manuscript, University of Wisconsin, Madison.

Rosenthal, Alan J. 1990. *Governors and Legislatures: Contending Powers.* Washington, DC: CQ Press.

Salmore, Stephen A., and Barbara G. Salmore. 1996. "The Transformation of State Electoral Politics." In *The State of the States,* ed. Carl E. Van Horn. Washington, DC: CQ Press.

Skaperdas, Stergios, and Bernard Grofman. 1995. "Modeling Negative Campaigning." *American Political Science Review* 89: 49–61.

Wattenberg, Martin P., and Craig Leonard Brians. 1999. "Negative Campaign Advertising: Demobilizer or Mobilizer? *American Political Science Review* 89: 891–900.

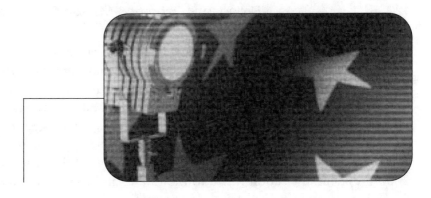

6

Message Tailoring in Spanish
Courting Latino Voters in the 2000 Presidential Advertising Campaign

Brendan J. Doherty
Melissa Cully Anderson

The rapidly expanding Latino[1] population in the United States has prompted considerable scholarship in recent years that assesses the role of Latinos in presidential elections, particularly as campaigns have spent increasing amounts of time and money to court Hispanic voters. In the election of 2000, both the Bush and Gore campaigns used television advertisements in Spanish to target prospective Latino voters. In this chapter we analyze English- and Spanish-language ads[2] sponsored by the two major presidential campaigns in the ten media markets in which the campaigns ran Spanish-language ads in the general election.[3] We assess whether the content and tone of ads differ by language, target audience, and by sponsor in ways that reflect scholars' expectations about the priorities of Latino voters and their relationship to the two major parties.

Our central question relates to how the candidates and parties perceive the role of Spanish-language advertisements in the context of their target audience. While research suggests that Spanish-language television is consumed largely by Latino viewers,[4] it is not clear whether *voters* of Hispanic origin receive their political information from Spanish-language television. Given this uncertainty, we wonder what the candidates and the two major party organizations are trying to accomplish by airing campaign advertisements in Spanish. We hypothesize that the campaigns might pursue one of two goals in the airing of Spanish-language ads. First, they may perceive such ads as an effective way to communicate with and court Latino voters. Alternatively, if they do not believe they will reach a substantial number of voters through Spanish-language ads, then the ads may simply be a symbolic gesture of outreach to the Latino community. To address this question, we explore the following relationships: first, how does the language of the message in the 2000 presidential election relate to the timing and tone of the message? Second, do the issues emphasized in these ads map onto the public policy priorities of prospective Latino voters?

We conclude that the Bush campaign exhibited much more similar patterns of issue priorities in Spanish and English than did the Gore campaign and that patterns of timing and geographic distribution of Spanish-language ads suggest that they represent an investment of key resources in an effort to reach out to prospective Latino voters. However, we find that the themes emphasized in Spanish ads by both campaigns do not map neatly onto the surveyed public policy priorities of various groups within the Latino community. Thus, while the candidates and parties seem to perceive the need to communicate with Latino voters, they still have yet to focus the content of their ads in Spanish on the issues most pressing to the Latino community. To support our conclusions, the rest of the chapter will: (1) discuss the political context and prior research that provide the backdrop for our study; (2) set forth our specific expectations with respect to the timing and content of the ads; (3) detail our findings; and (4) discuss the implications of our study and directions for further research.

Political Context and Prior Research

As illustrated in Table 6.1, the percentage of Latinos in the U.S. population has grown dramatically in recent years and is expected to increase steadily over the coming decades. They continue to remain relatively young when compared with other segments of the U.S. population—the median age of Latino residents in the United States is only 26 years, compared to 36 years for Anglo groups. Latinos are the fastest-growing voting population and currently comprise about 5% of all voters.[5]

Although Table 6.1 does not discern voters or even citizens, the chart illustrates the dramatic rise in the Latino population within U.S. borders. While the total U.S. population gain was 13% between 1990 and 2000, the rate of growth of Hispanic residents was 58%. Over half of that increase

Table 6.1 Change in U.S. Demographic Composition, 1990-2000

Demographic Group	1990 Census Population	% of Total	2000 Census Population	% of Total	% Gain, 1990–2000	% of all Latinos (2000)
Non-Hispanic	226,355,814	91%	246,116,088	87%	9%	
Mexican	13,495,938	5%	20,640,711	7%	53%	60%
Puerto Rican	2,727,254	1%	3,406,178	1%	25%	12%
Cuban	1,043,932	0%	1,241,685	0%	19%	5%
Other	5,086,435	2%	10,017,244	4%	97%	23%
Total Hispanic	22,354,059	9%	35,305,818	13%	58%	100%
Grand Total	248,709,873	100%	281,421,906	100%	13%	

Note: Columns may not add to 100% due to rounding.
Source: Compiled by the authors based on information from the Bureau of the Census. U.S. Census 2000. (Washington, DC).

came from Latinos of Mexican origin. Moreover, each Latino subpopulation taken alone, exceeded the growth rate of the entire nation. We expect that this growing population is likely to become increasingly prominent in the eyes of campaign strategists.

Our analysis of efforts to court Latino voters in presidential campaigns relates to research addressing message tailoring and the content of political communications.[6] The increasing salience of the Latino voting bloc has prompted many scholars to try to identify the critical issues facing Latinos and to assess the relationship between prospective Latino voters and the two major parties seeking to court them. A March 2002 policy brief by the Tomás Rivera Policy Institute, a think tank that focuses almost exclusively on Latino issues, uses a telephone survey of about 2,000 Latino registered voters from California, Texas, New York, Florida, and Illinois to determine the issues most important to Latino voters on election day.[7] Overwhelmingly, education is the top priority for the Latino community according to prospective Latino voters, regardless of national origin. Race relations, or civil rights, appears as a close second for certain groups in terms of issue urgency. Unemployment and immigration policy are also significant issues in the Latino community.

Did the 2000 election campaigns, through the airing of numerous ads in Spanish, respond to these priorities? Research suggests that not only does the Latino community avidly watch television but that the majority of bilingual viewers (57%) watch news channels exclusively in Spanish.[8] However, the same study acknowledges prior evidence that "Latinos who exclusively watch Spanish-language television were generally more recent immigrants to the United States."[9] To that end, some scholars suggest that the group of prospective Latino-American *voters* who receive most of their political information in Spanish is a small one. Rodolfo de la Garza explains, "the Bush people have long known that the way to reach Latino voters is in English. It's the immigrants who are Spanish dominant and who focus on Spanish language television."[10] Thus, the language choices of Latino voters with respect to television viewing are uncertain.

Expectations

We return to the questions at the center of our study: Did ads in Spanish represent symbolic outreach to the Latino community, or were they used in an attempt to mobilize prospective Latino voters? We will present an analysis of television advertisements aired during the general presidential election campaign of 2000 along the lines of language and party, reflecting variables such as timing, location, content, and tone. How were Spanish- and English-language ads presented by each party organization and campaign in the markets in which they chose to air ads in both languages?

Examining questions of location and timing of Spanish ads allows us to address whether advertising in Spanish was used to mobilize prospective voters or if it represented a symbolic attempt to build goodwill with Latinos. In an election as competitive as the presidential race of 2000, if these ads were merely a means of symbolic outreach, we would not necessarily expect to see the high level of ad activity as election day drew near that one might see if the goal were to mobilize voters in a close election. Similarly, if the ads were a key part of an electoral strategy, we might see a sharper focus on pivotal battleground states, while if the goal were symbolic outreach, we might see a broader geographic distribution of ads.

Second, we will turn to the issues emphasized in the ads. If the campaigns hope to court Latino voters through the messages they send in Spanish, we would expect that each campaign would emphasize issues in each media market that map well onto the issue priorities of the different Latino groups that dominate each city. Similarly, we would expect to see advertising strategies that reflect historical tendencies of different Latino groups to prefer Republicans or Democrats. If, instead, the campaigns' ads are largely a symbolic gesture, the issue coverage will not map as well to the priorities of Latino voters and will be more likely to match the content of English-language advertisements.

In order to develop some broad conclusions about the relationship between the issue content of Spanish-language ads and the Latino composition of each media market in which those ads were aired, we have used a three-step process. First, as all television advertisements are aired in certain media markets, we identified the counties comprising each media market in our study and noted the ethnic composition by national origin of the Latino communities and the voting outcomes within those counties for all voters in the 2000 presidential election. Second, we used data gathered through survey research to identify the political issues that are most salient to the Latino community. As we will see, these issues vary considerably by country of ancestry.

We then use the issue content of the ads aired in certain markets to examine the relationship between the national ancestry and policy priorities of the Latino electorate in these media markets. This link is tenuous at best as it requires making certain assumptions about representativeness and generalizability; the survey upon which we base our assumptions about the policy preferences of Latino voters was conducted in states that do not map directly those in which Spanish-language ads were aired.[11] In addition, the Census data that we use to distinguish among Latino origins, in each media market include all residents, not just citizens or voters. There is considerable variation in the composition of these two groups, depending on rates of naturalization and many factors affecting voter turnout. We acknowledge that these methodological issues render some of our conclusions somewhat tentative, but we hope, at the very least, to provide a starting point for more extensive research.

Data Source

This analysis draws from data compiled by the Wisconsin Advertising Project,[12] which used satellite technology to collect frequency data and content information on every ad airing in the top 75 U.S. media markets in the 2000 elections. In order to be able to make valid comparisons between ad airings in English and Spanish, we analyze the 10 media markets in which Spanish ads were run in the general election. As our goal is to analyze the strategies of the campaigns and their respective parties in the general election, we focus on ads sponsored only by the two major parties' committees and the two candidate campaign organizations, excluding from our study ads run by other groups and individuals.[13] Table 6.2 shows the distribution of general election English- and Spanish-language ads within the scope of our study by selected sponsors.

Examining the data, we see that independent expenditures by the Republican National Committee accounted for almost half of the ads aired in English during the general election campaign. Coordinated expenditures by the Republican National Committee (RNC), while dramatically less than their independent expenditures, still comprised the second largest category of ad airings by any sponsor. On the Democratic side, the Gore campaign and the Democratic National Committee (DNC) together sponsored the vast majority of Gore-friendly ads, while very few ads were sponsored by the DNC and coordinated with the Gore campaign. All together, the Republican sponsors ran more than twice as many ads in English as did the Democratic sponsors.

In contrast to the patterns in English, Democrats aired 34% more ads in Spanish than did Republicans, with the Gore campaign being the most prolific sponsor of Spanish ads. While the Democrats only aired 479 more Spanish-language ads than did the Republicans, the Democrats aired 4.2 ads in English for every ad they ran in Spanish. The Republicans, however, aired 13.7 ads in English for every ad that they ran in Spanish, illustrating that the Democrats made Spanish-language ads a proportionally larger part of their advertising strategies in these media markets.

For the remainder of our analysis we aggregate ad sponsors by party

Table 6.2 Ads Sponsored by Candidates and Campaigns, by Language

| | Selected Republican Sponsors | | | | Selected Democratic Sponsors | | | | Total |
	Bush	RNC	RNC/Bush	Subtotal	Gore	DNC	Gore/DNC	Subtotal	Total
English	2,721	12,340	3,988	19,049	3,539	3,622	645	7,806	26,855
Spanish	674	125	590	1,389	1,057	811	—	1,868	3,257
Total	3,395	12,465	4,578	20,438	4,596	4,433	645	9,674	30,112
% of All Ads	11%	41%	15%	68%	15%	15%	2%	32%	100%
% of Spanish Ads	21%	4%	18%	43%	32%	25%	—	57%	100%

Note: Ads sponsored by RNC and DNC represent independent expenditures made on behalf of the two major candidates. Ads sponsored by RNC/Bush and DNC/Gore represent expenditures that were coordinated between the campaigns and the party committees.

Source: Compiled by the authors based on information from Goldstein, Kenneth, Michael Franz, and Travis Ridout. 2002. "Political Advertising in 2000." Combined file [dataset]. Final Release. Madison, WI: The Department of Political Science at the University of Wisconsin-Madison and The Brennan Center for Justice at New York University. Hereinafter referred to as the Wisconsin Advertising Project.

affiliation, as we view the Republican National Committee and Democratic National Committee, practically speaking, as extensions of the Bush and Gore campaigns, respectively. The infrequency with which political parties were mentioned by any sponsor in either language as depicted in Table 6.3, particularly in the context of the large volume of ads sponsored by the parties, lends support to the perception of presidential campaigns as candidate centered.

Table 6.3 Mention of Political Party in Ads

	English Ads				Spanish Ads			
	Republican Sponsors		Democratic Sponsors		Republican Sponsors		Democratic Sponsors	
Party Mention								
Favored Party	887	5%	1	0%	-	0%	-	0%
Opposing Party	-	0%	40	1%	26	2%	-	0%
Both	-	0%	-	0%	-	0%	-	0%
None	18,162	95%	7,765	99%	1,363	98%	1,868	100%

Source: Compiled by the authors based on information from the Wisconsin Advertising Project.

Across the board, party labels played a minimal role in the ads in our study. Democrats never used party labels at all in Spanish ads, while Republicans never mentioned their own party in Spanish and mentioned the Democratic Party only 2% of the time. English-language ads exhibited only slightly higher rates of party mentions. Again, Democrats never mentioned their own party and only mentioned the opposing party in 1% of their ads. Republicans, in contrast, mentioned their own party in 5% of their ads in English but never mentioned the Democratic Party. Regardless of sponsor, parties were overwhelmingly not the focus of ads in either language.

To analyze variation by media market, and thus by the different Spanish-speaking ethnic groups in various locations, we stratified the ad airings by the ten media markets in which Spanish ads were run. Table 6.4 distinguishes the English- and Spanish-language ad airings by media market and party of sponsor and serves as the baseline for much of our analysis.

Once the ads are aggregated by candidate, we can see how each candidate and their sponsors distributed their resources by media market and by language. Table 6.4 distinguishes each media market and shows the number of ads shown by each sponsor group in each language and the percentage of those ads in each market that were aired in Spanish. Table 6.5 focuses on the Spanish-language ads and identifies the percent of all Spanish ads that each sponsor aired in any particular market.

These two tables, taken together, provide a descriptive summary that we use throughout the rest of this chapter. It is interesting to note how the two campaigns' sponsors differed in the allocation of Spanish-language ads. Gore sponsors aired about 500 more ads in Spanish than did Bush sponsors, and they were much more heavily concentrated in two major markets (Albuquerque/Santa Fe and Las Vegas) and only ran Spanish ads in four media markets in total.

Table 6.4 Distribution of General Election Ads by Language, Market, and
Campaign Organization

	Volume of Ads in Selected Markets							
	Republican Sponsors				Democratic Sponsors			
	English	Spanish	Total	% Span.	English	Spanish	Total	% Span.
Albuquerque/ Santa Fe	3,592	362	3,954	9%	3,952	894	4,846	18%
Chicago	2,005	—	2,005	—	1,375	51	1,426	4%
Denver	—	—	—	—	—	8	8	100%
Fresno/Visalia	1,540	75	1,615	5%	1	—	1	—
Las Vegas	2,015	190	2,205	9%	906	915	1,821	50%
Los Angeles	1,290	241	1,531	16%	—	—	—	—
Miami/Ft. Lauderdale	4,138	323	4,461	7%	1,572	—	1,572	—
New York	2	3	5	60%	—	—	—	—
Sacramento/ Stockton/ Modesto	2,052	74	2,126	3%	—	—	—	—
San Diego	2,415	121	2,536	5%	—	—	—	—
Total	19,049	1,389	20,438	7%	7,806	1,868	9,674	19%

Media Market (vertical label on left axis)

Source: Compiled by the authors based on information from the Wisconsin Advertising Project.

Republican sponsors, on the other hand, dispersed their Spanish-language ads more evenly among a larger number of markets, concentrating on Albuquerque/Santa Fe, Miami/Fort Lauderdale, Los Angeles, and Las Vegas, and running Spanish ads in eight different media markets overall. We look more carefully at these choices in the next section when we distinguish between battleground and non-battleground states.

Timing of Political Advertisements

Depicting the timing and volume of ads by month allows us to see trends by sponsor and language more effectively. While there was generally a consistent trend of increasing the volume of ads as the election approached,[14] the Democratic Spanish-language ads tailed off toward the end of the campaign. Democratic English-language ads, however, were initiated earlier in

Table 6.5 Percentage of Spanish-Language Ads in Each Media Market, by Sponsor

		Percent of All Spanish-Language Ads			
		Republican Sponsors		Democratic Sponsors	
		# of Ads in Spanish	% of All Spanish Ads	# of Ads in Spanish	% of All Spanish Ads
Media Market	Albuquerque/Santa Fe	362	26%	894	48%
	Chicago	—	—	51	3%
	Denver	—	—	8	0%
	Fresno/Visalia	75	5%	—	—
	Las Vegas	190	14%	915	49%
	Los Angeles	241	17%	—	—
	Miami/Ft. Lauderdale	323	23%	—	—
	New York	3	0%	—	—
	Sacramento/Stockton/Modesto	74	5%	—	—
	San Diego	121	9%	—	—
	Total	1,389	100%	1,868	100%

Source: Compiled by the authors based on information from the Wisconsin Advertising Project

the campaign and seemed to accelerate in volume much less dramatically than Republican ads, which peaked sharply in July and then again just before the end of the campaign. Spanish-language ads, too, were initiated earlier by Democratic sponsors than their Republican counterparts but leveled off in November while the volume of Republican ads increased noticeably (see Figure 6.1).

When we isolate battleground states, sharper contrasts emerge. We distinguish these ten media markets on the basis of whether they lie in states identified by CNN as battleground states.[15] These states were particularly contentious for the two campaigns and, according to our hypotheses, might provide insight as to the motives of advertising sponsors. We expect that if the sponsors believed the Spanish-language ads would reach likely voters, the volume of these ads would be high as the campaign reached its end. In contrast, if the sponsors used Spanish-language ads more symbolically to build goodwill with Latinos, we wouldn't expect to see investments of key resources in such ads in the final days of a close election.

Figure 6.1 Timing and Volume of Ads in All Media Markets Airing Spanish-Language Ads, by Language and Sponsor

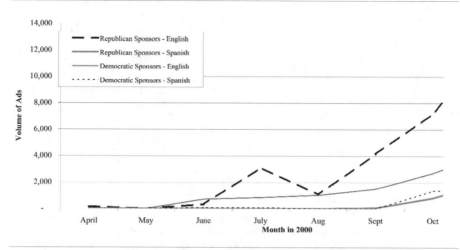

Note: Values for November have been pro-rated to reflect the shortened month
Source: Compiled by the authors based on information from the Wisconsin Advertising Project

In Figures 6.2 and 6.3, we disaggregated the data from the previous figure based on CNN's distinction between battleground and non-battleground states. Of the ten media markets in our analysis, four fall in battleground states for the 2000 election: Nevada (Las Vegas), New Mexico (Albuquerque/Santa Fe), Florida (Miami/Fort Lauderdale), and Illinois (Chicago). The remaining six media markets are in less competitive, non-battleground states: California (Sacramento/Modesto, Los Angeles, Fresno, and San Diego), Colorado (Denver), and New York (New York City). Figures 6.2 and 6.3 distinguish graphically the timing and volume of Spanish and English ads in battleground and non-battleground states.

Though we discovered while looking at all ads in the aggregate that the volume of Democratic ads seemed to increase at a slower rate than those sponsored by Republicans, even tapering off in the case of Spanish-language ads, that is not the case when we isolate the battleground states. In fact, Democratic sponsors in English ads seemed to nearly match the Republicans' rate of increase toward the finish line. Though still lower in volume than Republicans' English-language ads, Democrats were much closer to Republicans in these states. In Spanish, Democrats sponsored many more ads than Republicans, though as discussed earlier, the volume of these ads seemed to level off toward the end of the campaign.

Figure 6.2 Timing and Volume of Ads in Battleground States

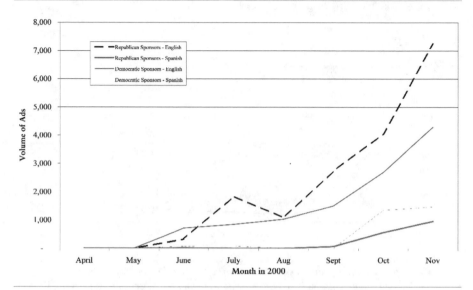

Note: Values for November have been pro-rated to reflect the shortened month
Source: Compiled by the authors based on information from the Wisconsin Advertising Project

In contrast, the non-battleground pool, which in our study is essentially California,[16] was overwhelmingly dominated by Republican sponsors. The volume of Republican ads in both English and Spanish in these states nearly matched that in the battleground states shown above, indicative in part of the almost two-to-one funding advantage that Republicans enjoyed over Democrats in the closing days of the 2000 campaign.[17] While the Democratic sponsors seemed to be much more selective by choosing to allocate their resources to the more competitive arenas and at the very end proportionally more toward English-language ads, Republicans seemed to be relatively consistent across the board in terms of language and venue with the exception of the peak in advertising in July, which may coincide with the timing of the Republican National Convention that month.

To review our hypotheses, we expect that sponsors who perceived Spanish-language ads as a symbolic gesture wouldn't necessarily invest resources in Spanish ads in the final days of a close election campaign like that of 2000. If, however, Spanish ads were aimed to mobilize prospective voters in the last stretch of a tight electoral contest, then the timing and volume of those ads would be more consistent with those of English-language ads. Similarly, sponsors hoping to target prospective voters would be more likely to run ads in the final days of the campaign in battleground states.

Figure 6.3 Timing and Volume of Ads in Non-Battleground States

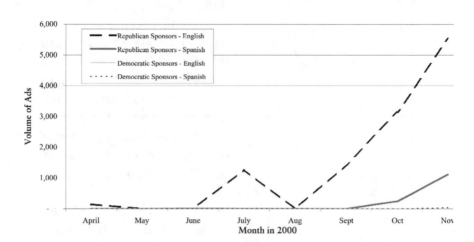

Note: Values for November have been pro-rated to reflect the shortened month
Source: Compiled by the authors based on information from the Wisconsin Advertising Project

The evidence yields a mixed picture for the two sets of sponsors. Looking at Spanish ads in all ten media markets, though Republicans' ads displayed no substantial distinction between the English- and Spanish-language ads in terms of volume and timing, Spanish ads sponsored by Democrats were more abundant than their Republican counterparts but seemed to level off in volume toward the end of the campaign. The Republican pattern seems to demonstrate a final push for Spanish-speaking as well as English-speaking voters, while the Democrats seem to have focused more on English-speaking voters in the final days of the campaign. This, of course, could be a function of the Republican advantage in campaign funding.

Dividing these data between battleground and non-battleground states, however, paints a clearer picture. The Republican sponsors invested significantly in English and Spanish ads in both competitive and noncompetitive states, suggesting that their advertising strategy was more programmatic than the Democrats' strategy, and perhaps reflected their greater financial resources. The Democrats, on the other hand, focused their resources almost exclusively on battleground states; in these states, they made a final effort in both English and Spanish, though the trend reflects a stronger push at the end for English-language ads. With fewer resources at their disposal, Democrats were forced to be much more selective in their decisions

Table 6.6 Focus of Ads, Miami Markets vs. All Markets

Focus	English Language				Spanish Language			
	All Markets		Miami		All Markets		Miami	
	Rep	Dem	Rep	Dem	Rep	Dem	Rep	Dem
Policy	13,175 69%	5,755 74%	2,607 63%	1,240 79%	1,017 73%	1,070 57%	200 62%	-
Personal	877 5%	375 5%	366 9%	- 0%	89 6%	- 0%	32 10%	-
Both	4,996 26%	1,634 21%	1,165 28%	332 21%	68 5%	484 26%	39 12%	-
Neither	1 0%	42 1%	- 0%	- 0%	215 15%	314 17%	52 16%	-
Total	19,049 100%	7,806 100%	4,138 100%	1,572 100%	1,389 100%	1,868 100%	323 100%	-
% of Total	100%	100%	22%	20%	7%	24%	23%	0%

Source: Compiled by the authors based on information from the Wisconsin Advertising Project

concerning where to allocate their ad dollars, perhaps explaining their near-exclusive concentration on battleground states. Notwithstanding this difference, the patterns of ad timing of the Bush campaign overall and the Gore campaign in competitive states suggest that both parties used Spanish-language ads in search of Latino votes in the final days of the 2000 campaign.

Content of Political Advertisements

The content of political ads also differed along the lines of language. To assess the difference between English and Spanish ads in terms of their substance, we analyze a few variables that evaluate the tone of the ad and the nature of the messages the ads aim to convey. Did the ad have content that focused on policy issues, personal issues, or both? Did the ad promote its sponsor, attack the opponent, or contrast the two? Finally, we evaluate the distinct policy issues that are covered in the ads. Which policy issues did the two campaigns and the party committees emphasize? In the following section, we illustrate a few distinctions in advertising content under the cover of language between Republicans and Democrats.

In our analysis of ad focus, we expect the Republican appeal to the Latino community on issues relating to family values will yield a stronger emphasis on personal issues in Spanish-language ads than in English-language ads. In particular, we distinguish the Miami media market from the other markets because the large Cuban population there provides an audience that should be especially responsive to ads favoring Bush.[18] As we can see from the numbers in Table 6.6, the emphasis on personal issues was not much stronger in the aggregate, but as we expected, Spanish ads by Republicans in Miami were almost twice as likely to feature only personal content (10% in Miami, compared with 6% across all selected markets) and more than twice as likely to feature both personal and policy content than all markets in the aggregate (12% and 5%, respectively). In addition, however, English-language ads sponsored by Republicans in the Miami market also tended to be more personal in nature than those in other markets, perhaps supporting de la Garza's suggestion that Republican outreach to Latino voters in Miami included ads in English as well.

With respect to the tone of the ad, we wondered in particular whether Spanish-language ads were more or less likely to be characterized as attack ads. Given research examining causal relationships between the use of attack ads and voter turnout,[19] we might expect each party to make strategic choices seeking to influence the turnout of the Latino electorate. If negative ads drive down turnout, and because the patterns of advertising timing we discussed earlier suggest that both campaigns were trying to reach out to new voters, we'd expect not to see as many attack ads in Spanish as in English. Alternatively, if a media market in a competitive state contains a large Spanish-speaking audience that might be predisposed to favor one candidate, we might see the other campaign use attack ads in Spanish to depress Latino turnout in that area. In particular, as Latino voters tend to favor Democratic candidates, with the exception of Cuban-Americans, we posit that Republicans might use attack ads in Spanish to depress turnout in media markets with large Latino voting populations.

Instead, we see Democrats using attack ads in both languages with much greater frequency than Republicans (Table 6.7). In fact, there were no Spanish-language ads sponsored by Republicans that were characterized as attack ads. Overwhelmingly, Republicans tended to promote Bush in Spanish-language ads with little contrasting. Even in English, Democratic sponsors were more likely to use attack ads than were Republicans.[20]

Examination of English ads aired in Miami yields patterns for both parties that are not markedly different in tone; both Republicans and Democrats showed a slightly stronger tendency to attack or contrast in English in the Miami market and a lesser tendency to promote. While the Republicans did not air attack ads in Spanish in any media market, their ads in Miami demonstrated a much greater likelihood to contrast the candidates than to promote compared with the patterns in the aggregate.

Given that Miami is the stronghold of Latino support for Republicans,

Table 6.7 Tone of Ads, Miami Markets vs. All Markets

Tone	English Language				Spanish Language			
	All Markets		Miami		All Markets		Miami	
	Rep	Dem	Rep	Dem	Rep	Dem	Rep	Dem
Attack	2,574 14%	1,981 25%	700 17%	473 30%	- 0%	575 31%	- 0%	-
Contrast	7,761 41%	2,002 26%	1,660 40%	506 32%	149 11%	- 0%	93 29%	-
Promote	8,714 46%	3,823 49%	1,778 43%	593 38%	1,240 89%	1,293 69%	230 71%	-
Unclear	- 0%	- 0%	- 0%	- 0%	- 0%	- 0%	- 0%	- 0%
N/A	- 0%	-	-	-	- 0%	-	- 0%	-
Total	19,049 100%	7,806 100%	4,138 100%	1,572 100%	1,389 100%	1,868 100%	323 100%	- 0%
% of Total	100%	100%	22%	20%	7%	24%	23%	0%

Source: Compiled by the authors based on information from the Wisconsin Advertising Project

the reluctance on the part of Republican sponsors to air attack ads in Spanish and the nonexistence of *any* Spanish-language ads sponsored by Democrats leads us to doubt the hypothesis that campaigns would use attack ads in Spanish to drive down voter turnout in media markets with strong Latino support for the opposition. Instead, the modest level of Spanish-language attack ads by both sets of sponsors in all markets supports the supposition that both parties were in fact trying to directly mobilize support within the Latino electorate.

Issue Coverage: Marketing the Message to the Audience

Next, we examine the issue content of the ads in our study and make some tentative conclusions about the relationship between that content and the policy priorities of the prospective audience in each market. We do not attempt to establish causal relationships between voter preferences and the choices made by ad sponsors in our study; however, interesting patterns emerge from introducing survey research results on Latino voting preferences and comparing them to issue coverage in Spanish- and English-language ads.

For the most part, the comparisons we make in this section distinguish the Miami media market from the other media markets because, as we mentioned in the last section, the vast majority of Latino residents in that area are of Cuban descent. Table 6.8 shows the residential Latino composition of selected media markets[21] according to country of origin as well as data on the outcome of the 2000 presidential election in each media market.

Table 6.8 Selected Latino Populations and Election

Media Market	Non-Latino Population	2000 Latino Population, by Origin (%)					Total Population	2000 Election Vote Choice for President	
		Mexican	Puer. Rican	Cuban	Other	Total		% Gore	Winner
Albuquerque	63%	14%	0%	0%	23%	37%	100%	48%	Dem
Chicago	84%	12%	2%	0%	2%	16%	100%	59%	Dem
Fresno	53%	41%	0%	0%	6%	47%	100%	41%	Dem
Las Vegas	78%	16%	1%	1%	5%	22%	100%	51%	Dem
Los Angeles	60%	30%	0%	0%	9%	40%	100%	54%	Dem
Miami	60%	1%	3%	18%	17%	40%	100%	59%	Dem
Sacramento	80%	16%	0%	0%	3%	20%	100%	45%	Repub
San Diego	73%	22%	1%	0%	4%	27%	100%	45%	Repub
Total	64%	20%	1%	2%	8%	30%	100%	53%	Dem

Note: The population information was aggregated from Census data for each country comprising the media markets. Thus it is not necessarily an appropriate point of departure for comment about voting patterns as it includes popluation figures from all residents. However, we feel it is a useful reference and have included it as such. Source: Compiled by the author based on the Bureau of the U.S. Census and "U.S. Cities by Designated Market Area," 2000-Nielsen Media Research.

As we can see, Miami's Latino population makes up 40% of the area's residents, nearly half of whom are of Cuban descent. By far, Miami's Cuban population is the largest in the nation.

We distinguish Cuban Americans as a voting population because survey research indicates that voters of Cuban origin, of all Latino voters, tend to provide the most support for the Republican Party. Table 6.9 shows survey results measuring candidate support for Bush and Gore just before the 2000

Table 6.9 Support for Presidential Candidates by Latino Sub-group[22]

| | | Support for 2000 Presidential Candidates | | |
		Bush	Gore	Undecided
Latino Sub-Groups	Mexican	21.70%	61.60%	16.70%
	Puerto Rican	18.50%	64.10%	17.30%
	Cuban	70.00%	19.70%	10.30%
	Other	28.10%	56.50%	15.40%

Source: Reproduced by the authors based on information from Barreto, de la Garza, Lee, Ryu, and Pachón, "A Glimpse into Latino Policy and Voting Preferences." The Tomás Rivera Policy Institute, March 2002 Policy Brief, p. 5.

election by Latino national origin.

Cuban Americans overwhelmingly supported Bush and reported the lowest rate of indecision. In contrast, the balance of registered Latino voters expressed a preference for Gore that ranged from solid to strong. As such, comparisons between Miami and the rest of the media markets provide interesting insights into the advertising strategies of the two sets of sponsors.

Survey research on issue priorities of prospective Latino voters provides the next mechanism for evaluating the issue content of English- and Spanish-language ads. Figure 6.4 shows the top priorities for the Latino community, according to national origin.

Education is found to be the top priority for the Latino community according to prospective Latino voters, regardless of national origin. Overwhelmingly, Mexican Americans emphasize this issue above all others; however, Puerto Ricans and Cuban Americans see race relations or civil rights as a close second in terms of issue urgency. Unemployment ranks high with Mexican Americans and Puerto Rican Americans, while prospective voters of Cuban descent, largely concentrated in Miami, are concerned with immigration policy. The economy, while present in the minds of many Latino voters, seems to be more modestly emphasized across all nationalities.

These observations serve as the point of departure as we move on to examine the issue content of actual ads, by language and by sponsor, in the 2000 presidential election. As we suggested in our hypotheses, our expectations about the relationship between the issue priorities shown in the prior chart and the issue content of the ads depend on the strategies employed

Figure 6.4 Issue Priority for the Latino Community by National Origin

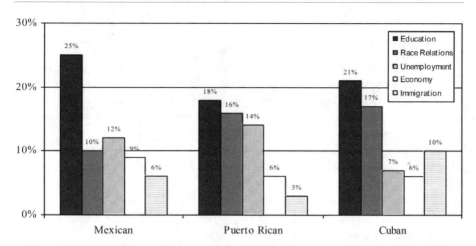

Source: Reproduced by the authors based on information from Barreto, de la Garza, Lee, Ryu, and Pachón, "A Glimpse into Latino Policy and Voting Preferences." The Tomás Rivera Policy Institute, March 2002 Policy Brief, p. 5.

by the sponsors. In particular, if the strategy of the sponsors was to actively court Latino voters, we expect to see a strong relationship between the content presented in Spanish and the issues emphasized within the Latino electorate. On the other hand, if the strategy of the sponsors was largely symbolic, then the content of the Spanish-language ads would not map as well to these priorities.

For this section we aggregated all of the issues covered by all ads;[23] the following figures (Figure 6.5, Figure 6.6, and Figure 6.7) do not distinguish between ads that cover different numbers of issues, nor do they differentiate the first issue mentioned in an ad from later ones.

Examining the issues emphasized in ads in English, we see that for Republicans, children and education and Social Security were the most prominent themes, followed by the deficit, spending, and the economy; health care and Medicare; and Bush's background and record. For Democrats, health care and Medicare, taxes, and Gore's background and record were the most frequently sounded themes. Figure 6.5 illustrates the Republicans' more frequent presence on the airwaves, as they used their superior financial resources to air many more ads and sound issues many times more often than did the Democrats.

Turning to ads in Spanish (see Figure 6.6), the pattern of dominance is reversed, with the Democrats airing more ads and emphasizing issues with

Figure 6.5 All Issues: English-Language Issues Coverage, by Sponsor

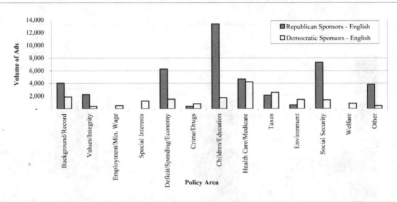

Source: Compiled by authors based on information from the Wisconsin Advertising Project

Figure 6.6 All Issues: Spanish-Language Issues Coverage, by Sponsor

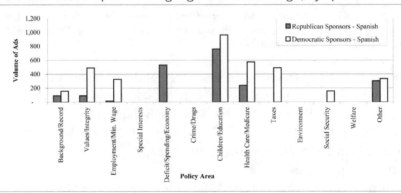

Source: Compiled by authors based on information from the Wisconsin Advertising Project

Figure 6.7 All Issues: Repubican Sponsorship of Ads in the Miami Market, by Language

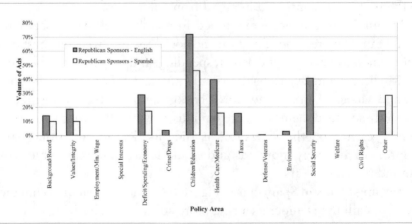

Source: Compiled by authors based on information from the Wisconsin Advertising Project

greater frequency than did the Republicans. As in English ads, Republicans devoted the most attention to children and education, followed by the deficit, spending, and the economy. But unlike their ads in English, the Republican ads in Spanish did not give extensive treatment to a wide range of issues. The Democrats, in contrast, sounded a wider variety of themes in their ads in Spanish than did the Republicans. Children and education jumped to the top of the Democrats' priority list, followed by health care and Medicare, values and integrity, and taxes.

In the aggregate, Democrats appeared to sound different themes in the two languages more so than did Republicans. With the exceptions of Social Security and taxes, which were emphasized heavily in the English but not in the Spanish, the Republicans' issue priorities seemed to be relatively consistent messages in the two languages, focusing most on children and education, followed by the deficit, spending, and the economy as well as health care and Medicare. The Democrats, on the other hand, were less consistent as they emphasized children and education, values and integrity, and employment and the minimum wage proportionately much more in Spanish than they did in English, while health care and Medicare as well as taxes were consistent themes in both languages. Interestingly, immigration, a theme that would arguably be of significant interest to the audiences of Spanish ads, was almost never addressed by either party in either language.

Given the large Cuban population in Miami, we thought the issue content presented by both parties might differ in this market compared to other markets. Therefore, we looked at the same questions for the Miami media market. Since Democratic sponsors did not air any Spanish-language ads in Miami, we confined our comparisons to Republican sponsors' ads in English and Spanish. We found that Republicans' treatment of the Miami market did not differ much from English to Spanish. As shown in Figure 6.7, the patterns mirrored those in the aggregate for Republicans. With the exceptions of Social Security and taxes, the relative emphasis placed on the various issues was similar in both English and Spanish.

We turn to the relationship between the issues emphasized by the campaigns in Spanish and the issue priorities of the Latino community. All three ethnic groups surveyed cited education as their first priority, and the campaigns did frequently air ads on education on Spanish in all markets, particularly in Miami. Aside from this issue, however, we see little correspondence between the surveyed issue priorities and the themes sounded by the campaigns. Race relations, the second most important issue to Cuban Americans and Puerto Ricans and the third key issue for

Mexican Americans, is not an issue emphasized in any market. Civil rights, perhaps the theme most closely related to race relations, was not prominent in all markets in the aggregate, and focusing on Miami, the issue is mentioned in a handful of ads that amount to less than 1% of the issues mentioned. Unemployment, the second most important issue for Mexican Americans and the third most important issue for the other two groups, was not addressed by Republicans in either language; Democrats barely addressed unemployment in English but did so more in Spanish. Neither party ran ads focusing on unemployment in Miami. Thus, the themes sounded in Spanish do not appear to map closely onto the supposed issue priorities of the Latino community.

Conclusions and Further Research

In this chapter we set out to discern whether the 2000 presidential candidates and their parties sought to use Spanish-language ads to target prospective voters or as a symbolic effort to reach out to the Latino community. We found a number of differences in many aspects of the ads along the lines of language, party of sponsor, and media market. The two parties varied in their geographic and temporal allocation of campaign resources, their use of Spanish-language ads, their focus on personal factors and policy issues, and their willingness to employ attack ads. Patterns of timing and geography offered limited support for the notion that the campaigns were indeed using ads in Spanish to reach out to prospective voters, as key resources were invested in the closing days of the campaign for Spanish ads in key states by both parties. With respect to the focus and tone of the ads, the use of Spanish-language ads, particularly by Republicans, suggests a distinct effort to reach out to new Latino voters. In addition, the paucity of attack ads in Spanish by Republican sponsors lends modest support to the hypothesis that their commitment to reaching out to new voters was strong. In the second part of our study examining the connection between Latino priorities and the issue coverage in Spanish-language ads, while the Bush campaign displayed much more consistent patterns of issue priorities in Spanish and English than the Gore campaign, the issues sounded in Spanish did not closely mirror the surveyed issue priorities of prospective Latino voters.

Overall, the timing, geographic distribution and focus, and tone of the ads suggest that both campaigns, and the Republican campaign in particular, invested key resources throughout the 2000 campaign to reach out to prospective Latino voters in Spanish. However, this conclusion is weakened by a failure on the part of both campaigns to tailor the content of their ads targeted at Latino voters to their audience's policy imperatives. Although both parties seem committed to communicating with Latino voters, they still have yet to focus on the issues most salient to the Latino community.

Why? We offer three suggestions. First, perhaps the parties have acknowledged the rising salience of Latino voters but have yet to tailor their message to the audience in a cogent manner. The rapid growth in the Latino electorate, in other words, has not yet commanded the full attention of the parties. Their effort to reach out to this group has resulted only in the existence of Spanish-language ads but not the content appropriate to the Latino audience. If this is the case, we should see an increase in the use of issues salient to the Latino voting community as the parties and campaigns adjust to this growing population over the upcoming elections.

Alternatively, perhaps the campaign organizations are aware of the issues most important to this group, but addressing these issues presents a conflict of interest to the campaigns concerning the messages they provide in English or the general policies they present in their platform. The parties might not be willing to say what Latino voters want to hear if it conflicts with their platform or with the messages they want to communicate to their constituents in English. If this is the case, the content presented in Spanish may continue to fail to map to Latino voter preferences as this population grows in salience.

A third possibility is the failure of campaigns to address issues salient to Latinos mirrors trends in the population at large. Voter apathy in recent decades might be attributed to a failure on the part of candidates and campaigns to address the issues that are most important to the majority of the population. In presidential elections, the disproportionate influence of certain states such as Florida may cause candidates to emphasize issues most salient to certain groups of prospective voters there, such as a prescription drug benefit for the elderly. If campaign messages are being driven by the need to curry the favor of electorally critical segments of the population, other potential voters may feel that their priorities are not being addressed in both English and Spanish.

While this study has revealed important patterns of efforts to target Latino voters in the 2000 presidential campaign, it calls to mind a number of directions for further research. We restricted our analysis to ads aired by the campaigns themselves and the national Democratic and Republican parties. A significant number of ads in Spanish were run by interest groups, most notably the Sierra Club; expanding this analysis to ads run by all sponsors, including third-party candidates, would provide a fuller account of political outreach in Spanish in the 2000 presidential election. Similarly, we discussed only the ads run in the ten media markets in which the campaigns ran ads in Spanish so that we could make comparisons about ads run in the same geopolitical context. Comparing our findings to advertising patterns in other media markets in which there were no Spanish ads run would more completely situate the Spanish ads in the context of the general election.

While we attempted to link the themes emphasized by the parties to the public policy priorities of various Latino ethnic groups, this analysis could draw more systematically on survey research to explore this relationship further. Additionally, detailed analysis of the relationships between advertising patterns and demographic, turnout, voting, and ad-viewing data would further illuminate the context and the consequences of the parties' strategic advertising choices. Adding a qualitative element to this study, perhaps by interviewing campaign strategists, would provide insight into the rationales behind the patterns of communication that we observed. Another potential avenue of investigation would be to analyze efforts to reach out to prospective Latino voters in the presidential primaries. Given the rising salience of Latinos in recent political campaigns, questions such as these will likely become increasingly important in upcoming political campaigns.

ENDNOTES

1. We use the words Latino and Hispanic interchangeably, referring to people of Latin American descent in the United States.

2. These materials are based on work supported by the Pew Charitable Trusts under a grant to the Brennan Center for Justice at New York University and a subsequent subcontract to the Department of Political Science at the University of Wisconsin-Madison.

3. The ten media markets are: Albuquerque, Chicago, Denver, Fresno, Las Vegas, Los Angeles, Miami, New York, Sacramento, and San Diego. We have included, for the purposes of this analysis, ads sponsored by the Bush campaign, the Republican National Committee (both independent and coordinated expenditures made on behalf of Bush), the Gore campaign, and the Democratic National Committee (both independent and coordinated expenditures made on behalf of Gore). We have not included other independent expenditures made on behalf of the two major candidates, such as those by interest groups, nor have we included ads aired on behalf of candidates other than Bush and Gore.

4. Louis DeSipio, "Latino Viewing Choices: Bilingual Television Viewers and the Language Choices They Make," May 2003.

5. Arturo Vargas, *Vital Speeches of the Day,* New York (January 1, 2000).

6. Scholars such as Miller and Sigelman (1978) and Goggin (1984) have argued that in certain policy areas, the audience does indeed play a key role in shaping political speech. Miller and Sigelman, for example, conducted content analysis of Lyndon Johnson's speech and found evidence supporting the hypothesis that presidents tend to manipulate their message to the specific audience to whom they are speaking. Although they readily caution that their conclusions might have limited generalizability, anecdotal evidence over the past several decades reinforces the idea that in this era of mass political communication, politicians and candidates alike are likely to modify the content and tone of their messages depending on the target of their communication.

7. "A Glimpse into Latino Policy and Voting Preferences," Barreto et al., March 2002.

8. DeSipio 2003.

9. DeSipio, 3.

10. Reported by John W. Fountain in the *New York Times,* November 6, 2000.

11. The survey was conducted in five states: California, Florida, Illinois, New York, and Texas. Our study covers Spanish and English ads aired in California, Colorado, Florida, Illinois, Nevada, New Mexico, and New York.

12. Goldstein, Kenneth, Michael Franz, and Travis Ridout. 2002. "Political Advertising in 2000." Combined file [dataset]. Final Release. Madison, WI: The Department of Political Science at the University of Wisconsin-Madison and the Brennan Center for Justice at New York University. A follow-up paper, discussing coding and reliability, was written by the primary investigators and is available at www.polisci.wisc.edu/~-tvadvertising/reliability.pdf.

13. Of the 970,428 ad airings captured, 301,521 related to the presidential campaign and were run in 73 media markets. Of these, only 4,376 ads were in Spanish. Our study focuses on the 3,257 ads that were run by campaigns and parties in Spanish in the general election, as well as the 26,855 ads run by campaigns and parties in English in the same 10 media markets.

14. Since the November numbers only reflect several days worth of ads, we prorated that number to reflect the shortened month. This is not an ideal remedy as the prorated numbers are likely to be somewhat overstated, but for graphical purposes we thought the trend would be more aptly captured.

15. CNN identified 20 battleground states in the 2000 presidential campaign; these states were believed to be potentially winnable by either campaign, and were the subject of much campaign and media attention.

16. Barely any ads were run in the two other media markets in non-battleground states. Only eight ads were run in Spanish in Denver, while only three Spanish ads were run in New York City. Thus, our analysis of patterns in non-battleground states is essentially a study of the four media markets in California.

17. Van Natta Jr. and Broder, *New York Times,* November 3, 2000.

18. Seventy percent of prospective voters of Cuban descent supported Bush in a pre-election survey discussed later in the chapter.

19. See Ansolabehere, Iyengar, Simon, and Valentino 1994; Ansolabehere and Iyengar 1996; Kahn and Kenney 1999; Lau, Sigelman, Heldman, and Babbitt 1999; Wattenberg and Brians 1999.

20. Investigators for the Wisconsin Advertising Project found that the question of whether ads promoted a candidate, attacked an opponent, or contrasted the two to be the most problematic in terms of inter-coder reliability. They posited that the negative tone of many ads that contrasted candidates led some coders to label them attack ads. For a full discussion of this, please see www.polisci.wisc.edu/~tvadvertising/reliability.pdf.

21. We have removed the Denver and New York media markets from this analysis, as only eight Spanish-language ads were aired in Denver and only three were run in New York.

22. These data were generated from a telephone survey conducted over a two-week period from October 8, 2000 to October 26, 2000. Reported by the Tomás Rivera Policy Institute.

23. In order to make the charts more legible, we hid two categories (civil rights and defense/veterans' issues) that had such little volume as to be nearly indiscernible. In addition, we combined categories that we felt were closely related: for example, the separate categories of "deficit," "spending," and "economy" were merged. We acknowledge that this approach may neglect interesting and important distinctions among the more specific issues

REFERENCES

Alvarez, Lizette. "Latinos Are Focus of New Brand of Ads." *New York Times,* October 28, 2002.

Ansolabehere, Stephen, and Shanto Iyengar. 1996. *Going Negative: How Political Advertisements Shrink and Polarize the Electorate.* New York: The Free Press.

Ansolabehere, Stephen, Shanto Iyengar, Adam Simon, and Nicholas Valentino. 1994. "Does Attack Advertising Demobilize the Electorate?" *American Political Science Review* 88 (4), 829–838.

Barreto, Matt, Rodolfo O. de la Garza, Jongho Lee, Jaesung Ryu, and Harry P. Pachón. "A Glimpse into Latino Policy and Voting Preferences." Policy Brief, Tomás Rivera Policy Institute. March 2002.

Bruni, Frank. "Courting the Hispanic Voter." *New York Times,* October 21, 2000.

DeSipio, Louis. "Latino Viewing Choices: Bilingual Television Viewers and the Language Choices They Make." Policy Brief, Tomás Rivera Policy Institute. May 2003.

Farney, Dennis, and Eduardo Porter. "Hispanic Voters Take on New Significance in Presidential Politics." *Wall Street Journal,* October 23, 2000.

Fountain, John W. "Candidates Woo Latinos with Ads, but Not Policy." *New York Times,* November 6, 2000.

Gimpel, James G., and Karen Kaufmann. "Impossible Dream or Distant Reality? Republican Efforts to Attract Latino Voters." Backgrounder, Center for Immigration Studies. August 2001.

Goggin, Malcolm L. 1984. "The Ideological Content of Presidential Communications: The Message-Tailoring Hypothesis Revisited." *American Politics Quarterly* 12 (3), 361–384.

Goldstein, Kenneth, Michael Franz, and Travis Ridout. 2002. "Political Advertising in 2000." Combined file [dataset]. Final Release. Madison, WI: Department of Political Science at the University of Wisconsin-Madison and The Brennan Center for Justice at New York University.

Kahn, K. F., and J. Geer. 1994. "Creating Impressions: An Experimental Investigation of Political Advertising on Television." *Political Behavior,* 16, 93–116.

Kahn, K.F., and P.J. Kenney. 1999. "Do Negative Campaigns Mobilize or Suppress Turnout? Clarifying the Relationship between Negativity and Participation." *American Political Science Review* 93, 877–889.

Lau, R. R., L. Sigelman, C. Heldman, and P. Babbitt. 1999. "The Effects of Negative Political Advertisements: A Meta-Analytical Assessment." *American Political Science Review* 93, 851–876.

Miller, Lawrence W., and Lee Sigelman. 1978. "Is the Audience the Message? A Note on LBJ's Vietnam Statements." *Public Opinion Quarterly* 42 (1), 71–80.

Nielsen Media Research. *Directory of U.S. Cities by Designated Market Area, 2001–2002.* 2002.

Ridout, Travis N., Michael Franz, Kenneth Goldstein, and Paul Freedman. 2002. "Measuring the Nature and Effects of Campaign Advertising." Working paper, Wisconsin Advertising Project.

Van Natta, Don, Jr. "Republicans Open a Big Drive to Appeal to Hispanic Voters." *New York Times,* January 15, 2000.

Van Natta, Don, Jr., and John M. Broder. "The 2000 Campaign: Fund-raising; with Finish Line in Sight, an All-Out Race for Money." *New York Times,* November 3, 2000.

Vargas, Arturo. "Latino Voters: The New Political Landscape." *Vital Speeches of the Day* 66 (6), 170–174. January 1, 2000.

Wattenberg, M. P., and C. L. Brians. 1999. "Negative Campaign Advertising: Demobilizer or Mobilizer?" *American Political Science Review* 93, 891–899.

Yardley, Jim. "The 2000 Campaign: The Texas Governor; Hispanics Give Attentive Bush Mixed Reviews." *New York Times,* August 27, 2000.

7

The Perfect Storm of Politics

Media and Advertising during the 2002 U.S.
Senate Campaign(s) in Minnesota

Amy E. Jasperson

*"It was like a combination of a number of factors and it all kind of came together in an
ugly mess. It's like the perfect storm of politics."*[1]
—Eric Mische, political director for U.S. Senator Norm Coleman

Introduction

In the early months of 2002, the Senate campaign in Minnesota was shaping up to be one of the most hotly contested and highly targeted races in the
country, with partisan control of the U.S. Senate hanging in the balance.
Democratic incumbent Paul Wellstone was a passionate, fiery liberal who
was not afraid to speak his mind, making him a lightning rod for conservative attacks. Republican Norm Coleman had been a Democrat who
endorsed Wellstone in his 1996 campaign, but after switching parties, he was
now a rising star in the ranks of the Republican Party. While pundits, practitioners, and the public anticipated a hard-fought battle, no one could
have predicted the rollercoaster campaign dynamics and crisis decision
making that characterized the historic race of 2002 and demonstrated the
importance of media coverage and advertising for campaign politics.

Past research demonstrates the significance of media and advertising in shaping attitudes of the electorate. In particular, studies show that news and ads can perform an agenda-setting function, not telling the voters what to think but rather telling them what to think *about* (Cohen 1963, McCombs and Shaw 1972). In addition, by framing a story in a particular way or selecting some aspect of the story to the exclusion of others, media can influence the interpretation of the public (Iyengar, 1991; Jasperson et al., 1998; Nelson et al., 1997). Further, media can prime attitudes or alter the criteria by which voters evaluate a candidate (Aldrich et al., 1989; Jacobs and Shapiro, 1994; Krosnick and Kinder, 1990). Finally, advertisements serve an educational function for voters. Positive ads can make candidates more likeable to voters. Contrast or attack ads can highlight important contrasts between candidates, helping voters to make a comparative choice. Ideally, the latter ads can have the intended effect, raising positive feelings about the sponsoring candidate or lowering evaluations of an opponent. Yet under some circumstances, attack ads have been shown to have unintended consequences harming the candidates they are intended to help (Garramone, 1984, 1985; Jasperson and Fan, 2002).

When Senator Wellstone and seven others were killed in a plane crash on October 25, 2002, just 12 days before voters were scheduled to go to the polls, the campaigns immediately shut down all activity and pulled their ads off of the air. A larger than usual number of viewers began tuning in to local television programming to get information about the breaking news.[2] Advertising and television messages were even more important in this context, and they became instrumental in communicating dynamic events to the public and making statements about the character of political actors in a crisis. Initially, the idea that sympathy toward Wellstone would spur goodwill toward his replacement seemed to suggest that Coleman's campaign was effectively over. Lessons from a similar unusual situation, the 2000 Carnahan/Ashcroft Senate race in Missouri, indicated that sympathetic emotions propelled Carnahan's name to victory over Ashcroft when Carnahan perished in a plane crash relatively close to election day. Despite this precedent, a number of critical factors strategically converged, defying expectations, to create the perfect set of circumstances for a Coleman victory in Minnesota.

Former Vice President and Ambassador to Japan, Walter Mondale, enjoyed an immediate lead over Coleman in opinion polls when his name emerged as a possible candidate to carry Wellstone's legacy forward. Stories about Wellstone dominated the media's agenda, yet the media's later live coverage and continued amplification of controversy surrounding the Wellstone memorial primed swing voters to negatively evaluate the Democrats. Just as Mondale became the official party candidate, his advantage over Coleman had dissipated, leaving the two candidates in a dead heat at the start of the "second campaign." While Mondale initially benefited from the emotional dynamics, he later became a casualty. Coleman carefully traversed the political waters and strategically managed his public communication based on lessons learned from Missouri. Given the unusual emotional mood of the battered electorate, any variation in these critical events and their coverage by media could have shifted swing voters and changed the outcome of the election.

While it was an unusual case, the 2002 U.S. Senate campaign in Minnesota still offers important lessons for scholars of political campaign communications. This case highlights the significance of political context and audience mood for the interpretation and understanding of campaign messages in the form of news and ads. Second, it reinforces the more specific point that expectations matter for the reception and processing of political message content and tone. Reporters and the public hold commonly understood norms of behavior, and when a public person violates those expectations, such behavior will become more salient than other information. Third, maintaining control of the message is essential in any public situation that occurs during a campaign. In a further tragedy for the Wellstone campaign, in its desire to be "nonpolitical" and provide a personal, unscripted tribute, it released control of the memorial message. Some unscripted memorial tributes, spoken from the heart by all involved, were interpreted as inappropriately political by media and critics. On the other hand, Coleman, who maintained smart strategic message control at all times through the mourning period and second campaign, was viewed as the figure acting in a respectful, nonpolitical manner. Finally, this case suggests that it is not only the events themselves, but the way in which they are framed and amplified by media, that can be important for determining the information environment that shapes the judgment of swing voters.

This chapter presents data from television news clips purchased from the *PR Newswire* and *Soundclips* databases as well as advertisements from the campaigns and ad buys collected from local television stations in the Twin Cities media market to create a measure of television news and advertising messages. In addition, in-depth interviews with the Wellstone, Coleman, and Mondale campaign consultants, the political parties, and members of the media provide a picture of the intentions of the political actors. Any complete understanding of the dynamics of this race must examine these factors in relation to how the media messages were understood by the voting public. Polling data from media outlets and the Wellstone, Coleman, and Mondale campaigns provided a measure of public response to the campaign dynamics.[3] As National Republican Senatorial Committee (NRSC) strategist, Chris LaCivita, commented, "There was no single issue. . .it was a combination of a fairly good media campaign. . .and the memorial"[4] that unexpectedly harmed Mondale, Wellstone's replacement candidate. Mike Bocian, a member of Mondale's polling team, commented, "There are so many things that came together, most particularly the memorial service and President Bush's visits. . .we knew we were in a tight race."[5] And, as Coleman political director Eric Mische noted in the opening quote, the perfect convergence of factors came together to elect Norm Coleman as the next senator from Minnesota, despite all initial expectations to the contrary.

Media Coverage

The Plane Crash and Campaign Suspension

When the Wellstone campaign plane crashed on October 25, Norm Coleman was left with a deceased opponent propelled to mythical stature within hours of his death, and Wellstone supporters were thrown into a state of devastating grief. As Coleman's campaign manager Ben Whitney explained, it was like a "15 round prize fight where both people have beaten the daylights out of each other, the opponent drops dead and you go to your corner and there is no outcome, no ending."[6] Ads from all political races were pulled off of the television and radio airwaves for a mourning period that lasted until Tuesday of the following week. A memorial planned for Tuesday night, October 29, was the most highly anticipated event in this mourning period. It would be the public remembrance of Wellstone that would transition from grief to confirming a replacement candidate and kicking off the "second campaign" and the affirmation of Wellstone's legacy.

Mourning and Sympathy

The tragedy unfolded immediately in breaking news as the media mourned live with the Minnesota public. Sympathy coverage for Wellstone dominated the news as national outlets began to descend upon the Twin Cities and the local news began to cover the memorial tribute wall that spontaneously arose outside of Wellstone headquarters. The most repeated message on all stations reflected the conclusion that even if you did not agree with him, you knew where Wellstone stood, and he commanded respect as a person of integrity. This tragic event, as communicated to the viewing public, led to an immediate rally of support, sympathy, and grief for the Wellstone family as throngs of people descended upon the State Capitol in St. Paul that evening for a televised candlelight vigil. Politicians and the public alike expressed positive views of the eight deceased individuals and condolences for their families.

Reporters and mourners on all sides of the political spectrum set aside political ideology and reflected upon Paul Wellstone, the person and the compassionate politician. Stories of the conflict and controversy from the past several months of the campaign were replaced with stories of loss and mourning. During the two weeks prior to the crash (October 11 through 24), local television media produced 95 news segments mentioning Coleman compared to 75 news segments mentioning Wellstone, but during the week after the crash, television news produced over 1,000 news segments devoted to the Senate campaign.[7] Analysis of news coverage reveals that it remained steady during the moratorium on campaigning, with most of the coverage focusing on positive coverage of Wellstone. Political frames were replaced with human frames. Media devoted continual news coverage to remembering Wellstone's life and reflecting on his legacy.

Strategy

Beyond the incredible tragedy of losing these lives, the aftermath of the plane crash left both sides in a difficult strategic position. According to Minnesota law, Wellstone's name had to be replaced on the ballot since he could not assume the office. A replacement had to be chosen by the Democratic Party no less than five days before the election. The party planned to hold a nomination convention the day after the Wellstone memorial. Also, both parties had a stake in deciding how to handle the absentee ballots that had already been cast with so little time remaining before election day. In a lawsuit brought by the Democrats, they argued that the absentee ballots should be thrown out and new ballots mailed to voters since Wellstone was no longer a candidate. On the other hand, Republicans wanted to protect the absentee ballots that had already been cast for Coleman and candidates in other races. A court ruling dictated that previously cast votes could be corrected, but the burden lay with the voter to request a new ballot rather than with the state to provide a new ballot.

Further, the Republicans were strategizing about how to best engage the public again in the campaign without a clear opponent and without offending public sensibilities about the tragedy. Meanwhile, the Democrats were trying to prolong the period of mourning as long as possible to sustain the sympathy for Wellstone, hoping it would help the succession candidate. Both positions were daunting, yet Coleman was just hitting his stride as the Democrats were forced to soldier on under a cloud of intense grief, with the additional burden of crushed hearts and spirits.

Coleman as Sympathizer

Coleman, who had been in the same area flying in another small plane at the time of the accident, immediately returned to the Twin Cities. During a strategy session with his closest consultants, the group discussed lessons from the Carnahan/Ashcroft race in Missouri in 2000. Unlike Ashcroft, who shut down his campaign permanently after Carnahan's death in a plane crash, Coleman knew that if he permanently shut down his campaign, it would ensure his defeat. Instead, he decided to call a press conference and to speak to the public as a mourner who commiserated with Minnesota's loss. He consciously became a part of Wellstone's sympathy rally, offering his condolences and prayers.

> This is a terrible day for Minnesota. Paul Wellstone and I were political opponents and that was it . . . I had the greatest respect for his passion, he was a fighter. The people of Minnesota are going to miss that . . . I am going to miss that. We have suspended all campaign activities. . . this is a time for folks to pray, and pray and mourn. [8]

Coleman's advisor, Eric Mische reflected, "Clearly they had a grieving process they had to go through.. . .We were deliberate about making sure that we were exercising the kind of respect that people would expect from us."[9] Coleman was challenged with the task of remaining visible through the campaign moratorium as a mourner, yet he needed to avoid violating expectations of respect and decency for the grieving families. This strategic decision was important for maintaining Coleman's presence, in a non-political manner, during the media agenda dominated by Wellstone's tragedy.

Mondale as Successor

Speculation began swirling around former vice president and ambassador to Japan, Walter Mondale, as the frontrunner for succeeding Wellstone as the Democratic candidate in the Senate race. Mondale began receiving calls on Friday urging him to run as Wellstone's replacement from former and current statesmen like Carter, Clinton, and Daschle.[10] Further, his name immediately surfaced as the only person who had the reputation and stature to step in and win. Local media reports began to highlight Mondale's statement at Wellstone campaign headquarters when he said, "If Paul were here he'd want us to think about one thing and that is to carry on the fight that he led with such brilliance and courage over all these years. And, Paul and Sheila, we intend to do that."[11] In a further sign, DFL (Democratic-Farmer-Labor) Party chair Mike Erlandson declared at a press conference that there were three names synonymous with DFL politics in Minnesota: Humphrey, Mondale, and Wellstone.[12] By Saturday morning, it was considered settled behind the scenes when representatives of the Wellstone family met with Mondale to ask him to carry on Wellstone's legacy. Although Mondale did not officially accept, a story was leaked to a local paper that he was strongly considering it in order to keep others out of the running.[13]

In many cases of tragedy, the replacement candidate is a spouse or family member. According to those close to the Democratic Party, neither of Wellstone's two surviving sons was considered for the race. While Mondale was not a Wellstone family member, he was considered part of the Minnesota DFL family and an integral part of the DFL party legacy in Minnesota. Just after the plane crash, news reporters showed touching images of Wellstone and Mondale walking and talking together in the hours of video tributes to Wellstone's legacy. The link between Wellstone and Mondale was strongly forged through constant news coverage and video images. Also, the fact that the Wellstone sons asked Mondale was an immediate focus of media attention.

This sympathetic coverage for Wellstone and the symbolic linking of Wellstone and Mondale proved to be important in the aftermath of the crash. Internal poll results collected over the weekend showed that Mondale enjoyed a clear advantage over Coleman. The Mondale group, led by campaign manager Tina Smith and pollster Al Quinlan, put a poll into the field over the weekend with results available early Tuesday morning. The Republican Party, as separate from the Coleman campaign in a purposeful effort to avoid the appearance of acting politically during this time, also conducted a poll. Strategists on both sides confirmed that Mondale had an eight-point lead over Coleman, and Mondale was the only candidate tested who beat Coleman with the public.[14] According to Smith, "We were in the advantage, and wanted to maintain it by using the press."[15] They hoped to ride the wave of sympathy to victory on election day.

Controversy Erupts in Media Coverage

While Mondale remained publicly silent out of respect for Wellstone, and Norm Coleman was only present on the air to announce that he, too, was still mourning Wellstone, both candidates received coverage of their "non-campaigning" in the press. Media increased their coverage after the weekend and began to cover more campaigning stories as well as mourning stories. Most of the coverage was speculative neutral reporting about Mondale and Coleman. However, conflict began to arise as the Minnesota Republican Party chair and the National Republicans began to turn up the heat on Mondale. Initially, these stories prompted criticism against the Republican Party for inappropriately campaigning too early. These criticisms contributed to the angry reaction later when Republicans, Independents, and the media framed the Wellstone memorial as a partisan rally.

On Sunday night, while commending Coleman for his grace in this difficult situation, Minnesota Republican Party chair Ron Eibensteiner opened fire on Mondale. In the national press, Newt Gingrich challenged the idea of Mondale as the replacement candidate, criticizing his term as vice president under President Carter. Further, in the local paper, Eibensteiner stated that a vote for Mondale would be a vote for a placeholder rather than someone who really wanted the job. The press framed the stories as the GOP refusing to roll over and give up. On Monday, while the victims' families attended multiple funerals and buried their dead, the Senate met in its chamber to honor Wellstone. Colleagues on both sides of the aisle gave moving tributes while news coverage showed his seat draped in a black shroud. At the same time, Eibensteiner issued a five-debate challenge to Mondale in an attempt to jump-start the political campaign. Former Republican Governor of Minnesota, Arne Carlson, scolded the move as inappropriate and urged the party leader to refrain from further political tactics. In the evening news coverage, controversy over partisan politicking was the main focus of the media's agenda, and controversy threatened to crumble the sympathetic mourning coverage.

The primary focus of Tuesday's news coverage was the public memorial that evening, signaling the official symbolic end of mourning and the return to campaigning Wednesday, yet controversy remained the focus of the day. In the context of a Bush tribute to Wellstone before a bill-signing ceremony, media sources reported that Bush would not attend the memorial service. The Wellstone staff tried to bring the coverage back to a focus on sympathy for Wellstone instead of the partisan wrangling. As Wellstone press secretary Jim Farrell declared, "This is not a day for politics. It's a day for Paul Wellstone, and a day to find a way to concentrate on Paul Wellstone's vision and energy."

The reporter followed with a comment that foreshadowed the expectations of the evening to come. "This statement begins to answer some of the concerns that Republicans are beginning to have at this point (about the Wellstone memorial). With an event like this with a theme which is 'stand up, keep fighting,' they are concerned it will turn into a GOTV rally as opposed to a memorial."[16] This news report illustrated how the Republican Party started to frame the memorial event as a rally for the press even before the event had begun. The reporter also noted correctly, "This is uncharted territory for both Democrats and Republicans. Nobody is sure exactly how to act in a situation like this. Both campaigns are being very careful and I am told by both sides that it is back to campaigning tomorrow."

Many of these stories indicated that in order to try to regain a presence on the media's agenda, the Republican Party attempted to refocus the coverage on the campaign again while the Democrats tried to continue the rallying sympathy coverage. These were risky tactics by the Republicans in that the media began to frame the conduct as inappropriate in a period of mourning. The statement by the former Republican governor signaled that criticism of these actions was warranted. Potentially, fallout from a continued Republican message strategy could have ended up harming Coleman, had it not been for the events to follow. The tone of the coverage leading up to the memorial was an important part of setting the context for processing the memorial itself, which many agree played into the Republicans' pre-memorial message. Election-oriented comments made in speeches during the memorial were seen as even more inappropriate given the criticisms of Republican politicking before the memorial. Television played a central role in bringing the Wellstone memorial to the public and presenting and interpreting the story that unfolded.

The Wellstone Memorial

Media reports provided details of the memorial service for the public and set expectations of the event. Memorial planner Alison Dobson maintained that they were clear about the event while members of the media acknowledged after the fact that they should have been more aware of what could have evolved. The event was scheduled at Williams Arena, the basketball venue at the University of Minnesota, because the Wellstone family wanted the event to be accessible to all, because of the Wellstones' commitment to education, and because all three of the deceased staff members also had ties to the university. The planners intended the memorial to be upbeat and inspirational as reflected in the program theme, "Stand up! Keep fighting," in a contrast to the somber funerals that those close to the families had been attending continuously since Monday morning. The campaign staff had a different perspective in the grieving process when planning the memorial since the public had not experienced the private somber services.

In retrospect, it is clear that no one knew what to expect, yet everyone had preconceived notions about what should and should not occur. In the Carnahan case in Missouri, the family held a state ceremony with a traditional somber funeral that was televised live. It is estimated that 10,000 mourners came to Jefferson City, the capitol, for the service. The theme of continuing Carnahan's legacy was communicated by his daughter when she "pledged that his supporters wouldn't 'let the fire go out.'"[17] While the themes at the memorial for the Minnesota crash victims were similar, the style, presentation, and tone were different. While many politicians spoke at Carnahan's service in 2000,[18] the Wellstone family limited the political speakers at the Wellstone memorial to Senator Tom Harkin of Iowa, Wellstone's best friend in the Senate. However, the Carnahan memorial was not perceived to be inappropriately political because of the somber, traditional tone of the event. A similar event in Minnesota presumably would have elicited little controversy.

In the Minnesota memorial, the speakers (personal friends chosen by the families) had been given no instructions other than to keep their comments to 20 minutes and to speak from the heart.[19] From the moment the crowds of attendees entered the arena to gospel music, the service did not have the feel of a typical memorial. The jumbotron above the stage was turned on so that the vast crowd could see the speakers. The mood was surprisingly upbeat and the crowd was energized. Both the arena and the stadium next door, linked through technology, were filled to capacity with reports of anywhere from 20,000 to 26,000 seats filled. Jumbotrons were also turned on outside for the overflow crowds who came and stayed despite the frigid temperatures. Members of the crowd cheered and occasionally booed as political dignitaries entered the arena and were captured by the media pool cameras. Two hours of the service program passed as relatives and personal friends eulogized Will McLaughlin, Tom Lapic, Mary McAvoy, Marcia Wellstone, and Sheila Wellstone. According to Tom

Mason, a Coleman consultant who attended the services, "In the first hour of that service, things were as sad as things can be, it was a tragedy. . . . It was really a sad service."[20]

After two hours of remembrances, Rick Kahn, Wellstone's best friend and former student, stood up to eulogize Paul Wellstone. Speaking from his heart, he began by making reference to Wellstone's speeches and the explosive emotional reaction they caused in moving people to want to act. He told stories of Wellstone's background in grassroots politics, and after about seven minutes, he struck a pleading tone. As if he were channeling Wellstone himself, Kahn whipped the audience of over 20,000 into an emotional catharsis when he shouted, "And then we're gonna organize, we're gonna organize, we're gonna organize!" The crowd chanted: "Wellstone! Wellstone! Wellstone!" About ten minutes into his speech, Kahn specifically made reference to the upcoming election. He asked the crowd not to bring Paul's legacy "forever to an end" and later pleaded, "I am begging you to win this election for Paul Wellstone!" He continued by speaking directly to Republicans who were friends of Wellstone by identifying them by name and asking, "Can you not hear your friend calling you one last time?" Four minutes later, Kahn ended his 20-minute speech. Wellstone's sons, David and Mark, followed, with the final speech given by Senator Harkin.

The entire memorial service was approximately 3 hours, 24 minutes total. Fourteen minutes of the 204-minute event, or just under 7%, made reference to winning the election for Paul Wellstone. Some critics argued that the tone of the memorial could be considered partisan from the moment it began, as the audience cheered for the Clintons and booed Republican Senator Trent Lott when they were shown entering the arena. On the other hand, defenders of the memorial wondered how anyone could criticize the way that the families and friends of those killed chose to mourn their loved ones. Some Republicans, such as Wellstone friend and Congressman Jim Ramstad and Secretary of Health and Human Services Tommy Thompson, downplayed the tone of the service when questioned by media. Others, such as Republican strategists Vin Weber and Sarah Janecek, immediately cried foul and attacked the Democratic Party in the media for appearing to exploit Wellstone's death for political gain. Now that the event itself had ended, the media swung into high gear to put the situation in context for the public.

The Media Perspective behind the Scenes

All news stations in the Twin Cities decided to cover the memorial service for the plane crash victims as a live news event. Most stations covered it nonstop starting with their 6:00 P.M. newscasts as it had merit as a news story separate from any political criteria.[21] However, given Wellstone's position as a senator, the news stations assigned political reporters to the arena with the election night team activated in their studio to give running commentary during the event. Even the media could not remove the political lens from their own conceptualization of how to cover the story.

The event was structured in a pooled arrangement where the various stations contributed different staff for the variety of jobs, and all stations shared the same news feed. When the director of photography for the event called for a shot of a political dignitary entering the arena, she realized that the image was broadcast on the jumbotron, and the audience reacted with cheers or boos. She noted that this tone was instigated by the crowd before the program even officially began. She reported struggling with the crowd to maintain control of the tone through her choice of camera shots. Oftentimes she would purposely pull back so as not to linger too long on a particular dignitary in order to let the public excitement diffuse.[22] The event producer noted struggling with the same dilemma.[23]

According to the local news directors and television anchors, chaos ensued at all of the stations during the Rick Kahn speech. As Kahn began to plead with the audience to "help win this election for Paul Wellstone," they faced a dilemma as the message had become political in nature. "When you hear the words memorial service, you expect emotion and spirit, but 'this is why we need to defeat Norm Coleman in the next election. . .' You kept waiting for them to do something to stop it."[24] The Channel 5 (KSTP) news director claimed that they "felt a bit bamboozled"[25] while the anchor for Channel 4 (WCCO) news initially felt "deceived" like they were "participants in a commercial for Walter Mondale's candidacy."[26]

Immediately, all three stations individually began discussing whether or not they should pull out of the coverage. They were concerned that if they pulled out, they had to cut it entirely, and the Wellstone sons had not yet spoken. Most were willing to give the sons great leeway in terms of their speeches, but they did not expect the election plea from Kahn. The news directors reported that the switchboards started lighting up, with most calls complaining about the partisan tone of the speaker and demanding equal time for the Republicans. To make matters worse for members of the media, the public was blaming *them*. "We became the vehicle through which this mistake was made."[27] The media was seen as "a tool of the Democratic Party"[28] according to feedback from angry viewers. The media had become part of the evolving story because of their decision to cover a live event over which they had no control.

Despite the pleas from callers and eventually from the state Republican Party leadership, the stations all decided that the equal time rule had not been activated. The equal time rule requires that if a candidate gives a political speech that is covered by the press, the other candidates are required to be given equal airtime by the stations. The stations determined that equal time did not apply in this case since no official candidate spoke at the memorial. Further, Mondale was yet to be nominated and confirmed by the Democratic Party. In addition, Mondale did not speak at the event even though the camera focused on him often over the course of the evening, eliciting cheers from the audience. Once the memorial ended just before the 10:00 P.M. news, the anchors and commentators put the memorial in context for their viewers to diffuse the angry feedback.

The Media Reaction on Air

During the live coverage prior to the 10:00 P.M. news, the anchors were visibly shaken and upset on KARE-11. Over the image of people clearing out of the arena, anchor Paul Magers claimed that the event turned into much more than a memorial; it became an "open and blatant political rally." Guest expert, University of Minnesota historian Hy Berman commented, "It was probably expected that some of it would be, in fact, a political rally. . .but what it turned out to be was a kind of *massive* political rally that perhaps went beyond the norms at some times." Magers responded, "When it was sold to all of us, I shouldn't say sold, but when we were approached about carrying it, we were told that it would be a memorial, a celebration, a celebration of six lives cut short and as you just mentioned, Hy, I think everyone probably has a reasonable expectation, we as broadcasters, we as journalists, that there will be some politics in there."

Magers concluded by defensively stating, "And the bottom line is this that for those of you at home who have taken the time to call or send an e-mail, we recognize what's taken place. Exactly what becomes of this, I have no idea, because it seems like there's a wide range of opportunities available to the Republican Party regarding broadcast air time." Berman stated, "They (the Republicans) have gotten a wedge in that they didn't have before. . .The Mondale people, or I assume the Mondale people, are going to regret this as an outcome of this memorial rally." Berman continued later, "It was a turn, a twist, I think I didn't fully anticipate. . .I thought some of it would be that way, and of course it is understandable that it would be that way, but the extent of it is what went over the edge."[29] These statements signify that the violations of expectations perceived by angry viewers were reflected in the commentary of experts through the news media. These opinion leaders told the public, some of whom may not have drawn their own conclusions, that the event went too far. Also, the media commentators drew a clear link between the memorial and the Mondale campaign, despite the fact that Mondale campaign and the local Democratic Party were not involved in the planning.[30] This media-forged link then worked to hurt Mondale's position in the second campaign.

Commentary also provided another reason for the reaction by the journalists and experts. Magers, the anchor, mentioned that the Republicans "were roundly chastised by the Democrats" for issuing a five-debate invitation to the DFL. Berman responded, "Correctly so. That was the wrong thing to do at that time and this is the wrong thing to do at this time." Berman characterized Kahn's speech as a "rip-roaring kind of partisan appeal that we would expect at a party rally but not at a memorial service." Magers anticipated hearing about it "tonight, tomorrow, and in the days ahead." So, while the memorial event itself had an impact on the more partisan viewers and the media anchors, directors and reporters, the ensuing media coverage of the event highlighted a small segment of that service and amplified it into the lead story, promising to continue talking about the controversy of the event for days to come.

Clearly these testimonials from the media demonstrated that a portion of the speeches violated their expectations of an appropriate memorial service. Further, the length of the service, at over three hours, violated journalistic norms and frustrated some television executives. Given that they did not know what to expect, some television media made certain assumptions that might have been incorrect. Finally, they lost advertising dollars during prime time programming.[31] According to memorial planner Alison Dobson, "We were very clear from a planning perspective that this was not a funeral with a draped coffin. There would be music and lovely speeches and things like that. The media never raised questions about that."[32] Yet when viewers became upset with the tone of the service, the media amplified this view on the air because they unwittingly had become a part of the controversial story.

The 10:00 p.m. News

The post-memorial coverage on the Tuesday night 10:00 P.M. newscast was just the beginning of an immediate on-air reaction that would last through the next day. Different stations selected various segments as illustrations of appropriate remarks. All stations framed the memorial as a service to commemorate the victims of the plane crash that got out of hand and became a partisan rally. All newscasts showed video clips of Rick Kahn begging the audience to "win this election for Paul Wellstone."

On KSTP-5, political reporter Tom Hauser concluded that the memorial was framed as "mostly a memorial for Paul Wellstone, but at times it became more political. The memorial was for the most part a celebration of six lives, the focus not on what was lost, but what was gained from their all-too-brief existence." At the end, Hauser's closing signified the dominant presence of this frame as he concluded, "Most of *the rally* was about the lives lost, but at times it did become political" (emphasis added).

The WCCO-4 coverage provided a different live lead in from the perspective of Norm Coleman, Wellstone's opponent. Reporter Esme Murphy opened by providing her own evaluation to contextualize the story by proclaiming that Coleman "was moved to a different part of the auditorium that would be a bit more friendly to him although it was hard to believe that he would find any friendly section with this very partisan crowd." "What's not clear is if he stayed for the entire service—what turned out to be a highly partisan memorial service." In the reporter's closing point she commented, "Officially, the Democratic line has been that they wouldn't be saying anything political until after Fritz Mondale was actually named the replacement candidate. That certainly changed here tonight."

In the KARE-11 coverage, the anchor, Magers, composed himself from his earlier visible agitation and opened the 10:00 P.M. newscast by saying, "Tonight's memorial service hit on every emotion from tears to laughter." Co-anchor, Diana Pierce, transitioned into the new frame, "But at some moments, the tribute sounded more like a rally for the Democratic Party." They concluded with a statement from Bill Walsh, the Republican Party spokesperson, deciding "much of the night was poignant and touching but in the end, it turned into a campaign rally." Magers added, "Boy, we can attest the phones were ringing off the hook here as well." While all reporters acknowledged the touching moments, the conclusion reached by all media sources was that something dramatic and inappropriate had happened. This reinforcement and amplification of the anti-Democratic frame continued to dominate the next day's television news.

The Day After: Continued Fallout from the Memorial

The politicization of the memorial was now the lead story on all stations. Despite efforts by the Wellstone campaign to take the memorial
issue off the agenda early on Wednesday, the story would not dissipate. While
the story's presence on the agenda was partly related to the personal feelings from the media described above, conflicting messages coming from the
Democrats and the Wellstone campaign probably did not help to defuse the
story. Wellstone's campaign manager, Jeff Blodgett, held a press conference
to take responsibility and to apologize for the memorial, but the DFL
Party spokesperson, Mike Erlandson, defended the Wellstone staff, saying
that the family and close friends were traumatized and the public should
understand.

By the 5:00 P.M. news, the media added another colorful opinion leader
who helped to prolong the charge against the controversial memorial.
Governor Jesse Ventura claimed that he walked out of the memorial because
he felt "violated and used." The lead-in for KARE-11 on the 5:00 P.M. news
indicated that Governor Ventura walked out because he was upset and he
was not alone in his disappointment. According to anchor Magers, "There
are fierce accusations that what started as a fitting memorial turned into a
blatant political rally." According to the co-anchor, "Complaints go beyond
party lines." The graphic behind the anchors asked, "memorial or political rally?" with a picture of Wellstone's friend who gave the controversial
speech. The segment reports that Ventura warned his wife that the memorial would turn political and echoed the dominant frame for viewing the event
as he proclaimed, "To turn a memorial service into a *political rally* I found
quite disturbing." Ventura then said that the Democrats' actions were hypocritical because they had been criticizing the Republicans for being too political prior to the memorial. Because of this, he pledged to appoint an
independent to fill the vacancy left by Wellstone's death. As the main
anchor on WCCO, the top-rated station for that week's election coverage
noted, Jesse Ventura should not be considered a litmus test for judgment,
but media "use him because he's good copy."[33]

Many of the campaigning stories from Wednesday and Thursday after
the memorial were critical of the Democrats despite the fact that the grieving Wellstone staff and family planned the memorial. They continued to focus
on the story of the surprising turn in the memorial service in part to justify their decisions to air the event live and to elaborate on their decision
to deny equal time to Republicans afterwards. In doing so, media were instru-

mental in further amplifying the message that the Democrats were being hypocritical and had violated expectations in a time of grief.

Although Mondale was not involved in planning the memorial, he was now inextricably linked to Wellstone and was becoming the target for angry feelings about the memorial from some key swing demographic groups, such as women and seniors. The initial angry reaction on the part of some viewers corrected for the surge of goodwill that initially characterized Mondale's support. According to the Mondale campaign, the impact of the memorial and the media coverage in the aftermath had a visible effect in the polls. While Mondale was up eight points on Monday before the memorial, by Thursday morning the poll numbers indicated that his lead was cut to 2%. According to Mondale consultant Mike Bocian, "We knew that those events were having a serious impact on our candidate, the late Senator Wellstone's image, and the race itself. We were no longer in a position of significant advantage, but it could still be a race."[34] Confirming the internal campaign polls, the *Star Tribune's Minnesota Poll,* conducted polls before and after the memorial service. The Monday October 28 poll

Table 7.1: Media and Mondale Campaign Polls for Senate Vote Question

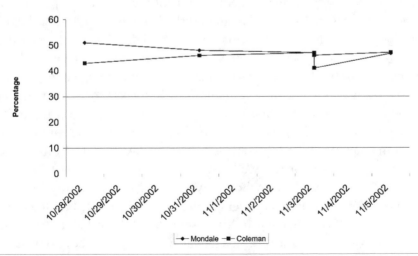

Sources: Star Tribune Minnesota Poll data were provided by Rob Daves. Margin of error reported for 11/3/02 poll was +/- 3.2%. Pioneer Press Mason-Dixon poll data were provided by Dave Peters. Margin of error reported for 11/3/02 poll was +/- 4%. Mondale campaign poll data were collected by Al Quinlan of Greenberg Associates and provided by Ted Mondale. Fox News poll data were provided by Daron Shaw, Associate Professor of Government at the University of Texas at Austin.

showed that Mondale was ahead 47% to Coleman's 39% (see Table 7.1). A poll conducted after the memorial showed that Mondale's lead had dropped to five points, within the poll's margin of error.[35]

This anger spilled over from the television coverage to talk radio, where the memorial was the focus of discussion through the end of the week.[36] By gaining a voice through media coverage, the angriest viewers were also able to resonate with some viewers who probably had not quite made up their minds about how to make sense of the event. While some on both sides acknowledged the damage of some undecided voters viewing the event live for themselves, Coleman consultant Tom Mason admitted, "People didn't know how to react. I think it was the media coverage of it that determined their reaction."[37] Mondale consultant Bocian concurred that, "If it hadn't been replayed again and again and again," the event might not have had such an impact.[38] As the second campaign between Mondale and Coleman began, Coleman continued to remain above the controversy while angry voters, led by some Republican spokespersons and Jesse Ventura, went after the Democrats in the press.

Media Coverage over the Weekend

Two of the most significant media events of the second campaign were the President Bush rally for Coleman and the live televised debate the day before the election between Coleman and Mondale. Despite the fact that Sunday is not typically an active news day, media crews were busy following both candidates. Fifteen news segments, many of them live, ran on different stations reporting on President Bush's speech for Coleman that afternoon. This was not the first time the president had come to Minnesota, yet media outlets felt compelled to give the event more coverage in the aftermath of the memorial. KSTP-5 decided to cover the rally live from 3:30 to 4:00 P.M. to make up for the Wellstone memorial from the past Tuesday. According to Don Shelby, anchor at WCCO-4, this was an event that might have received voiceover coverage and not a sound-bite because of the number of times Bush had come to Minnesota already on behalf of Coleman. "It was just another political rally. He was not going to talk about things important to the state of Minnesota. He was here to get his guy elected."[39] Yet in the aftermath of the memorial, they felt compelled "to throw full coverage at the event."[40]

The other most anticipated event of the second campaign was the live debate. The debate was broadcast live from the State Theatre on Minnesota Public Radio and KARE-11 television from 10:00 to 11:00 A.M. Typically

KARE-11 broadcast "soft local news programming" at this time with about 21.5% of all televisions tuned in during this hour. For the debate, 33% of all television households tuned in, and an additional 20% of household tuned in after the 10:00 P.M. news when it was rebroadcast.[41]

In addition, throngs of demonstrators came out in the cold, some to hold signs and rally for their candidate and others to protest against the exclusion of the Green and Independent Party candidates from the debate. The Independent Party candidate filed a lawsuit attempting to prevent the debate from going forward without his participation. Just before the debate was scheduled to start, Governor Jesse Ventura placed himself again on the media agenda by picking this moment to announce Wellstone's replacement for the remainder of the current term. He chastised the media for not including all voices in the debate and announced that he was appointing Dean Barkley, his Independent Party mentor, because of his displeasure with members of both main parties.

However, the media's primary interest for coming out of the debate was whether or not Mondale had a command of the issues after years away from politics. According to some media and political watchers who saw him at the Democratic nominating convention on Wednesday night, Mondale appeared to have "none of the zeal" that he used to have and they felt that "his (political) days were long past."[42] Everyone respected Mondale for coming out of retirement to carry on for Wellstone, but it was felt by many that he deserved to slow down and enjoy his family. The stakes were highest for Mondale as all eyes were on him.

As the moderators asked the questions, both candidates demonstrated that they were on the top of their game. Mondale showed that he was a tough debater who displayed a clear command of the issues and exceeded the expectations of those who reported the story to the public. Coleman was well versed as well since he had been debating with Wellstone for months. The debate was a clear contrast of ideology and perspective on issues of importance to the voters. After the debate, political reporter Kerri Miller from KARE-11 remarked that she was struck by Mondale's energy, vigor, and knowledge of the issues. Tom Hauser from KSTP-5 agreed but felt that Mondale came across as mean. In particular, Mondale referred to Coleman as "Norman" during the debate, "a name he probably hasn't been called since he was 12 years old."[43] Magers, one of the debate moderators, echoed Hauser's impression and conservative commentator Bob Novak's assessment that Coleman's calm demeanor had provided a stark contrast to Mondale's feisty style.

Given that the debate took place so close to election day, it is difficult to determine the true impact of the head-to-head match-up. Both sides felt that their candidate picked up significant support, and both denied collecting poll numbers. Further, local reporters were attentive to the fact that this late-event coverage could influence the way last-minute deciders cast their votes the next day. They were consciously mindful in framing their nightly news reports about the campaign in order to be fair to both candidates.[44]

Overall, with local television news arguably serving as a key source of evolving information for the voters, the balance of coverage was important for defining political discourse for the late deciders. While events themselves certainly had an impact, those who did not experience events firsthand received the dominant frame through media coverage of events. As events unfolded, negative coverage of the Wellstone memorial hurt Mondale, while some additional coverage of presidential visits boosted positive exposure for Coleman.

Advertising Content and Tone

This race is also a story of two different advertising campaigns punctuated by tragedy. The first campaign was a long endurance marathon fought over the course of almost ten months, with campaign ads peppering the airwaves, at first positive, then turning to contrasts and attacks. While the barrage of negative ads was a common occurrence on Twin Cities television during the final months of the campaign season given the number of hotly contested races, the Minnesota Senate race was relatively positive in tone overall because of the delay in attacks and the forced positive tone of the second advertising campaign. While the Wellstone campaign was able to level an effective attack against Coleman's character, Coleman was able to battle back with his own positive character spot. This spot from the first ad campaign laid the foundation for him to make a compelling case for himself during the second positive ad campaign.

During the Coleman/Mondale campaign, both candidates' consultants believed that the emotional context of the tragedy limited them to a positive ad strategy. In addition, Mondale was handicapped by the shortened time frame. While he was guaranteed equal access in buying ad slots despite the last-minute timing, it would be risky to attack Coleman without a significant amount of time to reestablish his own positive image with the voters. Further, given the sensitive emotional context, attacks by either side could have been interpreted as inappropriate, just as the memorial had been interpreted as improper, leading to a backlash against the attacking candidate. While attack ads helped to chip away at Coleman's favorability in the first campaign, Mondale refused to engage in attacks. Yet an attack ad sponsored by Coleman's party against Mondale could have become a problem for Coleman that shifted the advantage back to Mondale. When the Republican Party pulled the attack ad just before it was scheduled to air, they took the controversy off of the media's agenda and kept the issue from derailing Coleman's campaign.

The First Advertising Campaign: Wellstone vs. Coleman

In the first campaign, Coleman and Wellstone focused on getting their message out through early political advertising. Ads had not started airing during Wellstone's 1996 race until May of that year, but during 2002 Coleman went up on the airwaves in February, and the DFL party began airing ads in March, many months before the election. This race reflected a trend of candidates and parties running ads earlier and earlier in the election cycle in order to define themselves before their opponents could define them. Poll results revealed that most people had already formed their opinions about the two well-known candidates early in the year with only 12% undecided in February. However, with a 40% favorability rating for Coleman compared to 48% for Wellstone, Coleman was eager to go on the air to win over more undecided voters.[45] Coleman was barely trailing Wellstone in the horserace question, with 46% favoring Wellstone compared to 42% for Coleman. Given that Wellstone was the incumbent, Coleman's team felt they were well within striking distance. Wellstone's camp was equally as confident, given that Wellstone had won his past two races, yet rarely received over 50% of the vote. He was comfortable at 46% to 48% support.

During the summer, when most voters were not as attentive to political races, the airwaves were filled with positive image and issues ads highlighting each candidate. The only exceptions were some attention-grabbing independent group advertisements. These groups primarily focused on Wellstone's candidacy, either supporting him or attacking him as the incumbent. Despite the presence of groups such as the AFL-CIO, the Sierra Club, the United Seniors Association, and Americans for Job Security, independent groups did not play as significant a role in the race as the candidates and parties.[46] The candidates and parties had a heavy presence for months, spending millions of dollars in advertising buys. Between $20 and $25 million were spent on television advertising, with relatively equal amounts spent by candidates and parties on each side.[47]

However, by the end of the summer, the race remained in the same dead heat that existed earlier in the year. According to Chris LaCivita of the National Republican Senatorial Committee (NRSC) and Andy Grossman of the Democratic Senatorial Campaign Committee (DSCC), both parties wanted to run ads critical of their candidates' opponents earlier in the campaign cycle in order to try to open up a lead. In 1996 Republican candidate Rudy Boschwitz had been labeled a negative campaigner because of a barrage of attack ads run from May through October against Wellstone by the NRSC. These ads contributed to a decline in Boschwitz's favorability and assisted in Wellstone's 1996 victory (Jasperson and Fan, 2002). Both parties wanted to avoid this type of unintended backlash from negative ads in 2002 by delaying attacks on the opponent so the other candidate would look like the aggressor.

In 2002 both parties spoke of using contrast ads—ads that raised doubts about the target candidate of the ad while reaffirming confidence in the sponsoring candidate. Oftentimes candidates can lower the favorability of their opponents without causing any backlash against them by using contrast spots, as opposed to pure attacks (Pinkleton, 1997). The Minnesota senate race "was a race in which a lot of us wanted to go contrast, as opposed to negative, earlier. It was just, they weren't going negative. And if they weren't going negative, we didn't want to be labeled as a negative campaigner . . .It was really right after Labor Day that we both just said, 'Gloves off.'"[48]

Two ads in particular were the most important in defining the first campaign. In early October, the Wellstone campaign decided to level a direct hit on Coleman's character by unveiling a long-awaited ad entitled, "Join Me" (All ads discussed in this chapter can be found on the web site for this book [see "Note to Reader" on page vii].) This ad showed actual video footage of Coleman giving a DFL Party convention speech in 1996 endorsing party nominees Paul Wellstone for Senate and Bill Clinton for president. The ad concluded by asking the viewer, "Can you trust Norm Coleman?," implying that voters could not trust a man who switched parties and had endorsed his current opponent in his last campaign. As Coleman pollster Glen Bolger explained, "It was not that he had switched parties but what that meant to voters about his character" that caused the damage.[49] A "truth test" conducted by WCCO television determined that this ad was indeed true, making it a credible attack on Coleman's word. After "Join Me" began airing on September 29th, Coleman's favorability dropped from 54% to 42%

Figure 7.1: Candidate Favorable Ratings (Wellstone/Coleman).

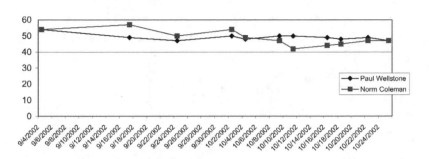

Source: Wellstone polls conducted by Diane Feldman of The Feldman Group. Data provided by Wellstone campaign. Sample size is 600. Very favorable and favorable ratings are combined.

between October 2 and October 11. By October 11, Wellstone's internal polls showed that Coleman's unfavorable rating had increased by 12 points from 30% to 42% (see Figures 7.1 and 7.2).

Wellstone dodged his own problems in late September when a new issue surfaced with the potential to cause serious damage. In his attempt to bring a national focus to the elections, President Bush sought authority from Congress to take preemptive action against Iraq as part of the war on terrorism. An NRSC ad airing at the same time took Wellstone to task for not doing enough to support a strong military. While a media truth test on October 2 claimed that the ad was misleading, the ad itself received widespread airing, and the Wellstone campaign staff was concerned about the possible fallout from Wellstone's position on the issue. Much of the Minnesota public, as well as the American public, supported a popular president on the Iraq issue. On October 3, Wellstone spoke on the Senate floor in opposition to the resolution granting Bush unilateral authority to launch an attack. He was the only senator up for reelection to oppose this resolution when the vote was taken a week later.[50] Both supporters and opponents thought he might be self-destructing by taking such a position, although Wellstone was known for standing up for his convictions regardless of the consequences.

After Wellstone spoke out, his favorability dropped only two points. He bounced back and held steady at around 50% favorability through October 11, the day after the official vote. A week later on October 16, Wellstone was still at 49% favorability, and the difference between his favorables and unfavorables was approximately 8% in his favor. According to ad consult-

Figure 7.2: Candidate Unfavorable Ratings (Wellstone/Coleman).

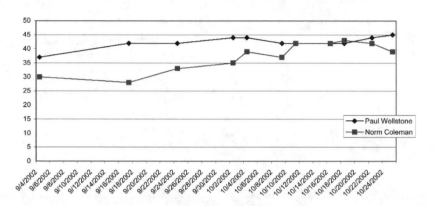

Source: Wellstone polls conducted by Diane Feldman of The Feldman Group. Data provided by Wellstone campaign. Sample size is 600. Very unfavorable and unfavorable ratings are combined.

ant Mandy Grunwald, this vote proved that Wellstone had not changed as a candidate as his detractors had claimed. She concluded that voters regained their appreciation for Wellstone's dedication to always voting his conscience. He proved that he would do what he thought was right. Originally, the strategy team had discussed creating an ad to explain his vote on Iraq, much like he had explained his vote against Clinton's welfare reform bill in 1996. However, after looking at the poll numbers, it appeared that his vote was "making sense to people," and they did not want "to do anything that would appear to politicize it."[51] The poll numbers at this time put him in a stronger position than Coleman, who showed no net advantage in favorability.

Given the state of Coleman's favorability ratings, this was the ideal time for the Coleman campaign to unveil the ad that many claim to be the most memorable, touching, and effective in deflecting criticism during the first campaign. In "My Dad," Coleman's young daughter, Sarah, spoke to the voters about her father. The idea came to ad consultant Scott Howell as Coleman told him about his previous political defeat in 1998. He claimed that people were not seeing who he really was, and he repeated feedback that his daughter offered, "Dad, just show more of your heart." Howell felt that if the voters saw Coleman through the eyes of his daughter, they would become invested in him, viewing him as a real person and a good guy.[52]

In "My Dad," Sarah made the case, in a humorous way, that her father was a man of character and follow-through. "If you don't do your homework, you *will* get grounded. Just ask my brother." The ad also showed Coleman playing outside with his family and trying to juggle for his daughter. This ad humanized Coleman, stabilizing his favorability ratings and counteracting a new Wellstone ad that began airing at the same time. This ad made it less likely for Wellstone's attacks to continue to stick despite the fact that most of the Wellstone campaign's ad buy during this time focused on criticizing Coleman. The impact of not promoting himself was seen in Wellstone's slight decline in favorability during this period. Coleman's positive "My Dad" ad resonated well with voters, and his favorability rating increased 5% by the time the ad stopped airing on October 21.

This late mixture of both hard-hitting and positive character spots had tightened the race into a close competition leading into October 25. In the head-to-head horserace question between the two, poll numbers fluctuated over time and depended upon the source. Polls from the campaigns indicated that the race was too close to call with both candidates hovering around 43% support. The difference between the two front-runners, whether in a two-candidate or four-candidate question structure, fell within the margin of error (see Table 7.2). Despite these close numbers, both campaigns claimed that their candidate was on his way to victory. However, without other clear data showing a magnitude of difference beyond measurement error to confirm these claims, the true outcome is impossible to know.

Newspaper polls in the Twin Cities painted a different picture. In the last media poll before the plane crash, which was released in mid-October, the *Star Tribune* showed that Senator Wellstone had begun pulling ahead of Coleman 47% to 41%, just at the poll's 3% margin of error[53] (see Table 7.3). With the additional GOTV grassroots mobilization that Wellstone was known for, academics began reaching the conclusion that "the shift had occurred" in Wellstone's direction.[54] Further, coverage of this information in the news could have caused a self-fulfilling prophecy leading into the final week and a half.

The Planned Finale

As election day approached, news about the advertising strategy unfolded daily. On October 23, 2002, an article ran in the *Star Tribune* describing a $1 million ad buy made by the independent group, Americans for Job Security, for the final ten-day campaign. This buy would have created a huge influx of negative information against Wellstone during the final two-week period leading up to election day. According to Kathleen Hall Jamieson from the Annenberg School at the University of Pennsylvania, "the sheer magnitude of such an ad buy could change the course of the election."[55] This amount of information critical of Wellstone caused concern among his staff despite Minnesota voters' rejection of negative campaigning and their reelection of Wellstone in 1996. Given the concern about this influx of money, the Wellstone consultants created an ad to tie the actions of this group to Coleman and to call on him to expose the group or reject the ad.[56]

When the plane crashed on October 25, Americans for Job Security pulled their advertising buy, and neither ad was ever aired. The Wellstone campaign's final ad, written in part by Wellstone, was the only ad shown in a final tribute by local television news stations after the plane crash. The ad entitled "Represent" contained Wellstone's favorite credo: "I don't represent the oil companies or the Enrons of this world, but they already have great representation in Washington. I represent the people of Minnesota." This ad launched the media rally for Wellstone and his legacy, mentioned in the prior section.

Overall, the advertising battle between Wellstone and Coleman during the first campaign, with the parties and independent groups weighing in, was a spirited fight where criticism of the opponent's record was a necessary strategy to cause movement for or against each candidate. Wellstone

Table 7.2: Candidate Polls: Wellstone v. Coleman for horserace question

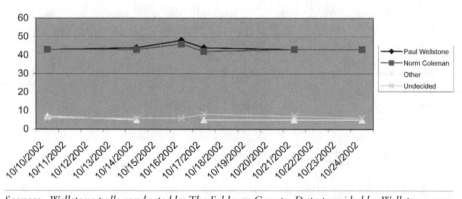

Sources: Wellstone polls conducted by The Feldman Group. Data provided by Wellstone campaign. Coleman polls conducted by Public Opinion Strategies. Data provided by Coleman campaign.

Table 7.3: Media Polls for Senate Horserace Question (Wellstone v. Coleman).

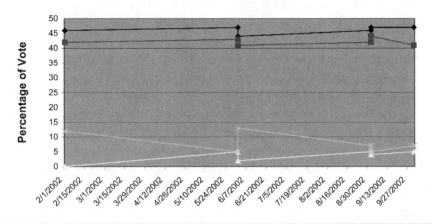

Sources: Star Tribune Minnesota Poll data were provided by Rob Daves. Pioneer Press Mason-Dixon poll data were provided by Dave Peters.

was successful in nailing Coleman on the question of integrity and position-switching while Coleman was successful in reemerging by establishing a compassionate personal image that had been missing prior to hiring Howell in late summer. As stated by Wellstone's press secretary, Jim Farrell, it was essential for Wellstone to hammer on Coleman's inconsistencies and "keep a foot on his neck" to prevent him from "morphing" into another candidate.[57] As long as the Wellstone campaign could continue to pin Coleman down, Farrell was confident Wellstone would win.

Because of the number of early positive ads aired along with late positive ads, academics characterize the 2002 Senate campaign as a positive race overall. Almost 70% of Wellstone ads were positive compared to over 66% of Coleman's ads. Further, the party ads for Wellstone and the independent group ads for Wellstone were more positive than negative, while the independent group ads aimed at benefiting Coleman were attacks on Wellstone.[58] Yet the final few weeks of the Wellstone/Coleman race saw a barrage of contrast and attack spots that most Minnesota viewers remember, giving credibility to the assessment that both sides had been "pounding the snot out of each other"[59] in paid media during the final weeks. It is clear that this tone would have continued into election day in order to move the late-deciding voters until tragedy changed everything. Yet the voters seemed to forget the bitter battle of the first ad campaign as they made judgments during the second campaign.

The Second Advertising Campaign: Coleman v. Mondale

The second ad campaign began immediately for Coleman as he launched his tour around the state on Wednesday morning, October 30—the day after the Wellstone memorial. Mondale was scheduled to be confirmed by the Democratic Party at the convention later that evening, so he was not yet in official campaign mode. Wednesday also saw the end to the moratorium on advertising as most other candidates jump-started their ad campaigns around the state. Despite the challenge of going on the air again, both Coleman and Mondale were eager to move forward with sympathetic, positive ads, appropriate for the political context.

This was another lesson learned by the Coleman campaign after speaking with Missouri consultants. Ashcroft did not offer personal condolences publicly to the Carnahan family after the 2000 Missouri plane crash. While he was trying to appear respectful, to the Missouri public this appeared heartless and cold. Coleman's camp knew that they had to go on the air to continue to reconnect emotionally with the public. Coleman began aggressively by running two ads. The first ad, "Look Forward," was one of the most pivotal and delicate ads of this new campaign. It represented the transition from mourning to campaigning and needed to be sincere and respectful.

Coleman signaled that he commiserated with Minnesotans and spoke directly into the camera from an outdoor field on a cold Minnesota day. The ad communicated a two-part message. First, Coleman expressed his grief and sadness about the deaths of those associated with his opponent's campaign. The ad then cut to a slightly closer and brighter image of Coleman asking Minnesotans to join with him in looking to the future. He made the case that he had been talking to the people for the past two years as he campaigned around the state. His message implied a clear contrast with Walter Mondale, a political leader from the past who had been drafted into the position out of necessity.

A second ad brought his daughter Sarah back for an emotional spot designed to pull at the heartstrings and remind the public that they already knew "Norm" was "a good guy."[60] In the spot, "Me Again," she tells Minnesotans there is more that they should know about her dad. She repeated some of the same points about Coleman's character that she made before in "My Dad," but closed by saying "and he has a really big heart. I just thought you should know." These ads were designed to bring the focus back to campaigning but accomplish it in a compassionate and sensitive way. These ads allowed Minnesotans to like Norm Coleman and to support him without feeling guilty because he was communicating in a respectful and appropriate way. "Look Forward" ran until Friday, and "Me Again" remained on the air through election day. Coleman wrapped up his message with "Big Finish," his final ad reminding voters about the same issues that had been a part of his campaign agenda prior to the plane crash. While members of the Wellstone team believe that Coleman's emotional statements were "crocodile tears," these ads were necessary gestures used to convince the Minnesota public that Coleman was an empathetic guy who was also truly affected by the tragedy and deserved a chance in this second campaign against Mondale.

Mondale went on the air after his official confirmation by the party committee on Wednesday night. The Mondale ads were filmed on Wednesday afternoon and began airing on Thursday. "My Friend" was Mondale's transition ad into campaigning. Appearing as a compassionate elder, he spoke directly to the people of Minnesota as he commiserated: "Minnesotans lost a great champion last week, and I lost a dear friend, but working families should not lose their voice in the Senate and you won't." He spoke of his experience and knowledge of the Senate and his heartfelt eagerness to carry on the fight for Wellstone's issues. "I'll continue Paul's fight for people, and I hope you'll join me." It was a clear choice to mention and reference Wellstone out of respect for the prior campaign. Further, many of Wellstone's former staff members were now volunteers for Mondale, and the Wellstone supporters were driven to "win the election for Paul." However, neither the former Wellstone staff nor the new Mondale staff was yet aware of how significant the memorial fallout would be when this ad was created and sent to the stations to air.

A second ad with a more upbeat tone began airing along with "My Friend" on Friday November 1. This second ad spoke of values and a commitment to public service while depicting Mondale in action working on the various issues that he had come to understand through his decades of experience. In the closing tag line, the speaker said, "In an uncommon time, an unparalleled record of service. . .Walter Mondale, carrying on the fight," making another implied reference to Wellstone's legacy. This ad successfully transitioned further in the direction of reminding the Minnesota public of Mondale's separate impressive credentials yet continued to retain the emotional link to Wellstone.

The final Mondale ad, which aired on Monday and Tuesday (election day), showed a complete break with the implied references to Wellstone. This ad showed a series of white words on a black screen. "Integrity.

Honesty. Experience. Walter Mondale, a lifetime of working for people."
It mentioned his involvement in authoring Medicare, the Civil Rights Act
and the Camp David Peace Accord and listed his positions as ambassador
to Japan, vice president, and senator. This time, the announcer closed by
saying, "Serious challenges demand serious experience," with no mention
of Wellstone. Clearly at this point the Mondale campaign realized the
damage caused through association with the Wellstone memorial, and they
were moving beyond mentioning the legacy to let Mondale's experience and
merit stand on its own. However, with the memorial fallout placing both
candidates in a dead heat, the race had become a case of convincing the voters
to take the risk of voting for Mondale, an unknown quantity who had been
campaigning for five days, or voting for Coleman, a better-known quantity who had been campaigning for over a year. Further, given the prior assessment by Wellstone's press secretary about the need to pin Coleman down,
critical ads were necessary for raising doubts about Coleman and reducing
his favorability. However, such ads were not considered a viable strategy
in such an emotionally sensitive political context.

Despite the challenge of mounting a last-minute campaign, Mondale succeeded in raising over $2.5 million. Because of campaign finance law, the
Wellstone campaign could donate only $1,000 directly to Mondale. The rest
of the money was raised by the party, local fundraising efforts, and the
MoveOn.org Website, which took in $700,000 in less than a week.[61] In addi-
tion, because the stations were obligated to provide equal access to air time,
Mondale was able to compete equally with Coleman on the airwaves. In
fact, ad buy data reveals that Mondale aired more ads than Coleman
during the short campaign.[62] However, Mondale was at a natural disadvantage in starting from scratch and introducing himself to Minnesotans after
nearly 20 years out of the spotlight. After the negative fallout from the
Wellstone memorial, it was even more imperative for Mondale to mount
a clear, credible, positive message in his advertising.

One final wrinkle had the potential to turn the entire race on its head.
During the campaign moratorium before the Wellstone memorial, the
NRSC was concerned that Coleman was lagging behind Mondale. On
Wednesday night after the memorial, the true fallout was still unclear and
the NRSC tested ads in focus groups to try to bring Coleman back into the
race. They tested four attacks and two positive spots and decided to send
the best attack spot to Minnesota television stations. The ad was a 30-second
spot with visuals of headlines from the Carter/Mondale era. Headlines
such as "Double digit inflation," "Soviets invade Afghanistan," and

"Hostages taken in Iran," were typed in black letters on a white screen. These words all started mixing in with each other and the announcer asked, "Times have changed. Has Walter Mondale?" According to Chris LaCivita of the NRSC, the focus group response indicated that "it was brutal, brutally effective."[63] By Thursday, the ad was at stations awaiting traffic instructions from the NRSC.

On Thursday afternoon, Kerri Miller, political reporter for KARE-11, was planning to break a story on the 10:00 P.M. news that National Republican Party ad attacking Mondale was waiting at the stations, ready to run the next day. Miller had already taped an on-camera reaction from the Democratic Party. When she called the Coleman people for a reaction, they told her they would call her back. The next phone call she received was from Chris LaCivita at the NRSC telling her that she could not air the ad in her story.[64] According to LaCivita, the Coleman campaign had serious concerns about airing an attack ad in Minnesota at this time. "Coleman called me up and raised hell. Ultimately, it's our decision, not his."[65] The NRSC decided not to run the attack because it would focus attention on the process and not the message that they wanted to communicate.

Since the traffic order to run the ad had not yet been authorized, the NRSC pulled the attack ad and ran a positive ad in its place. Yet once the party had arrived at a decision, it did not want the attack ad to be aired, and LaCivita threatened to sue the station if Miller showed the ad in her segment. Miller still ran the story about the NRSC attack without showing the ad itself. In a related smart strategic move, Coleman immediately released a public statement condemning negative ads in the campaign. According to Minnesota state Republican Party chair Ron Eibensteiner, the way it played in the media gave Coleman another "opportunity to be a hero" by rejecting the negative ad. The NRSC sent out the ad "and Norm put the kibosh on it. The intention was to let Democrats know that we were prepared to play hardball"[66] in case they had planned to run negative attacks against Coleman.

Only a few stories aired about the attack ad, and the party's removal of the ad took the story off the media's agenda, and Coleman's management of the potential problem allowed him to take the high road as he had done during the entire second campaign. The short-lived controversy over the negative ad highlighted the risk of attack advertising in terms of strategy as well as content in such an emotional context. Since generally consultants feel that some types of negative ads are effective in moving voters, the NRSC wanted to attack Mondale immediately to tighten the race. The National Republican

Party was reportedly frustrated by Coleman's position when he publicly made a statement against attack advertising, but Coleman strategists in Minnesota argued that those in Washington did not have a sense of the mood in the state at the time. According to a Coleman consultant, they were convinced that an attack ad would have thrown "a big bucket of cold water on voters, especially swing voters."[67] Some Coleman strategists were afraid that the ad would lead to a backlash and shift sympathy back in the direction of Walter Mondale.

Clearly, not all strategists agreed and it was a point of contention within the Republican ranks. As LaCivita noted, "Personally, I think we would have won by more" had the ad run.[68] By airing the positive ad instead, the issue of negative advertising was taken off the table as a campaign conflict, and there was no test of whether or not negative attacks would boomerang with the voters in such an emotionally volatile mood. However, media and public reaction to other "typically political" behavior resulted in negative consequences. It is reasonable to consider that unintended fallout could have occurred in response to negative advertising as well.

Election Day Results

Norm Coleman defeated Walter Mondale by a vote of 49.5% to 47.3%, with approximately 3% going to the other candidates, including Wellstone. Exit polls revealed a very polarized electorate. The *Pioneer Press*'s Mason Dixon poll showed that 71% of Coleman voters and 86% of Mondale voters had made up their minds about who they were going to vote for prior to Wellstone's death.[69] In other words, a strong majority of Democratic Party voters were solidified before the memorial service (i.e., even before Mondale was an officially nominated candidate) and did not change their position. These voters did not change course when media coverage started covering conflict. The *Star Tribune* poll showed that 97% of strong Republicans voted for Coleman, and 93% of strong DFLers voted for Mondale on election day. However, this poll also showed that 22% of Coleman supporters, many of them swing voters or soft support, came on board after the memorial service, presumably in reaction to information gleaned from media over the last days of the campaign.[70]

In addition, internal Mondale polling showed that perceptions changed about whether or not to continue the Wellstone legacy or chart a new direction for Minnesota. Before the memorial, 48% wanted to continue Wellstone's legacy compared to 43% who wanted to see things move in a new direction. These percentages flipped so that on November 3, 48% preferred to move in a new direction. Feeling thermometer ratings also showed Mondale dropping 6 points from a mean score of 60 before the memorial to a score of 54 after the memorial. Most striking, Wellstone's score dropped 10 points from 67 on October 28 before the memorial to 57 just before election day. Coleman's rating increased from 52 before the memorial to 55 just before election day.[71] Momentum during the final days was working against Mondale and in favor of Coleman.

Newspaper polls indicated that the public's interest in the race continued to grow over time. In mid-October, 88% of those polled expressed interest in the campaign, while 96% reported interest in the campaign just before election day. During the entire Mondale/Coleman campaign, over 90% of people surveyed reported being interested in the campaign. Analysis by grassroots coordinators showed that while turnout in democratic base areas was very high, the biggest turnout increases were in Republican-leaning suburban and exurban areas that had shown population increases. The exurban voters, or those voters living just beyond the suburban precincts, made the difference for Coleman by coming out in large numbers.[72]

Over 79% of Minnesota voters cast their ballots in the 2002 U.S. Senate race, an amazing participation rate by any election standards. In areas where Democratic performance was lower, turnout was 16% higher than a baseline turnout measure. In the high Democratic performance areas, turnout was 14.6% higher than past turnout and 13.2% higher than expected.[73] In other words, turnout figures were well above predicted levels for both Democratic and Republican areas, with a greater edge for Republicans.

Coleman consultant Tom Mason commented on the impressive engagement of the Republican voters:

> The Wellstone coalition is the highly praised turnout organization. Republicans just never get that kind of enthusiasm! I was astounded, the morning after the memorial service. . .but we had a 6:00 A.M. and Norm was leaving to jump on a plane, which in itself was symbolic. . .250 people at 5:30 A.M. in St. Paul—it was inspiring. . .it was the base of course, but you need the base. And, to be perhaps too candid, Norm Coleman is not among the more conservative Republicans in Minnesota, the base can sometimes be a challenge to motivate and get them out. That was not a problem in the last week of the campaign.[74]

Overall, Minnesota's turnout was the highest in the country, and it was the highest of any non-presidential election year in Minnesota in the last decade.[75] These findings suggest that the events had engaged, rather than depressed, citizen participation.

Conclusion

The Wellstone memorial dissipated the good feelings toward Mondale among the weaker support and late-deciding voters, but it also gave rise to a rally of support for Coleman that mobilized the Republican base like never before. Strong Wellstone/Mondale supporters were activated by emotion after the memorial in their desire to "win it for Paul." Both bases were energized, and independents were motivated to think hard about the choice of who to elect as their next senator.

Media played a pivotal role in giving significant coverage and amplification to changing events, and particularly by framing the memorial as a political rally rather than an emotional tribute by grieving friends and supporters. Television media, in particular, played a unique role in setting the agenda for print and radio. Because they were the conduits of the live memorial broadcast, they reflected both on air and behind the scenes about the unscripted live event that had unfolded before them. Also, media attention to the potential use of attack ads by the NRSC and to Mondale's aggressive approach to debating with Coleman suggests that even the most standard criticism during a traditional campaign elicited close scrutiny and concern in this extremely sensitive context. Therefore, both candidates stuck with a positive advertising strategy, making it possibly one of the most positive campaigns during the 2002 season. Further, it appears that the decision not to air the attack ad from the NRSC was a crucial strategic decision that allowed momentum to continue working in Coleman's favor. While some argue it could have opened up a further lead, in such a sensitive context, media were primed to find further controversy.

Initially, it seemed impossible that Coleman could win a campaign when tributes to Wellstone, interspersed with images of Mondale and mourning politicos from all parties, dominated the airwaves. Indeed, Coleman characterized running against Mondale as Wellstone's successor as somewhat akin to "running against Mt. Rushmore." However, this lead in the polls did disintegrate over time because of the convergence of several factors, including the media coverage of critical events as well as strategically executed advertising decisions. The directions of these breaks then created a true head-to-head political battle between the two candidates as Norm Coleman got a second chance. In the end, by a 3% margin, an incredibly engaged voting public chose the battle-worn candidate who had been making his case to the people of Minnesota for 10 months rather than the dutiful, noble statesman who only had 5 days in the race. The 2002 U.S. Senate campaign concluded in the perfect storm of politics.

ENDNOTES

1. Author interview with Eric Mische, political director for Senator Norm Coleman, 7/21/03.

2. Nielson data obtained from Mandy Sween, Research and Station Projects Director, KARE-11, 10/23/03.

3. I would like to thank the Wellstone, Coleman, and Mondale campaigns and consultants for their insights and access to data to make this analysis possible. Further, I thank all media personnel who assisted with this study, including staff at Soundclips and PR Newswire. Finally, I appreciate the contributions of William Flanigan, Ken Goldstein, David Magelby, Quin Monson, Daron Shaw, and Jennifer Williams who generously shared data to serve as a point of comparison for my own data collection. Any errors are the sole responsibility of the author.

4. Author interview with Chris LaCivita, NRSC, 8/13/03.

5. Author interview with Mike Bocian, Greenberg & Associates, 1/7/04.

6. Author interview with Ben Whitney, Coleman campaign manager, 1/9/03.

7. Information about television news clips obtained through PR Newswire and Soundclips databases.

8. Coleman press conference, 10/25/02.

9. Author interview with Mische.

10. Author interview with Ted Mondale, 1/8/03.

11. Newsclips, Kare-11 5pm news, Kerri Miller reporting, 10/26/02.

12. Newsclips, Kare-11, 5pm news, Kerri Miller reporting, 10/26/02.

13. Author interviews with Tina Smith, Mondale campaign manager, and David Lillehaug, Mondale consultant, 1/9/03 and 1/8/03.

14. This general trend is confirmed by Smith from the Mondale campaign and Glen Bolger from Public Opinion Strategies, Coleman pollster, and Tom Mason, Coleman media consultant.

15. Interview with Smith.

16. KSTP newscast, 6:00 P.M., 10/29/02.

17. Von Sternberg, B. "Death Stirs Eerie Memories of Missouri Race," *Star Tribune,* October 30, 2002, A9.

18. Author interview with Michael Smith, political science professor at Kansas State University, 11/21/03.

19. Author interview with Rick Kahn, Wellstone friend and eulogist, 7/24/03.

20. Author interview with Tom Mason, Coleman media consultant, 8/14/03.

21. Author interview with Tom Lindner, news director at KARE-11, 1/7/03.

22. Author interview with Sue Hartley, director of photography for memorial (KARE-11), 7/25/03.

23. Author interview with Andrew Wittenberg, memorial producer (KSTP-5), 11/11/03.

24. Author interview with Lindner.

25. Author interview with Scott Libin, news director at KSTP, 1/10/03.

26. Author interview with Don Shelby, news anchor at WCCO-4, 10/27/03.

27. Author interview with Shelby.

28. Author interview with Paul Magers, news anchor at KARE-11, 10/27/03.

29. These comments were made on the air in discussion after the memorial and before the 10:00 P.M. news.

30. According to interviews with Mondale staff and Mike Erlandson, DFL Party spokesperson, 11/27/02.

31. According to a background interview, one station official at KSTP-5 was already jumping up and down at 7:15 P.M., yelling at the Democrats about not getting any revenue for the night.

32. Interview with Alison Dobson, memorial planner and communications staff for Wellstone, 8/11/03.

33. Interview with Shelby.

34. Interview with Bocian.

35. Von Sternberg, B. "Minnesota flows to the right," *Star Tribune,* November 10, 2002, A1, A24.

36. Interview with Shelby. KSTP Radio clip from 10/30/02.

37. Interview with Mason.

38. Interview with Bocian.

39. Interview with Shelby.

40. Interview with Shelby.

41. Nielsen ratings provided by Mandy Sween, KARE-11.

42. Interview with Magers.

43. Interview with Magers.

44. Author interview with Pat Kessler, political reporter for WCCO, 11/4/02.

45. *Pioneer Press* Mason-Dixon poll, 2/2002.

46. CMAG data available through Ken Goldstein, University of Wisconsin. Also, see David B. Magelby, J. Quin Monson, and the Center for the Study of Elections and Democracy, CSED 2002 Soft Money and Issue Advocacy Database [dataset]. Provo, UT: Brigham Young University, Center for the Study of Elections and Democracy [producer and distributor], 2002.

47. See Table 4.5 in Flanigan, William H., Miller, Joanne M., Williams, Jennifer L., and Nancy Zingale. 2003. "The Minnesota U.S. Senate Race and the Second Congressional District Race," *PS On-line,* E-symposium, July.

48. LaCivita quoted in Pew Foundation Symposium, "The Last Hurrah: Soft Money and Issue Advocacy in the 2002 Congressional Election," National Press Club, February 3, 2003.

49. Author interview with Glen Bolger, Public Opinion Strategies, 12/26/03.

50. Associated Press. "Wellstone Opposes Iraq Resolution." 2002.

51. Author interview with Mandy Grunwald, Wellstone ad consultant, 10/29/03.

52. Author interview with Scott Howell, second Coleman ad consultant, 10/17/03.

53. Note that several Republicans claim that the *Star Tribune* method of sampling is biased toward under-selecting Republicans and over-selecting Democrats.

54. Interview with David Schultz, Hamline University professor, 7/25/03.

55. Patricia Lopez, "Mysterious group spends $1 million on anti-Wellstone campaign," *Star Tribune*, 10/23/02.

56. Interview with Grunwald.

57. Author interview with Jim Farrell, Wellstone/Mondale press secretary, 1/7/03.

58. See Flanigan et al., 2003(b).

59. Interview with Mische.

60. Interview with Howell.

61. See Flanigan et al., 2003(a).

62. Local ad buy data collected by author from public political file at stations showed 269 Mondale spots compared to 231 Coleman spots. National CMAG data, which appeared to under-report actual spots airing, showed 197 Coleman spots compared to 161 Mondale spots. See endnote 46.

63. Interviews with LaCivita.

64. Author interview with Kerri Miller, KARE-11 political reporter.

65. Interviews with LaCivita.

66. Author interview with Ron Eibensteiner, MN State Republican Party Chair, 1/10/03.

67. Interview with Mason.

68. Interviews with LaCivita.

69. Rachel E. Stassen-Berger, "Poll shows independents tipped scales to GOP," *St. Paul Pioneer Press*, November 10, 2002, 1A, 10–11A.

70. Bob von Sternberg, "Minnesota flows to the right," *Star Tribune*, November 10, 2002, A1, A24.

71. Mondale polling data from Al Quinlan at Greenberg Research, provided by Ted Mondale, 9/18/2003.

72. Interview with Mason; also see Cramer 2003.

73. Interview with Bocian.

74. Interview with Mason.

75. Minnesota Secretary of State Website, 2003.

REFERENCES

Aldrich, J., Sullivan, J. L., and E. Borgida. 1989. Foreign affairs and issue voting: Do presidential candidates waltz before a blind audience? *American Political Science Review,* March 123–141.

Cohen, B. 1963. *The press and foreign policy.* Princeton, NJ: Princeton University Press.

Cramer, D. 2002 Election analysis. *Grassroots Solutions,* January 2003, 1–8.

Flanigan, W. H., Miller, J. M., Williams, J. L., and Zingale, N. 2003a. The Minnesota U.S. senate race and the second congressional district race, *PS On-line,* E-symposium, July.

Flanigan, W., Miller, J., Williams, J., and Zingale, N. 2003b. The television campaign in the 2002 Minnesota U.S. senate race, Paper presented at the 2003 Annual Meeting of the Western Political Science Association, Denver, CO, March 29.

Garramone, G. 1984. Voter responses to negative political ads, *Journalism Quarterly,* 61 (summer), 250–259.

Garramone, G. 1985. Effects of negative political advertising: The role of sponsor and rebuttal, *Journal of Broadcasting and Electronic Media,* 29 (2), 147–159.

Iyengar, S. 1991. *Is anyone responsible? How television frames political issues.* Chicago: University of Chicago Press.

Jacobs, L., and R. Shapiro. 1994. Issues, candidate image, and priming: The use of private polls in Kennedy's 1960 presidential campaign, *American Political Science Review* 88, 3, 527–540.

Jasperson, A. 2003. The sympathy vote: Reality or illusion. Paper presented at the 2003 Annual Meeting of the American Political Science Association, August 28–August 31, 2003, Philadelphia, PA.

Jasperson, A., and D. Fan. 2002. An aggregate examination of the backlash effect in political advertising: The case of the 1996 U.S. senate race in Minnesota. *Journal of Advertising,* 31, 1 (spring), 1–12.

Jasperson, A., Shah, D., Watts, M., Faber, R., and D. Fan. 1998. Framing and the public agenda: Media effects on the importance of the federal budget deficit, *Political Communication* 15, 205–222.

Kropf, M. E., Simones, A., Jones, E. T., Neuman, D., Hayes, A., and M. Gilbride Mears. 2001. The 2000 Missouri senate race, *PS On-line,* June.

Krosnick, J., and Kinder, D. 1990. Altering the foundations of support for the president through priming, *American Political Science Review,* 84 (2), 497–512.

McCombs, M., and Shaw, D. 1972. The agenda-setting function of mass media, *Public Opinion Quarterly,* 36, 176–187.

Minnesota Secretary of State's Office Website, *http://electionresults.sos.state.mn.us/*

ElecRslts.asp?M=S&Races=allstate.

Minnesota U.S. Senate Campaign [dataset]. From *SoundClips* television clips database. 2002, 2003. Minneapolis, Minnesota.

Minnesota U.S. Senate Campaign [dataset]. From *PR Newswire* television clips database. 2002 and 2003. Bloomington, Minnesota.

Nelson, T., Clausen, R., & Oxley, Z. 1997. Media framing of a civil liberties conflict and its effects on tolerance, *American Political Science Review* 91 (3), 567–584.

Pinkleton, B. E. 1997. The effects of negative comparative political advertising on candidate evaluations: An exploration, *Journal of Advertising*, xxvi (1), 19–29.

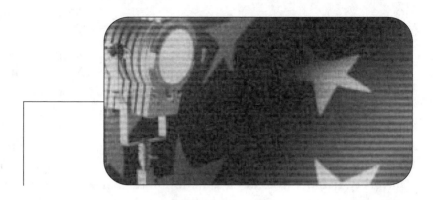

8

Bowling with Erskine and Down Home with Dole

Re-packaging the Candidates in the 2002 Senate Race in North Carolina[1]

Timothy Vercellotti

Introduction

Former Clinton White House Chief of Staff Erskine Bowles and Elizabeth Dole, a cabinet member in two Republican presidential administrations, faced similar tasks as they began their 2002 campaigns to succeed Jesse Helms as one of two U.S. senators from North Carolina.

Each candidate was a seasoned veteran of Washington power politics. Bowles, an investment banker whose father had run for North Carolina governor in 1972, had directed the Small Business Administration during President Clinton's first term in office. As White House chief of staff during Clinton's second term, Bowles had brokered a balanced budget agreement with Republican leaders in Congress. Dole had served as secretary of transportation under President Reagan and as secretary of labor under President George H. W. Bush. She also briefly sought the 2000 Republican presidential nomination and was married to the party's 1996 presidential nominee, former Senate Majority Leader Bob Dole.

Translating that experience, however, into personas that would resonate with voters across North Carolina was the task awaiting both Bowles and Dole. The candidates had to convey the right mix of images to show that while they were comfortable in the marble corridors of Washington, they also could relate to their future constituents: the tobacco and cotton growers and hog farmers Down East; the soccer moms and dads in the suburbs of Raleigh, Greensboro, and Charlotte; retirees along the coast and in Southern Pines and Pinehurst; and the textile workers in the Piedmont's rapidly dwindling manufacturing base.

In addition, both candidates had negative images they needed to dispel. Elizabeth Dole, a native of Salisbury, North Carolina, and a graduate of Duke University, had not lived in the state for more than 40 years. When Helms announced his retirement from the Senate in August 2001 and Dole mulled over a run for the seat, the North Carolina Democratic Party wasted no time in characterizing her as a "carpetbagger" (Speizer and Wagner 2001).

Bowles had his own image dilemma. In addition to his political pedigree and background in banking, his positions in the Clinton administration were his major selling points in the campaign. But those posts had the potential to be his greatest weaknesses as well. Clinton had been a polarizing figure for North Carolina voters in 1992 and 1996, and he lost the state handily both times to President Bush and Bob Dole, respectively. Bowles, while citing his government experience, had to take care not to link himself too closely with Clinton for fear of alienating conservative Democrats.

Bowles also had an additional problem that Dole did not have: poor name recognition. Given her high-profile cabinet posts and her husband's 1996 presidential campaign, Dole was widely known in North Carolina. An Elon University Poll of 622 adults conducted in early October 2001 found that 93.6% of those surveyed recognized Dole's name. Only 39.5% recognized Bowles's name (see Table 8.1).

Dole and Bowles relied heavily on campaign advertising to repackage their images in such a way as to gloss over their weaknesses while emphasizing their strengths. The candidates and political parties poured a total of $26 million into the campaign, making the North Carolina Senate race one of the most expensive in the state's history (Quinterno 2003). An examination of the advertising and public opinion in North Carolina showed that the candidates had difficulty ameliorating their image problems through advertising as election day approached in November 2002. Some of the earliest images of the candidates (Dole as carpetbagger and Bowles as Clinton aide) remained potent through the end of the campaign. One of the key lessons from this particular contest is that citizens appear to latch onto public personas early in campaigns, and those personas become increasingly difficult to change as the campaign progresses. This seems to be especially true

Table 8.1 Name Recognition

"We are now going to switch to questions that are more specifically related to North Carolina politics. I am going to begin by reading to you the names of several individuals who are active in public life. After I mention each name, I would simply like you to tell me if you recognize that individual." Dole and Bowles were among seven potential candidates for the U.S. Senate at the time of the survey. All seven names were rotated in random order in the survey. Percentages might not total 100 percent due to rounding.

	Elizabeth Dole	Erskine Bowles
Recognize	93.60%	39.50%
Does not recognize	5.80%	60.10%
No response	0.60%	0.30%

Note: N = 622 adults.
Source: Elon University Poll, October 1-4, 2001. Elon University, Elon, North Carolina.

for candidates who were already in the public eye before they embarked on their campaigns.

This chapter will use the 2002 Senate race in North Carolina as a case study of the dynamics of reshaping public images through campaign advertising. After a review of the literature on the use of campaign advertising to establish and refine candidate images, I will explore the impact of campaign advertising in the Dole-Bowles race, which Dole won handily by a margin of 54% to 45%. Data for this study come from two sources: the Elon University Poll, a statewide public opinion survey conducted six times per year, and Campaign Media Analysis Group, a private firm that uses satellite technology to capture and catalog campaign ads that air on television.

The Cultivation of Candidate Images Using Advertising

While the normative ideal of campaign advertising is that it focuses on issues and candidate positions on those issues, a significant proportion of ads stress candidate characteristics such as personality, integrity, family life, previous professional experience, and competence. All of these features combined help voters to form images of the candidates, with some variation based on voters' characteristics and predispositions (Kaid and Chanslor 1995).

Kaid and Chanslor's definition of image is helpful in framing the discussion. The authors define image as "a combination of appearance dimensions and candidate characteristics relevant to job performance (honest, able, qualified, etc.) as perceived by voters and interacting with each voter's own characteristics and predispositions" (p. 84).

A large number of ads focus on the candidates' images. Joslyn (1980) found that presidential candidates tend to stress issues most often, followed by candidate characteristics in advertising. Some of the personal traits stressed in ads include leadership, honesty, responsiveness to citizens, strength, and determination. West (1997), however, concluded that it is difficult to distinguish between issues and candidate images in ads "because many ads are based on a combination of substantive matters and character attributes" (p. 39). In an examination of 379 ads aired in presidential campaigns from 1952 to 1996, West found that the greatest concentration, 32%, focused on the personal qualities of the candidates.

The qualities that candidates emphasize tend to vary according to the circumstances of the electoral contest. Kahn and Kenney (1999) interviewed managers of campaigns for U.S. Senate seats and found that incumbents and challengers stress different traits. By necessity, challengers focus more on their personal backgrounds in an attempt to introduce themselves to voters, the authors found. Incumbents, on the other hand, focus on the extent to which they have succeeded in empathizing with their constituents.

The degree of competition between the candidates will also determine ad content, Kahn and Kenney found. If a race is lopsided, the leading candidate is more likely to emphasize his or her personal traits as opposed to issue positions. If a race is tight, candidates are more likely to air negative ads that attack their opponents on a personal level. This is especially true when there is an open seat, according to Kahn and Kenney. Examining ads that stressed the candidates' personal traits in campaigns for open Senate seats, the authors found several consistent themes: 33% of the ads stressed an opponent's Washington ties in a negative manner; 20% of the ads accused an opponent of negative advertising; 13% stressed that the opponent lacked integrity, and the remainder spread across a number of other themes.

The timing of the campaign is also important. Researchers have found that candidates tend to stress personal characteristics to a greater extent in the period leading up to a primary compared to the general election phase of the campaign (Marshall 1983, West 1997). The inherent logic is that, in a primary contest, issue positions between candidates of the same party are less likely to conflict with each other, forcing the candidates to emphasize their personal characteristics or criticize their opponents' traits. Marshall also notes that competitors in a primary may be less likely to stress ideological or issue differences to prevent a party split in the approaching general election campaign.

Does any of this matter to voters? Previous research suggests that it does. Voters evaluate candidates along personal dimensions. Markus (1982) found that public attitudes about presidential candidates' personal traits could be separated into two categories: (1) beliefs about the personal competence of a candidate and (2) beliefs about personal integrity. Marshall (1983) found that voters were most likely to focus on personal characteristics in races where there was an open seat, largely because, with the absence of an incumbent, voters are unable to engage in retrospective voting on issue positions. Miller (1990) argues that the weight of personal traits is greater for legislative races than for presidential contests. Also, voters use different evaluative criteria in sizing up the personal traits of Senate candidates versus House candidates. For Senate candidates, voters are more likely to rely on issue positions and assessments of candidate competence and integrity. In House races, voters are more likely to focus on candidates' personal appeal and responsiveness to their constituents (Miller, 1990).

Voters are most likely to focus on personal characteristics early in the campaign. Marshall (1983) found that voters cited personal traits most often in explaining why they liked or disliked presidential candidates in January 1980, early in the campaign season. Roberts (1981) reported similar findings and noted that early formation of opinions about candidates based on personal qualities could result in selective exposure to subsequent information about candidates' issue positions. Patterson (1980) and Pfau and Burgoon (1989) also found that once voters form images of the candidates, those images are unlikely to change as a result of new information. Patterson also found that voters' impressions of candidates became more general over the course of the campaign, but the overall focus of their opinions did not change.

> As a candidate's image develops, a final noteworthy pattern emerges as part of its structure: people's impressions of the candidate become progressively more general. In the final six months of the 1976 election, specific impressions of Carter (such as, "He's a peanut farmer," "He smiles a lot") decreased in number, while general impressions (such as, "He's honest," "He's incapable") increased 50 percent. Even as impressions become more general, however, the overall focus of those impressions remained constant. (Patterson 1980, pp. 137–138)

Taking into account previous research, it is clear that voters focus on the personal traits of candidates early in the campaign. Thus ads that stress candidate images are more likely to be effective early in a campaign. West

(1994) found this to be the case, noting that advertising that aired before primary elections influenced opinion concerning name recognition, favorable and unfavorable impressions of candidates, and whether candidates appeared to be viable.

Measuring Voters' Exposure to Ads

Given that campaign advertising plays a key role in the development of voters' impressions of candidates, the next question to consider is how to accurately measure the effects of advertising on voters as they form their opinions. Ansolabehere and Iyengar (1995) argue that using surveys to measure voters' recollections of ads may underestimate exposure to the ads because of faulty memories. West (1997) argues that there is also the potential for social desirability bias when using surveys to ask voters whether campaign ads influenced their decision making.

> When asked directly whether television commercials helped them decide how to vote, most voters say ads did not influence them. . . . But this is not a meaningful way of looking at advertising. Such responses undoubtedly reflect an unwillingness to admit that external agents have any effect. Many people firmly believe that they make up their minds independently of the campaign. Much in the same way teenagers do not like to concede parental influence, few voters are willing to admit that they are influenced by television. (West 1997, p. 10)

Voters in the 2002 Senate race in North Carolina were no exception. Two weeks after the November 5, 2002 election, when asked to indicate the most important factor in their decision making, 40.4% of voters said candidate issue positions were the most important factor. Eighteen percent said the candidate's experience in government, and 17.1% said the candidate's party affiliation were the most important factors. Only 4.6% pointed to television and radio ads (see Table 8.2). These assessments came despite the fact that the two candidates had spent a combined total of $26.1 million running for the Senate (Quinterno 2003), with a considerable portion of that money going toward campaign advertising. And although voters claimed that ads did not play a major role in their decision making, the vast majority of those voters offered an assessment of the ads that aired in the contest. When asked to describe the tone of the ads in the Senate race, 65.1% said "mostly negative"; 24.1% said they were "evenly divided between positive and negative," and 5.6% described the ads as "mostly positive" (see Table 8.3).

Thus, while voters might not view ads as playing a key role in their decision-making process, it is clear that they see the ads and form opinions

Table 8.2 Name Recognition

What was the most important factor in making your choice for the Senate? Was it the candidate's:

Position on the issues?	40.40%
Experience in government?	18.00%
Political party?	17.10%
Other?	11.00%
Television and radio ads?	4.60%
Experience in the private sector?	4.60%
Gender?	1.50%
Don't know	2.10%
No response	0.60%

Note: N = 473 registered voters who said they voted in the November 5, 2002, U.S. Senate race. Response categories were rotated in random order. Percentages may not total 100 percent due to rounding.
Source: Elon University Poll, November 18-21, 2002.

of them. Those opinions may influence their decision-making process on a conscious or unconscious level. The question remains, however, how best to measure that influence. An alternative to the survey approach is to conduct experiments in which people view the ads, then fill out questionnaires afterward that measure their reactions to the ads (see, for example, Ansolabehere and Iyengar 1995). The primary drawback of this approach is that experiments inject a measure of artificiality into research. Experimental subjects are likely to have viewed the ads in an institutional setting and may not respond to them in the same way that they might have had they viewed the ads at home in the natural course of their day.

A third possibility, using survey research, is to employ a proxy measure for exposure to televised campaign advertising. One such measure would be exposure to television newscasts. A national study of election coverage and campaign advertising by the Norman Lear Center at the University of Southern California and the Department of Political Science at the University of Wisconsin-Madison during the final seven weeks of the 2002 midterm elections found that local newscasts on 122 randomly selected television stations featured stories about political campaigns just over 40% of the time. But 80% of the newscasts contained at least one campaign ad. Almost half of the newscasts had three or more campaign ads (Local TV News Coverage of the 2002 General Election, 2003, p. 5).

Given that a significant percentage of campaign ads air during newscasts, one could measure the amount of exposure to local and national news-

Table 8.3 Tone of Ads in Senate Race

How would you describe the tone of the television and radio ads that were aired on behalf of the Senate candidates?

Mostly negative	65.10%
Evenly divided between positive and negative	24.10%
Mostly positive	5.60%
Don't know	4.00%
No response	1.20%

Note: N = 676 adults.
Source: Elon University Poll, November 18-21, 2002.

casts during an election season on the assumption that individuals will see campaign advertising during those programs. If one can quantify that ads have appeared regularly during the newscasts, one can use exposure to newscasts as a rough measure of exposure to campaign advertising. That is the approach that I take in this analysis. In addition to asking people whether they had seen campaign advertising or could recall specific ads, I surveyed their viewing habits in terms of local and national television newscasts. I then matched those responses to a database of campaign advertising from the 2002 Senate race in North Carolina. I discuss the database in detail in the next section.

Exposure to Campaign Advertising in the Dole-Bowles Race

I obtained a database of campaign ads from Campaign Media Analysis Group (CMAG), an Arlington, Virginia, firm that uses sophisticated technology to monitor the airing of campaign advertising on national and cable networks and local television stations. The company catalogues paid advertising in the nation's top 100 media markets, six broadcast networks and 26 national cable networks (for additional information, see CMAG's web site at www.politicsontv.com). Each time a commercial airs, CMAG captures the commercial, records its content, and documents the date, time, television station, and program on which the ad appeared.

Scholars who have worked with CMAG data maintain that the data have a high degree of validity. Freedman and Goldstein (1999) assessed CMAG data from the 1996 presidential campaign. Drawing on spending reports and interviews with officials from the campaigns of Bill Clinton and Bob Dole, they concluded that CMAG had captured the depth and breadth of the advertising with only a few exceptions. "The staffers reported only a handful of discrepancies out of the tens of thousands of ads aired. It should be noted that, in these cases, the campaign staffers usually trusted the CMAG findings, believing that the stations aired the wrong commercial or aired a commercial at an incorrect time" (Freedman and Goldstein 1999, note 4).

CMAG monitored advertising in the four largest A. C. Nielsen media markets in North Carolina during the 2002 Senate race: Charlotte; Greensboro, High Point, and Winston-Salem; Raleigh, Durham, and Fayetteville; and the South Carolina market of Greenville and Spartanburg, which also reaches across the state line into Asheville, North Carolina. Approximately 60 different ads touting or criticizing Elizabeth Dole and Erskine Bowles aired a total of 26,079 times in the four markets between February 1, 2002, and the general election on November 5, 2002. Ads aired most frequently in the Raleigh-Durham-Fayetteville market, followed by the Greensboro-High Point-Winston-Salem market; Charlotte; and Asheville (see Table 8.4).

The distribution of campaign advertising across 2002 reflected the unusual rhythms of the 2002 Senate race. Candidates had to file to run for the seat by March 1, 2002, and the primary was scheduled for May 7, 2002, but in mid-March 2002 the North Carolina Supreme Court voted to delay the May 7 primary indefinitely while the court considered a legal challenge to the state's newly redrawn state legislative districts (Dyer 2002). The legal challenge continued until mid-July, when a trial court judge, on the instructions of the state Supreme Court, redrew legislative districts for the 2002 election. The state Board of Elections rescheduled the primary for September 10, 2002 (Bonner 2002).

The candidates and their supporters and detractors began airing advertising in February, with the number increasing in March until the state Supreme Court postponed the primary indefinitely. Advertising tapered off

Table 8.4 Frequency of Airing of Senate Ads by Nielsen Market, February 1-November 5, 2002

Market	Total Number of Airings of Ads
Raleigh-Durham-Fayetteville	8,527
Greensboro-High Point-Winston-Salem	8,136
Charlotte	6,796
Greenville-Spartanburg, SC, Asheville, NC	2,620

Source: Campaign Media Analysis Group, Arlington, Virginia.

in April, May, and June, then increased again in July and August. More than 80% of the advertising occurred in the final 10 weeks of the campaign, from September 1 through November 5 (see Table 8.5).

The ads highlighted each candidate's personal and professional backgrounds early in the campaign, with the focus shifting to issue positions after Dole and Bowles handily won their party's respective nominations in the September 10, 2002, primary. The key issues in the general election portion of the campaign included disagreements over Dole's stance on privatizing Social Security, competing claims over who would be more effective in bringing new jobs to North Carolina, and whether granting presidents "fast-track" authority to negotiate trade agreements had contributed to the decline in the textile industry in the state.

The majority of the campaign advertising (55%) aired during local and network TV newscasts. The concentration of ads during television newscasts makes it possible to measure exposure to the ads without relying entirely on survey respondents' memories, particularly when days or weeks have passed since the airing of the ads.

The first round of ads that aired in the Dole-Bowles contest provides evidence to support the notion that measures of exposure to newscasts can serve as proxies for measures of exposure to campaign ads. The North Carolina Democratic Party began airing a 30-second ad on February 1, 2002 that criticized Dole for attending a "secret fundraiser" hosted by former Enron Corporation Chairman Kenneth Lay (Zalinger 2002a). The fundraiser

Table 8.5 Frequency of Airing of Senate Ads in North Carolina by Month, February 1-November 5, 2002

Month	Number of Airings of Ads	Daily Average
February	517	18.5
March	719	23.2
April	429	14.3
May	0	0
June	409	13.6
July	827	26.7
August	1,993	64.3
September	6,329	211
October	12,158	392.2
November (November 1–5)	2,698	539.6

Source: Campaign Media Analysis Group, Arlington, Virginia.

took place on September 20, 2001, and Dole attended despite having said previously that she would suspend campaigning temporarily following the September 11, 2001, terrorist attacks.

The script for the ad consisted of the following:

Announcer: September 11. Elizabeth Dole promises she'll put her campaign on hold. But then, on September 20th, flies to a secret fundraiser hosted by Kenneth Lay, the chairman of Enron. The *Winston-Salem Journal* says, "While Dole's campaign was publicly stating it had its activities on hold, it was conducting fundraisers at the house of a scoundrel." Her campaign "lied," says the *Journal*. Tell Elizabeth Dole we expect the truth. (Zalinger 2002a)

The ad aired on stations in the Charlotte, Greensboro-High Point-Winston-Salem, and Raleigh-Durham-Fayetteville media markets 266 times over the next 10 days, according to the CMAG data. Within hours of the first airing of the ad, the National Republican Senatorial Committee responded with a 30-second spot entitled "Ugly," in which the Democratic Party was taken to task for its ad (Connors 2002a). The script consisted of the following:

Announcer: America must be one nation. And President Bush is bringing us together. Yet some politicians are trying to tear us apart. The Democrats have launched another negative smear campaign, this time attacking Elizabeth Dole, former head of the Red Cross, questioning her patriotism. It's ugly politics, and it all leads to Washington. It's hypocritical and wrong. Tell the Democrats to keep their negative attacks in Washington. North Carolina deserves better. (Connors 2002a)

The committee's ad aired in the same three markets 251 times between February 1 and 10, 2002.

Elon University Poll data collected between February 11 and 15, 2002, immediately after the ads stopped running, found that 65.1% of adults in the three media markets where the ads aired remembered seeing the Democratic Party's ad. Of those who reported seeing the ad, however, 74% said the ad had not changed their opinion of Dole. Only 12.8% said the ad prompted them to think less highly of Dole (see Table 8.6).

Of the 266 airings of the Democratic Party's ad, 223 airings or nearly 84% occurred during local and national television newscasts. This concentration of advertising was reflected in the Elon University Poll data. The percentage of respondents who recalled seeing the Democratic Party's ad was

Table 8.6 Impact of Enron Ad on Perceptions of Elizabeth Dole

Have you seen a television advertisement that criticized Elizabeth Dole for attending a private fundraising event for her Senate campaign on September 20th?

	Number	Percent
Yes	265	65.10%
No	127	31.20%
Read or heard about it	14	3.40%
Don't know/No response	1	0.20%

Note: N = 407 adults in the three largest A.C. Nielsen media markets where the ad aired (Charlotte; Greensboro-High Point-Winston-Salem; and Raleigh-Durham-Fayetteville). Percentages may not total 100 due to rounding.

The following question was asked of those who said they had seen the ad: After seeing the ad, is your opinion of Dole:

	Number	Percent
More favorable?	24	9.00%
Less favorable?	34	12.80%
Opinion has not changed	196	74.00%
Don't know/No response	11	4.20%

Note: N = 265; Percentages may not total 100 due to rounding.
Source: Elon University Poll, February 11-15, 2002.

much higher among those who frequently viewed local and national television newscasts. Among survey respondents who reported watching local television newscasts five or more days out of the previous seven days, 76.1% remembered seeing the ad. For respondents who reported watching a national television newscast at least five of the previous seven days, 80.3% said they saw the ad (see Table 8.7).

Using a chi-square test, one can determine whether frequency of viewing newscasts is related to having seen the ads. In these instances, the chi-square statistics are large and statistically significant. The p-values associated with the statistics are quite small, indicating that the probability that the variables are related only by chance is less than 1/100 of 1%.

One might argue that those who frequently watched local television newscasts might have seen a news story about the controversial ad, but that argument is less plausible when one considers that national newscasts were unlikely to cover a story about campaign advertising in a Senate race in North Carolina so early in the campaign season. Indeed, the results suggest that when campaign advertising occurs frequently during television newscasts,

Table 8.7 Variation in Recall of Enron Ad by Frequency of Viewing Newscasts

Have you seen a television advertisement that criticized Elizabeth Dole for attending a private fundraising event for her Senate campaign on September 20th?

	Frequent Viewer of Local News		Frequent Viewer of National News	
	No	Yes	No	Yes
Yes (Saw ad)	39.3% (48)	76.1% (217)	46.7% (86)	80.3% (179)
No	54.1% (66)	21.4% (61)	47.3% (87)	17.9% (40)
Read or heard about it	6.6% (8)	2.1% (6)	5.4% (10)	1.8% (4)
Don't know/ No response	0.0% (0)	0.4% (1)	0.5% (1)	0.0% (0)
Total	(122)	(285)	(184)	(223)

Notes: Chi Square = 52.3 3 df p < .0001 50.3 3 df p < .0001.
N = 407 adults in the three largest A.C. Nielsen media markets where the ad aired (Charlotte; Greensboro-High Point-Winston-Salem; and Raleigh-Durham-Fayetteville).
Source: Elon University Poll, February 11-15, 2002.

Frequent viewers are those who reported having watched a newscast during at least five of the previous seven days.

Raw numbers are in parentheses. Percentages are column percentages. For example, 76.1% of frequent viewers of local newscasts recalled seeing the ad, compared to 39.3% of infrequent viewers. Column percentages may not total 100 percent due to rounding.

exposure to those newscasts can serve as an indicator of exposure to the advertising.

Using Ads to Shape Images

After the initial dust-up between the parties, campaign advertising in the Senate race focused on the more conventional task of introducing, or reintroducing, the candidates to the voters. Bowles began airing ads in early March 2002 that stressed his experience in public service, including stints as chair of the North Carolina Rural Prosperity Task Force, head of the U.S. Small Business Administration, and White House chief of staff under Bill Clinton (Connors 2002b). Bowles also sought to boost his name recognition by bowling a few frames in an ad set in a bowling alley (Connors 2002c). The ad, entitled "Erskine Bowls," began airing in early April 2002 and had the following script:

Bowles: "Thank you so much. Hey, guys, how are you? Good to see you."
Man #1: "Erskine bowls."
Announcer: "Erskine Bowles. He grew up in Greensboro. Raised a family
    in Charlotte. He's one of North Carolina's most successful business-
    men. A strong advocate for education and a leader in the fight to bring
    good jobs to every part of our state."
Man #2: "Erskine bowls?"
Man #1: "Like I said, Erskine Bowles."
Announcer: "Erskine Bowles. Strikingly experienced for North Carolina."
    (Connors 2002c)

In introducing himself to voters, Bowles sought to stress his credentials as
White House chief of staff while not drawing too much attention to his
former boss, President Bill Clinton. Indeed, in an early ad in which Bowles
stressed his role in negotiating a balanced budget with Republican leaders
in Congress in 1997, Bowles included a picture of himself with Republican
Senator Trent Lott of Mississippi, then the Senate majority leader. The ad
drew complaints from Lott and other Republicans who supported Dole
(Romano 2002). The Bowles campaign also aired an ad touting Bowles's
role in coordinating the Clinton administration's response to the Oklahoma
City bombing in 1995 (Zalinger 2002b). Neither ad mentions President
Clinton by name.

The ads focusing on Bowles's White House experience aired in March
and April 2002. While Bowles took care not to mention his former boss in
the ads, Dole's supporters were eager to remind voters of Bowles's ties to
Clinton. Later in the campaign, when the focus of the ads for both candidates shifted from biographical information to issue positions, the National
Republican Senatorial Committee claimed that Bowles was using negative
campaign tactics that he learned while serving in the Clinton White House.
In an ad entitled "Shameless," which began airing in mid-September 2002,
the National Republican Senatorial Committee argued that Bowles had mis-
stated Dole's position on privatizing Social Security:

Announcer: Erskine Bowles and his allies are shameless. Attacking
    Elizabeth Dole after telling us he wanted to run a clean campaign.
    Distorting her record on Social Security. Where did Erskine Bowles learn
    his negative tactics? Bill Clinton's White House. Truth is, Erskine
    Bowles supported Bill Clinton's 1993 tax increase on Social Security,
    making it tough for seniors to make ends meet. Tell Erskine Bowles
    his Clinton-style attacks have no place in North Carolina. (Rodeffer
    2002a)

While Bowles had to contend with attempts to link him overtly to Clinton, Dole had her own Achilles' heel. While she had grown up in Salisbury, North Carolina, and received her bachelor's degree from Duke University, she had not lived in North Carolina for more than 40 years. News media and Democrats raised questions about Dole's absence from the state in August 2001, when Dole first expressed interest in the Senate seat. Although neither Bowles nor the Democratic Party raised the issue in ads, the Dole campaign's early advertising strategy attempted to address the matter through ads that emphasized Dole's North Carolina roots.

The Dole campaign began airing ads in June 2002. One of the first ads, entitled "Salisbury," stressed Dole's experiences growing up in small-town North Carolina (Rodeffer 2002b). Among those appearing in the ad were Dole's 101-year-old mother, Mary Hanford, who still lived in the family home in Salisbury, and Dole's husband, former Senate Majority Leader Bob Dole. According to the script:

Announcer: About Elizabeth Dole, much has been written. How did a small-town girl grow up to accomplish so much? It began here in Salisbury.
Woman #1: She's a kind and a very real person, like her mom.
Man #1: "She learned how to run a business.
Woman #2: Just like her dad.
Mary Hanford: I think she's human, but she does her darnedest to do something that she feels is worthwhile.
Man #3: The apple doesn't fall too far from the tree.
Bob Dole: She's a person of great faith, and she practices that in her daily life.
Man #4: You take the hard work and the experience?
Man #5: And you add the rock-solid values you get growing up in a small North Carolina town?
Woman #1: And there you've got Elizabeth Dole.
Woman #2: I think that she's a lot like me.
Announcer: Elizabeth Dole for North Carolina. (Rodeffer 2002b)

A second ad featuring Dole's mother began airing July 1, 2002 (Rodeffer 2002c). The ad also attempted to burnish Dole's image as a North Carolinian by pointing out that Dole at that point lived with her mother in Salisbury. Dole purchased the family home from her mother for $350,000 in December 2001 and moved in there order to establish residency in North Carolina (Associated Press, 1/13/02). According to the script:

Elizabeth Dole: Mother and I talk every day. She lives with me here in Salisbury.

Mary Hanford: We talk about family affairs, that's important to her, old friends.

Elizabeth Dole: Mother's 101, so we talk a lot about doctors and prescription drugs. I know why it's so important to talk to doctors, not bureaucrats—and why we need a Medicare prescription drug benefit.

Mary Hanford: Mothers know best. (Rodeffer 2002c)

In late July the Dole campaign began airing a third biographical ad, this one highlighting Dole's professional accomplishments. The ad, entitled "Growing Up," contained the following:

Woman #1: When I was growing up women didn't go to Harvard Law School.

Woman #2: They didn't work for five presidents.

Woman #3: They didn't become Secretary of Transportation or head of the Red Cross.

Woman #4: But Elizabeth Dole did. She made it OK for me to try.

Man: She's smart; she works way too hard and she knows the right people.

Woman #5: She has those qualities of caring that's so badly needed.

Woman #6: Elizabeth Dole would be the one for the job. (Rodeffer 2002d)

The emphasis of the advertising for both campaigns shifted from candidate images to issue positions by late summer 2002. Instead of touting their professional backgrounds or attempting to reassure voters that they were just plain folks, Dole and Bowles began to focus on key points of difference, such as their positions on whether to privatize Social Security and how best to provide a prescription drug benefit for senior citizens. Were the image ads successful? Was Bowles able to demonstrate his competence in government while not drawing too close a connection to his old boss, Bill Clinton? Was Dole able to blunt the criticism that she had only recently moved back to North Carolina? In the next section of this chapter I present empirical evidence concerning the relative effectiveness of the candidates' attempts to shape their public images.

Were the Ads Effective?

Dole's image as someone who had long ago left the state to pursue her career proved to be difficult to change. Despite airing ads that stressed her roots in North Carolina, public opinion on the issue did not shift significantly during the campaign. The Elon University Poll, in statewide surveys conducted in October 2001, March 2002, and October 2002, posed this question (with a minor word change once Dole reestablished residency in

North Carolina during the campaign): "Elizabeth Dole is among the candidates running for the U.S. Senate. Until recently, Dole had not lived full-time in the state of North Carolina for 40 years. How important will this factor be for you in deciding whom to support in this year's election?" The data suggest (see Table 8.8) that Dole's image as an outsider persisted despite her campaign ads, with nearly one-third of the voters citing the issue as very important or important in making their choice for the Senate seat. A follow-up question posed in the October 2002 survey, with just a few weeks left in the campaign, showed that not only was the issue important for some, but it also mattered in a negative way. For those who considered the issue to be very important or important, a sizable majority (67.6%) said it was a negative factor (see Table 8.9).

What role did campaign advertising play in this issue? The biographical ads that Dole aired during the summer either had very little impact or the impact was short lived. To test the impact of the ads, I used two proxy measures of exposure to advertising—the number of times in the previous seven days that individuals watched a local or national newscast. Given that a majority of ads aired in the 2002 race during newscasts, those measures provide a rough indicator of how often survey respondents may have seen ads for the candidates.

I classified individuals as frequent viewers of newscasts if they watched a news program on at least five of the previous seven days. I then created two dichotomous variables to reflect whether individuals were frequent viewers of either local or national news. But cross-tabulations of the frequent

Table 8.8 Importance of Elizabeth Dole's Residency Status

Elizabeth Dole is among the candidates running for the U.S. Senate. Until recently, Dole had not lived full-time in the state of North Carolina for 40 years. How important will this factor be for you in deciding whom to support in this year's election?

	October 2001	March 2002	October 2002
Very important	20.2%	18.3%	24.5%
Important	10.3%	8.3%	9.8%
Somewhat important	20.0%	17.7%	11.4%
Not important at all	44.4%	52.8%	50.9%
No opinion / No response	5.2%	2.9%	3.5%
N = (Registered voters)	466	650	633

Source: Campaign Media Analysis Group, Arlington, Virginia.

viewer variables with measures of the importance of the issue and the positive or negative direction of the importance revealed no significant relationships. Survey respondents attached varying levels of importance to the residency issue regardless of whether or not they were frequent viewers of newscasts, and therefore frequent viewers of campaign ads. The same held true in cross-tabulations of frequent news viewers and the measure of whether Dole's absence was important in a positive or negative way. No significant relationships emerged, suggesting that ads emphasizing Dole's roots in North Carolina did little to blunt concerns about her absence from the state.

Campaign advertising does appear to have played a role in shaping Bowles's image, however. In the October 2002 Elon University Poll respondents were asked the following question: "Erskine Bowles, the other major party candidate for the Senate seat, served as White House chief of staff in the Clinton administration. How important will this factor be for you in deciding whom to support in this year's election?" Forty-four percent of those surveyed said Bowles's experience would be very important or important to them in choosing a candidate for the Senate. When asked whether Bowles's service in the Clinton administration would be important in a positive or negative way, 53% said positive and 44.8% said negative (see Table 8.10).

The influence of campaign advertising surfaces when one considers the news consumption habits of the survey respondents. Those who watched local and national newscasts on at least five of the previous seven days were more likely to rate Bowles's experience as very important or important in making their decision than were individuals who had watched newscasts on four or fewer days (see Table 8.11). Chi-square tests show that the relationships between viewing newscasts and the importance of Bowles's White

Table 8.9 Positive and Negative Importance of Elizabeth Dole's Residency Status
Is the information important in a positive or negative way? (Posed only to those who rated Dole's time away from North Carolina as a very important or important issue in choosing a Senate candidate.)

	Percent
Positive	26.80%
Negative	67.60%
Don't know	4.60%
No response	0.90%

Note: Percentages may not equal 100 percent due to rounding.
Source: Elon University Poll, October 21-24, 2002.

Table 8.10 The Importance of Erskine Bowles's White House Experience
Erskine Bowles, the other major party candidate for the Senate seat, served as
White House chief of staff in the Clinton administration. How important will this factor
be for you in deciding whom to support in this year's election?

	Percent
Very important	29.10%
Important	15.00%
Somewhat important	16.00%
Not important at all	36.40%
No opinion / no response	3.50%

Note: Percentages may not equal 100 percent due to rounding.
Source: Elon University Poll, October 21-24, 2002.

Is the information important in a positive or negative way? (Posed only to those
who rated Bowles's service as chief of staff as a very important or important issue
in choosing a Senate candidate.)

	Percent
Positive	53.00%
Negative	44.80%
Don't know	1.40%

Note: Percentages may not equal 100 percent due to rounding.
Source: Elon University Poll, October 21-24, 2002.

House experience are statistically significant. The probability that the relationships are simply due to chance is less than 1/100 of 1% for local newscasts and less than 1% for national newscasts.

Whether the information is important in a positive or negative way also varied by frequency of viewing newscasts, but this was true only for those who frequently viewed national newscasts.

Among frequent viewers of national newscasts, 50.2% felt that Bowles's White House background was important in a positive way, while 49.8% felt it was important in a negative way (see Table 8.12). This differed from the distribution of opinions among infrequent viewers of national newscasts. In that group, 64.9% considered Bowles's experience to be important in a positive way, while 35.1% viewed the information in a negative light. A chi-square test shows that the relationship between the two variables is statistically significant at the level of $p < .05$.

The differences of opinion about Bowles between frequent and infrequent viewers of national newscasts suggest that campaign ads that ran during

Table 8.11 Importance of Bowles's White House Experience by Frequency of
Viewing Newscasts

Erskine Bowles, the other major party candidate for the Senate seat, served as
White House chief of staff in the Clinton administration. How important will this factor
be for you in deciding whom to support in this year's election?

	Frequent Viewer of Local News		Frequent Viewer of National News	
	No	Yes	No	Yes
Very important	20.6% (35)	32.3% (149)	24.5% (53)	31.5% (131)
Important	7.1% (12)	18.0% (83)	10.2% (22)	17.6% (73)
Somewhat important	22.9% (39)	13.4% (62)	22.7% (49)	12.5% (52)
Not important at all	45.3% (77)	33.1% (153)	38.4% (83)	35.3% (147)
No opinion / No response	4.1% (7)	3.2% (15)	4.2% (9)	3.1% (13)
Total	(170)	(462)	(216)	(416)

Notes: N = 632 registered voters
Chi Square = 28.0 4 df p < .000117.5 4 df p < .01
Frequent viewers are those who reported having watched a newscast during at least five of
the previous seven days.
Raw numbers are in parentheses. Percentages are column percentages. For example, 32.3%
of frequent viewers of local newscasts said Bowles's White House experience was very
important, compared to 20.6% of infrequent viewers. Column percentages may not total
100 percent due to rounding.
Source: Elon University Poll, October 21-24, 2002.

those newscasts had an effect on voters' perceptions about Bowles. But the
differences that emerge are counterintuitive, given that Bowles's ads
attempted to cast his White House experience in a positive light. Instead,
frequent viewers of national newscasts were more likely than infrequent viewers to consider Bowles's ties to Clinton in a negative manner. This may reflect
the influence not so much of Bowles's positive ads that aired in the spring
but that of critical ads aired by the Dole campaign and the National
Republican Senatorial Committee in September and October.

One example of that critical advertising was the spot entitled,
"Shameless," which accused Bowles of engaging in negative campaign tactics and charged that he learned those tactics as a member of the White House
staff. The ad, sponsored by the National Republican Senatorial Committee,
also claimed that Bowles had backed raising taxes on Social Security ben-

Table 8.12

Bowles's White House Experience as a Positive or Negative Factor by Frequency of Viewing Newscasts

Is the information important in a positive or negative way?

	Frequent Viewer of National News	
	No	Yes
Positive	64.9% (48)	50.2% (100)
Negative	35.1% (26)	49.8% (99)
Total	(74)	(199)

Notes: N = 273 registered voters
Chi Square =4.6 1 df p < .05
Frequent viewers are those who reported having watched a newscast during at least five of the previous seven days.
Raw numbers are in parentheses. Percentages are column percentages. For example, 50.2% of frequent viewers of local newscasts said Bowles's White House experience was very important or important in a positive way, compared to 64.9% of infrequent viewers. Column percentages may not total 100 percent due to rounding.
Source: Elon University Poll, October 21-24, 2002.

efits while working as an aide to Clinton in 1993 (Rodeffer 2002a). The spot aired 558 times in the Charlotte, Raleigh-Durham-Fayetteville, and Greensboro-High Point-Winston-Salem markets from September 18, 2002, to October 17, 2002, according to the data collected by Campaign Media Analysis Group. Another ad, entitled "Taxes," claimed that Bowles "worked to pass the largest tax increase in American history—including higher taxes on Social Security." (Rodeffer 2002e) The spot, sponsored by the Dole campaign, aired 582 times in the four largest media markets in North Carolina from Sept. 28, 2002, to Oct. 7, 2002, according to the Campaign Media Analysis Group data. These and other ads critical of Bowles's tenure at the White House may have contributed to the negative assessment of Bowles among frequent viewers of national newscasts.

Conclusion: Conditions under Which Ads Do or Do Not Shape Candidate Images

Were the candidates able to remake their public images through campaign advertising? The evidence presented here indicates that the Dole ads that stressed her roots in North Carolina did little to alter perceptions about the length of time that she spent living outside of North Carolina. The percentage of respondents who said the residency status was a very important or important issue actually rose between March and October 2002, despite the airing of the biographical ads over the summer. That Dole was unable to address this concern through advertising gives further evidence to support the argument that voters develop images of candidates early in a race, and those images become increasingly difficult to alter over time.

On the other hand, campaign advertising appeared to influence perceptions about Bowles relative to his service in the Clinton administration. Frequent viewers of national newscasts, at least some of which included campaign advertising, were more likely than infrequent viewers to assess Bowles's tenure at the White House in a negative manner.

Why the different effects of campaign advertising for the two candidates? Two explanations come to mind. First, Dole's biographical ads aired over the summer of 2002, and the latest wave of survey data concerning her residency was gathered in October 2002. It may be that any effect that the ads might have had worn off between the summer and October. The second possible explanation is rooted in the varying degrees of familiarity that voters had with the candidates going into the race. Recall that in March 2002, 93.6% of survey respondents recognized Dole's name, while only 39.5% recognized Bowles's name. Voters may have entered the campaign season with greater knowledge of Dole, given her long history of public service, and they may have had more firmly rooted attitudes about Dole that were difficult to alter through ads. Bowles, on the other hand, while known to some segments of the electorate because of his previous experience in public life, still had more of an opportunity to shape his image with voters. But that kind of latitude is a two-edged sword, because it also gave Dole and her supporters a greater opportunity to define Bowles in negative terms.

These conclusions require some caveats. The measures of exposure to advertising—frequency of viewing local and national newscasts—are indirect in nature. Also, in using survey data to test the effects of campaign ads, one can never be entirely sure that the survey respondents saw the ads in question. To achieve that certainty one would have to show the ads to study participants in a controlled experimental setting but with the attendant trade-off in external validity for the findings. Also, this research encompasses one campaign, and as such serves more as a case study than as a broad exploration of the effects of campaign advertising on candidate images.

But even with those cautions, the results reported here add to the existing evidence that reshaping candidate images through campaign advertising is a formidable task. Ads can help to alter a candidate's image, but the effects will vary along at least two dimensions. First, when a candidate is well known going into a race, as was the case with Dole, voters form their impressions early, and those impressions become more difficult to alter later in the campaign. Second, when it is possible to shape a lesser-known candidate's image, as in the case of Bowles, his or her opponent also may use ads to define the candidate in less than flattering terms. The effects of the positive, image-oriented ads may be offset or even overshadowed by the effects of the negative ads. The image that results may be a far cry from what the candidate hoped to create.

REFERENCES

Ansolabehere, Stephen, and Shanto Iyengar. 1995. *Going Negative: How Attack Ads Shrink and Polarize the Electorate.* New York: The Free Press.

Associated Press. 2002. "Elizabeth Dole Pays $350,000 for Mother's Salisbury Home." January 13, 2002.

Bonner, Lynn. 2002. "Assembly OKs Voting Plan." *Raleigh (N.C.) News & Observer,* July 17, 2002, p. B5.

Connors, Ryan. 2002a. "NRSC Returns Fire in Tar Heel State." NationalJournal.Com, February 5, 2002. *http://nationaljournal.com/members/adspotlight/2002/02/0205nrsc.htm.*

———. 2002b. "Bowles Pumps Experience, Challenges." NationalJournal.Com, March 8, 2002. *http://nationaljournal.com/members/adspotlight/2002/03/0308ebnc1.htm.*

———. 2002c. "Bowling for Senate." NationalJournal.Com, April 12, 2002. *http://nationaljournal.com/members/adspotlight/2002/04/0412ebnc1.htm.*

Dyer, Eric. 2002. "Board Delays May 7 Primaries." *Greensboro (N.C.) News & Record,* March 13, 2002, p. A1.

Freedman, Paul, and Ken Goldstein. 1999. "Measuring Media Exposure and the Effects of Negative Campaign Ads." *American Journal of Political Science* 43: 1189–1208.

Joslyn, Richard A. 1980. "The Content of Political Spot Ads." *Journalism Quarterly* 57: 92–98.

Kahn, Kim Fridkin, and Patrick J. Kenney. 1999. *The Spectacle of U.S. Senate Campaigns.* Princeton, NJ: Princeton University Press.

Kaid, Lynda Lee, and Mike Chanslor. 1995. "Changing Candidate Images: The Effects of Political Advertising." In *Candidate Images in Presidential Elections.* Kenneth L. Hacker, ed. Westport, CT: Praeger Publishers.

Local TV News Coverage of the 2002 General Election. 2003. Report by the Norman Lear Center, Annenberg School of Communication, University of Southern California, and the Department of Political Science, University of Wisconsin, Madison. *http://www.learcenter.org/pdf/LCLNAReport.pdf.*

Markus, Gregory B. 1982. "Political Attitudes during an Election Year: A Report on the 1980 NES Panel Study." *American Political Science Review,* 76: 538–560.

Marshall, Thomas R. 1983. "Evaluating Presidential Nominees: Opinion Polls, Issues and Personalities." *The Western Political Quarterly,* 36: 650–659.

Miller, Arthur H. 1990. "Public Judgments of Senate and House Candidates." *Legislative Studies Quarterly* 15: 525–542.

Patterson, Thomas E. 1980. *The Mass Media Election: How Americans Choose Their President.* New York: Praeger Publishers.

Pfau, Michael, and Michael Burgoon. 1989. "The Efficiency of Issue and Character Attack Message Strategies in Political Campaign Communication." *Communication Reports* 2: 52–61.

Quinterno, John. 2003. "Rough Parity Emerges in Senate Spending." *North Carolina DataNet,* March 2003, p. 10.

Roberts, Churchill L. 1981. "From Primary to the Presidency: A Panel Study of Images and Issues in the 1976 Election." *The Western Journal of Speech Communication* 45: 60–70.

Rodeffer, Mark H. 2002a. "Parties Trade Shots in North Carolina." NationalJournal.Com, September 20, 2002. *http://nationaljournal.com/members/adspotlight/2002/09/0920ncsen1.htm.*

———. 2002b. "Dole Hits TV Touting N.C. Roots." NationalJournal.Com, June 19, 2002. *http://nationaljournal.com/members/adspotlight/2002/06/0619ednc1.htm.*

———. 2002c. "Dole, Mother Return to Airwaves." NationalJournal.Com, July 11, 2002. *http://nationaljournal.com/members/adspotlight/2002/07/0711ednc1.htm.*

———. 2002d. "Ad Touts Dole as Pioneer for Women." NationalJournal.Com, July 30, 2002. *http://nationaljournal.com/members/adspotlight/2002/07/0730ednc1.htm.*

———. 2002e. "Dole Hits Bowles on Taxes, Social Security." NationalJournal.Com, October 1, 2002. *http://nationaljournal.com/members/adspotlight/2002/10/1001ednc1.htm.*

Romano, Lois. 2002. "Clinton Ties Put Ex-Aides in Campaign Bind." *Washington Post,* April 14, 2002, p. A4.

Speizer, Irwin, and John Wagner. 2001. "Liddy Dole Comes Home." *Raleigh (N.C.) News & Observer,* August 25, 2001, p. A1.

West, Darrell. 1994. "Political Advertising and News Coverage in the 1992 California U.S. Senate Campaigns." *Journal of Politics* 56: 1053–1075.

———. 1997. *Air Wars: Television Advertising in Election Campaigns,* Second Ed. Washington, DC: Congressional Quarterly Inc.

Zalinger, Jason. 2002a. "Dems Assail Dole for Enron Ties." NationalJournal.Com, February 1, 2002, *http://nationaljournal.com/members/adspotlight/2002/02/0201ncd1.htm*.

———. 2002b. "Bowles Touts Role in OKC Bombing Response." NationalJournal.Com, March 28, 2002. *http://nationaljournal.com/members/adspotlight/2002/03/0328ebnc1.htm*.

ENDNOTE

1. This research was funded in part through a grant from Elon College, the College of Arts and Sciences at Elon University.

9

From Saxophones to Schwarzenegger
Entertainment Politics on Late-night Television

David A. Schultz

Politics makes strange bedfellows. Yet politics and late-night talk shows make even stranger sleeping companions. Arnold Schwarzenegger's August 6, 2003, declaration on the *Tonight Show* that "I am going to run for governor of the state of California" and Leno's subsequent decision to introduce Arnold at his victory rally on October 7 were the culmination of a trend begun over a decade ago when Bill Clinton played the saxophone on the *Arsenio Hall Show.* That trend has fused politics to entertainment and made late-night talk shows such as Letterman and Leno increasingly important players in American politics. Be it in terms of the political jokes told in the monologues on Leno, Letterman, Conan, *Politically Incorrect!,* and the *Daily Show* with Jon Stewart, candidate appearances on these shows, or political skits on *Saturday Night Live,* the political influence of late-night talk shows, appears to be growing, fueled by numerous trends that have accelerated the merging of politics and entertainment.

This chapter examines the growing use of television talk shows both as a new form of political campaigning and as a forum of political news and information. It explores the role that these shows play in campaigns and candidate behavior. It will argue that the political role of late-night television is the product of several forces, including the changing structure of for-profit corporate news; a merger of entertainment and politics; and a rise of what shall be called a politainer culture ushered in by the likes of President Clinton and Jesse Ventura. The thesis will be that the emerging political role of late-night television is not an aberration but a convergence of several trends forcing a merger between politics and entertainment. The result, as some studies have confirmed, is a new source of political information and influence directed first at young and uninformed voters but also at other voters by means of the way politainment has affected traditional political coverage.

The Rise of Entertainment Journalism

The press and the news are important to democratic theory and practice. Both are critical in providing important information about the government to citizens so that the latter can make informed choices and hold public officials accountable (Schultz 2000, pp. 15–17). In addition, community newspapers and other news services operate as expressions of local sentiments, serving to support, as Alexis DeTocqueville argued, voluntary associations, which he saw as the lifeblood of American democracy. Yet the news does not simply serve the needs of citizens. The corporate structure of the media dictates that the production of news must be for a profit, and therefore what appears as news is shaped by the need for making money.

American news production has always been marked by private ownership, but this ownership structure did not always dictate that news was supposed to be simply a for-profit enterprise. The production of news passed from local newspapers by printers to political parties (Hamilton 2004). As voices of political parties, the presses promoted political dialogue, and as revolutionary rags they attacked the British (Davis 1996, 24–40). Today, as a result of the changes in media ownership and deregulation, the media are market driven as opposed to the nineteenth century when they were party driven (Hamilton 2004, p. 165; Grossman 1995, p. 85). What are the implications of news being a for-profit industry? There are several, but the most important factor is that news is business. According to Richard Salant: News is a special kind of business, but it is a business—a part of the free enterprise system this nation has chosen. It has to make money in order to spend money. The *New York Times* boasts "All the News That's Fit to Print," while the former Aspen *Flier*, a small paper, more modestly (and accurately) announced, "As Independent as Revenues Permit" (Salant 1999, p. 140).

News and information are commodities to be bought and sold like mouthwash, toilet paper, and soda (Lyotard 1979, p. 5; Wolf 1999, p. 109).

Industries that produce news wish to maximize revenues and will seek to present those news items that are most likely to generate readers, viewers, listeners, and profits. John Welch, former chairman of General Electric, the parent company that owns NBC, required every division, including news, to maintain the same profit margin (Grossman 1995, p. 75). Media services, thus, must be profitable, and that they have become. Media companies are an attractive corporate investment because for every dollar of revenue, 30 to 35 cents are profit, if not more (Parenti 1995, p. 166). As a result of this high profitability, the media and news industry has become the source of corporate takeovers and increased concentration in the last 20 to 30 years.

While media concentration is less in America than Europe, the trend nonetheless has been toward concentration of the media and news production into fewer and fewer corporate hands (Picard 1998, 201). For example, the number of controlling firms in the media—daily newspapers, magazines, radio, television, books, and movies—has shrunk from 50 corporations in 1984 to 26 in 1987 to 23 in 1990, and fewer than 10 in 1996. Federal Communications Commission (FCC) decisions in 2003 to allow media conglomerates to own more radio and television stations as well as other media outlets promise even more concentration in 2004 and beyond.

Corporate owners such as General Electric (GE) use the media they own to support their companies and their other interests, and studies suggest that corporate chains are more likely to pursue profit than traditional editorial policy (Underwood 1995, 119). GE, for example, is a large company with military and consumer products, power distribution systems, computer, financial, medical, and, yes, even media services. The increased corporate nature of news and media means that it not only represents a profit-making division for a larger company but that the news or media division is also encouraged to secure corporate objectives and goals that support the vast holdings of these companies. These news producers are less attached to their community than previously. As noted above, General Electric required NBC to maintain the same profit margin as every other division. This means that GE is more concerned with profits than with necessarily representing diverse interests and voices or providing news that is critical to citizens making informed political choices.

The increasingly corporate structure of the media means that news is not simply an objective presentation of political events where the needs of democracy dictate what will be aired or printed. In making decisions regarding what is produced as news, the logic of for-profit journalism means that "rational news departments should compete with each other to offer the least expensive mix of content that protects the interests of the sponsors and investors while garnering the largest audience advertisers will pay to reach" (McManus 1994, 85). In addition, as media outlets expand (even if ownership does not), each station, newspaper, or Website seeks to appeal to a specific demographic or audience, and that niche marketing has led both to an increased entertainment focus in the news (as news competes for viewers) and a change in the content of what news providers offer (Hamilton 2004).

If news is for profit, it must compete against other sources of entertainment for audience attention (Hamilton 2004, 175). For some, such as former PBS and NBC News president Lawrence Pressman, the result is that the "firewall that separates politics from entertainment has all but disappeared" (Grossman 1995, pp. 108–109).

The fact that journalism and media are increasingly market driven means that audiences are seen not as citizens to be informed but consumers to attract. The imperative of market needs comes into conflict with democratic needs (McManus 1994, 3), producing news that is less about the government and more focused on attracting audiences, regardless of the content. News, in short, has become entertainment (Timberg 2002, pp. 147–148).

Entertainment-focused journalism, however, is not simply a product of the internal drive for profits by mainstream or established news or media services. Instead, the "new media," including talk shows such as *The Jerry Springer Show* and *Oprah Winfrey* as well as information providers or media services such as MTV, the Internet, and the World Wide Web, shows such as *Hard Copy,* and even magazines such as *People,* also serve as competition for the more traditional news services and media outlets (Davis and Owen 1998). These highly profitable shows are in competition for audiences with more traditional news services, thus forcing mainstream news to change its product if it wishes to maintain audiences and revenues. In fact, as James Hamilton (2004) aptly argues, in the effort to attract young female viewers—one of the most prized and profitable demographics that advertisers will pay for—news will often run more of what is considered soft news, such as stories about entertainment or issues affecting the consumer or the family, because these viewers are more interested in stories about these items than they are about hard news. This means that competition for additional viewers drives the choice of news stories, seeking to set a mix of stories that will hold many traditional consumers of hard news, while at the same time increasing the market share of soft news consumers. The result is that news programs may demonstrate a spectrum of hard and soft news offerings, depending on the niche market they are seeking.

The new media have the potential to inform, to educate, and facilitate public discourse, yet even the "new media's promise is undercut by the commercial and entertainment imperatives that drive them" (Davis and Owen 1998, p. 7). It is a profit-making fare that competes against mainstream news, forcing even the latter to change (p. 18). The new media cover politics but only politics as it entertains, in part, because the audience the new media attract is a less politically interested audience than traditional news audiences, which are rapidly disappearing (p. 18).

One result is that traditional national evening news on ABC, CBS, and NBC now have relatively little hard news in a 30-minute format, with soft news and non-news and commercials occupying the lion's share of the broadcast ("Around the News in 22 Minutes" 1991). One study suggested less than 1% of the news covered is political news (Purdum 1999).

Overall, the drive to maximize profits has driven television news away from providing the important news and information citizens need to make informed choices about candidates. Instead, market-driven journalism has pushed news increasingly into a more entertainment-oriented mode, joining entertainment and politics.

The Rise of Politainment

Profit-driven journalism has emerged alongside a second cultural trend, which has forged a merger between politics and entertainment. However, this mixing of politics and entertainment is not a recent phenomenon. Dating back to the 1950s, candidates have a long history of appearing on late-night shows or on other entertainment television. For example, Richard Nixon appeared on the *Tonight Show* with Jack Paar in 1963 and played the piano. Nixon also appeared on *Laugh-In* in 1968. In 1992 Vice President Dan Quayle found himself entangled in a debate with Candice Bergen's television character on *Murphy Brown* over whether single mothers could be good parents and what constituted a family.

There are two critical turning points in the merger of politics and entertainment prior to Schwarzenegger's gubernatorial declaration on *Leno* and his clearly made-for-TV campaign that was carried on nightly on the

Tonight Show via the opening monologue. First there was Bill Clinton's appearance on the *Arsenio Hall Show* in 1992 playing his sax, while sporting dark sunglasses. No question that Clinton attempted to ape an image that would appeal to Baby Boomers and young people. In so doing, his appearance there as well as on MTV moved him more toward appearing as an entertainment figure. Alas, it was perhaps no coincidence that Clinton was considered a good friend of many in Hollywood.

A second and perhaps more significant turning point in the fusion of entertainment and politics can be seen in the example of celebrity-turned-politician, Jesse Ventura. He is but one clear indication of how media, politics, and popular culture became increasingly intertwined in our lives and in the lives of politicians. Here, an individual named James Janos rose to fame as a popular, cult-like, outlandish personality in the televised world of wrestling with the assumed persona of Jesse Ventura. From there he appeared in several films popular with teenagers and college students; then he moved on to be a controversial host of several AM radio talk shows in Minnesota. As a host he was known for his brash, hard-talking, "take no prisoners" views, which often criticized the political establishment. Jesse carried that persona over into his surprise run for governor, using it as a way to distinguish himself from the political establishment and to demonstrate that, if elected, he would be a different kind of governor.

And elected he was. Using his media image in televised debates and even in commercials that featured "Jesse Ventura action figures," Jesse Ventura did shock the world. After his election he became an international celebrity, merging his role as governor with that of professional wrestler into a unique figure in American politics.

After taking office, Ventura capitalized on his fame, selling his action figures and other merchandise bearing his name, and returning to the wrestling ring as governor to referee a 1999 World Wrestling Federation "Summer Slam" event. The media pop culture icon's personality and his role as governor have become indistinguishable. Jesse's power and value as a politician came not just from his use of a particular venue. Because Jesse was a politician who is also an entertainer, he has become what other politicians, such as Schwarzenegger, want to be—a politainer.

Emergence of the Politainer

Jesse Ventura emerged from a long line of predecessors who are celebrities (actors, newscasters, and athletes) turned politicians: Ronald Reagan,

Sonny Bono, Clint Eastwood, Jack Kemp, Bill Bradley, and Fred Grandy (*Love Boat's* "Gopher"), to name just a few. While following in the footsteps of such notable politicians, who have traded in their celebrity for political power, Jesse forged his own distinct political path. He took the trend of entertainer turned politician one step further because he was more than just a celebrity turned politician; he was simultaneously an entertainer *and* a politician; he is, in other words, a politainer.

Jesse's path was marked by many firsts for an American politician: action figures modeled after his television persona; a not-for-profit company ("Ventura for Minnesota, Inc.") that sold official licensed Jesse Ventura paraphernalia, along with a trademarked name; a tell-all autobiography published in his first few months as governor of Minnesota; a second book published (and aggressively promoted and publicized) just over a year later; an appearance on the soap opera *The Young and the Restless;* an appearance as the referee in a World Wrestling Federation match; and a weekly Minnesota radio show. His meteoric rise into the statewide, and now the national, political scene has been incredibly instructive for those who follow and study politics.

From Jesse's colorful activities one can deduce the characteristics of a politainer. A politainer is simultaneously an entertainer and a politician; his persona is a fiction; his persona is a commodity; and he uses multimedia venues (many of which are entertainment outlets) and sophisticated mass-marketing techniques to distribute his message and/or to market himself as a politician and as an entertainer.

Simultaneously an Entertainer and a Politician

A politainer has a dual career: he uses his entertainment career to benefit his political career, and he uses his political career to benefit his entertainment career. Jesse Ventura's autobiography, *I Ain't Got Time to Bleed,* his appearances on the late-night shows (Jay Leno and David Letterman), a controversial interview in *Playboy,* and the sale of Jesse Ventura action figures might not have occurred had he never run for governor. Likewise, it would have been impossible for Jesse to become governor without the celebrity status that accompanied his role as Jesse Ventura, the wrestler. Much like Schwarzenegger, he capitalized on his entertainer status, ran for governor as a publicity stunt, and much to his and everyone's surprise, was elected.

Entertainment Persona Is a Fiction,
Yet We Elect the Persona Rather Than the Person

James Janos is his real name, yet Minnesotans elected Jesse Ventura™, a man with a trademarked name fashioned after a coastal Californian city and a persona fashioned as an over-the-top wrestler. Ventura the wrestler/governor beat up "special interest man"; he sold officially licensed bumper stickers that said "My governor can beat up your governor"; and he refereed a World Wrestling Federation wrestling match. For Jesse Ventura the wrestler/governor, politics became the crucible in which he forged his persona as the tough-talking renegade wrestler.

Where James Janos ends and Jesse Ventura begins, or where the entertainer or governor begins and ends, was never clear to the public, the media, or perhaps Ventura, as he never could explain to people when he was in his persona as governor or entertainer. But there was no doubt that the Jesse Ventura persona was a fiction—a fiction that he sold to the public and upon which he had built his political base. The public has traditionally made a distinction between the public and the private sides of politicians' personalities and lives. For a politainer, the public/private tension is far less relevant than the tension between fiction and nonfiction.

Indeed, the public allows a politainer to get away with behavior that falls within expected parameters of that particular politainer's entertainment persona. Since Jesse had always been over-the-top, people allowed and even expected him to be consistent with that persona, even if his behavior was very different from what we might expect from an ordinary politician. He was blunt, used coarse and vulgar language, and referred to his critics as "gutless cowards," and the public viewed each instance as simply another example of the governor telling it like it is, even at the end of his term as governor, despite his waning popularity.

Ventura was examined not through the lens normally used to evaluate elected officials but instead through the magnifying glass normally used on movie stars and celebrities. Such a standard is less critical and introspective and tolerant of the latest foibles so long as they entertain and amuse us. And just like in an all-star wrestling match, the public suspends its beliefs in order to participate in the myth and fiction of Jesse "the Body" Ventura—the wrestler in the governor's office. He is the postmodern version of the Horatio Alger story: anyone can grow up and become famous, and the television viewer vicariously participates in the story. In its desire to be entertained, the public is willing to leave its critical faculties at the door and accept behavior from the politainer that they would not accept from another elected official.

Entertainment Persona Is a Commodity

The last two to three decades of the twentieth century were distinguishable from any others in their increasingly widespread and rampant consumerism. It is in this context that our culture (with the help of marketers and our mass media) has broken new ground in its ability to commodify almost anything. While the political world has never been immune to the influence of the marketplace, one could argue that the politainer becomes a commodity like Mountain Dew or Snickers bars. Jesse's use of a trademarked name, his enforcement of his rights, and his precluding others from capitalizing on his fame, and all the accompanying paraphernalia reinforce this fact (Caple 1998). In fact, in an August 1999 news conference he refused to rule out any future product endorsements (Ragsdale 1999).

Use of Multimedia Venues and Marketing Techniques

Politicians throughout U.S. history have made use of the media in their campaigns and during their terms of office. Political campaigns have continually adapted to the media and marketing practices of their times. In his book, *Adcult USA,* James Twitchell cites the "defining event of political maneuvering" in advertising as the 1952 election campaign of Dwight Eisenhower. A man named Rossier Reeves masterminded a highly successful campaign called "Eisenhower Answers America"—a campaign in which Eisenhower answered on television a series of questions that were generated by Reeves but asked on camera by average citizens. Decades later, "Reagan did exactly what Rossier Reeves was attempting to do for Eisenhower. He traded intellectual content for emotional appeal" (Twitchell 1996, pp. 121-122).

John F. Kennedy innovatively used television. Common wisdom has it that it was Kennedy's appearance on the first televised presidential debate with Nixon that helped him win the election. Kennedy's superb television presence contrasted so greatly with Richard Nixon's lack of presence that some say it cost Nixon the election. Bill Clinton, too, pushed his use of the media farther than any previous president when he went on MTV, and when he played the saxophone on the *Arsenio Hall Show.* He and Hillary periodically used morning and prime time interview shows (e.g., the Barbara Walters specials, and the *Today Show*) to get particular messages out.

Clearly there is historical precedent for politicians' use of the media. What is different about a politainer's use of the media is the degree to which it is done. What the politainer represents is the complete saturation of politics by media and marketing.

Thus, television's increasingly market-driven traits have resulted in a more profit-oriented news that is more entertainment focused. This has helped fuel the ground for the emergence of a change in American politics that is now really politainment. A politainment culture thereby sets the stage for late-night talk shows, becoming the new public forum and political soap-box for politics and for why Schwarzenegger's appearance on *Leno* was not unique but a culmination of a trend fusing politics and entertainment.

The Impact of Late-Night Talk Shows

Late-night talk shows became political focal points during the 2000 presidential race. Jay Leno and David Letterman hosted candidates John McCain, George W. Bush, and Al Gore. David Letterman even employed a long-running stunt, Campaign 2000, in a successful effort to hype ratings by enticing New York Senate candidate Hillary Clinton to appear on his show. For Letterman the purpose was clear: better ratings. But for the candidates, the free exposure was invaluable, and the result was a faint effort at emulating Ventura's success in bridging the politics and entertainment gap. In fact, Ms. Clinton, who used running as "Hillary!" as her slogan (reminiscent of other first-name-only celebrities such as Madonna and Cher), seemed poised to make a bid for public office by using her first name much like a brand name for a product. "Buy Hillary! New and Improved!" Overall, the trend towards celebrity news (Hess 2000) dovetails with the emergence of celebrity politicians.

But what impact do late-night talk shows such as *Leno* and *Letterman* have on American politics? There are several dimensions along which one can measure their new prominence.

Candidate Appearances

Give the Oval Office one heck of a scrubbing.
—the #2 item on the "Top 10 Changes George W. Bush Will Make in the White House," read by Bush on the *Late Show with David Letterman*

Remember America, I gave you the Internet and I can take it away.
—the #9 item on the "Top 10 Rejected Gore-Lieberman Campaign Slogans," read by Al Gore on the *Late Show with David Letterman*

David Letterman: How do you look so youthful and rested?
George Bush: Fake it.
David Letterman: And that's pretty much how you're going to run the country?
    —Exchange between Letterman and Bush on the *Late Show*,
    October 19, 2000

When once asked why he robbed banks, Willie Sutton reputedly remarked, "Because that is where the money is." Why would the likes of Al Gore, George Bush, and Hillary Clinton appear on these shows? Because that is where the undecided voters are.

As noted earlier, candidates and public officials have occasionally appeared on talk shows in the past, but it was not until the 2000 presidential race that candidate appearances on late-night talk shows took off. As Tables 9.1 and 9.2 demonstrate, from January 1, 2000, to election time, 2001, late-night talk shows hosted many of the major presidential candidates.

Table 9.1 2000 Presidential Candidate Appearances on the *Tonight Show with Jay Leno*

Al Gore, October 31, 2000
Tipper Gore, August 16, 2000
George Bush, October 30, 2000
Ralph Nader, September 12, 2000
John McCain, February 4, 2000, March 1, 2000
Hillary Clinton, August 11, 2000

Table 9.2 2000 Presidential Candidate Appearances on the *Late Show with David Letterman*

Hillary Clinton, January 12, 2000
George Bush, March 1, 2000
Al Gore, September 14, 2000
Ralph Nader, September 28, 2000
George Bush, October 19, 2000

Table 9.3 2000 Presidential Candidate Appearances on Other Talk Shows

Gore on *The Oprah Winfrey Show*, September 12, 2000
Bush on *The Oprah Winfrey Show*, September 20, 2000
Gore on *The Queen Latifah Show*, October 9, 2000
Gore on *Live with Regis and Kelly*, June 10, 2000

Bush on *Live with Regis and Kelly,* October 9, 2000
Gore on *The Rosie O'Donnell Show,* October 21, 2000

In addition to appearing on *Leno* and *Letterman*, as Table 9.3 chronicles, George Bush and Al Gore appeared on several other talk shows, such as *Live with Regis and Kelly* or *The Oprah Winfrey Show,* but even beyond the presidential candidates, Hillary Clinton, the president's wife and candidate for United States senator in New York, also made the trek to late-night television in search of politainer fame and votes.

The 2000 presidential race did not end the rush to late-night television. Since the 2000 election, candidates, politicians, and news show or media hosts have continued to be regular guests on *Leno* and *Letterman*, for example. A selected review of these two shows (2001 through 2003) alone indicates that Leno has hosted Hillary Clinton, Laura Bush, George Bush, Al Gore twice, Dick Cheney, and John McCain. Jesse Ventura, Dick Gephardt, Tom Ridge, and Rudy Giuliani have also made appearances. News or media show hosts Tim Russert, Chris Matthews, Bill Maher (twice), and Bill O'Reilly have also appeared.

Letterman has hosted John McCain three times since 2000, along with Al Gore, Hillary Clinton, Bill Clinton, Rudy Giuliani (twice), and Michael Bloomberg. A host of reporters, especially Tom Brokaw, seem to be regulars on *Letterman*—all signs that news, politics, and entertainment have blurred and that politicians and news people want to be seen as entertainment figures. They are seen as personalities, not politicians or serious journalists, telling jokes and sitting next to rock musicians and actors, competing for the same viewers by projecting their personalities into the public mind in ways no different than product marketing and advertising.

Besides going where the voters are, what value does appearing on late-night television have? Media exposure and face time are the answer. According to the Center for Media and Political Affairs, the total air time for election coverage on the news during the 2000 campaign was 12.6 minutes per night, compared to 24.6 minutes in 1992. Most of stories that did appear were either negative reports about the candidates, the horse race (who is ahead according to the polls), or involved the reporters and not the candidates speaking. At the same time, candidates increasingly received less face time. The average candidate soundbite was 7.8 seconds in 2000. This compares to 8.2 seconds in 1996; 8.4 in 1992; and 9.8 in 1988 (Media Monitor 2000). Compare this to 1968 when the average sound bite was 60 seconds (Hallin 1997, p. 60)!

In comparison to the paltry coverage on the news, George Bush received 13 minutes on *Letterman* on October 19, 2002, which was more than his total on television news for three major stations during that month. Similarly, Al Gore's appearance on *Letterman* on September 14, 2002, gave him more coverage than he received on three networks in the entire month of September (Media Monitor 2000).

Appearances on late-night television and talk shows thus serve as an important alternative to the decline in real coverage that the candidates should have received on the news but did not get. But beyond the drive toward politainment, another factor dictating the decrease in face time and coverage on the news gets at the central importance of television in American culture. Specifically, besides television and the media occupying an important democratic role in informing citizens, television is also the major source of information people use to learn about politics. As such, at least at the presidential level, this translates into candidates increasingly spending more and more money on television ads to reach voters. This means that the media have a huge financial incentive not to provide news coverage to candidates. Denying television news coverage forces candidates to buy ads on television, and candidate appearances on late-night television boost ratings, thereby increasing media profits.

Powerful incentives stemming from the corporate ownership of the media and by market-driven news deny candidates sufficient coverage in the more traditional forums where citizens used to gather political information. Why give free candidate-centered coverage when one can force them to buy expensive air time? Why give face time on the 6:30 P.M. news when an appearance on *Letterman* or *Leno* will produce higher Nielsen ratings and more profits? These economic forces clearly explain the motives of the networks, but they also help explain why candidates go on these shows.

Political Jokes and Public Opinion

A second way to assess the growing impact of late-night television is to examine its influence on public opinion. One way these shows influence opinion is through the jokes and opening monologues Leno, Letterman, Conan, and Stewart among others tell.

For years the Center for Media and Political Affairs has been tracking political jokes and humor on late-night television. They note that that the trend since 1988 to 2000 has been an increase in political humor, with political jokes on late-night television taking off in 1992. During the 2000 presidential race, George Bush was the target of 254 general election jokes and Al Gore the target of 165. In total for 2000, Bush was the target of 910 jokes, Bill Clinton 806, Al Gore 530, Hillary Clinton 186, and Dick Cheney 155.

If one were watching these shows and listening to the jokes, what would one have heard about the two major candidates? Among other things, the major candidates for the presidency were liars, dummies, and drunks!

> Republicans are calling the Bush-Cheney ticket the 'Wizard of Oz' ticket. One needs a heart and the other needs a brain.
> —*Tonight Show* host Jay Leno
> Vice President Gore has announced that he will make campaign finance reform the cornerstone of his campaign. And he also announced that for $10,000 you can have your name inscribed on that cornerstone.
> —*Tonight Show* host Jay Leno
> Bush has a new campaign slogan. It's 'Reformer with Results,' which I think is a big improvement on the old one: 'A Dumb Guy with Connections.'
> —*Late Show* host David Letterman
> As you know, Florida is the lynchpin to the presidency. Florida—home of the wet T-shirt contest.
> —*Daily Show* host Jon Stewart
> There is still no winner. There is a state of confusion and not knowing in America. So I guess the Bush era has begun.
> —*Politically Incorrect* host Bill Maher
> When asked if officials should consider hanging chads, George W. Bush said, "Yeah, let's hang him. Who is he? Let's do it."
> —from *Saturday Night Live's* "Weekend Update"

For Gore, stories about him being stiff, boring, and wooden were pervasive. Jokes about Gore's claim to have invented the Internet also were common fare. In turn, Bush was described as a dumb frat boy with drinking problems. Overall, as Marshall Sella put it, the choice before the voters in 2000 who watched late-night television was between the stiff and the dumb guy (Sella 2000).

Do these jokes or late-night shows have any real impact or do voters and viewers simply dismiss all this information as entertainment? Increasingly there are indications that these shows do, in fact, matter.

For one, Wolf Blitzer, a CNN reporter, argues that these jokes have an impact, helping to shape public perceptions of candidates in the popular culture (Sella 2000). Jokes frame the way candidates are thought of in popular culture, influencing the way people and ultimately the news describe or depict candidates. As Duerst, Koloen, and Peterson (2001) contend, voters who received no other information about politics in 2000, except by way of late-night talk shows, would have received a negative view of politics, devoid of issues (except for Bush's strong support of the death penalty), and they would have seen Bush as dumb and Gore as stiff and wooden. In addition, Jamieson and Waldman (2003) note how late-night television affects candidate behavior. For example, they report that Al Gore was forced to watch how he was depicted on *Saturday Night Live* (p. 68), presumably to learn how he was being framed and thus how to diffuse the impression created by those depictions.

Second, in February 2000, the Pew Research Center for the People and the Press released a report subtitled "The Tough Job of Communicating with the Voter." In this February 5, 2000, study, Pew noted a decline in traditional media viewing for news and the rise of talk shows as a new source of news, based upon polling data it had obtained. In its survey, Pew noted that 24% rely on national TV news for political information; 25% rely on local news for campaign coverage; 31% rely on newspapers; and only 15% relied on news magazines such as *Time* or *Newsweek* as their primary source. The study also found that political activists received much of their news from papers but that marginal voters received much of theirs from news magazines. More surprisingly, 51% of those surveyed indicated that they gleaned information from comedy programs such as *Saturday Night Live*, and 9% said they regularly received political information from Letterman or Leno.

For those under age 30, 47% indicted that they were regularly informed by late-night comedy shows. Clearly, late-night television, especially for younger and less-involved or less-informed voters, had become a staple of political information and knowledge. In fact, Goldthwaite (2002) finds evidence that there is some priming effect from late-night television among those who have less political knowledge. That means that late-night television provides cues for the politically uninformed, offering them some knowledge about candidates, which they eventually use when making up their minds about voting.

Fernando (2003) also examined the impact of late-night television on viewers under 30 years of age. He found that Letterman's largest demographic was the 18 to 30 age group (p. 80), and they were most likely to get news from late-night television (p. 81). While Fernando did not find that political participation was affected by viewing late-night television (89, 91), he did find that it affects the images of candidates (p. 87), especially among those who have less formal education and are less politically active (18 to 24). Put into perspective, Gerald Pomper (2001) indicated that 18- to 29-year-olds represented approximately 17% of the voters in the 2000 presidential race. This means that 18,840,000 individuals in this age group voted (p. 139). While it is not certain what percentage of this demographic considers themselves politically active or informed, if the Pew study is accurate, around nine million of these individuals received political information from Letterman, Leno, and the other talk shows.

Matthew Baum (2002) more directly measures the impact of talk shows, using as a case study the appearance of Gore and Bush on *The Oprah Winfrey Show*. Here Baum notes that Gore's appearance on the show caused a spike, where his lead went from 2 to 6.6 points, but Bush's subsequent appearance on the show a few days later reduced it to 3 points (p. 3). In examining the viewer demographics and content of traditional news shows versus what he calls e-shows (entertainment and talk shows), Baum notes that more Democrats than Republicans watch daytime television talk shows. He also found traditional news to be 5 to 15 times more partisan than e-shows (p. 16), with Al Gore depicted favorably 96% of the time on e-shows as opposed to 57% and 58% on traditional news shows. Bush was depicted favorably 95% of the time on e-shows and only 65% and 42% on traditional news shows (p. 16). In addition, e-shows give fewer partisan cues but also one-third fewer policy cues than traditional news shows (p. 19).

Besides getting more air time, another incentive candidates have for appearing on talk shows is that they will be more favorably and less critically examined than on traditional news shows. They will be cast less in partisan terms and seen more in terms of their personalities. In contrast, their appearances on traditional news shows are more partisan and critical. The value of appearances on traditional news shows is that they appeal to the more informed and partisan viewers and often reinforce or solidify supporters. But appearances on e-shows have a different impact. According to Baum, e-shows appeal to the politically uninformed. For example, the 18- to 34-year-old age group is the largest demographic for day and evening talk shows. For those who are least interested, watching e-shows increases interest in politics but for those who are most interested, watching e-shows decreases interest (p. 20). Perversely, among the least politically engaged Democrats, e-shows increased the probability of voting for Bush and decreased the chances of voting Gore; for the least politically engaged Republicans, it increased the probability of voting for Gore and decreased the probability of voting for Bush (p. 25)!

While these boomerang results seem odd, they do suggest an interesting pattern emerging for candidates. Candidates have to repackage their message to a fragmented market and to people who do not watch the news (p. 5). Thus, there are at least two basic markets served by television. The first includes those partisans and the better informed who watch traditional news shows or who gather their political information from more mainstream news sources, such as newspapers. These are the individuals who respond to partisan cues and most probably have already made their voting decisions early on. The second television market is those who are politically uninformed, less or nonpartisan, and they are perhaps undecided regarding how they will vote. It is this group of voters that watches late-night or e-tv, and are perhaps the swing voters who will decide the outcome of the election. Thus e-tv, while it has little impact on more educated or partisan voters, is aimed at the 10 to 20% of the electorate that is undecided (Hershey 2001, p. 58).

Hillary Clinton Does Letterman

From The Home Office in Chappaqua, New York: The Top Ten Reasons That, I, Hillary Clinton, Finally Decided to Appear on *The Late Show*.

10. I lost a bet with Tipper.
9. I did think this was a show where you answer a couple of easy questions and you win $1,000,000.
8. If Dan Quayle did it, how hard can it be?
7. I was already in town to interview for the Jets' head coach position.
6. Four words: severe lapse of judgment.
5. I needed an excuse to get out of dinner with Donald Trump.
4. When they threw in a *Late Show* tote bag, I said, "Gas up the Taurus, Bill, we're going to Dave's."
3. I have not been in the Ed Sullivan Theater since I was dating Ringo.
2. To tell you the truth, Dave, I thought Johnny hosted this show.
1. If I can make it here, I can make it anywhere!

Talk shows compete with other shows that are profit centers in their own right (Timberg 2002, pp. 4–5). Each talk show has its own script, providing an opportunity to view the candidates as persons. Yuking it up with the host is a good way to diffuse jokes being told about them and also to recast themselves as cool or hip. The political and electoral results are often profound, demonstrating how such an appearance can affect public opinion—and one's electoral chances.

Hillary Clinton's January 12, 2000, appearance on *Letterman* was a classic. It was a defining moment in her campaign for the United States Senate. Until that time, Letterman was a harsh critic of Ms. Clinton and described her as a carpetbagger. Her appearance on the show was the culminating event of Letterman's "Campaign 2000," wherein he staged a series of stunts aimed at getting her to appear on the show. A January 11, 2000, poll had Ms. Clinton behind New York Mayor Rudy Giuliani 49% to 40%, but her performance on the show was nothing short of remarkable. Opening with the statement: "I knew if I were going to run for the Senate, I had to sit in this chair and talk to the big guy," Clinton answered a supposed pop quiz on New York State (it was later found that she was briefed on the questions) and offered her own version of a Top Ten List.

According to the *New York Post,* her joking with Letterman was so successful that the night was seen as a "major facelift on her campaign." Her appearance was also a major facelift for Letterman: The normal audience for the show was about 4 million, but 11.2 million watched the show that night. According to Nielsen ratings, the January 12 show was the first time Letterman won that time spot in 5 years. Not only did Hillary Clinton's appearance on Letterman boost the bottom line for the show, but as a result, Clinton pulled even with Giuliani (according to the polls), and eventually went on to win the New York Senate race (BBC News 2000). Since that appearance, Senator Clinton has continued to ride the coattails of politainment, engaging an author tour in 2003 to sell her book and encourage rumors of her presidential candidacy and political future.

Schwarzenegger and the Future of Late-Night Television

Late-night television impacts politics. By way of jokes, comedy routines, and candidate appearances, it frames campaigns and candidates by reaching uninformed and undecided voters (perhaps the "Jaywalking" segments on *The Tonight Show* symbolize the typical voter who watches these shows). Late-night television defines popular culture's depictions of the candidates, which, in turn, influence the news. Candidates are thus forced to respond, appearing on late-night television both as a replacement for the decreasing coverage they receive in an increasingly entertainment-driven news media and as an alternative to more traditional news, seeking to appeal to swing and uninformed voters.

For candidates, late-night television has become another campaign stop and political forum. Candidates can either be passive objects of jokes that often negatively frame them, or they can actively use Letterman, Leno, and Conan as a new way to campaign and mold their images. For the talk shows, the payoff is also huge—ratings! Arnold Schwarzenegger's appearance on *Leno* resulted in Nielsen ratings of 7.1 rating/17 share, with a 20 share in San Francisco and a 23 share in Los Angeles (Gerhart 2003). Almost one in four televisions on in Los Angeles—the second largest television market in the country—was turned to the show that night. The Schwarzenegger campaign, much like Ventura's, involved a candidate whose media image on television and films overshadowed and framed the campaign. Arnold's declaration of his candidacy on late-night television was proof positive that politainment triumphed as a new cultural manifestation, fusing politics to entertainment and giving late-night television a new role in American politics.

In fact, the 2003 California recall was a perfect, made-for-TV politainment event. With 135 candidates vying for their 15 minutes on camera, many ran not with the hope of being governor but to get publicity. Gary Coleman, former child star; Arianna Huffington, celebrity journalist; *Hustler* publisher Larry Flynt; and porn star Mary Carey all appeared to being using their candidacies for self-promotional purposes, and Leno fed into that cause, making the recall a regular staple of his jokes.

Leno, the *Tonight Show,* and Schwarzenegger all helped one another. As Leno launched the Schwarzenegger candidacy, the constant drumbeat of jokes and monologues reinforced the carnival atmosphere of the recall, downplaying the substantive policies and problems underlining California's politics. Arnold generally stayed clear of issues, preferring to let entertainment and political reporters simply give him coverage on television. It was not important that he was a real candidate with real issues; he merely needed to act or play a candidate on the tube looking "gubernatorial." Television is a visual, not an aural medium—people watch and do not listen to it. All the criticism from political reporters, either in print or on television, did not matter because exposure was the key—and he got it.

The recall and campaign implied troubling questions for television. Oprah Winfrey had both Arnold and Maria on her show—and no other gubernatorial candidates—giving the Terminator free air and plenty of time to portray himself as a good husband and father and thereby reassure female voters that he was not a sexist jerk. Oprah's decision to give him free time, along with Leno's, raises important ethical questions about the role of the media in politics. Perhaps Oprah favored Arnold for governor, but perhaps it really was about ratings for her. If it was about ratings, it suggests that she and her producers were either completely unaware of or did not care about the ethical issues that were raised by his appearance on her show.

The same is even more true for Leno. His decision to introduce Schwarzenegger at the latter's victory party clearly crossed the ethical line. No longer can one claim that Leno was politically neutral in his jokes. How that will affect viewers in the future will be interesting to see, but here again, ratings and dollars were more important than ethics. Jeff Zucker, head of entertainment for NBC, knew of the Leno appearance at the victory rally and had "no problem" with it (Carter, October 10, 2003a). Perhaps the "no problem" stemmed from the fact that Leno was drawing two million more viewers per night than Letterman, making over $1 billion for NBC over the years (Carter, November 3, 2003b). Profits über ethics is the message one draws from this, and perhaps NBC might have thought differently were Leno not so popular.

Schwarzenegger's candidacy thus was a perfect embodiment of politainment. He is married to Maria Shriver, a member of the first family of political television (the Kennedys), and the lure of using the Kennedy mystique and tying Camelot to the Terminator played well in many circles as Ms. Shriver sought to reassure Democrats and women (especially in light of the many allegations of her husband's sexual harassment) that Arnold was okay to vote for (Nagourney amd Rutenberg 2003). Arnold's acting persona, framed by movies such as *Terminator* and *Conan the Barbarian,* defined his political persona such that women's groups condemned his Hollywood movie interviews as if they were political positions. Perhaps this tough persona, like Jesse Ventura's in Minnesota, is what made him popular with voters who thought they knew who Schwarzenegger was and saw in that persona one who could better handle California's problems that the wimpy Gray Davis. Arnold was thus the new lead actor to play governor. In the end, the delineation between the politics of the gubernatorial recall and showbiz has all but disappeared.

For 2004 and beyond, entertainment venues will be an important and powerful resource for candidates seeking to reach undecided or swing voters, and it will be these shows that will drive mainstream news and popular culture depictions of candidates and politics. The reason for this, to a large extent, is the emergence of a politainment culture and the desire of the media to maximize ratings and profits. In 2003, as the presidential race was heating up and Howard Dean was taking off as the frontrunner, former General Wesley Clark was given potent air time as he debated entering the race. A former general and hero makes a wonderful lead actor in a presidential race, adding nice drama to it. In fact, the press he received was so favorable that despite little initial name recognition and almost no preparation for the issues, he quickly moved to the number two slot among Democrats in opinion polls.

Politically, while many may wish to condemn this trend toward entertainment, there may be little to be done about it unless one wishes to adjust campaign laws, strategy, and public financing in relation to this new phenomenon or change the media ownership laws to prevent the further concentration of media ownership or even reinstate or adopt new fairness rules that limit the ability of shows to push candidates unless they give equal time to others.

REFERENCES

"Around the News in 22 Minutes." 1991. *New York Times,* July 7, B1.

Bagdikian, Ben H. 1997. *The Media Monopoly.* 5th ed. Boston: Beacon Press.

Baum, Matthew. 2002. "Rocking the Vote: What Happens When Presidential Candidates Hit the Talk Show Circuit?" Paper delivered at the Annual American Political Science Association Convention, San Francisco, CA, August 29 to September 2.

BBC News, 2000. "Hillary Clinton Does Letterman," *http://news.bbc.co.uk/1/hi/world/ americas/601609.stm* (July 1).

Caple, Jim. 1998. "Ventura Won't Let Others Cash in on His Cachet." *St. Paul Pioneer Press,* December 24, 1998: A1.

Carter, Bill. 2003a. "NBC Supports the Politically Partisan Leno." *New York Times,* October 10, A22.

Carter, Bill. 2003b. "Late at Night, That's NBC Crowing." *New York Times,* November 3, C1.

Center for Media and Political Affairs: Election Watch. 2003. *www.cmpa.com/politics/ elections/joketime.htm* (June 30).

Davis, Richard. 1996. *The Press and American Politics: The New Mediator.* 2nd ed. Upper Saddle River, NJ: Prentice Hall.

Davis, Richard, and Diana Owen. 1998. *New Media and American Politics.* New York: Oxford University Press.

Duerst, Lindsey, Glory Koloen, and Geoff Peterson. 2001. "It May Be Funny, but It Is True: The Political Content of Late-Night Talk Show Monologues," Paper delivered at the Annual American Political Science Association Convention, San Francisco, CA, August 29 to September 2.

Fernando, Mark Phillip. 2003. "The Late-Night Effect: Late-Night Television's Effect on the Perception of Political Figures." Master's thesis, Georgetown University, May 1.

Gerhart, Ann. 2003. "A Barbarian at the Gate of Camelot." *Washington Post,* August 8, C1.

Goldthwaite, Dannagal E. 2002. "Pinocchio v. Dumbo: Priming Candidate Caricature Attributes in Late-Night Comedy Programs in 2000 and the Moderating Effects of Political Knowledge." Paper delivered at the 2002 Annual APSA Convention, August 29–September 1, 2002.

Graber, Doris A. 1997. *Mass Media and American Politics.* 5th ed. Washington, DC: Congressional Quarterly Press.

Grossman, Lawrence K. 1995. *The Electronic Republic.* New York: Penguin Books.

Hallin, Daniel C. 1997. "Sound Bite News: Television Coverage of Elections." In Shanto Iyengar and Richard Reeves, eds. *Do the Media Govern?: Politicians, Voters, and Reporters in America.* Thousand Oaks, CA: Sage Publications.

Hamilton, James T. 2004. *All the News That's Fit to Sell: How the Market Transforms Information into News.* Princeton, NJ: Princeton University Press.

Hershey, Majorie Randon. 2001. "The Campaign and the Media." In Gerald M. Pomper, *The Election of 2000,* New York: Chatham House Publishers, pp. 46–72.

Hess, Stephen. 2000. "Federalism & News: Media to Government: Drop Dead." *Brookings Review* (Winter 2000): 28–31.

Jamieson, Kathleen Hall, and Paul Waldman. 2003. *The Press Effect: Politicians, Journalists, and the Stories That Shape the Political World.* New York: Oxford University Press.

Lyotard, Jean-François. 1979. *The Postmodern Condition: A Report on Knowledge.* Minneapolis: University of Minnesota Press.

McManus, John H. 1994. *Market-Driven Journalism: Let the Citizen Beware?* Thousand Oaks, CA: Sage Publications.

Media Monitor: Campaign 2000 Final: How TV News Covered the General Election Campaign. *www.cmpa.com/Mediamon/mm1112000.htm* (June 30).

Nagourney, Adam, and Jim Rutenberg. 2003. "Recall Race's No Longer 'Secret' Weapon." *New York Times,* October 9, A1.

Parenti, Michael. 1995. *Democracy for the Few.* 6th ed. New York: St. Martin's Press.

Pew Research Center for the People and the Press. 2002. "Audiences Fragmented and Skeptical: The Tough Job of Communicating with Voters." Press release, February 5.

Picard, Robert G. 1998. "Media Concentration, Economics, and Regulation." In *The Politics of News, The News of Politics,* ed. Doris Graber, et al. Washington, DC: Congressional Quarterly Press, pp. 193–217.

Pomper, Gerald M. 2001. "The Presidential Election." In Gerald M. Pomper, *The Election of 2000,* New York: Chatham House Publishers, pp. 125–154.

Purdum, Todd S. 1999. "TV Political News in California Is Shrinking, Study Confirms,"*New York Times,* January 13, A11.

Ragsdale, Jim. 1999. "Ventura Lambasts His Critics on Radio." *St. Paul Pioneer Press,* *August* 21, A1.

Reeves, Richard. 1997. *Do the Media Govern? Politicians, Voters, and Reporters in America,* Thousand Oaks, CA: Sage Publications, pp. 57–65.

Salant, Richard S. 1999. *Salant, CBS, and the Battle for the Soul of Broadcast Journalism: The Memoirs of Richard S. Salant.* Edited by Susan Buzenberg and Bill Buzenberg. Boulder, CO: Westview Press.

Schultz, David. 2000. "The Cultural Contradictions of the American Media." In David Schultz (ed.) *It's Show Time! Media, Politics, and Popular Culture.* New York: Peter Lang, pp. 13–28.

Sella, Marshall. 2000. "The Stiff Guy vs. the Dumb Guy." *New York Times Magazine.* September 24, 72–80, 108.

Timberg, Bernard. 2002. *Television Talk: A History of the TV Talk Show.* Austin, TX: University of Texas Press.

Twitchell, James B. 1996. *Adcult USA.* New York: Columbia University Press.

Underwood, Doug. 1995. *When MBA's Rule the Newsroom.* New York: Columbia University Press.

Wolf, Michael J. 1999. *The Entertainment Economy: How Mega-Media Forces Are Transforming Our Lives.* New York: Times Books.

Woodward, Gary C. 1997. *Perspectives on American Political Media.* Boston: Allyn and Bacon.

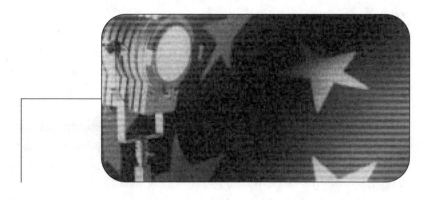

10

Lights, Camera, and an Action Hero!
Arnold Schwarzenegger and the Media Frenzy in the California Recall

David L. Schecter

On an overcast Monday morning in Sacramento, November 17, 2003, 56-year-old Arnold Alois Schwarzenegger was sworn in as the 38th governor of the state of California. In addition to the 7,500 invited guests attending the inaugural, including dignitaries from thirteen countries, there were 740 television and print reporters and 50 TV satellite trucks. Journalists from Japan, Australia, France, Germany, the United Kingdom, and Schwarzenegger's native Austria attended (Chorneau 2003), and shortly after it was all over former Los Angeles Mayor Richard Riordan proclaimed: "There are more cameras and newspaper people here than there are attending the inauguration of the president of the United States" (Fitzenberger 2003).

Such was the state of California politics following the historic recall election that had rocked the Golden State a month earlier. In that special election, called to remove sitting Governor Gray Davis, political neophyte Arnold Schwarzenegger swept into office after one of the most interesting and brief campaigns in American history. The events surrounding the campaign and Schwarzenegger's rise to power could not have taken place without the media coming on board for the ride. While print and television media have always played a major role in our politics, as the other chapters included in this volume attest, in the California recall the media drove the election along from the very beginning. In fact, it will be argued here that without the media there would have been no Governor Schwarzenegger.

This chapter follows the role of the media in this race from its beginning in the spring of 2003 through the October election and the November inauguration. Specific attention is given to the media frenzy surrounding the Schwarzenegger campaign from the start and how his handlers used those very media to their advantage throughout the race. The term *media frenzy,* a term synonymous with sharks partaking in a feeding frenzy, may be an understatement in the case of the recall. In this particular case, the bait may have gotten the best of the sharks. During a slow summer of news coverage, where the main events of the day were the Laci Peterson murder investigation taking place in California and the ongoing war in Iraq, the California recall became *the* center of the storm—*the* news event that combined the allure of a Hollywood movie star with political intrigue, advertising wars, a dash of courtroom drama, and an audience willing to tune in seemingly 24 hours a day, seven days a week. This was truly a made-for-TV event that the American political system had never seen before. The impact of this election on future campaigns across the nation may be felt for decades.

Background

Some background on the recall process itself is necessary to help set the stage for the recall campaign. Only one governor in U.S. history, Lynn J. Frazier of North Dakota (1921), had ever been recalled prior to Gray Davis being pulled from office in the 2003 race. While 18 states allow for the recall of state officers, governors are rarely touched by the provision. Occasionally state judges or members of the legislature have had to face a recall ballot, but for the most part the recall is a phenomenon of local governments throughout the nation. As a cousin to the more popular Progressive-era direct democracy reforms, such as the initiative and referendum, its use at the statewide level has been sporadic and often unsuccessful. In almost all of the states that have the provision in their Constitution relative to statewide officeholders, citizens are required to submit a certain number of signed petitions to the state calling for the removal of the official, which is followed by a certification of voter signatures and the placement of the recall question on a future statewide ballot.[1]

Since the recall provision was placed into the California Constitution in 1911 (art. II, sec. 13–20), on 31 separate occasions governors had been faced with opposition that threatened to use the recall and went so far as gather signatures to place it on a future ballot. As Gregg Jones and Evan Halper of the *Los Angeles Times* reported on July 8, 2003, none were successful in getting past the signature stage. In other words, in the largest state in the union, no governor had really ever had to take the threat of the recall very seriously. This all changed in 2003 for a variety of reasons, the crux of which focused on the leadership of sitting Democratic governor Gray Davis. During a stellar career in state politics, Davis had moved up the political ladder and had held positions as state controller (1987 through 1995) and lt. governor (1995 through 1999) before being elected as governor in 1998. Prior to this election, one longtime follower of state politics said Davis was "perhaps the best prepared governor-in-waiting that California has ever produced" (Trounstine 2003, 19 . His first term was marked by several controversies, but the voters reelected Davis to a second, and final, four-year term in November 2002. This followed tradition, as California voters had reelected every single governor to a second term since the 1940s, and Davis was no exception.

The gubernatorial race in the fall of 2002 was a particularly boring affair with only one debate between the candidates, and Davis won the race easily, 47% to 42%. The Republican primary in the spring of that year was a different story. The primary produced the candidate Davis would beat, Bill Simon, but it was a raucous affair when Republican delegates selected Simon to carry their banner in the general election. He was a multimillionaire businessman with no prior political experience, and he took the party nomination over Secretary of State Bill Jones and former Los Angeles Mayor Richard Riordan. Riordan was seen by many as the candidate most able to defeat Davis due to his more moderate positions on certain social issues and his excellent name recognition in the state, but the Davis camp spent nearly $10 million of its own money in the Republican primary to push down Riordan and bolster Simon (Schecter 2003).

The strategy worked. Simon won the nomination and Davis was able to defeat him handily in November. This story of Republican infighting is important to the recall race because much of the support for Schwarzenegger in 2003 came from Republicans who felt they had learned a lesson in 2002 and simply wanted to back the candidate they perceived as most electable when the chance rolled around within a year.

Another important background element from the 2002 campaign that will help us understand the state of affairs in California prior to the recall concerns the energy crisis that had hit the state in 2001 and the growing state deficit of 2001–2002. With energy prices soaring under deregulation and the state in panic mode in 2001, Governor Davis was accused of acting too slowly on the issue and procrastinating on a number of important decisions to stabilize energy prices. On the deficit front, like many states at the time, California was in dire straits, but Davis was accused during the 2002 governor's race of misleading the public as to the actual size of the deficit. This came back to haunt him following his victory in November. [2]

It should be noted that future governor Arnold Schwarzenegger was also involved in the 2002 general election campaign but not as a candidate as might be expected. During that campaign Schwarzenegger was getting his feet wet, so to speak, barnstorming the state on behalf of a ballot initiative he was supporting—Proposition 49. This proposition earmarked roughly $500 million each year for after-school programs, and Schwarzenegger spent nearly $1.1 million of his own money to push the initiative along. He was the number one donor to the cause, beating out even the California Teachers Association by $500,000 (California Online Voter Guide 2002). Prior to the November 2002 election, Schwarzenegger repeatedly traveled the state on behalf of Prop 49 and made no secret of the fact that he was supporting education this time around and supporting his own political ambitions at the same time.[3] In short, while Schwarzenegger has been accused of being a newcomer to California politics, this is not really the case. He did not hold public office before 2003, but he did campaign on behalf of many candidates and issues prior to the recall campaign, building up a nice Rolodex for himself filled with the state's most important players and interest groups.

The Stage Is Set

Against this backdrop and immediately following the November election, a small group of Republican leaders began circulating a petition to recall Gray Davis. Media coverage of this signature stage of the process was relatively light. Most political reporters, pundits, and academics understood that other governors had faced the threat of recall before and that only one governor in history had ever been removed from office. The media coverage became more intense, however, after the state Republican Party convention was held in Sacramento on Saturday, February 22. Nearly 1,400 Republicans attended the convention; every major newspaper in the state covered the event and noted the convention rallying cry: "Dump Davis!" In an article titled "Davis Recall Bid Has Supporters and Doubters at GOP

Convention," published in the *Los Angeles Times,* February 23, 2003, Michael Finnegan reported that the "nascent move to try to oust the Democratic governor in a special election became a centerpiece of the state Republican convention here as a few hundred delegates and other Davis foes held a demonstration outside the Capitol to show support for a recall." Key Republicans, however, including top leaders in the assembly and senate were not very supportive of the recall idea, stating that "key resources" would be wasted on such an effort and that talk of a recall would jeopardize their ongoing discussions with Davis concerning the latest state budget.

The anti-tax group, People's Advocate (led by Republican Ted Costa), was the real driving force behind the recall, and Costa was quick to point out in interviews that this was a nonpartisan effort with support from Democrats and independents. A few months down the road Costa would be proven correct as signatures were gathered and votes were counted.

Governor Davis's initial reaction to the pro-recall events at the GOP convention was reported in the *San Francisco Chronicle* on February 24, 2003. John Wildermuth quoted Davis as saying: "This is simply sour grapes. My opponents lost the election fair and square. Now they want another election. I'm focused on the job they elected me to finish. I'm not going to forecast the results of this recall." It proved to be more than just sour grapes as the recall effort proceeded into early March.

With the war in Iraq looming on the horizon, Ted Costa and the main recall proponents began the arduous task of collecting signatures from throughout the state. They needed roughly 900,000 signatures to get the recall on the ballot—the number deemed necessary by the constitution after calculating 12% of the nearly eight million votes cast in the previous November governor's election. Nearly a million signatures is a daunting task, and the recall supporters were hitting some tough roadblocks early on. By March 25 they had filed all of the necessary paperwork with the secretary of state's office to begin collecting signatures, and they put together a Website to help raise funds (www.recallgraydavis.com). Much of the media was being distracted by international issues at this time, however, and paying signature-gathering firms to collect the signatures was an increasingly expensive undertaking.

By the end of April much of the media focus on the recall began to fade temporarily, and headlines such as the "Davis Recall Drive Hurting for Cash" appeared in the *San Francisco Chronicle* on April 27. Across San Francisco Bay, however, the *Oakland Tribune,* and in Southern California, the *San Diego Union-Tribune,* were running stories that same weekend about a well-

known United States congressman from California, Darrell Issa, who was
rumored to be interested in bankrolling the recall effort. With some mixed
messages coming from Issa, Steve Geissinger reported in the Oakland paper
on April 25 that: "Issa said he would not donate directly to the recall campaign but that he might contribute funds to independent efforts aimed at
advancing the cause." Within ten days Issa made up his mind and pledged
$100,000 to the pro-recall efforts. He also began gearing up his own not-
so-subtle campaign to replace Davis if the recall succeeded. Within weeks
Issa would pledge nearly $1.5 million of his own money to the cause, and
for a while he looked like the only candidate who could afford to face Davis
and be willing to put his money where his mouth had been.

By mid-May it was widely known that the pro-recall forces, literally
thanks to Issa's cash infusion, had begun gathering enough signatures to put
the question on the ballot, and candidate names were popping up daily with
respect to "who else" would run against Davis. Paraphrasing Ross Perot,
an op-ed piece by Daniel Weintraub of the *Sacramento Bee* pointed out on
May 15 that the recall had become "the crazy aunt who won't go away."

On the Democratic side of the ledger, most potential candidates by mid-
May were sticking with the party line that the recall was a Republican "coup"
attempt, and they stuck by their newly reelected governor. No Democrat
wanted to be the first to break ranks and come forward, and it is important to review the structure of the recall ballot momentarily to see why this
is the case.

As shown in Appendix A, the recall ballot in California is actually divided
into two questions on which the voters had to choose.[4] The first question
pertained only to Gray Davis and asked: "Shall Gray Davis be recalled
(removed) from the office of governor?" Voters were asked to simply say
"Yes" or "No" to this question. They then proceeded down the ballot to
view a list of names of those qualified by the secretary of state to run for
the seat.

To provide a random element to the listing of names, the state used a
lottery system to rearrange the alphabet and list names according to that
new arrangement. This new "alphabetical list" (which began with the letters R, W, Q, O, J, M, V, A, H, B, S, G , etc.) was standardized for all ballots but was rotated by assembly district throughout the state. In this
manner, in Assembly District 1 the names appeared as first determined by
the random alphabet. In Assembly District 2, the candidate who appeared
first in Assembly District 1 dropped to the bottom and the other candidates

moved up one position and so on throughout the 80 districts (Secretary 2003).

In other words, all candidates wishing to challenge the governor, in the conventional sense, do not really do so on this ballot. The governor in question must beat the recall on the first ballot question, and in doing so, no successor is even needed. If the sitting governor gets less than 50% of the "No" vote, he or she is removed from office, and the replacement is chosen from among those qualified on the second question. There is no run-off, either, in this type of format; a simple plurality of votes determines the winner. In theory, if there were 135 final names on the second ballot question, as was the case here, the next governor, if Davis was removed, could win with anywhere from a few votes to 40% to 50% of the vote or more, depending on how the other candidates fared. They just had to get the *most* votes on Question 2.

This presented a problem for the Democrats because it was widely believed that if any prominent Democrat came forward to challenge Davis, he/she could take votes from him on Question 1, by providing a reasonable Democratic alternative to the voters and raise the chances of his defeat. For Davis and his supporters to win they needed to impress on voters that this was a Republican-led effort that should not be supported by loyal Democrats and that all votes and campaign cash should be steered toward Davis and Davis only. By mid-June, however, a number of prominent Democrats began questioning this logic, and several felt that providing a reasonable alternative to Davis on Question 2 might keep the governorship in their hands.

This wrangling over strategy played out for several weeks, and the media spent a considerable amount of time during these weeks diagramming the ballot possibilities for voters and explaining the awkwardness of the recall ballot even though the exact number of candidates would not be determined for nearly two months. Media coverage at this point revolved around the technicalities of the recall, the positioning of party leaders, and the rumors concerning which candidates were likely to run against Davis besides Darrell Issa.

One thing was certain, however—Davis's popularity at the polls was dwindling. As the respected Field Poll announced on July 16: "Likely voters favor Davis's recall by a 51% to 43% margin." While voters expressed mixed feelings about whether the recall itself was justified, only 6% of likely voters were undecided on their feelings toward the governor. Of the Republican names put before the voters former Los Angeles Mayor

Richard Riordan was favored at 21%, followed by Arnold Schwarzenegger at 15% and Bill Simon at 12% (Field 2003).

Polling would prove to be a crucial piece of the recall puzzle and helps explain the strange relationship between the recall itself and the media. There was no shortage of polls taken during the recall, and Table 10.1 gives an overview of just a few of the most prominent polls in the state and how they were gauging the electorate over several months. Near-weekly polling led to reporters covering those polls and pundits predicting winners based on the latest numbers available. The coverage of the "horse race" has always been a major part of reporting on important elections, and the recall provided a ton of fodder for the media to dish out. As pointed out by others,

Table 10.1 Recall Poll Results

Date	Agency	Bustamante	Schwarzenegger	McClintock	Camejo	Other	Undecided
8/13	Field Poll	25%	22%	9%	2%	23%	19%
8/21	LA Times	35%	22%	12%	1%	21%	9%
9/7	Field Poll	32%	27%	14%	2%	7%	18%
9/8	Stanford/ Knowledge Networks	28%	40%	8%			
9/8	Survey USA	29%	39%	16%			
9/12	LA Times	30%	25%	18%	2%	20%	5%
9/28	Field Poll	31%	30%	19%	3%	4%	13%
10/1	Field Poll	26%	36%	16%	6%	3%	13%
10/1	LA Times	32%	40%	15%			

Sources: Compiled by the author from:

(1) http://www.surveyusa.com/2003_Elections/ CA030909RecallReplace.pdf

(2) http://www.knowledgenetworks.com/info/press/releases/2003/ 091003_carecall.htm

(3) http://www.latimes.com/news/local/timespoll/state/

(4) http://www.field.com/fieldpollonline/subscribers/RLS2095.pdf

Date	Agency	Recall Davis?	Yes	No	Undecided
4/6*	Field Poll	46%	43%	11%	
7/4	LA Times	51%	42%	7%	
7/13+	Field Poll	51%	43%	6%	
8/13+	Field Poll	58%	37%	5%	
8/21	LA Times	50%	45%	5%	
9/7+	Field Poll	55%	40%	5%	
9/8	Stanford/ Knowledge Networks	62%	38%		
9/8	Survey USA	62%	37%		
9/28+	Field Poll	53%	43%	4%	
10/1+	Field Poll	57%	39%	4%	
10/1	LA Times	56%	42%	2%	

*Conducted among all registered voters
+ Among likely voters

Sources: Compiled by the author from:

(1) http://www.field.com/fieldpollonline/ subscribers/RLS2095.pdf

(2) http://www.latimes.com/news/local/timespoll/state/

(3) http://www.knowledgenetworks.com/info/press/releases/2003/091003_carecall.htm.

(4) http://www.surveyusa.com/2003_Elections/CA030909RecallReplace.pdf

the media often "treat campaigns . . . as a competition for office. The focus is on the race itself . . . and 'human interest' trivia" (Parenti 1986, p. 15).[5] By late July this appeared to be the case concerning the buildup to a recall vote, but things would get ramped up considerably in the next two weeks. What had previously been a fascinating story that had begun to garner national attention and curiosity became, almost overnight, the most fascinating political story in the nation. Among analysts estimating a $40 million spending binge just for recall campaign commercials expected to hit the airwaves, Los Angeles political consultant Hal Dash noted: "It's gravy time for the media" ("Online" 2003.

The Megastar

On July 23, 2003, 120 days after initiating the recall drive, proponents had obtained the proper amount of signatures and Secretary of State Kevin Shelley, a Democrat, certified their number. Fulfilling his constitutional duties, on the following day Lt. Governor Cruz Bustamante, also a Democrat, called for a special election on October 7 to pose the recall questions to the voters. As Erica Werner of the Associated Press reported in a July 9, page-one story for the *Oakland Tribune*, the pro-recall forces were ready to go: "We can't rest on our laurels just because we gathered the signatures. We have to now make sure that people go out and vote the way we want them to," acknowledged Dave Gilliard of the Rescue California Recall Gray Davis Committee. Gilliard claimed they had $13 million to spend on the recall effort, and they would spend heavily on "television advertisements and direct mail." Supporters of Governor Davis claimed they would match that spending dollar for dollar. For the state, Kevin Shelley's office reported that the estimated cost of the election would be between $53 million and $66 million.

It was official—California would have its first recall election for a governor and candidates were given until Saturday, August 9 to submit nomination papers to their local election office. The threshold to qualify was tremendously low. Candidates were only required to complete their paper work correctly, pay the $3,500 filing fee, and submit 65 valid signatures from registered voters from their own party. By August 6th, 621 individuals had pulled papers to run.

Returning to Lt. Governor Cruz Bustamante, it would turn out that he would play an even larger role in the election than might have been considered in late July. A former speaker of the assembly, Bustamante hailed from the Central Valley of California and was elected to the lieutenant governor's position in 1998 and 2002. A formidable figure in the Hispanic community, he had risen through the ranks and made no secret of his interest in the governorship. A number of other prominent Democrats also held key statewide executive positions, however; some with greater financial resources available than Bustamante. For these Democrats it was hard to weigh the benefits of entering this strange race against their own sitting governor versus biding their time until the seat was open again in 2006. During June and July, Bustamante stated repeatedly he would not enter the fray and that he would support Davis.

As the first week of August rolled around he had a change of heart. A number of prominent Democrats stayed loyal to Davis, most notably former San Francisco mayor and current U.S. senator Dianne Feinstein, but some began to speak publicly for the first time about Davis's expected chances and how the Democrats should not simply give up the seat without a fight. Against this backdrop Bustamante began to consider the run more seriously, and many political analysts knew that his personal relationship with Davis was frosty, at best.

Around this same time there were increasing reports that Richard Riordan, who had lost the Republican gubernatorial nomination to Bill Simon the previous year, was going to throw his hat in the ring. A millionaire and a moderate Republican, Riordan was a close friend of Arnold Schwarzenegger, and his staking out a position before the August 9 deadline made it appear as if Schwarzenegger would probably not run and would just defer to the senior statesman. The press was reporting as late as Saturday, August 2 that Riordan was likely to run, and speculation about his chances was positive. Democrats appeared concerned with this and recognized Riordan's strengths. One Democratic consultant put it this way: "Clearly, Riordan is somebody who's run statewide . . . and has a base in the largest media market in the state" (*Fresno Bee* 2003).[6] In the meantime, Arnold Schwarzenegger announced that on Wednesday, August 6 he would appear on NBC's *The Tonight Show with Jay Leno* and make an official announcement about his plans. The former *Dating Game* contestant was wrapping up his world tour promoting his latest film, *Terminator 3: Rise of the Machines,* and would return to Southern California for the late-night television appearance.

During this stretch it should be noted that Gray Davis was also ratcheting up his media time and launching an offensive of his own. Davis was filling his schedule with interviews on national television, and one event on

CNN's *Late Edition* showed the strategy the Davis camp was taking at this time. He blasted Issa through most of the interview, calling him a "right-winger" who was out of touch with the values of most Californians. The media, then, became *the* tool for Davis and all of the potential candidates to spread their message and reach the voters during the start of what everyone knew would be a frenetic and accelerated campaign. The media was more than willing to oblige and knew they had an exciting race on their hands. Unfortunately for Davis, however, his star did not shine as brightly as Schwarzenegger's and the others on television, and for a governor so adept at discussing the issues, his media appearances were unable to light anybody on fire.

Wednesday, August 6 was the day everyone had been waiting for, and professional actor Arnold Schwarzenegger did not let them down. There are numerous, competing explanations of exactly who knew what and when, but Schwarzenegger certainly made the most of his moment in the national spotlight and stunned the political world with his announcement. After all, how many governors or governors-in-waiting can be guests on the most popular late-night show in America and surprise everyone in attendance at the same time?

Of all of the accounts of the incident, Karen Tumulty and Terry McCarthy of *Time* magazine do a good job capturing the moment. They report that prior to the show Jay Leno asked Schwarzenegger if he was going to run, and the former star of the film *Running Man* said he would not, adding: "I am bowing out." His top advisor, George Gorton, a former advisor to previous Republican governor Pete Wilson, stood on the set of the show, and as Schwarzenegger was introduced, Gorton was holding the "concession speech" that they had prepared. At that moment, Schwarzenegger "threw a muscular arm around his shoulder and said, 'Let's do it.'" (Tumulty and McCarthy 2003).

The show tapes in the afternoon on the West Coast, and as Schwarzenegger announced his intentions to the live studio audience they went crazy. As reported by Tumulty and McCarthy of *Time*, Gorton, at first, thought Schwarzenegger was possibly joking with the crowd, and after the first commercial break he was ejected from the studio for "using his cell phone to begin alerting Schwarzenegger's other clueless advisers." During the taping Schwarzenegger spoke excitedly with Leno and promised to "pump up Sacramento" because the politicians there were not doing their jobs.

He blamed Davis by name and paraphrased a famous scene from the film *Network* by stating: "We are mad as hell and we're not going to take it anymore." Adding, "I know they're going to throw everything at me and say I have no experience and I'm a womanizer and I'm a terrible guy . . . [but] I do not have to bow to any special interests. I have plenty of money. No one can pay me off. Trust me: No one." With that, Schwarzenegger left the stage and held an impromptu press conference with reporters. While there had been earlier concerns that his wife, Maria Shriver of the famous Kennedy clan, had not wanted him to run, he immediately said that she supported him "no matter what."

With this appearance political media entered a new era. The line was now completely blurred between entertainment, news, reality television, and politics. Never before had a candidate announced on national television that he would run for governor, and while aging actors had run for the seat before and won (Ronald Reagan served from 1967 to 1975), none were of the magnitude of Schwarzenegger with seven of his movies grossing more than $100 million each. Entertainment reporters now had their biggest story of the year and political reporters had theirs as well. National and international coverage of the television spectacle over the next few days was swift and often humorous. With an abundance of Schwarzenegger movie titles to play off of, headlines included: "Total Recall," complete with full-color, front-page pictures of Schwarzenegger in character from his films (*New York Daily News*); "Governator" (*New York Post*); "The Day After: Calif. Recall Election Is Script-Worthy" (*USA Today*); and "Ahhnold!?" (*Time*).

People from the Hollywood film industry also chimed in concerning the newest story to cross political and entertainment boundaries. On August 8 *USA Today* reporters Ann Oldenburg and Andy Seiler quoted veteran TV producer Harry Thomason giving a slight warning to Schwarzenegger by saying, "The difference between the entertainment business and politics is that people in the entertainment business are nice." In that same story, longtime movie critic Leonard Maltin praised the new candidate by saying, "Nobody plays the game of self-promotion better than Arnold Schwarzenegger. He has always understood how to work the media." By the end of the election, Maltin's words would prove to be prophetic not just relative to the entertainment media but to the political media as well, who were never quite able to get a handle on the Schwarzenegger campaign and were often pushed aside for exclusive interviews with the mainstream entertainment press.

And how did Gray Davis react to the hullabaloo surrounding the Jay Leno announcement? In a post-election interview with Beth Fouhy of the Associated Press published November 9 in the *Fresno Bee,* Davis "recalled

the sinking feeling he had" when Schwarzenegger made the announcement. "I knew it wasn't good news. These superstars are in the subconscious
of all Americans—we've seen these folks for years. And the only reason
they're superstars is there's a reservoir of good will for them. I've beaten plenty
of wealthy people, but they were just mere mortals. I had to take down a
megastar."

Bring on the Other Players

While Richard Riordan provided plenty of commentary about the
Schwarzenegger appearance in the days that followed, it was said he too
was caught by surprise by the televised announcement and was not happy
with his friend for surprising him in this manner. He signaled immediately
that he would not enter the race, though, and would support the actor-turned-
politician. Darrell Issa's retreat from the scene was not so calm, cool, and
collected. After basically bankrolling the entire signature-gathering drive,
the 49-year-old Issa understood the star power associated with
Schwarzenegger, and in an emotional, teary-eyed news conference on
Thursday, August 7 he backed out of the race. He stated that his mission
was "accomplished" and that "in 61 days [Davis] will be gone."[7]

The same day in front of nearly 50-odd members of the media,
Schwarzenegger picked up his filing papers in Los Angeles and got a taste
of what the political media was interested in. His first question from
reporters that day was: "What is your plan to cut the state budget?" He
responded by saying that, "we will have a plan very soon," but he avoided
any more specifics. Political reporters throughout the campaign would
soon find out things would not get much better, and this was all part of the
Schwarzenegger campaign plan from the beginning. Ted Harbert, a former
top executive at NBC and friend of Schwarzenegger, told Bernard Weintraub
of the *New York Times* on August 10 that Schwarzenegger's plan was
always to save money "by using free media. When you have name recognition like him, you can go directly to the people." In a *Philadelphia
Inquirer* story of Sunday, August 10 by Reuters writer Arthur Spiegelman,
veteran journalist and Reagan biographer Lou Cannon stated bluntly: "I
don't have a quarrel if the whole country thinks California is crazy, but there's
nothing unusual about a film star running for office. It is a major industry
in the state."

Continuing on the Republican side, former gubernatorial candidate Bill
Simon was still flirting with running as was former baseball commissioner

and 1984 Olympics organizer Peter Ueberroth. Little-known Republican state senator Tom McClintock also took out papers to run and was gearing up for the campaign. McClintock had been an outspoken supporter of the recall at the February GOP convention and was considered a solid, classic conservative with strong support from some members of the business community and religious right. As with the 2002 gubernatorial race, the Republican leadership was divided on the type of candidate to support early on, with many fearing that Schwarzenegger's centrist views on abortion and gun control signaled he was really a RINO (Republican in Name Only). Also, it was reported that he had not voted in five of the past 11 statewide elections. What Schwarzenegger's people understood early, however, was the atypical structure of this election and that no real primary vote was going to take place. As discussed earlier, the names of all qualified candidates were going to be listed on the ballot, Democrat, Republican, and independent alike.

On the Democratic side, State Insurance Commissioner John Garamendi toyed with the idea of entering the race for several days but decided against it. So by August 8 all eyes were on Cruz Bustamante. His earlier statements about avoiding the race seemed meaningless now as Bustamante was clearly positioning himself to run.

On that historic Friday night, the day before hundreds of people filed to run against him, Gray Davis appeared live on HBO's *Real Time with Bill Maher* to denounce the recall again, stating: "Leadership is more than snappy one-liners." The next day the California Highway Patrol reported that a motorcade carrying the governor sped 94 mph in a 55-mph zone in San Luis Obispo County. The entourage was chased for five miles before a CHP officer, who was part of the motorcade, asked the pursuing officer to "back off." The officer in charge of the motorcade was reprimanded for breaking traffic laws, but no citations were written. A strange ending to a tough week for Davis.

On Saturday the 9th there were not too many surprises. As Dean Murphy wrote the following day in the *New York Times:* "In keeping with the recall's metastasis from grass-roots democracy to sureality TV, spectators and camera crews outnumbered candidates at some county election offices . . . [and] a cattle pen was set up outside" one of them near Los Angeles "for the paparazzi." Schwarzenegger, Bill Simon, Peter Ueberroth, Tom McClintock, and Bustamante all filed to run.

A new name also surfaced, that of political columnist Arianna Huffington, who chose to file as an independent. Huffington's ex-husband, Michael, had challenged Diane Feinstein during her reelection bid in

1994 but lost in a tight race. Arianna Huffington had never run for political office before although she had been a strong supporter of Republican candidates in the past. She now vowed to run against the parties as the only serious female candidate in the race. Her personal fortune, in the millions, seemed to make her a formidable challenger, but her biggest claim-to-fame early on was showing up at the same elections office as Schwarzenegger on the day he filed to try and steal some of the media spotlight. She was roundly criticized in the press for the move. The other serious candidate in the race was Green Party hopeful Peter Miguel Camejo. He had run for the governorship under the Green label in 2002 and had received nearly 5% of the statewide vote. While admittedly underfunded, Camejo would prove to be a formidable debater later in the campaign, and he and Huffington made a few joint appearances early on since both were trying to go after the same type of independent-minded voters, who were upset with the two major parties. Neither would ever get nearly the coverage of the early frontrunners, Schwarzenegger and Bustamante.

The list of other candidates who filed that Saturday and eventually made the cut was a who's who of oddballs, former stars, and wannabes. *Hustler* magazine publisher Larry Flynt joined the group, as did child-star Gary Coleman (from the 1970s show *Diff'rent Strokes*). Many dubbed Coleman "the other Arnold," because of the name of his famous television character. His trademark "What you talkin' 'bout, Willis?" was resurrected from the lexicon and used throughout the campaign. The comedian Gallagher of watermelon-smashing fame got involved, as did an electrical engineer named Michael Jackson; an Edward Kennedy; a Richard Simmons; a Dan Feinstein; a George B. Schwartzman; a Los Angeles billboard model named Angelyne; Ned Roscoe, owner of the Cigarettes Cheaper! discount chain; Jack Grisham, front man for the punk band TSOL; a porn star; and a gentleman named Trek Thunder Kelly who asked people to vote for him, "thus breaking the Seventh Seal and incurring Armageddon." The media occasionally covered some of these individuals but mainly as a sideshow to the larger event.

After all was said and done there were 135 candidates whose names appeared on the October 7 ballot—50 Democrats, 42 Republicans, and 43 independents or third-party individuals. These numbers are particularly interesting considering the early charge by Davis that the recall was a blatant attempt by the right to take over the governorship. It appeared there were more Democrats than Republicans willing to replace him, with the floodgates partially being opened by Bustamante's entrance in the race.

Meanwhile, Schwarzenegger made the cover of *Time, Newsweek,* and *People* (with Maria) that week and appeared on *Today, Good Morning America,* and a number of other national shows. Former governor Jerry Brown stated unequivocally in an interview with Martin Kasindorf of *USA Today* on August 11 that the former body builder was clearly "on top. It's his to lose." On CNN's television interview show *Aaron Brown's Newsnight* that same evening, political analyst Jeff Greenfield said Schwarzenegger's entrance into the race was "a perfect storm for the media age." GOP consultant Ed Rollins, in the same show, remarked: "I've never seen anything like it." Adding, "California is the ultimate television state," and that Schwarzenegger would be an excellent candidate because, as an actor "he's gonna listen to people. . . . he's used to taking directions . . . [and] he's surrounded by a strong team."

Two interesting side issues came up at this time, however, concerning the media. The National Association of Broadcasters sent an alert to its California members concerning the equal-time provision. While covering the Schwarzenegger campaign it was apparent that equal time would not have to be given to all 134 of Schwarzenegger's opponents each day, but the Federal Communications Commission rules were clear that the networks should not be showing any Schwarzenegger movies, which could be seen as supporting his candidacy. All agreed and cooperated.[8] Some media outlets were getting criticized as well for too much coverage of the Schwarzenegger campaign. This came up throughout the eight-week campaign and can be summarized in a scathing letter to the editor printed in *USA Today* on August 13. A reader warned the paper that it had become Schwarzenegger's de facto "public relations firm" and continuously used a "large picture" of the actor alongside "small" photos of Davis and Bustamante. These were interesting angles on the larger media story that are worth reflecting upon.

Additionally, a number of national columnists and political writers of all political stripes became jaded with the recall process and the nonstop media coverage. In an editorial column published August 15 in the *Fresno Bee,* E. J. Dionne Jr. of the *Washington Post Writers Group* called the affair a "national scandal" after quoting an Associated Press bureau chief's admission that they were covering the recall, "pretty much all day, all the time." Dionne lamented that the coverage resulted in "a vicious cycle that leads to the infantilization of politics," with television telling "voters almost nothing about what is going on." He argued that citizens had become mere "spectators to a distant clash in which celebrity is the only thing that matters." Political scientist Larry Sabato of the University of Virginia wrote a commentary for the *Los Angeles Times* editorial page August 22 calling the process a "mob-ocracy" that would only lead to a flurry of recalls by "transient majorities." Fox News was accused of "political assassination" in its coverage of Cruz Bustamante by *Universal Press Syndicate* writers Roberto Rodriguez and Patrisia Gonzales on September 8 in one of their columns. George Will, also of the *Washington Post* Writers Group, declared October 9 in a *Fresno Bee* editorial that the recall was simply "a riot of millionaires masquerading as a 'revolt of the people.'"

The Eight-Week Campaign

Over the next two weeks the candidates assembled their campaigns and tried to raise money for the inevitable television advertising assault in ways that were occasionally sophisticated and often not very sophisticated at all. Gallagher received press attention for standing outside of the U.S. Treasury in Washington, D.C., with a giant steel bucket trying to collect funds, and other candidates tried to get as much free media as possible or collect funds on their Websites. The frontrunners, Schwarzenegger, Bustamante, Simon, Ueberroth, Huffington, Camejo, and McClintock traveled the state looking for support anywhere they could find it and also used the national Sunday news shows, such as *Meet the Press*, when they could get the coverage. Talk radio became an important tool for many, but Schwarzenegger consistently had the upper hand, and he vowed to spend whatever it would take to win. Estimates of his personal fortune ranged from $200 to $800 million, and he was clearly the wealthiest person who had ever run for governor of California. He also began to surround himself with top names from business and politics, naming former U.S. Secretary of State George Schultz and billionaire investor Warren Buffett to his team of economic advisors. Many members of former governor Pete Wilson's team also joined the Schwarzenegger camp including Don Sipple, Sean Walsh, and Bob White. These were individuals who understood California politics and could keep the candidate on message.

Schwarzenegger's first ads began running Wednesday, August 20, two weeks after the Jay Leno appearance. The ads were mostly 60-second spots with the candidate talking into the camera about his background and leadership skills. He spent over $200,000 alone in the San Francisco market during this first one-week buy and approximately $1.5 million statewide. For media companies the recall was turning out to be the source of a nice chunk of change during an otherwise unremarkable advertising season. In late August financial consulting firms Legg Mason and J.P. Morgan estimated, in separate reports, that over $50 million would be spent on political ads during the recall. Among radio, television, and direct mail, that number would prove to be fairly accurate when all was said and done.[9] But free media was still the name of the game for the Schwarzenegger camp. At a press conference in Los Angeles on August 21, roughly 160 journalists were on hand, and Schwarzenegger was garnering a lot of attention on the talk-radio circuit. Things were also going well in that media owners were getting on board the Schwarzenegger train. A. Jerrold Perenchio, the Republican chairman and chief executive of Spanish-language Univision Communications Inc. (and former contributor to Gray Davis), joined Schwarzenegger's team of economic advisers that same week.

In a brief broadcast made from a Sacramento television station August 23, Bill Simon quietly dropped out of the race, and pressure was building on the other two key Republicans, McClintock and Ueberroth, to do the same. The first major debate of the race took place September 3 sans Schwarzenegger; it was a dry affair in which only McClintock, Ueberroth, Huffington, Camejo, and Bustamante participated. After a poor showing in which he confessed he was "not a politician" and did not "do good on TV," Ueberroth bowed out within a week.

The Schwarzenegger strategy was to purposely avoid these earlier debates to make sure he could control his message more effectively and to ensure limited free media coverage for his opponents. As expected, the remaining leading candidates called for debates at every turn and attempted to turn Schwarzenegger's absences into an issue, but voters just never seemed to mind his lack of participation. After all, Schwarzenegger was making himself available, just not in the normal way. While the regular candidates debated in relative obscurity in one three-day stretch in September, Schwarzenegger appeared on *Oprah* (with Maria), Howard Stern's radio show, and *Larry King Live*. Schwarzenegger was truly going national with the campaign and getting the media coverage needed to keep it all going. As campaign aide Mike Murphy stated on MSNBC after the election, as reported in a *Los Angeles Time* story of October 10 by Ronald Brownstein, "participating in more debates would have trapped the candidate 'in a conventional political campaign' that would have diluted his unconventional appeal."

As the *Sacramento Bee* reported later in its online edition October 3, "Schwarzenegger topped the most-mentioned list in an August review of

8,000 newspapers, magazines and television news show transcripts. The review by commercial information service Factiva showed 3,404 Schwarzenegger mentions, followed by Davis with 3,166. Lt. Gov. Cruz Bustamante finished a distant third at 1,450." Factiva's own news release for the week ending September 7 showed that the August numbers were no fluke, with Schwarzenegger maintaining a sizable lead over everyone else in the race, including Davis (Factiva 2003).

Republicans held another convention the weekend of September 13, and tremendous pressure was put on Tom McClintock to follow the lead of Simon and Ueberroth and get out of the race, which he never did. He was having money woes at the time, however, and as former state party chairman John Harrington noted in a September 17 article appearing in the *Fresno Bee* by Knight Ridder Newspapers reporter Steven Thomma: "TV is the name of the game, and it can cost $3 million to $4 million a week on TV in L.A. County alone. Tom has not raised that kind of money." Delegates seemed to be falling right in line behind Schwarzenegger, and the weekend coverage went well for the movie star. As John Ellis of the *Fresno Bee* reported on September 20, over 260 media credentials were distributed for the convention (roughly five times the normal number), guaranteeing saturation coverage.

Over the next week the Democrats were gearing up for the final three weeks of the campaign by bringing in some heavyweights of their own. Former president Bill Clinton campaigned with Davis and Bustamante in Los Angeles, and in the days to come he was followed by former vice president Al Gore, the Reverend Jesse Jackson, and several U.S. senators. This garnered the best press coverage for Davis to date, and he was as energetic as ever on the campaign trail.

For Bustamante, fundraising was going reasonably well, and, in opposition to some other polls, a *Los Angeles Times* poll released that week showed him with a slight lead over Schwarzenegger. His main concern was that he was getting some negative coverage for accepting several million dollars in campaign contributions from Indian gaming tribes, and Schwarzenegger began running ads against him saying that he was, essentially, in the pocket of these special interests. In other words, Bustamante was getting caught in an odd Catch-22. He desperately needed money to compete with the others and he was having some success in this area, but the criticism of his reliance on gaming funds was hurting him on other fronts.

If there was a partial momentum shift in this race, it came during this stretch in mid-September where the Democrats appeared to be almost holding their own against the Schwarzenegger juggernaut. All of it came to a halt rather suddenly, however, when a strange court case concerning the recall and the first real debate of the race took center stage.

Adding a courtroom drama to a political race is nothing new in American politics, and one need only remember the five-week court challenge in Florida in 2000 that helped determine the presidency. Nearly a dozen court cases had been moving through the system as the recall campaign played itself out, and many had been around since the spring of 2003. Early cases focused on the legitimacy of signature-gathering firms, the legality of the recall petitions, and other technical issues. Cases had been brought by pro-recall forces to speed things up, and Davis's camp had countered with some cases of their own just to slow things down or delay the vote. While most of these had wound themselves down by this point, a three-judge panel of the federal appellate court based in San Francisco threw a wrench in the works on September 15 declaring that the vote should officially be postponed.

The essence of this case, *Southwest Voter Registration Education Project v. California Secretary of State Kevin Shelley,* was that a number of counties in California were using outdated, punch-card systems in the October 7 election, and the machines had been ruled "significantly prone to error." These were the same machines that had caused the problems in Florida in 2000, and California was in the process of phasing them out before the 2004 presidential primaries. The plaintiffs in the case argued that going ahead with the October 7 recall using faulty equipment could disenfranchise hundreds of thousands of voters. The state took the position that they would be happy to wait until new machines were put in place in these counties, but they simply *had* to call the recall election for when they did, and so the machines in question would have to be utilized one last time.[10]

For several days it was unclear if the recall would actually go forward, and every major paper in the state covered the story in great detail. A full, 11-judge panel of the Ninth Circuit Court of Appeals agreed to hear oral arguments in the case on September 22, and observers waited patiently to see what would happen. After an exciting hour of arguments, broadcast live throughout the state on many networks (including C-SPAN), the larger panel voted to overrule the earlier panel's recommendation to halt the election. Things would go forward as planned. Most of the candidates publicly stated that they had hoped this would be the case, but it was an obvious interruption in the momentum gained by the Democrats. The biggest event of the campaign would come two days after the court case and prove to be the beginning of the end for Governor Davis and Cruz Bustamante.

Billed by Arnold Schwarzenegger as the "Super Bowl," all five remaining serious candidates held their first and only debate as a group at California State University, Sacramento, on the night of September 24. The 90-minute event was planned by the California Broadcasters Association and was heavily hyped by the press. The candidates sat at two long tables, partly facing each other in a kind of V-formation. Schwarzenegger, McClintock, and Camejo sat at one table and Huffington and Bustamante sat at the other. In the center, Association president Stan Statham acted as moderator. Historians will surely differ on the potency of this debate, but few would argue that it was regal, informative, or well organized. It was a zoo.

In an obvious ploy to get Schwarzenegger to participate, the broadcasters released the questions that were to be asked at the debate days in advance. In front of millions of viewers, Statham defended this tactic in the first three minutes of the broadcast, stating that they wanted to create "a debate of debates" and had been "successful" in doing so. Statham editorialized throughout the evening, interrupted some candidates and not others, diverted from the given questions on numerous occasions, and generally let the candidates simply shout at each other most of the time. Barbs and insults flew back and forth, and at one point Huffington interrupted Schwarzenegger; Schwarzenegger then interrupted Huffington, and she shot back: "This is completely impolite. This is the way you treat women." Bustamante, Camejo, and McClintock generally remained civil for most of the debate, although Bustamante was roundly criticized afterward for being too sarcastic in some comments and for acting too aloof, à la Al Gore in his first 2000 debate with George Bush. At one point a clearly gleeful but exasperated Statham said: "Ladies and gentlemen, this is not Comedy Central."

The crowds loved it. Many Californians watched the debate, and afterward it appeared that Schwarzenegger's gamble to only show up at one debate had paid off. He did not shoot himself in the foot in any way and came across as reasonably knowledgeable on state issues. He was calm much of the time and unlike most of the others showed a sense of humor. His supporters seemed pleased that they now had the "cover" they were looking for to continue to support his candidacy with less than two weeks remaining in the race. While Bustamante needed a knockout blow at the event to show he could go toe to toe with Schwarzenegger, things did not go that well for him. Camejo and McClintock looked the most knowledgeable of all of the candidates, but in polls released right after the debate it did not prove to help them at all. Within a week Arianna Huffington came to realize she was not going to do well in the election and dropped out of the race.

This left Schwarzenegger, Bustamante, Camejo, and McClintock as the most serious candidates on the second part of the recall ballot ten days out from the election; Gray Davis began to get even more aggressive in these closing days. It was reported that his internal poll numbers, mainly from polls taken by the state teacher's union, were not looking good, and on Friday the 26 he publicly challenged Schwarzenegger to a debate, "right here, right now." Followers of American political campaigns know that for the most part, incumbents avoid their opponents at all costs, and it appeared here that Davis was breaking this cardinal rule in a last-minute attempt to save his job. CNN's Larry King offered to host a debate between the two candidates that weekend, but the Schwarzenegger camp declined immediately. As Erica Werner of the Associated Press wrote in the *Fresno Bee* of September 30, Davis humorously countered, "I don't know what Mr. Schwarzenegger is afraid of. I mean I never participated in a Mr. Universe contest. I weigh maybe 165 pounds on a good day. [Why is he] on the run?"

A majority of California newspapers weighed in that Sunday with their endorsements, and it did not look good for the Democrats. The *Los Angeles Times, San Jose Mercury News,* and *Sacramento Bee* did urge a "no" vote on the recall, but declined to endorse any candidates as a replacement. The *San-Diego Union-Tribune* called for Davis's removal and supported Schwarzenegger as a reasonable replacement. In total, Schwarzenegger received the endorsement of four major dailies; Bustamante and the others received none.

Relative to the money race just in the last reporting period of the campaign, Dan Morain and Joel Rubin of the *Los Angeles Times* reported on September 26 that: "campaign spending had reached $50 million dollars" in the race, and Schwarzenegger was well ahead of any of his rivals. The actor raised $13.6 million up to that point and had spent $13.4 of it mostly on television ads—$5.4 million on production and air time and $1.4 million on printed ads in the previous four-week stretch. (By the time it was all over Schwarzenegger had invested over $8.5 million of his own money in the race, the largest contribution of any single individual to any candidate or committee. His campaign brought in $21.9 million in total.)[11] Bustamante had raised and spent nearly $9.4 million, almost all of it on television ads, and Richie Ross, his campaign manager, stated: "We've been in a day-to-day battle for money to buy TV ads." Davis had raised and spent nearly $9 million; McClintock, $1.6 million, and Camejo approximately

$50,000. When Huffington left the race it was reported that she was approximately $138,000 in debt.

Free media continued to help all of the candidates, but Schwarzenegger, as frontrunner, benefited the most in the final month of the campaign. George Raine of the *San Francisco Chronicle* quoted an Associated Press study in a (page A-13), September 30 story showing the extent of coverage the recall was getting nationally. According to the study, from August 1 to September 25, the nightly newscasts on NBC, ABC. and CBS devoted a total of 127 minutes to the recall versus 36 minutes going to all nine Democratic candidates running for president.

In the final days one other major story appeared, and this one presented the biggest problem to date for Schwarzenegger. The *Los Angeles Times* ran a scathing story on Thursday, October 2, claming that six women had come forward to say they had been touched by Schwarzenegger in a sexual manner without their consent. As Schwarzenegger stated on the *Tonight Show* two months previously, he knew allegations of womanizing would be tossed at him, but the credibility of the *Times* story was tough to question. One of the story's writers was a former Pulitzer Prize winner, and the *Times* vowed they had vetted the story properly and would never have run it unless they felt the reporting was accurate. Each of the women explained to reporters that Schwarzenegger had harassed her, and the Schwarzenegger camp decided that the best defense was to go on the offensive. Schwarzenegger admitted that day that he had behaved "badly" in the past and that he would clear up the accusations after the election. He accused the *Times* of holding the story until the last weekend of the race to upset undecided voters and that the report was "trash politics." The *Times* stood by the piece, and the impact it had on voters seemed to be negligible. It appears most voters had already made up their mind about the recall, and turnout at Schwarzenegger events remained as strong as ever. Maria Shriver also began appearing with her husband at most events during this period.

Schwarzenegger spent the final days before the vote touring the state in a bus caravan with each bus named after one of his movies. His personal bus was called *Running Man;* his staff followed on *Total Recall,* and literally 200 reporters and camera people followed on *Predators One, Two,* and *Three.* Hurting for stories, the media actually began just interviewing other media for much of this trip, and a humorous account of these stories can be found in the *California Insider* writings of Daniel Weintraub of the *Sacramento Bee* ("Online" 2003). On October 3 the Associated Press reported: "Television networks are sending their big guns to California for

Tuesday's recall vote, eager to tap into the political circus that could make Arnold Schwarzenegger the state's next governor. Tom Brokaw, Peter Jennings, and Dan Rather will be heading West, and cable news networks CNN, Fox News Channel, and MSNBC have put special election-night plans in place to cover a race that has shoved other political news to the side." Meanwhile, it was reported that in Sacramento the Davis administration had ordered nearly 350 empty archival boxes from the state library to begin packing away important state papers.

Election Day

When Tuesday October 7 rolled around it was relatively clear to most observers that Gray Davis was not going to be able to save his seat, and Arnold Schwarzenegger would be the next governor. Following a turnout rate of roughly 51% in November 2002, turnout on this day was strong— 61% of eligible voters, or 15.4 million Californians. On the first ballot question to recall Davis the official votes were 55.4% (4,976,274) "Yes," 44.6% (4,007,783) "No," and 4.6% (429,431) chose not to cast a vote. Davis became only the second governor in U.S. history to be removed from office by the voters. On the second question of who should become the new governor, the results were startling: Schwarzenegger won outright with 48.6% (4,206,284), Bustamante came in a distant second with 31.5% (2,724,874), McClintock came in third with 13.5% (1,161,287), Camejo came in fourth place with 2.8% (242, 247), and Huffington rounded out the top five with 0.6% (47,505). Of note, just following Peter Ueberroth in sixth place, Larry Flynt pulled in 17,458 votes in seventh place, and Gary Coleman came in eighth with 14,242.[12]

On election night Gray Davis conceded at 9:50 P.M. (PST) from his election night headquarters at the Millennium Biltmore Hotel in Los Angeles. He stated in his gracious speech that he accepted the "judgment" of the voters and that he had "placed a call to Mr. Arnold Schwarzenegger" to congratulate him on the victory. He asked all Californians to "put the division behind" them, and he appeared loose and sincere. Among those standing with Davis on the podium were his wife Sharon and the Reverend Jesse Jackson. Two nights later Davis would make a cameo appearance on the *Late Show with David Letterman* and read a Top Ten List of suggestions for Schwarzenegger to consider. They included: "When you realize you don't know what you're doing, give me a call" and "To improve your approval rating, go on Leno; when you get kicked out, go on Letterman."

Following Davis's concession, Schwarzenegger appeared on a stage at the Century Plaza Hotel in Los Angeles following an introduction by none other than Jay Leno. Leno received loud applause from the crowd as he departed the stage and made way for Governor-Elect Schwarzenegger, his wife Maria and her parents, Eunice and Sargent Shriver. Schwarzenegger's speech was also a gracious one, and he promised the crowd that: "I will not fail you; I will not disappoint you and I will not let you down."

Bustamante and McClintock both gave concession speeches that evening from their hotels in Sacramento, and McClintock made a point in his speech of pledging "his wholehearted support" for Schwarzenegger.

Final Thoughts on the Media and the Recall

The day before the election it was said by Jim Rutenberg of the *New York Times* that the Schwarzenegger campaign prompted a "role reversal among [the] media," and this seems like an accurate way to describe the unprecedented campaign. As noted earlier, most media frenzies have the media devouring the victim, but here the reverse was the case. It is important to note, however, that the reversal was particularly painful for the daily political press. Unlike the entertainment press, they had virtually no one-on-one contact with Schwarzenegger, and when they did, it was in an extremely controlled environment. Their frustration showed through in story after story as the campaign progressed, and the voters did not seem to mind terribly that their main source of information about the actor came from paid ads and television shows like *Entertainment Tonight*. Mainstream political reporters were pretty much cut out of the loop early on, and there was not much they could do about it. Lengthy pieces on candidate positions were virtually nonexistent during the abbreviated campaign, and the Schwarzenegger camp in particular doled out specifics in very small quantities and on their time frame—no one else's.

Implications for this kind of campaign and for the media influence in the race are far reaching. In a reflective piece titled "Schwarzenegger Approach Would Be Hard to Copy," Ronald Brownstein of the *Los Angeles Times* speculated on October 10 that Schwarzenegger's victory might "encourage the recruitment of more celebrity candidates" and those "with the resources to largely fund their own campaigns." Granted, wealthy candidates have always been appealing to the parties, but they may have even more incentive to enter races now based on Schwarzenegger's success and seemingly easy ride. Brownstein quotes GOP pollster Frank Luntz in adding: "What defines qualified to the media is different than to the public . . . [they have] a completely different evaluation of whether or not Arnold is qualified." Brownstein concludes by stating that: "Schwarzenegger's strategy wasn't cost free: an exit poll conducted for the television networks found that 63% of voters believed he hadn't sufficiently addressed issues facing the state." Thus, the public does not appear to be well served by this kind of campaign.

The media certainly appeared to benefit in several ways from the race, however. In addition to the advertising dollars, Nielsen reported that television stations in the Los Angeles market nabbed some of their highest ratings for their election coverage and late local news. The *Arts and Entertainment* network stated it was "fast-tracking production on an original biopic about [Schwarzenegger] titled *See Arnold Run*" (Romano 2003). And on the video front, sales of Schwarzenegger films heated up, including rereleases of almost everything in his catalog. Marc Rashba, vice president of catalog marketing for Columbia TriStar home video, stated it best: "The media circus and frenzy it created and how it renewed interest in a single human being, that's something I don't think anyone, all the studios combined, could have paid for. It was ubiquitous" (Germain 2003).

Dan Walters, longtime columnist for the *Sacramento Bee,* penned an editorial piece on October 12 in which he claimed that the recall "was the most unusual campaign for high political office that California had ever seen, one that broke many—perhaps all—of the informal rules in the book." He quoted Schwarzenegger adviser George Gorton as saying: "This [was] not a position election. This [was] a character election," and Walters suggested that as a campaigner Schwarzenegger "was nearly flawless." In a column published November 24, Walters added: "it makes one long for the days when a reporter could simply walk into the Capitol suite . . . and talk to whomever was around, even the governor."

What else can be learned concerning the recall race relative to the uniqueness of the Schwarzenegger campaign? Was this some kind of fluke? Can anything really be generalized from this race concerning other candidates for office? I think that the Schwarzenegger campaign represents the third or fourth major race of its type in the last few decades that concerned itself with entertainers from outside the normal political realm who ran successful, interesting races at just the right time.

In California, any discussion of this type of campaign would have to begin with Reagan's victory in 1966 but would be followed by a look at Sonny Bono's successful campaign for Congress and Clint Eastwood's successful run for the mayorship of Carmel. California's political culture is particularly accepting of entertainers-turned-politicians, but it is not alone in this regard. Governor Jesse Ventura's election in Minnesota might be the most interesting example outside California to point to, and his voluntarily leaving office after just one term illuminates the problems that some of these individuals run into. In their recent book, *Celebrity Politics,* Darrell West and John Orman (2003) explore the careers of many of these individuals and help us understand that their track record is mixed. As West and Orman point out, entertainers-turned-politicians often have difficulty governing and maintaining the same coalition of support that held their campaigns together.

In many ways it appears entertainers-turned-politicians begin to resemble the very individuals they usually rail against in their campaigns once they see how complicated things actually are away from the campaign trail. Governing is a complicated business, and some of these individuals lack the political skills necessary to enact promised legislation or "clean house" in the way they promised to the voters. This recall race does tell us, however, that celebrity politics remains alive and well in America, and the voters appear continually accepting of these kinds of candidates. Celebrity *governance* is a different story, though, and it is my feeling that Arnold Schwarzenegger may go the way of Jesse Ventura and opt out of running for another term. I say this for two reasons: (1) Plain and simple, Schwarzenegger does not need the money, power, or prestige that comes with the position and is often sought by officeholders. As one of the top movie stars in the world he has already attained all of these things, and while the governorship gives him a certain kind of national legitimacy that he has not enjoyed previously, I would question whether his appetite for political life in Sacramento will remain strong. (2) When we usually discuss governors' styles in the political science literature (Harrigan and Nice 2001), one of the categories that often gets mentioned concerns a type of governor known as The Frustrated Warrior. The trademark of these types of individuals is that they sincerely hope to change the political system and they run their campaigns as motivated elements of change. Upon governing, however, Frustrated Warriors are unable to get many of their programs adopted. This fact, along with the fact that the personality traits of these types can lead to poor communication with legislative leaders, leads me to believe that Schwarzenegger, while always the warrior in his movies, may find the task too frustrating over time.

What does this race tell us about the media, politics, and political advertising in general and for the future? Several things are apparent about the latest relationship among these entities looking back at the California recall.

1. Most of the public is still getting the vast majority of their political information from the mass media and advertisements. The public was literally educated by television and radio during the recall, which is not terribly different than in most races, but during an abbreviated campaign this was not to their advantage. As noted earlier, time was rarely given to candidate platforms during the race, and much of the focus related to scandal-style stories and personality issues. On the scandal front, Bustamante was continually blasted for accepting so much money from Indian gaming, and Schwarzenegger faced repeated stories (not just in the final days of the campaign from the *Los Angeles Times*) about infidelity, his lack of participation in substantive debates, and his cloudy prescriptions for fixing the budget mess in Sacramento. While there is often criticism leveled in some arenas when campaigns drag on too long, in the case of the recall the public would have been much better served by a lengthier, more thoughtful campaign. This style of campaign was not what the Schwarzenegger camp wanted or encouraged, but the media did a disservice to the voters by consistently emphasizing style over substance. The old chestnut "just giving the people what they want" would not necessarily have rung true in this race because the voters became so caught up in the process so quickly that I am unsure if their needs were ever truly gauged. From day one of the campaign, flashy visual images, clichés, and sound bites ruled the day. Also, while California voters are used to raucous, expensive campaigns, they are also used to careful deliberation of candidates and lengthy direct democracy ballot questions that have been put before them in the past. For the recall much of that seemed to be thrown out the window as the entire political system "turned topsy-turvy" (Rutenberg 2003).

2. There was reasonable, critical coverage of some political advertisements during the campaign, and this practice should be encouraged in the future. The *Los Angeles Times* and *Sacramento Bee* ran series throughout the race titled "Ad Watch," where the most important ads were analyzed for accuracy and fairness. This process allows voters to gauge the truth behind political ads, but unfortunately its impact on election outcomes is unclear. There is an irony to all of this as well. While most parts of the media were being fed by the recall machine, the credibility of other, more critical parts of the media seems less plausible. Again, it is hard for voters to really know just what to believe in a cam-

paign of this sort where the lines between news and entertainment are so blurred. The onus here is on the media to highlight important aspects of the campaign and provide the most objective coverage possible, but this was the exception and not the rule for the California recall. To be fair, the onus is also on the voters to be more analytical of media coverage and to encourage their local media outlets to cover more substantive issues. In theory, this suggests that a two-way dialogue between the media and those being served is the best way to approach a political campaign of this sort.

3. On a final point, candidates should be aware that the media "honeymoon," which often occurs during a campaign after one or the other candidate becomes the media darling, can be over rather quickly. Candidates, no matter how popular, should be braced for this inevitability and realize that the media can be a fickle partner. While Ronald Reagan enjoyed somewhat of a lengthy honeymoon as the Teflon President, this is certainly not the case for most elected officials. For Schwarzenegger, in particular, if the entertainment press begins to cover him less and the political press increases their coverage, he could be in for a difficult time in Sacramento. This is the probable scenario given the accelerated 24-hour news cycle and the entertainment media's appetite for new material.

As Schwarzenegger took the oath of office from state Supreme Court Chief Justice Ronald George on November 17, one very positive aspect of the media coverage did come to light. A number of state television stations were considering opening up Sacramento bureaus for the first time in over two decades, and coverage of state politics was expected to rise. Lou Cannon, Ronald Reagan's biographer, quoted an anonymous Los Angeles television producer at the time as saying: "We gave Arnold so much coverage, good and bad, that we can't drop out now because we've helped create an interest in what he does next" (Cannon 2003, p. 29). Schwarzenegger himself agreed to be more open with the media, and in an interview covered by Gary Delsohn of the *Sacramento Bee* published November 19, the new governor proclaimed: "We will share everything with the press. This will be a very unusual situation here. We will have many press conferences in the future because, as I have said to you all many times before . . . everything that I've done in my life, the press has been always a very essential and important part."

APPENDIX A

OFFICIAL BALLOT / BOLETA OFICIAL
STATEWIDE SPECIAL ELECTION / ELECCIÓN ESTATAL ESPECIAL
OCTOBER 7, 2003, FRESNO COUNTY / 7 DE OCTUBRE DEL 2003, CONDADO DE FRESNO

INSTRUCTIONS TO VOTERS: You must use a black pen, blue pen or No. 2 pencil to completely fill in the oval to the left of your choice.
INSTRUCCIONES AL ELECTOR: Utilice usted una pluma o bolígrafo de tinta negra o azul, o bien un lápiz No. 2, para llenar completamente el óvalo al lado izquierdo de su preferencia.

Fill in oval like this ●   Llene el óvalo así ●

STATE / ESTADO

Shall GRAY DAVIS be recalled (removed) from the office of Governor?
¿Debería ser GRAY DAVIS destituido (removido) del cargo de Gobernador?

○ YES, SÍ
○ NO, NO

Candidates to succeed GRAY DAVIS as Governor if he is recalled:
Los candidatos a suceder a GRAY DAVIS como Gobernador en caso de que sea destituido:

Vote for One   Vote por Uno

Candidate	Occupation	Party
FRANK A. MACALUSO, JR.	Physician/Medical Doctor / Médico	Democratic/Demócrata
PAUL "CHIP" MAILANDER	Attorney / Abogado	Democratic/Demócrata
DENNIS DUGGAN MCMAHON	Banker / Banquero	Republican/Republicano
MIKE MCNEILLY	Artist / Artista	Republican/Republicano
MIKE P. MCCARTHY	Used Car Dealer / Vendedor de automóviles usados	Independent/Independiente
BOB MCCLAIN	Civil Engineer / Ingeniero civil	Independent/Independiente
TOM MCCLINTOCK	State Senator / Senador estatal	Republican/Republicano
JONATHAN MILLER	Small Business Owner / Propietario de pequeña empresa	Democratic/Demócrata
CARL A. MEHR	Businessman / Hombre de negocios	Republican/Republicano
SCOTT A. MEDNICK	Business Executive / Ejecutivo de empresa	Democratic/Demócrata
DORENE MUSILLI	Parent/Educator/Businesswoman / Madre/educadora/mujer de negocios	Republican/Republicano
VAN VO	Radio Producer/Businessman / Productor de radio/hombre de negocios	Republican/Republicano
PAUL W. VANN	Financial Planner / Planificador financiero	Republican/Republicano
JAMES M. VANDEVENTER, JR.	Businessman / Hombre de negocios	Republican/Republicano
BILL VAUGHN	Structural Engineer / Ingeniero estructural	Democratic/Demócrata
MARC VALDEZ	Air Pollution Scientist / Científico de contaminación del aire	Democratic/Demócrata
MOHAMMAD ARIF	Businessman / Hombre de negocio	Independent/Independiente
ANGELYNE	Entertainer / Artista	Independent/Independiente
DOUGLAS ANDERSON	Mortgage Broker / Agente hipotecario	Republican/Republicano
IRIS ADAM	Business Analyst / Analista empresarial	Natural Law-Ley Natural
GEORGE B. SCHWARTZMAN	Businessman / Hombre de negocios	Independent/Independiente
MIKE SCHMIER	Attorney / Abogado	Democratic/Demócrata
DARRIN H. SCHEIDLE	Businessman/Entrepreneur / Hombre de negocios/empresario	Democratic/Demócrata
BILL SIMON	Businessman / Hombre de negocios	Republican/Republicano
RICHARD J. SIMMONS	Attorney/Businessperson / Abogado/hombre de negocios	Independent/Independiente
CHRISTOPHER SPROUL	Environmental Attorney / Abogado ambiental	Democratic/Demócrata
RANDALL D. SPRAGUE	Discrimination Complaint Investigator / Investigador de quejas de discriminación	Republican/Republicano
TIM SYLVESTER	Entrepreneur / Empresario	Democratic/Demócrata
JACK LOYD GRISHAM	Musician/Laborer / Músico/obrero	Independent/Independiente
JAMES H. GREEN	Firefighter/Paramedic/Nurse / Bombero paramédico/enfermero	Democratic/Demócrata
GARRETT GRUENER	High-Tech Entrepreneur / Empresario de alta tecnología	Democratic/Demócrata
GEROLD LEE GORMAN	Engineer / Ingeniero	Democratic/Demócrata
RICH GOSSE	Educator / Educador	Republican/Republicano
LEO GALLAGHER	Comedian / Comediante	Independent/Independiente
JOE GUZZARDI	Teacher/Journalist / Maestro/periodista	Democratic/Demócrata
JON W. ZELLHOEFER	Energy Consultant/Entrepreneur / Consultor de energía/empresario	Republican/Republicano
PAUL NAVE	Businessman/Prizefighter/Father / Hombre de negocios/boxeador/padre	Democratic/Demócrata
ROBERT C. NEWMAN II	Psychologist/Farmer / Psicólogo/agricultor	Republican/Republicano
BRIAN TRACY	Businessman/Consultant / Hombre de negocio/consultor	Independent/Independiente
A. LAVAR TAYLOR	Tax Attorney / Abogado impositivo	Democratic/Demócrata
CHARLES "CHUCK" PINEDA, JR.	State Hearing Officer / Funcionario de audiencias estatales	Democratic/Demócrata
HEATHER PETERS	Mediator / Mediadora	Republican/Republicano
ROBERT "BUTCH" DOLE	Small Business Owner / Propietario de pequeña empresa	Republican/Republicano
SCOTT DAVIS	Business Owner / Propietario de empresa	Independent/Independiente
RONALD J. FRIEDMAN	Physician / Médico	Independent/Independiente
GENE FORTE	Executive Recruiter/Entrepreneur / Reclutador de ejecutivos/empresario	Republican/Republicano
DIANA FOSS		Democratic/Demócrata
LORRAINE (ABNER ZURD) FONTANES	Film Maker / Cineasta	Democratic/Demócrata
WARREN FARRELL	Fathers' Issues Author / Escritor de temas relacionados con padres	Democratic/Demócrata
DAN FEINSTEIN		Democratic/Demócrata
LARRY FLYNT	Publisher / Editor	Democratic/Demócrata
CALVIN Y. LOUIE	CPA / Contador público certificado	Democratic/Demócrata
DICK LANE	Educator / Educador	Democratic/Demócrata
TODD RICHARD LEWIS	Businessman / Hombre de negocios	Independent/Independiente
GARY LEONARD	Photojournalist/Author / Periodista fotográfico/escritor	Democratic/Demócrata
DAVID LAUGHING HORSE ROBINSON	Tribal Chairman / Presidente tribal	Democratic / Demócrata
NEIL ROSCOE	Cigarette Retailer / Vendedor de cigarros al detalle	Libertarian/Libertario
DANIEL C. "DANNY" RAMIREZ	Businessman/Entrepreneur/Father / Hombre de negocios/empresario/padre	Democratic/Demócrata
CHRISTOPHER RANKEN	Planning Commissioner / Comisionado de planificación	Democratic/Demócrata
JEFF RAINFORTH	Marketing Coordinator / Coordinador de mercadotecnia	Independent/Independiente

◯ **BROOKE ADAMS** — Business Executive / Ejecutiva de empresas — Independent/Independiente
◯ **ALEX-ST.JAMES** — Public Policy Strategist / Estratega de política pública — Republican/Republicano
◯ **JIM HOFFMANN** — Teacher / Maestro — Republican/Republicano
◯ **KEN HAMIDI** — State Tax Officer / Funcionario impositivo estatal — Libertarian/Libertario
◯ **SARA ANN HANLON** — Businesswoman / Mujer de negocios — Independent/Independiente
◯ **IVAN A. HALL** — Custom Denture Manufacturer/Fabricante dentaduras postizas media — Green/Verde
◯ **JOHN J. "JACK" HICKEY** — Healthcare District Director / Director de distrito de atención de la salud — Libertarian/Libertario
◯ **RALPH A. HERNANDEZ** — District Attorney Inspector / Inspector de fiscalía — Democratic/Demócrata
◯ **C. STEPHEN HENDERSON** — Teacher / Maestro — Independent/Independiente
◯ **ARIANNA HUFFINGTON** — Author/Columnist/Mother / Escritora/columnista/madre — Independent/Independiente
◯ **ART BROWN** — Firm Writer/Director / Guionista y director de cine — Democratic/Demócrata
◯ **JOEL BRITTON** — Retired Meat Packer / Empacador de carne jubilado — Independent/Independiente
◯ **AUDIE BOCK** — Educator/Small Businesswoman / Educadora/prop. de pequeña empresa — Democratic/Demócrata
◯ **VIK S. BAJWA** — Businessman / Hombre de negocios — Democratic/Demócrata
◯ **BADI BADIOZAMANI** — Entrepreneur/Author/Executive / Empresario/autor/ejecutivo — Independent/Independiente
◯ **VIP BHOLA** — Attorney/Businessman / Abogado/propietario de empresa — Republican/Republicano
◯ **ED W. BEARD** — Businessman / Hombre de negocios — Republican/Republicano
◯ **ED BEYER** — Chief Operations Officer / Funcionario principal de operaciones — Republican/Republicano
◯ **JOHN CHRISTOPHER BURTON** — Civil Rights Lawyer / Abogado de derechos civiles — Independent/Independiente
◯ **CRUZ M. BUSTAMANTE** — Lieutenant Governor / Vicegobernador — Democratic/Demócrata
◯ **CHERYL BLY-CHESTER** — Businesswoman/Environmental Engineer/Mujer de neg./ingeniera amb. — Republican/Republicano
◯ **B.E. SMITH** — Lecturer / Conferencista — Independent/Independiente
◯ **DAVID RONALD SAMS** — Businessman/Producer/Writer / Hombre de negocios/productor/escritor — Republican/Republicano
◯ **JAMIE ROSEMARY SAFFORD** — Business Owner / Propietaria de empresa — Republican/Republicano
◯ **LAWRENCE STEVEN STRAUSS** — Lawyer/Businessperson/Student/Abogado/hombre de neg./estudiante — Democratic/Demócrata
◯ **ARNOLD SCHWARZENEGGER** — Actor/Businessman / Actor/hombre de negocios — Republican/Republicano

◯ **WILLIAM TSANGARES** — Businessperson / Hombre de negocios — Republican/Republicano
◯ **PATRICIA G. TILLEY** — Attorney / Abogada — Independent/Independiente
◯ **DIANE BEALL TEMPLIN** — Attorney/Health/Businessman/Abog./salud/hombre de neg. — American Ind./Ind. Americano
◯ **MARY "MARY CAREY" COOK** — Adult Film Actress/Artist de películas para adultos — Independent/Independiente
◯ **GARY COLEMAN** — Actor / Actor — Independent/Independiente
◯ **TODD CARSON** — Real Estate Developer / Promotor inmobiliario — Republican/Republicano
◯ **PETER MIGUEL CAMEJO** — Financial Investment Advisor / Asesor de inversiones financieras — Green/Verde
◯ **WILLIAM "BILL" S. CHAMBERS** — Retired Switchman/Boilerman / Guardagujas y guardafrenos ferroviario — Republican/Republicano
◯ **MICHAEL CHELI** — Businessman / Hombre de negocios — Independent/Independiente
◯ **ROBERT CULLENBINE** — Retired Businessman / Hombre de negocios jubilado — Democratic/Demócrata
◯ **D. (LOGAN DARROW) CLEMENTS** — Businessman / Hombre de negocios — Republican/Republicano
◯ **S. ISSA** — Engineer / Ingeniero — Republican/Republicano
◯ **BOB LYNN EDWARDS** — Attorney / Abogado — Democratic/Demócrata
◯ **ERIC KOREVAAR** — Scientist/Businessman/Científico/hombre de negocios — Democratic/Demócrata
◯ **STEPHEN L. KNAPP** — Engineer / Ingeniero — Republican/Republicano
◯ **KELLY P. KIMBALL** — Business Executive / Ejecutivo de empresa — Democratic/Demócrata
◯ **D.E. KESSINGER** — Paralegal/Property Manager / Asistente jurídico/administrador de propiedades — Democratic/Demócrata
◯ **EDWARD "ED" KENNEDY** — Businessman/Educator / Hombre de negocios/educador — Democratic/Demócrata
◯ **TREK THUNDER KELLY** — Business Executive/Artist / Ejecutivo de empresa/artista — Independent/Independiente
◯ **JERRY KUNZMAN** — Chief Executive Officer / Funcionario ejecutivo principal — Democratic/Demócrata
◯ **PETER V. UEBERROTH** — Businessman/Olympic Advisor/Hombre de neg./consultor juegos olímpicos — Republican/Republicano
◯ **BILL PRADY** — Television Writer/Producer / Escritor y productor de televisión — Democratic/Demócrata
◯ **DARIN PRICE** — University Chemistry Instructor / Instructor universitario de química — Natural Law/Ley Natural
◯ **GREGORY J. PAWLIK** — Business Owner / Propietario de empresa/hombre de empresa/artista — Republican/Republicano
◯ **LEONARD PADILLA** — Law School President / Presidente de facultad de derecho — Independent/Independiente
◯ **RONALD JASON PALMIERI** — Gay Rights Attorney / Abogado de derechos de homosexuales — Democratic/Demócrata

◯ **KURT E. "TACHIKAZE" RIGHTMYER** — Middleweight Sumo Wrestler / Luchador sumo peso mediano — Independent/Independiente
◯ **DANIEL W. RICHARDS** — Businessman / Hombre de negocios — Republican/Republicano
◯ **KEVIN RICHTER** — Information Technology Manager / Gerente de tecnología informática — Republican/Republicano
◯ **REVA RENEE RENZ** — Small Business Owner / Propietaria de pequeña empresa — Republican/Republicano
◯ **SHARON RUSHFORD** — Businesswoman / Mujer de negocios — Independent/Independiente
◯ **GEORGY RUSSELL** — Software Engineer / Ingeniera de software — Democratic/Demócrata
◯ **MICHAEL J. WOZNIAK** — Retired Police Officer / Oficial de policía jubilado — Democratic/Demócrata
◯ **DANIEL WATTS** — College Student / Estudiante universitario — Green/Verde
◯ **NATHAN WHITECLOUD WALTON** — Student / Estudiante — Independent/Independiente
◯ **MAURICE WALKER** — Real Estate Appraiser / Tasador inmobiliario — Independent/Independiente
◯ **CHUCK WALKER** — Business Intelligence Analyst / Analista de inteligencia empresarial — Republican/Republicano
◯ **LINGEL H. WINTERS** — Consumer Business Attorney / Abogado de consumidores y empresas — Democratic/Demócrata
◯ **C.T. WEBER** — Labor Official/Analyst / Funcionario laboral/analista — Peace and Freedom/Paz y Libertad
◯ **JIM WEBER** — Community College Teacher / Profesor de universidad comunitaria — Democratic/Demócrata
◯ **BRYAN QUINN** — Businessman / Hombre de negocios — Republican/Republicano
◯ **MICHAEL JACKSON** — Satellite Project Manager / Gerente de proyecto de satélite — Democratic/Demócrata
◯ **JOHN "JACK" MORTENSEN** — Contractor/Businessman / Contratista/hombre de negocios — Independent/Independiente
◯ **DARRYL L. MOBLEY** — Businessman/Entrepreneur / Hombre de negocios/empresario — Republican/Republicano
◯ **JEFFREY L. MOCK** — Business Owner / Propietario de empresa — Republican/Republicano
◯ **BRUCE MARGOLIN** — Marijuana Legalization Attorney / Abogado de legalización de marihuana — Democratic/Demócrata
◯ **GINO MARTORANA** — Restaurant Owner / Propietario de restaurante — Republican/Republicano
◯ **PAUL MARIANO** — Attorney / Abogado — Democratic/Demócrata
◯ **ROBERT C. MANNHEIM** — Retired Businessperson / Hombre de negocios jubilado — Democratic/Demócrata
◯ Write-in

TURN OVER AND VOTE BOTH SIDES
VOLTIE Y VOTE AMBOS LADOS

FRONT Card 3 Rpt/Rpt 22-22 "0000022"

ENDNOTES

1. For an excellent summary of the historical roots of the recall and its use at the state level, see Zimmerman, 1997. For a review of the history of direct democracy in California, see Allswang, 2000.

2. Much has been written about the California energy crisis, and the budget crisis which is being summarized here simply to aid in our discussion of the recall. For a strong review of both of these matters, see Hyink and Provost, 2004.

3. Discussing the "Warren Way," after former California governor Earl Warren, M. Dane Waters of the Initiative and Referendum Institute wrote that this is "the strategy by which a candidate uses a statewide ballot initiative to increase his or her name recognition" for future political runs (Waters 2001).

4. The sample ballot in Appendix A comes from Fresno County, CA. There were two initiatives on the statewide ballot that day, but they are not included here. Proposition 53 dealt with dedicating part of the state general fund to infrastructure needs, and Proposition 54 prohibited state and local government from classifying any person by race, ethnicity, color, or national origin. Both propositions were defeated by wide margins on October 7. Also note that not all counties used the ballot shown here where an oval is filled in with a pen or No. 2 pencil. Thirty-four of the 58 counties in California do use this Optical Scan system, but others use the (in)famous punch-card ballot, used during the Florida presidential recount of 2000, and a few use the newest touch-screen system where the voting machine resembles an ATM-type device and voters walk through a menu of choices to cast their vote. See the California Voter Foundation Website at http://www.calvoter.org for a "voting technology resources page" and a map of the state showing the various equipment utilized in the recall election.

5. More than 60% of the news stories covering the 2000 presidential primaries focused on tactics or strategy, rather than issues, according to a study by the Norman Lear Center at the University of Southern California's Annenberg School of Communication. (Kaplan and Hale 2000)

6. Except as otherwise noted in the remaining sections of this chapter, the chronology of events and specific quotes from reporters were taken from *The Fresno Bee* 1 August–7 October, 2003. Copies of these articles and all materials quoted in this chapter are available from the author upon request.

7. It is difficult to gauge the exact amount Issa spent during the recall campaign, as there were numerous pro-recall committees gathering signatures and coordinating efforts, and it appears he gave to nearly all of them. Figures ranging from $1.3 million total to $1.5 million to $1.73 million to $2.96 million were reported at different times during the campaign. The figure most often cited is $1.5 million, which is why it is used here.

8. It was reported that most, but not all, cable channels complied with the request, so as not to "run afoul of the federal laws" ("Pulling" 2003). The FCC law in question is the 1934 Communication Act, sec 315(a).

9. I am unable to go into great detail in this chapter on the variety of direct mail pieces used during the campaign, but they are numerous and most were well crafted. I have over 30 different pieces that were collected throughout the state, and I would be happy to make them available upon request.

10. An outstanding legal Website is www.FindLaw.com. They have maintained a special section devoted to the recall highlighting all of the major cases dealt with during the campaign: http://news.findlaw.com/legalnews/lit/recall/index.html.

11. This number was provided by California Common Cause. CCC lists major contributions to all candidates and committees for the entire recall campaign on its website: http://recallmoneywatch.com/recallwatch/home/index.html. Additional information, based on specific numbers reported to the secretary of state can be found at: http://www.calvoter.org/recall/candidates.html.

12. For complete results see the Secretary of State Website: http://www.ss.ca.gov/elections/sov/2003_special/sum.pdf

REFERENCES

Allswang, John M. 2000. *The Initiative and Referendum in California, 1898–1998.* Stanford: Stanford University Press.

California Online Voter Guide: A Project of the California Voter Foundation. 2002. Top Ten Contributors to California Propositions. Available from http://www.calvoter.org/2002/general/propositions/topten.html.

Cannon, Lou. 2003. "The Arnold Show." *California Journal,* December 29.

Chorneau, Tom. 2003. "Schwarzenegger Sworn in as Governor of California." *Fresno Bee,* November 17.

Factiva Index. 2003. "For the Second Week in a Row, Schwarzenegger Is the Most Covered Candidate." Available at http://www.businesswire.com/webbox/bw.090803/232515846.htm.

Field Poll. 2003. Available at http://field.com/fieldpollonline/subscribers/RLS2075.pdf. July 16.

Fitzenberger, Jennifer. 2003. "Gov. Schwarzenegger Takes Oath of Office." *Fresno Bee,* November 18.

Fresno Bee. August 1–October 7, 2003.

Germain, David. 2003. "He's Everywhere." *The Fresno Bee,* November 12, E5.

Harrigan, John J., and David C. Nice. 2001. *Politics and Policy in States and Communities.* San Francisco: Longman.

Hyink, Bernard L., and David H. Provost. 2004. *Politics and Government in California.* San Francisco: Pearson Education.

Kaplan, Martin, and Matthew Hale. 2000. "Local TV News Coverage of the 2000 Primary Campaigns." Publication of the Norman Lear Center at the University of Southern

California. Available at: http://www.learcenter.org/html/publications/?c=online+-publications

"Online California Recall Election." 2003. *Sacramento Bee,* August 19.

Parenti, Michael. 1986. *Inventing Reality: The Politics of the Mass Media.* New York: St. Martin's Press.

"Pulling the plug." 2003. Editorial. *Fresno Bee,* August 19, B8.

Romano, Allison. 2003. "Arnold's New Role Cost $16m." *Broadcasting and Cable* Issue #41, October 13.

Rutenberg, Jim. 2003. "Schwarzenegger Prompts Role Reversal among the Media." *New York Times,* October 6.

Schecter, David L. 2003. "Poison in the Well: A Depensation Model Explanation for Voter Behavior in Primary Elections." Paper presented at the Western Political Science Association, Denver, CO, March 27–30.

Secretary of State, California. 2003. "Results of Randomized Alphabet Drawing." Available from http://www.ss.ca.gov/elections/statewide_special_random_alpha.htm.

Trounstine, Philip J. 2003. "Democratic Daze." *California* Volume 34, Number 11, November 19–21.

Tumulty, Karen, and Terry McCarthy. 2003. "All That's Missing Is the Popcorn." *Time,* August, 23–26.

Waters, M. Dane. 2001. "Do It the Warren Way," *Campaigns and Elections* Vol. 22, Number 6, August, 56.

West, Darrell M., and John Orman. 2003. *Celebrity Politics.* Upper Saddle River, NJ: Prentice Hall.

Zimmerman, Joseph F. 1997. *The Recall: Tribunal of the People.* Westport, CT: Praeger.

ADDITIONAL RESOURCES

These Websites are currently up and running and contain two to three commercials each for Gray Davis and Arnold Schwarzenegger.

http://www.no-recall.com/mediaroom.asp

http://joinarnold.com/en/press/videocenter.php

These two Websites may be helpful for readers and provide lighthearted looks at the recall through the eyes of comedians, late-night talk show hosts, editorial cartoonists, and others.

http://politicalhumor.about.com/cs/california/

http://www.sacbee.com/content/opinion/cartoons/babin/. See the section marked "Recall Gallery."

11

Political Advertising in Canada

Paul Nesbitt-Larking
Jonathan Rose

Introduction

Not quite married and yet unlikely to experience an ugly separation, Canada and the United States can be described as comfortable if asymmetrical cohabitants of the North American continent. The complex relationship that has evolved over almost 250 years is foundational to the Canadian identity if not quite to the American. The continued existence of Canada as a sovereign state had been rearticulated and reasserted in every generation as a deliberate act of collective will. The pull of the United States—culturally, economically and strategically—has grown throughout the past fifty years as the United States has emerged as the global superpower. Canadian popular culture is saturated by American media, such as TV shows, magazines, movies, and music. Canadian security and defense initiatives are intricately bound to those of the United States through our membership in NATO and NORAD. Canada is an export-dependent economy, and over 80% of its exports go to the United States. Living in a multicultural and radically decentralized federation in which the sum of the parts often appears to be greater than the whole, Canadians are fervent in their quest for an identity. The only certainty seems to be that Canada is not the same as the United States.

The consequence of Canada's coexistence with the United States is the simple and yet compelling impulse to remain politically independent. There is a dialectic between the impulse of assimilation and integration into the American orbit on the one hand and the abiding compulsion of the European heritage on the other. Canada's political economy, political culture, and state formations are rooted in the tensions between the negative freedoms of liberal possessive individualism (the American way) and the more positive freedoms of communitarianism (the European heritage). This is why McRae (1964) and Horowitz (1966) describe Canada's ideological characteristics as fundamentally liberal but with conservative and socialist influences. It is for this reason, too, that while Lipset (1990) states that the political cultures of Canada and the United States share much in common, Canadian political culture is "more class-aware, elitist, law-abiding, statist, collectivity-oriented, and particularistic (group-oriented)" (p. 8) than the United States. The very connotations of the word *liberal* are discursively distinct in Canada and the United States, and such a distinction illustrates the more general ideological gap. To be liberal in the United States is to occupy the progressive, equality-based end of the American ideological spectrum and has in many quarters a pejorative connotation. In Canada, liberal encompasses a much broader range from the progressive and egalitarian to the classical/business and freedom-oriented end of the scale.

The tensions between the American model of liberal individualism and the European traditions of solidaristic collectivism have prompted Mendelsohn (2002) to remark (on the basis of his empirical analyses of public opinion) that at the beginning of the twenty-first century, Canada remains: "more collectivistic, more open to diversity, more supportive of state intervention, more deferential, and more prepared to find solidarity with people in other countries than its southern neighbour" (p. 1). The remarkable longevity of Canadian political cultural distinctiveness is noteworthy, according to Mendelsohn, in light of the impact of a decade of globalization, continental economic integration, federal and provincial neoliberal fiscal policies, and the consequent erosion of the Canadian welfare state.

The characteristic patterns of ideological tendency in Canada and the United States are mirrored in their respective patterns of political advertising. In general, advertising constitutes a sensitive measure of the cultural character of a time and place, and careful analyses of advertising can reveal much about core values and beliefs. While political advertising in Canada exhibits marked trends toward the American model, there are key moments of distinction and divergence. As a quintessentially possessive individualistic practice, our analysis anticipates that despite the similarities, political advertising in the United States is relatively more widespread, less regulated, freer in expression, and less culturally reserved than in Canada.

Our chapter consists of four substantive sections. These explore, in turn, the political economy of advertising, the regulative role of the state in political advertising, the mutual interplay of political advertisements and the Canadian political culture, and Canadian governments as political advertisers. According to Lynda Lee Kaid, political advertising can be defined as: "the communicative process by which a source (usually a political candidate or party) purchases the opportunity to expose receivers through mass channels to political messages with the intended effect of influencing their political attitudes, beliefs, and/or behaviours" (Kaid in Romanow et al., 1999, p. 12). This American definition is a useful general definition but immediately illustrates the fundamental distinctions between the two polities. In Canada, political advertising not only includes a substantial quantum of *free* exposure but has been increasingly subsidized and supported by the state in recent years. Moreover, governments themselves have become major players in political advertising. We now turn to an examination of these points of distinction.

Canadian Political Economy and Political Advertising

Canada and the United States share much in common when it comes to the political economy of advertising. Both polities have developed free markets in which rights to basic civil freedoms are taken for granted. It is not at all surprising that advertising in general, and political advertising in particular, is a multimillion-dollar business in both countries and that, as the junior partner, Canada's trends in political advertising borrow from and replicate American advertising techniques and trends after the customary election cycle time gap. In Canada, advertising is a $9 billion per annum industry. In the United States, advertising contributes over $183 billion to the economy each year (Rose, 2000, p. 45). Advertising is clearly a vital component of each nation's economic prosperity. However, according to the total populations of the two countries in 2002 (Canada: 31.5 million; United States: 280.5 million), advertising expenditures should be 9.2 times as great in the United States as in Canada, other things being equal. In fact, the Americans spend 20.3 times as much on advertising—over double the per-capita rate of Canadians. When it comes to political advertising, the differences are even larger. While Canada is a capitalist country, its economic development has emerged historically in the context of the strong, even dirigiste state and a political culture that is powerfully communitarian. The United States is grounded in a tradition of less restrained and cautious capitalism. This is evident in comparative data on entrepreneurial risk taking, venture capital, public spending and taxation, macroeconomic and microeconomic indicators of fiscal prudence, and investment in innovation.

American elections are highly expensive. In comparison with the hundreds of millions of dollars devoted to election spending in the United States, Canadian parties spend quite modestly.

To place matters in perspective, Bush and Gore between them spent over $305 million in 1999–2000 during the American presidential election. The combined spending of the five major political parties in the Canadian general election of 2000 was between $22 and $23 million expressed in American dollars (Elections Canada). Dianne Feinstein's successful contestation of a California Senate seat in 2000 saw her spending more than the entire Liberal Party of Canada spent in that year to win their third term (Federal Elections Commission; Elections Canada). John R. Thune, running for Congress in South Dakota in 2002, disbursed almost as much in his state (with a population of 756,000) as did the Canadian Alliance in its *national* campaign to unseat the Liberal Party in 2000 (Federal Elections Commission; Elections Canada).

When it comes to the manner in which total election spending is distributed, the contrasts between Canada and the United States are interesting and significant. On the whole, American candidates and parties devote between two-thirds and three-quarters of their total campaign spending to political advertisements (Kaid et al., 1986, p. xiii; Paletz, 1998). In Canada, the proportion is smaller and has varied between one-half and two-thirds for the major parties since the 1970s (Fletcher, 1988, p. 164; Kline et al., 1991, p. 284; Fletcher and MacDermid, 1998, p. 1). The entire business of elections in Canada is understated. Owing to Canada's parliamentary system, election campaigns are shorter in comparison with their American counterparts (MacDermid, 1997, p. 86), and there are far fewer full-time political consulting firms in Canada. There are, as Leiss et al. (1990, p. 390) put it, too few elections to support consultants specializing only in political work.

The proportion of total campaign spending devoted to political advertising in the Canadian federal election of 2000 by political parties was as follows: Canadian Alliance: 78.3%; Liberal Party: 61.4%; Progressive Conservative Party (PC): 48.1%; New Democratic Party (NDP): 30.7% and the Bloc Quebecois (BQ): 23.1% (Elections Canada). The variations among the Canadian parties suggest some important realities. First, the two traditional parties of government (Liberals and PCs) devoted approximately half their budgets to the political advertising campaign. Second, the grassroots parties (NDP and BQ) employed interpersonal communication strategies rather than the mass media for the dissemination of their views. Finally, the Canadian Alliance was the only party to approximate the American style of campaign spending and needed to do so in order to convey their message to the voters of Ontario with only minimal campaign staffs in the ridings. The Canadian Alliance data are particularly instructive. Of the major political parties in Canada, the Canadian Alliance (formerly the Reform Party of Canada) emerged as the most pro-American in its policy orientations and the most "American" in its structure, policies, and style. Despite some powerful regional support in Alberta and British Columbia, the party failed to make an electoral breakthrough in the heavily populated core provinces of Ontario and Quebec. (In December, 2003, the Canadian Alliance and the Progressive Conservative Party united to form the new Conservative Party of Canada.)

If the American style and policies of the federal Canadian Alliance have anything to do with its limited success in Ontario, the picture is complicated by the fact that a provincial party, the Progressive Conservative Party, has enjoyed great success on the basis of a broadly similar ideological and operational character. Under their leader, Mike Harris, the Ontario Progressive Conservatives (PCs) won a famous come-from-behind electoral victory in 1995 (MacDermid, 1997; Fletcher, 1999; MacDermid and Albo, 2001). The impressive and unexpected victory of the Harris PCs in 1995 was grounded in an American-style managed campaign built around the marketing of the party platform, referred to as "The Common Sense Revolution." Harris's campaign team included Tom Long, who had worked for Ronald Reagan, and Leslie Noble, who had worked for Republican candidate Jack Kemp. Long brought in American attack ad specialist Mike Murphy, who worked with Long, Noble, Paul Rhodes, and Jaime Watt to create the television advertising campaign of 1995. It was masterful in its execution. Taking the incumbent New Democratic Party and the Liberal Party by storm, the Harris team strategically purchased TV time that would bring them to the maximum number of their most desired demographic groups for the least advertising dollars. The ads themselves were a skillful combination of populist rhetoric and attacks on carefully chosen targets, notably welfare recipients, criminals, and beneficiaries of employment equity programs.

In January 1999, the governing PCs introduced changes to the Election Finances Act of Ontario that permitted substantial increases in campaign contributions, increased spending limits, and increased the amount of campaign time during an election campaign in which it would be permissible to advertise. The government also allowed the more widespread use of soft money donations by declaring important campaign costs such as polling expenses, furniture and equipment, office rentals and professional fees to be no longer reportable and regulated campaign costs. The combined impact of these changes was to the advantage of those political parties with existing financial resources and those parties able to attract further financial resources. The built-in positive impact of these changes for the incumbent PCs was formidable. In the 1999 provincial election, the Harris team had far more money to spend than the other parties. The 1999 provincial election was also preceded by a flurry of PC political ads criticizing the Liberal Party and its leader, who were caught out by the (then) unconventional decision to launch advertisements before the official start to the campaign. The benefit of this was that expenditures on advertising spent outside of the election period are not regulated by the Elections Financing Act.

While recent developments in Ontario suggest a trend toward the Americanization of political advertising, matters seem to be moving in the other direction at the federal level. However, before moving to a consideration of the Canadian state and political advertising, it is noteworthy that following the controversial and divisive 2000 Presidential Election in the United States, Congress passed the Bipartisan Campaign Reform Act in 2002, thereby "Canadianizing" American federal practices to some extent. The act places restrictions on the use of soft money and attack ads hitherto disguised as "issue advocacy." The new legislation increases hard money limits but requires disclosure of campaign contributors. Business, trade, and labor associations are now barred from "electioneering communication" (Briffault, 2002). Each of these developments is designed to enhance transparency, to reduce the impact of big money in future elections, and to diminish the undignified assaults of attack campaigns. In subsequent sections of this chapter, it will become apparent that even with such changes in place, the character of American political advertising is likely to remain less regulated than that in Canada. Moreover, it seems certain that the law will be subject to strong constitutional challenge. Whatever else can be said, however, it does represent the aspiration of people who have hitherto resisted regulatory instruments that there must be some limits to the unfettered power of money to buy tools of mass persuasion.

The Canadian State and Political Advertising

The Canadian Constitution underwent a profound shift in the early 1980s. Then Prime Minister Trudeau undertook the twin tasks of patriating the Constitution and underwriting it with a Charter of Rights and Freedoms. Patriation abolished the last remnants of British colonial regulation of the Canadian Constitution. The Charter of Rights and Freedoms, while not supplanting British common law nor ending Parliamentary supremacy, entrenched a range of justiciable rights and freedoms that gave Canada its own "Bill of Rights." Freedom of expression has long been a characteristic of Canadian civil society, under the common law traditions, but the Charter rendered this and other freedoms more certain. By the 1990s, Romanow and his colleagues could say (1999, p. 181):

> On both sides of the border, constitutional free-speech provisions support a system of paid political advertising. This in turn means that there are limits upon the limits that can be imposed on advertising. It also means that moral arguments can take up where legal boundaries end.

Canada's freedoms of expression, of the press, and other media of communication have self-consciously evolved in the context of the sacred respect accorded to First Amendment rights of free speech in the United States. In one of her rulings, Canadian Supreme Court Justice L'Hereux-Dube stated: "it may be helpful to look at the American experience, not with a view to applying their decisions blindly but rather to learn from the process through which they were derived" (L'Hereux-Dube in Trudel and Abran, 1991, p. 42). Recent rulings by the Supreme Court of Canada reflect self-conscious moves toward the elevation of freedom of speech to a constitutional principle that is equal in importance with the right of the accused to a fair trial and to the principles of peace, order and good government.

Despite these important similarities and apparent convergences there are significant differences between the two nations in the relationship of the polity to the state. The American polity developed in spite of the state; the Canadian polity developed because of it. Canada's longstanding dependency on the state finds expression in the field of political advertising. Every major government report on Canadian broadcasting or culture from the Aird Report in 1929 stresses the centrality of the Canadian state in promoting and protecting a Canadian mass media.

The 1986 Caplan-Sauvageau Task Force on Broadcasting Policy said: "Unlike American communications legislation which was designed primarily for co-ordination purposes, Canadian broadcasting policy has always pursued social and cultural objectives" (Trudel and Abran, 1991, p. 66). Given the asymmetry of the North American binational relationship, the United States has always exerted the most powerful economic, cultural, diplomatic, and political pressures on Canada to conform. The Canadian state has been obliged to devise strategies and structures to preserve and promote Canadian identities, if not always Canadian unity. Without these safeguards, and the necessity to ritually reinvent them each generation, Canadian culture would quite naturally be pulled into the American orbit. This is why Fletcher and MacDermid (1998, p. 30) offer the following balanced assessment:

> Canada has a long history of borrowing campaign techniques from the United States. However, it has retained important areas of distinctiveness: expenditure limits, a limited period for broadcast advertising, the availability of free as well as paid time, and a party-centred campaign process appropriate for a parliamentary system.

Americans are proud of their First Amendment freedoms of speech and the press. Even when fairly conclusive evidence has been offered that advertisements have caused harm, there is great reluctance to limit freedom of expression. Freedom of speech and the media is almost an absolute guarantee in the United States, but even in the United States these rights have been hedged in certain ways by the evolution of legislation needed to sustain minimal order and assist in the promotion of limited standards of equity in the face of societal inequalities. While limited, the heart of federal legislation on political advertising is the Federal Election Campaign Act (FECA), first passed in 1974 and amended frequently since then, which regulates the conduct of both presidential and congressional elections.

Despite such regulation, an early attempt to limit the amount Political Action Committees (PACs) could spend in an election campaign was ruled unconstitutional in the 1976 case *Buckley v. Valeo*. The U.S. Supreme Court ruled that the law limiting election spending by third parties, such as PACs, was unconstitutional because it limited freedom of speech. In its findings, the Supreme Court indicated that demonstrable waste, excess, and stupidity were insufficient criteria to permit governments to determine spending ceilings for PACs. If free speech was vitriolic and vindictive, it was the people who should evaluate it, not the government that should limit it in advance. PACs grew into the thousands in the 1980s and 1990s and came to dominate both the funding of election campaigns and the character of the advertisements. (Ansolabehere and Iyengar, 1995; Diamond and Bates, 1992; Jamieson, 1992)

Both Canada and the United States operate with certain legal safeguards against the dissemination of certain kinds of advertisements, including political advertisements. Depictions deemed to be offensive, obscene, or liable to incite violence are subject to criminal prosecution. It is always open to candidates to issue civil suits against any advertisements they deem to be defamatory. In both polities, however, the bar is set high, and prosecutions on both criminal and civil criteria are almost nonexistent. There appears to be an implicit acceptance of the fact that in politics there are no false or unjust claims. Agencies exist in both countries to protect consumer rights and enforce advertising standards. While they are similar in many respects, it is interesting to note how the primary emphasis in Industry Canada's Office of Consumer Affairs is on "protection," while the first terms employed in the American Federal Trade Commission's mandate statement are to ensure that "the nation's markets are vigorous, efficient and free of restrictions" (Canada; Federal Trade Commission).

The overall statute for controlling political advertising in Canada is the Canada Elections Act. The fundamental provisions of the act have been in place since 1974. Political parties are legally and formally recognized and thereby granted certain rights and responsibilities. In return for openness in reporting all receipts and expenditures, they are granted reimbursement by the state of a proportion of their expenses for advertisements and other costs. Moreover, the state grants them a quantum of free election advertising time. Perhaps most importantly, generous tax concessions are available to individual donors to political parties. For most modest donors, a 75% tax refund is available for financial support given to their party of choice. The Canada Elections Act is altogether more restrictive than the American FECA when it comes to electoral advertising. Like the American legislation, the Act stipulates that messages must be authorized (section 320) and that services offered to one party or candidate must be offered to all and be made available at the cheapest rates. However, the Canada Elections Act goes much further. It stipulates that each broadcaster must make available a maximum of six and one-half hours of paid prime-time broadcasting to the parties (section 335), and that these hours must be divided according to a formula in which various indicators of the parties' electoral and legislative strength are factored into the evaluation of an equitable share (section 338). New official political parties are guaranteed a minimum number of purchasable minutes (section 339), and a certain number of free broadcast minutes (up to three and one-half hours) must also be made available to the parties on the basis of their established shares of the paid time (section 345). The Canada

Elections Act further stipulates a number of regulations concerning the quantity and quality of election advertisements. For instance, there is an advertising blackout on election day, and all advertisements must name the sponsor (section 320).

The Canada Elections Act (sections 346 and 347) further delegates the task of issuing guidelines to broadcasters to the Canadian Radio-television and Telecommunications Commission (CRTC). The CRTC communicates with each licenced station within days of receiving the order from the chief electoral officer. The CRTC also supervises the administration of the act during and immediately after each election. Stations are required to log each advertisement and its sponsor and to ensure that the allocation of paid and free time among candidates is equitable. The CRTC issued *Les Enterprises* in 1991, a document whose language reflects the distinctly public service character of Canadian agencies vis-à-vis the conduct of elections (Trudel and Abran, 1991, p. 78):

> The . . . provisions of the [Elections] Act unequivocally attest to Parliament's intent that, in supervising the use of radio frequencies, which are public property and limited in number by the radio spectrum, the greatest possible emphasis be given to the affirmation of the right to freedom of expression, subject to the requirement for programming of high standard and subject to achieving an intelligent harmony with the requirement for balance in the discussion of matters of public concern.

In a dramatic move away from the Americanizing trend toward big spending campaigns and access to soft money purchases, the federal government has recently passed legislation that limits the rights of certain groups to donate to political campaigns (Bill C-24). This initiative sets it on a course that contradicts trends set in the Progressive Conservative governments of Ontario under Mike Harris and Ernie Eves. (The Liberal government of Dalton McGuinty, elected in 2003, seems likely to follow federal trends in campaign regulation.) The legislation limits corporate and union donations dramatically to $1,000 per annum. Individuals will now be permitted to donate up to $5,000 per annum. The quantity of public money available to parties has been increased to compensate for anticipated shortfalls. Eligibility thresholds for reimbursement of election expenses have been lowered from 15% to 10%. The reimbursement rate for registered parties has been doubled to 50%, bringing it into line with the current reimbursement rate for candidates. The Income Tax Act has been amended to substantially increase the levels of individual donations that are partially refundable. Any person making a donation of up to $400 per annum (up from $200) will receive a 75% tax refund. These new provisions are applicable for the first time to riding associations, leadership contestants, and party nomination contestants. With these sweeping changes it is anticipated that the amount of public money in federal party coffers will increase from the current level of about 60% to about 80%.

The historical tension in Canada between negative and positive freedom, between unfettered freedom of expression and state-promoted equity, has been nowhere more evident than in the ongoing struggle to develop appropriate and constitutionally sound public policy on the issue of "third-party advertising." Third-party election advertising can be defined as material funded and disseminated to influence the outcome of the election by persons other than official candidates and parties. Initial legislation to limit the capacity of third parties to fund election campaigns was challenged in the Alberta Court of Appeal in 1984. The court ruled that the Canada Elections Act violated the free speech provisions of the Charter. The federal government decided not to appeal the ruling to the Supreme Court, and in the 1988 federal election campaign, third-party spending, notably by groups opposed to abortion and in favor of free trade, reached historically high levels. Many commentators became alarmed at the perception that those with the resources to buy advertising time on television were able to exert undue influence over public debate. Alarm diminished somewhat in 1992 when, despite enormously outspending their opponents, the "Yes" side was defeated by the "No" side in a major and comprehensive referendum on constitutional change, known as the Charlottetown Accord.

In May 2000 the federal government introduced an elaborate new set of clauses into an amended Elections Act. These facilitated third-party advertising under certain conditions but set limits on spending levels. The Alberta Court of Appeal ruled the government's third-party legislation unconstitutional in December 2002. The court agreed with the appellant, Stephen Harper, that third parties should not have to limit their spending or disclose their donors. The current situation with respect to third-party advertising is unclear as the Harper decision is under appeal, and in the meantime Elections Canada are abiding by the Alberta appeal court decision. The complex vacillation on this issue reflects the reality of the Canadian approach to political advertising, balanced uneasily as it is between freedom and responsibility. The role of the Canadian state is likely to be further challenged in the months and years to come, not merely from the seemingly inexorable pressure of political deregulation, which originates in a globalizing political economy, but also from the sheer diffusion of techniques of mass and niche marketing.

The CRTC has given up on any attempt to control the Internet and existing attempts by Elections Canada to regulate Internet use have proven inadequate. The future role of the Canadian state in political advertising will be conditioned by new trends in Internet distribution techniques, rapid and computerized dialing techniques, and sophisticated database demographic marketing tools that permit highly specialized direct mailing campaigns. In the end, what Canadians will or will not accept with respect to political advertising is a matter of the evolving political culture. The economic forces of globalization or the political impact of regulations notwithstanding, Canadian citizens are agents with the capacity to choose or refuse.

Canadian Political Culture and Political Advertising

As an increasingly integrated region in the North American market, Canada has readily adopted and followed most of the principal developments in advertising techniques and strategies (Leiss et al., 1990). Trends in political advertising made popular in the United States have been replicated in Canada following a lag of a few years. As we shall see, however, not all developments in political advertising have been welcome in Canada.

The earliest modern advertisements emerged in the radio age in 1930s Canada. Prime Ministers Borden and King both employed advertising agencies, and the first major controversy over political advertisements arose in the 1935 federal election. The Conservative Party aired political advertisements, known as the "Mr. Sage" advertisements, which attacked the Liberal Party of Mr. King without identifying the Conservative Party as sponsor. Despite the advertisements, King won the election and subsequently introduced electoral legislation that included a ban on dramatizations in political advertisements and a requirement that sponsors be named. By the 1950s and 1960s, the television era necessitated the further sophistication of campaign techniques, and the Liberal Party's Keith Davey introduced strategic planning into election campaigns with the assistance of Kennedy's pollster, Lou Harris. By the 1970s, Kline and his colleagues (1991, p. 227) could report that "the integration of polling, advertising, touring and media exposure" had become "essential to efficient campaign management." Following American cultural trends, Michael Posner stated in the early 1990s that, "Just like a box of soap, a can of soup or a carton of cornflakes, they [politicians] require marketing strategies, promotion campaigns and plenty of spin to grab that all-important market share" (Posner, 1992, p. 40). The existence of American-style political advertising in

Canada is undeniable, and yet it has never occupied the central cultural role that it has in the United States.

There is, in the political culture of Canada, a resistance to the glibness and superficiality of political advertisements and the manner in which they devalue reflective judgment, slow deliberation, and social responsibility. In the United States, because American creed is so deeply embedded, political debate is a matter of *genuine* market choice. In Canada, the parliamentary traditions of government and opposition, in combination with the relentless search for a political identity, render political debate altogether more philosophical and ideological. In this context, it is relatively less acceptable to present politicians, issues, and parties as brands and labels. Moreover, in the Canadian parliamentary system, there is less need for the kind of American candidate identification advertisements that package the fresh face and introduce the person to the voters (Diamond and Bates, 1992).

Most leaders are already known to the people through their apprenticeships in their parties as backbenchers and cabinet ministers. Whereas in the United States political advertising is largely a matter of consumer choice and should therefore remain largely unfettered, in Canada there is a greater sense of equity and seriousness in ensuring that each side is presented adequately in any public debate. Perhaps it is for this reason that Fletcher and MacDermid (1998) report that Canadian political advertisements tend to be more party centred than their U.S. counterparts.

Despite the abundant intellectual distaste for attack ads and a generalized mood of revulsion among the Canadian public, such advertisements have been employed in Canada since the 1980s. In the 1988 federal election campaign, political advertisements by the Liberal Party called Brian Mulroney a liar, and advertisements by the Progressive Conservative Party referred to John Turner as a liar. The 1993 federal election campaign contained the now-notorious Progressive Conservative ads that captured images of Jean Chretien with his naturally twisted mouth accentuated. The voice-over referred to Chretien as "an embarrassment." While attack ads decreased in the campaign of 1997, the Reform Party produced a composite of four Quebecois political leaders on a poster with lines drawn through their faces (Fletcher and MacDermid, 1998). The idea was to make the point that Canada has had too many leaders from Quebec, and that by inference, that is why those Quebecers always get what they want at "our" expense. Jean Charest and Jean Chretien were two of the four politicians shown. Charest called it "bigoted," and Chretien said that it was "the most divisive campaign in Canadian history."

Romanow and his colleagues (1999) conducted the principal study of attack ads in Canada in their exploration of the 1993 federal election. Their principal conclusion—that extensive use was made of attack ads in that election—is in our judgment an exaggeration. In order to be classified as an attack ad, the material should meet Taras's (1990, p. 219) criteria of: "ridicule . . . savaging of their character. . . . The competence, motives, intelligence, and integrity of opponents are brought into question. The object is to draw blood, to inflict irreparable damage." The object of the attack can be an individual or a class of individuals. Attack ads tend to be unsubstantiated, insinuating, and often resort to ad hominem arguments (Gauthier, 1994). On the basis of these definitions, not many of the 1993 ads studied by Romanow and his colleagues meet the criteria.

In fact, our reanalysis of their classification system confirms the judgement of Wearing and Tilley (in Romanow et al., 1999, p. 6) that while Americans prefer a personal attack on politicians, Canadians emphasize political scandal. Despite the fact that the 1997 federal election was genuinely a cleaner campaign than 1993, Fletcher and MacDermid's (1998) analysis of the attack mode in the latter election generates a more accurate image of the scope of attack ads in Canadian elections. They acknowledge that very few of the hard-hitting advertisements were "directed at the competence or character of the leaders" (Fletcher and MacDermid, 1998, p. 21). In fact only 9 of the 87 spot advertisements they classified in the 1997 campaign contained attacks on personal character or style. They conclude that "it could not be said that the spots were 'down and dirty'" (Fletcher and MacDermid, 1998, p. 21).

Irrespective of the cultural response of Canadians to negative ads and to the degree to which one can claim that they have been employed in Canadian elections, what can we say of their more specific impact on Canadian audiences? Based on his studies of the 1988 federal election, Jean Crete (1991, p. 17) concludes that attack ads only work if they attack the issues. He also offers some more general insights into the matter of audience reception of political ads. First, less-informed voters are most likely to derive information content from spot advertisements (p. 23), and second, political advertisements of any kind rarely change minds; rather they serve to reinforce existing opinion (p. 27). Citing Palda's (1973) research, Canadian Environics polls, and American research, Crete concludes (1991, pp. 29–30) that advertisements can be effective and that there is a tendency for those who spend the dollars to get the results. Fletcher and MacDermid

(1998, p. 7) claim that in Canada, "advertising has had significant effects on campaign dynamics and voter choice and exposure is high."

Certainly the advertising strategy of Allen Gregg and his Progressive Conservative team seemed to pay dividends in 1988. Following the leadership debates in mid-campaign, the Progressive Conservatives were alarmed to see that John Turner and his Liberal Party were rising rapidly in popularity. Gregg produced a series of negative ads attacking Turner's credibility (Taras, 1990, p. 222). They seemed to work and the remainder of the campaign saw the PCs increasing in popularity and ultimately winning. Of course, part of the success can be attributed to the fact that the numerical dominance of the PCs in the 1984 federal election gave them more minutes of free and paid television advertising time according to the Elections Act formula. It is also probable that the PCs benefitted from the enormous sums of third-party money devoted to promoting the free trade cause. In the light of this mixed evidence of Canadian revulsion and yet some limited impact, what can we conclude? To some extent, the cautionary words of MacDermid (1997, p. 74) are salutary:

> The prospect of coming up with a research design that could study the effects of advertising free from experimental effects and in a true election environment is still distant and probably nonexistent.

We should also pay attention to Andre Pratte's claim that it is what goes on in the campaign itself and how the media cover the campaign trail that exert the most impact on election outcomes. Political advertising, he claims, only really exerts a strong impact when it is not well done (Institute for Research on Public Policy, 2003).

Government Advertising in Canada

As with political advertisements between Canada and the United States, there are some significant differences in government advertising between the two nations. The same pattern emerges in government advertising as with political advertising. Specifically, the differences between the two countries can also be traced to different cultural traditions and differing beliefs about the role of the state in national life. In Canada, the federal government spent over $200 million on advertising in 2000 and over $212 million in 2001, when it was the third largest advertiser in the country (AC Nielsen data).

In comparison, the United States government spent over $1 billion in 2001 but came in twenty-fourth in terms of expenditures. In per-capita figures the difference is clear. We demonstrated earlier that Americans spend much more on advertising expenditure per capita (almost twice as much as Canadians). On government advertising, however, the data are reversed. In 2001 the American government spent $3.57 per capita on advertising while the Canadian government spent $6.34 per capita. While clearly an important player in advertising, the U.S. government has never been in the top 12 advertisers in any medium (television, magazine, newspaper, cable television, outdoor advertising, or radio) according to *Marketing* (Hiscock, 2002, p. 24). Political advertising by government is an important and ongoing concern for governments, opposition parties, and the media in Canada. In the United States it is not an important concern either in popular debate in the media or in the scholarly literature on advertising.

In fact, like its political culture, Canada is a hybrid of American and British practices and beliefs in its government advertising efforts. As a result of this or perhaps as a result of the fusion of power in parliamentary systems, Canadian government advertising bears a closer resemblance to British government advertising than American. In both Canada and Britain, recent governments have come under attack for using advertising as a partisan vehicle of party propaganda. Scandals, which bear more than a passing similarity to Canadian government advertising scandals, have appeared in the British press alleging that "government is using taxpayers' money for unnecessary information campaigns" (Kleinman, 2003, p. 3). Moreover, both Canadian and British governments have been accused of using advertising as a means of patronage and tendering lucrative government advertising contracts to political friends. COI Communications, which is the British government's advertising arm, was the largest advertiser in 2001 beating the number two advertiser, Procter & Gamble, by £28 million by spending £142.5 million (Hiscock, 2002, p. 24). This pattern of state advertising largesse in Canada bears a much closer resemblance to British practices than it does American.

How governments in the United States and Canada advertise also tells an important story. The Canadian government's top three advertisers in 2001–2002 were the Departments of Tourism, Health and Welfare, and the Canadian Information Office. While we might understand the need for a large tourism advertising budget and see that the provision of information on health issues warrants a significant expenditure in that, the third largest spender in the government is telling. Until it was recently disbanded, the Canadian Information Office was a scarcely hidden propaganda arm of the federal government. Now subsumed under Communications Canada, its goal, according to its own euphemistic description, is to "listen actively to the opinions of Canadians so that the Government of Canada can respond."

Given the perilous place of Quebec in federation, one of the main purposes of state advertising in Canada is to extol the virtues of a united Canada to soft Quebec nationalists. This is compared to the United States where the Department of Defense (and now Homeland Security) regularly is among the top three government spenders. The little academic attention that government advertising has received in the United States focuses on issues of economic inefficiencies in government advertising (Mullen & Bowers, 1979, p. 39) or concerns about the government dominating the airwaves (Yarwood & Enis, 1982, p. 37). In Canada, like the United Kingdom, there is much greater concern about the state using advertising as a vehicle of propaganda or for national unity purposes.

Advertising by the state in Canada has a long history and, given the precarious nature of the Canadian identity, has been used to foster nationalism and create citizenship. It has been used less for the provision of information than it has in the creation of myths. According to Northrop Frye, these myths are important stories that are passed on from one generation to the next. They give meaning to community and help create allegiances to the state and pride in citizenship. For Jacques Ellul (1972), these myths are the basis of *integration propaganda* and serve an important and positive function. Advertising by the state in Canada differs from American government advertising in this regard. In Canada this integration propaganda has primed and shaped the public conversation, sometimes overtly, at other times in a subtle and sophisticated manner.

One of the most early overt examples of this was early twentieth-century immigration ads, which in a verbal and visual sleight of hand that would put present-day Madison Avenue to shame, extolled the virtues of Canada's winter climate. Yes, it was true, as one ad famously boasted, Winnipeg was free from malaria in winter. Another campaign dreamed up by Clifford Sifton, Prime Minister Laurier's minister of the interior, used the government's policy of "free land" as a readymade slogan in its ads. All of them, however, placed in American newspapers, laid the foundation for much of the current mythology of Canada as a nation of open spaces and rugged beauty as well as establishing a precedent that the state ought to be involved in creating national mythologies. Historian Pierre Berton (1984, p. 18) writes how these early campaigns were truly a multimedia affair:

> tens of thousands of pamphlets and exhibits at state fairs, 200,000 pamphlets distributed at the St. Louis Fair in 1904 alone; one thousand lantern-slide lec-

tures in England in a single year; one thousand inquiries a month at the High Commissioner's office in London; and a thirty-five thousand dollar arch at the coronation of Edward VII, trumpeting the advantages of immigration.

The most obvious manifestation of myth-making government advertising in Canada is the recurring Canada Day campaigns. They are myth-making because they use an ostensibly non-contentious celebration to make contentious arguments about federalism. The first large-scale advertising of this began with Expo '67 in Montreal. The federal government used Expo to tie ads into Canada's 100th anniversary of confederation and to counter the nascent but growing sovereignty movement in Quebec. Taking its lead from Clifford Sifton in earlier times, the federal Liberal government began a coordinated marketing campaign ostensibly to encourage Canadians to visit Expo but having the result of strengthening Canadians' loyalty to a united Canada. It marked the beginning of a maple-leaf branding campaign that Jean-Francois Lisee has called a "never-before-seen sociopolitical experiment aimed at leading to a rebirth of feelings of Canadian identity as a way of reducing the sovereigntist vote" (Kucharsky, 2000, p. 19).

Again in 1992 when Canada celebrated its 125th anniversary, the federal government began an aggressive advertising campaign whose goals seemed innocuous, but whose real purpose was to prime a federalist vote in the referendum on a set of constitutional changes in the same year. The massive spending by the federalist side was highlighted by a series of televised ads featuring prominent Canadians such as Olympic athletes and astronauts who spoke of the beauty of Canada from outer space or the pride felt by an Olympian on hearing the national anthem. As if that weren't enough, the television campaign also highlighted Canada's number one ranking by the United Nations based on life expectancy, education, and purchasing power and brought out one of the most powerful symbols of nationhood, the RCMP (Royal Canadian Mounted Police) musical ride.[1]

Advertising on constitutional issues or fiscal imbalance has been one way that the federal government in Canada has participated in important national deliberations. So entrenched in political life are ads by government that advertising has been used by one government to communicate to another. In the 1999 federal budget, for example, the government of Quebec spent over $300,000 to tell Quebecers that, according to the Premier of Quebec, "there will be less money for health than we had hoped" (Gamble & Cherry, 1999, p. A1). The centerpiece of that campaign was a powerful and visually evocative ad that showed two blood bags, a larger one labeled "Ontario" and a smaller one labeled "Quebec." The tag line was a succinct

"How do you feel now?" (see Figure 11.1). In a semiotic flourish, the federal government responded with an ad that showed Quebec literally dominating Canada with fleur-de-lis and dollar signs over a map of the country. Its tag line was an equally stark "24% of the population [but] 34% of new transfer payments" (see Figure 11.2).

Figure 11.1: Government of Quebec advertisement, 1999.

Sources: http://politics.queensu.ca/~rosej/figure1.tif

On constitutional matters the government's advertising has been more subtle. In 1982 when the Canadian constitution was being patriated from Britain even though Canadians democratic assent was not formally required, the federal government ran a now-famous ad, "Flight," which merely showed a slow-motion flight of Canada geese taking off from water. "Oh

Figure 11.2: Government of Canada advertisement, 1999.

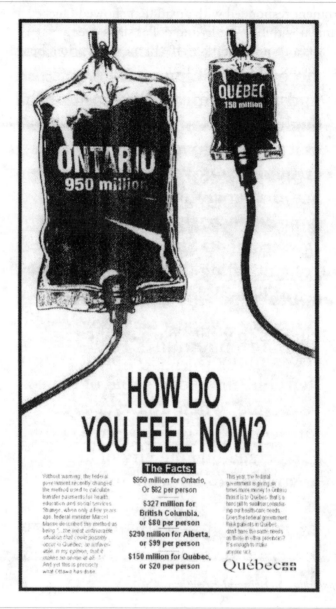

Sources:http://politics.queensu.ca/~rosej/figure2.tif

Canada" is hummed in the background while the narrator intones the virtues and importance of freedom to Canadians.[2] Two years prior to that, during the first referendum on sovereignty in Quebec, the federal government spent millions touting the importance of the federal presence in Quebec. Flags were flown on all federal buildings; tours by senior cabinet ministers were undertaken, and extra money was allocated to Quebec programs. All of these activities were, of course, supported by a massive federal advertising campaign in support of the federalist "no" side. Typical of the pervasiveness of the advertising the federal government ran a vigorous anti-smoking campaign that said in large letters "SAY NO!" In smaller letters below was "to smoking." The ad, of course, was an argument for the federal position in the referendum.

Until recently, the United States government did not use advertising as a way to create consensus on important policy issues. September 11 changed all that and launched the U.S. government in a myth-making exercise previously unknown in peace time. The efforts of the U.S. government went beyond government advertising or promotion. It represented what Van Ham (2001) calls the ascendancy of "state branding," the pervasive and systemic application of marketing and advertising principles to all aspects of public life.

The task of branding the United States fell to Charlotte Beers, the U.S. undersecretary of state for public diplomacy, whose job was to "shape effective messages explaining U.S. policies in new and ongoing issues" (State Department Website). She was hired just days after the U.S. invasion of Afghanistan in October 2001 and given an unprecedented amount of resources for selling America and its values to the Muslim world in particular. She has described the United States as a "beautiful brand" and television as a "fast delivery system" for the American government's message (McKenna, 2003, p. A4). Some of her techniques, like dropping pamphlets in Afghanistan, have failed miserably. Others, such as the $15 million (U.S.) shared-values campaign featured Muslims talking in glowing terms about their life in the United States, were quietly and quickly scrapped by the State Department. The campaign was decried by many who believed that it was misguided because it did not respond to the perceived problems in U.S. policies but merely papered them over with ads.

While the jury may be still be out on the success of the undersecretary of state for public diplomacy, the U.S. Army has followed its lead. The Army has become a significant advertiser and has attempted to radically refashion its brand beginning with changing their longstanding slogan "Be All That You Can Be" to "An Army of One"—a more individualistic slogan designed to appeal to the short attention span of their target audience—72 million Generation Y kids. The aggressive advertising campaign exists alongside an interactive Website that includes a downloadable video game called "America's Army: Operations," a four-man team arriving at colleges, high schools, or fraternities in a huge yellow Hummer with spray-painted images of army life; and a vehicle giving away army branded hats, jerseys, headbands, wristbands, and dog tags (Joiner, 2003).

While Canadian government advertising is still much more significant than American advertising in creating and developing nationalism, the newest development post-September 11 may change that in the United States.

Conclusion

A case study of American and Canadian political ads tell us much. They remind us how similar the two countries are in terms of the centrality of advertising. They also remind us of crucial differences, born of different political cultures and beliefs about the role of the state in national life. Though significant differences exist, we see a broad convergence in the style and arguments found in campaign ads in the two countries. There are however, significant differences in the way in which governments use advertising. Canadian advertising by the state has a much more robust history of being used to support federalism than in the United States. Still, similarities persist. In both Canada and the United States advertising is deeply embedded in the practice of democracy. Politicians have used rhetoric accessible to citizens since the days of Cicero's orations in Rome. Advertising, in some ways, is merely the most recent manifestation of this kind of public discourse, but perhaps more worrisome, as Daniel Borstin reminds us, "advertising is the characteristic rhetoric of modern democracy." (Borstin, 1962, p. 3) One of the important lessons to be drawn from this study—and any study of political ads—is that a study of modern politics cannot be divorced from an understanding of the actions and behaviors of symbolic handlers who routinely organize, plan, and manage the communications of political actors. The fact that increasingly the way in which we talk about politics is through the lens of advertisements leads not only to an abdication of governing according to Bruce Newman (1999) but also a devaluation of politics itself.

ENDNOTES

1. These ads may be viewed by following the "Government of Canada Ads" link on the Website http://politicalads.ca

2. This ad, "Flight," is also accessible on http://politicalads.ca via the "Government of Canada Ads" link.

REFERENCES

Ansolabehere, Stephen, and Shanto Iyengar, *Going Negative: How Attack Ads Shrink and Polarize the Electorate* (New York: Free Press, 1995).

Bellah, Robert N., Richard Madsen, William M. Sullivan, Ann Swidler, and Steven M. Tipton, *Habits of the Heart: Individualism and Commitment in American Life* (New York: Harper and Row, 1985).

Berton, Pierre, *The Promised Land: Settling the West 1986–1914* (Toronto: McClelland & Stewart, 1984).

Borstin, Daniel, *The Image: A Guide to Pseudo-Events in America,* 1st ed. (New York: Atheneum, 1962).

Briffault, Richard, "Soft Money, Issue Advocacy and the U.S. Campaign Finance Law," *Electoral Insight* 4 (2002), 9–14.

Canada. *Competition Act.* Department of Justice. [http://laws.justice.gc.ca/en/c-34/34286.html] (Accessed 21 January 2003).

Canada. Industry Canada. Office of Consumer Affairs. [http://strategis.ic.gc.ca] (Accessed 4 March, 2003).

Clark, S. D., *The Developing Canadian Community,* 2nd ed. (Toronto: University of Toronto Press, 1971).

Crete, Jean, "Television, Advertising and Canadian Elections." In Fred Fletcher, ed. *Media and Voters in Canadian Election Campaigns.* Volume 18 of the Research Studies. Royal Commission on Electoral Reform and Party Financing (Toronto: Dundurn Press, 1991), 3–43.

Devlin, L. Patrick, "An Analysis of Presidential Television Commercials, 1952–1984." In Lynda Lee Kaid, Dan D. Nimmo, and Keith Sanders, eds., *New Perspectives on Political Advertising* (Carbondale and Edwardsville: Southern Illinois University Press, 1986), 21–54.

Diamond, Edwin, and Stephen Bates, *The Spot: The Rise of Political Advertising on Television,* 3d ed. (Cambridge: MIT Press, 1992).

Easterbrook, W. T., and M. H. Watkins, eds., *Approaches to Canadian Economic History* (Toronto: McClelland and Stewart, 1967).

Elections Canada, *Election Financial Data.* [http://www.elections.ca] (Accessed 24 March 2003).

Ellul, Jacques, *Propaganda: The Formation of Men's Attitudes* (New York: Knopf, 1972).

Endicott, Craig, "100 Leading Advertisers," *Advertising Age* (June 24, 2002).

Federal Elections Commission (United States), *Financial Summary Reports*. [http://hern-don1.sdrdc.com/cgi-bin/cancomsrs/] (Accessed 24 March 2003).

Federal Trade Commission. *Guide to the Federal Trade Commission* [http://www.ftc.gov/bcp/conline/pubs/general/guidetoftc.html] (Accessed 26 February 2003).

Fletcher, Fred, "Playing the Game: The Mass Media and the 1979 Campaign." In Howard Penniman, ed. *Canada at the Polls, 1979 and 1980: A Study of the General Elections* (Washington, DC: American Enterprise Institute, 1981), 280–321.

Fletcher, Fred, "The Media and the 1984 Landslide." In Howard Penniman, ed., *Canada at the Polls, 1984: A Study of the Federal General Elections* (Durham: Duke University Press, 1988), 161–189.

Fletcher, Fred, "Political Communication and Public Discourse," *Canada Watch* 7, December 1999. [http://www.robarts.yourku.ca/canadawatch/vol_7_6/default.htm] (Accessed 22 January 2003).

Fletcher, Fred, and Robert MacDermid, "The Rhetoric of Campaign Advertising in Canada: An Analysis of Party TV Spots in 1997." Paper prepared for the 1998 Annual Conference of the International Association for Media and Communication Research, Glasgow, Scotland. July 29, 1998.

Frizzell, Alan, Jon H. Pammett, and Anthony Westell, *The Canadian General Election of 1988* (Ottawa: Carleton University Press, 1990).

Gamble, David, and Paul Cherry, "Bouchard Defends Bloodbag Campaign," *Montreal Gazette,* February 23, 1999, A1.

Gauthier, Gilles, "Referential Argumentation and Its Ethical Considerations in Televised Political Advertising: The Case of the 1993 Canadian Federal Election Campaign," *Argumentation and Advocacy* 31 (1994), 96–110.

Grant, George, *Lament for a Nation* (Toronto: McClelland and Stewart, 1965).

Hiscock, Jennifer, "Top 100 Advertisers," *Marketing* (February 21, 2002), 24.

Horowitz, Gad, "Conservatism, Liberalism, and Socialism in Canada: An Interpretation," *Canadian Journal of Economics and Political Science* 32 (1966), 143–171.

Howlett, Michael, Alex Netherton, and M. Ramesh, *The Political Economy of Canada: An Introduction,* 2nd ed. (Toronto: Oxford University Press, 1999).

Innis, Harold A., *Essays in Canadian Economic History* (Toronto: University of Toronto Press, 1962).

Innis, Harold A., *The Bias of Communication* (Toronto: University of Toronto Press, 1971).

Institute for Research on Public Policy, *Transparency, Disclosure and Democracy: Assessing the Chief Electoral Officer's Recommendations* (Montreal, IRPP: 2003).

Jamieson, Kathleen Hall, *Dirty Politics: Deception, Distraction, and Democracy* (New York: Oxford University Press, 1992).

Johnson, Karen S., and Camille Elebash, "The Contagion from the Right: The Americanization of British Political Advertising." In Lynda Lee Kaid, Dan D.

Nimmo, and Keith Sanders, eds., *New Perspectives on Political Advertising* (Carbondale and Edwardsville: Southern Illinois University Press, 1986), 293–313.

Joiner, Whitney, "The Army Be Thuggin' It," *Salon Magazine* [http:salon.com], October 17, 2003.

Kaid, Lynda Lee, Dan D. Nimmo, and Keith Sanders, "Introduction." In Lynda Lee Kaid, Dan D. Nimmo, and Keith Sanders, eds., *New Perspectives on Political Advertising* (Carbondale and Edwardsville: Southern Illinois University Press, 1986), xi–xx.

Kleinman, Mark, "Government Reins in Spending on Ads," *Marketing* (July 17, 2003), 3.

Kline, Stephen, Rovin S. Deodat, Arlene Shwetz, and William Leiss, "Political Broadcast Advertising in Canada." In Fred Fletcher, ed. *Election Broadcasting in Canada*. Volume 21 of the Research Studies. Royal Commission on Electoral Reform and Party Financing (Toronto: Dundurn Press, 1991), 223–301.

Kucharsky, Danny, "Waving the Flag: Ottawa and Quebec City Step up the Use of Ads as Overt, and Covert, Weapons in Their Ceaseless War of Words," *Marketing Magazine* (June 12, 2000), 19.

Legislative Assembly of Ontario. *Proceedings*. 36th Parliament. 1st Session. 149. January 22, 1997.

Leiss, William, Stephen Kline, and Sut Jhally, *Social Communication in Advertising: Persons, Products and Images of Well-being*, 2nd ed. (Toronto: Nelson, 1990).

Lipset, Seymour Martin, *Continental Divide: The Values and Institutions of the United States and Canada* (New York: Routledge, 1990).

MacDermid, Robert, "TV Advertising Campaigns in the 1995 Ontario Election." In Sid Noel, ed. *Revolution at Queen's Park: Essays on Governing Ontario* (Toronto: James Lorimer, 1997), 74–106.

MacDermid, Robert, and Greg Albo, "Divided Province, Growing Protests: Ontario Moves Right." In Keith Brownsey and Michael Howlett, eds., *The Provincial State in Canada: Politics in the Provinces and the Territories* (Peterborough: Broadview Press, 2001), 163–202.

Macpherson, C. B., *The Political Theory of Possessive Individualism* (London: Oxford University Press, 1962).

McDowall, Duncan, ed., *Advocacy Advertising: Propaganda or Democratic Right?* (Ottawa: Conference Board of Canada, 1982).

McKenna, Barry, "Chief Pitchwoman for U.S. Resigns Post, Citing Health Reasons," *Globe & Mail*, February 18, 2003, 27.

McRae, Kenneth, "The Structure of Canadian History." In Louis Hartz, ed., *The Founding of New Societies*. (New York: Harcourt, Brace and World, 1964), 219–274.

Mendelsohn, Matthew, *Canada's Social Contract: Evidence from Public Opinion*. Discussion Paper P101. Public Involvement Network. Canadian Policy Research Networks, November 2002.

Mullen, James, and Thomas A. Bowers, "Government Advertising: A Runaway Engine?" *Journal of Advertising* (Winter 1979), 39–44.

Nesbitt-Larking, Paul, *Politics, Society and the Media: Canadian Perspectives* (Peterborough: Broadview Press, 2001).

Newman, Bruce, *The Mass Marketing of Politics: Democracy in an Age of Manufactured Images* (Thousand Oaks, CA: Sage, 1999).

Oliver, Robert E., "Advertising Control Institutions in Canada." In Benjamin D. Singer, ed., *Communications in Canadian Society,* 2nd ed. (Toronto: Addison-Wesley, 1983), 121–130.

O'Neil, Helen, and Stephen Mills, "Political Advertising in Australia: A Dynamic Force Meets a Resilient Object." In Lynda Lee Kaid, Dan D. Nimmo, and Keith Sanders, eds., *New Perspectives on Political Advertising* (Carbondale and Edwardsville: Southern Illinois University Press, 1986), 314–337.

Palda, Kristian S., "Does Advertising Influence Votes? An Analysis of the 1966 and 1970 Quebec Elections," *Canadian Journal of Political Science* 6 (1973), 633–655.

Paletz, David L., *The Media in American Politics: Contents and Consequences* (New York: Longman, 1998).

Posner, Michael, "Repositioning the Right Honorable," *Canadian Business* (May 1992), 40–43.

Putnam, Robert, *Bowling Alone: The Collapse and Revival of American Community* (New York: Simon and Schuster, 2000).

Richards, Jef I., and Clarke L. Caywood, "Symbolic Speech in Political Advertising: Encroaching Legal Barriers." In Frank Biocca, ed., *Television and Political Advertising: Volume 2. Signs, Codes, and Images* (Hillsdale, NJ: Lawrence Erlbaum, 1991), 231–256.

Romanow, Walter, Walter Soderlund, and Richard Price, "Negative Political Advertising: An Analysis of Research in Light of Canadian Practices." In Janet Hiebert (ed.), *Political Ethics: A Canadian Perspective,* Volume 12. The Royal Commission on Electoral Reform and Party Financing (Toronto: Dundurn Press, 1991), 165–193.

Romanow, Walter I., Michel de Repentigny, Stanley B. Cunningham, Walter C. Soderlund, and Kai Hildebrandt, *Television Advertising in Canadian Elections: The Attack Mode, 1993* (Waterloo: Wilfrid Laurier University Press, 1999).

Rose, Jonathan, "Government Advertising in a Crisis: The Quebec Referendum Precedent," *Canadian Journal of Communication* 18 (1993), 173–196.

Rose, Jonathan, *Making "Pictures in Our Heads": Government Advertising in Canada* (Westport, CT: Praeger, 2000).

Rose, Jonathan, "The Advertising of Politics and the Politics of Advertising." In Benjamin D. Singer, ed., *Communications in Canadian Society,* 5th ed. (Toronto: Thompson, 2001), 151–164.

Rose, Jonathan and Alasdair Roberts, "Selling the Goods and Services Tax: Government Advertising and Public Discourse in Canada," *Canadian Journal of Political Science* 28 (1995), 311–330.

Rutherford, Paul, *Endless Propaganda: The Advertising of Public Goods* (Toronto: University of Toronto Press, 2000).

Sandel, Michael, *Democracy's Discontent* (Cambridge: Harvard, 1996).

Singer, Benjamin D., "Advertising: A Sociocultural Force." In Benjamin D. Singer, ed. *Communications in Canadian Society,* 4th ed. (Toronto: Nelson, 1995), 122–137.

Soderlund, Walter C., E. Donald Briggs, Walter I. Romanow, and Ronald H. Wagenberg, *Media and Elections in Canada* (Toronto: Holt, Rinehart and Winston, 1984).

Taras, David, *The Newsmakers: The Media's Influence on Canadian Politics* (Toronto: Nelson, 1990).

Trudel, Pierre, and France Abran, "The Legal and Constitutional Framework for Regulating Election Campaign Broadcasting." In Fred Fletcher (ed.) *Election Broadcasting in Canada,* Volume 21. Royal Commission on Electoral Reform and Party Financing. Research Studies (Toronto: Dundurn Press, 1991), 39–150.

Van Ham, Peter, "The Rise of the Brand State: The Postmodern Politics of Image and Reputation," in *Foreign Affairs* 80:5 (September–October 2001), 2–6.

Yarwood, Dean, and Ben Enis, "Advertising and Publicity Programs in the Executive Branch of the National Government: Hustling or Helping the People," *Public Administration Review* 42:1 (January 1982), 37–47.

12

Moving Voters in the 2000 Presidential Campaign
Local Visits, Local Media

David C. King
David Morehouse

Running for office. That phrase, with an emphasis on the word *running*, conjures for us memories of candidates darting among cities in the closing days of a campaign, of klieg lights on tarmacs, of caffeinated staffers and the tangible yearning among candidates to have their voices heard, to connect with voters, and to be a hundred places and on a million minds simultaneously.

Candidates want to reach potential voters, but more than reaching voters, they want to *move* them. This difference between reaching potential voters and actually moving voters to be supporters is crucial in campaigns, and it is at the heart of our proposition in this chapter: there is a poorly understood trade-off between spending money on television commercials and having candidates make campaign appearances.

Local campaign appearances generate tremendous free local media coverage, which often offsets the "costs" of appearing before relatively small audiences in out-of-the-way parts of America. Indeed, in many instances, local campaign appearances likely move the vote more than higher-priced advertisements.

Running candidates from place to place and running commercials in various places are mainstays of presidential campaigns. We expect, though, that on a dollars-per-vote basis, candidate trips to key regions are very often a more effective way to move voters than blanketing an area with television advertisements. This chapter explores the effects of Vice President Gore's August 2000 Mississippi River trip on moving voter preferences. With a working knowledge of the Gore campaign in particular (one of the authors was a senior advisor and trip director for Vice President Gore), we share new data about the impact of local visits on local polls of likely voters.

A candidate's time is the most precious commodity in presidential campaigns. Money, the fruit of an investment of personal time by candidates, makes it possible for campaigns to use television, radio, print, the Internet, and personal visits. The goal, naturally, is to reach as many voters as possible with a persuasive message or image, then move them to vote for the candidate, and to do so in the most cost-effective ways. The Gore campaign spent $44.6 million on television ads and media consulting services from September through November 2000. Over the same period, $10.7 million went to travel expenses including, among other things, costs for airplanes, hotels, event equipment, and decorations. Based on our analysis of Federal Election Commission reports covering those critical months, $4.14 was spent on television for every $1.00 spent on campaign visits.

Is that ratio, 4.14 to 1, even close to being an optimal trade-off between running commercials and running the candidate? In precise terms, that is an unanswerable question without a randomized control-group experiment, but in general terms, we can make headway in understanding how to assess the trade-off. Recent work by Alan Gerber, Don Green, and David Nickerson at Yale University gives us an indication of how much money it takes to increase voter turnout (which is not the same as turning out a voter for a specific candidate). Using experiments in which potential voters were randomly assigned to control and treatment groups, the Yale studies estimate that door-to-door visits by campaigns cost from $12 to $20 per vote as do phone banks run by volunteers. Professionally run phone banks mobilize relatively few voters and cost $140 to $150 per vote, which is far more costly than direct mail, at $40 per vote (Gerber & Green 2003, 2001a, 2001b, 2000a, 2000b; Gerber, Green, & Nickerson 2003). In a similar set of experiments focusing on a partisan turnout campaign for Michigan Governor Jennifer Granholm in 2002, Friedrichs (2003) found slightly lower costs per vote, but his analysis confirms the futility of relying so heavily, as most presidential campaigns do, on paid phone banks.

The Yale studies have important lessons for presidential campaigns. Candidates will want to avoid cost-ineffective techniques, such as paid phone banks, yet in the 2000 campaign and again in the 2004 Democratic primaries, these phone banks were used in record numbers. The distinction that campaigns need to make, once again, is between reaching voters and moving them. Phone calls reach but do not move many voters. Television advertisements may well reach voters if they are not channel-surfing during commercials, but the advertisements may not move many voters from the "undecided" column. Indeed, voters have become more skeptical of the charges and claims made in campaign ads, and in highly competitive races, viewers may quickly reach a saturation point (Just et al., 1996). Ken Goldstein and his colleagues tracked an astonishing 302,450 presidential spots in the 2000 campaign (Goldstein 2004).

The Bush and Gore campaigns made thousands of strategic choices about allocating both time and money between candidate visits and television advertising buys. Scholarly literature on this falls in two groups, one focusing primarily on local visits (Holbrook 2002, 1996, Campbell 2000, Shaw 1999b, Jones 1998), and the other largely examining the impact of television ads (Shaw 1999a, Freedman & Goldstein 1999, Ansolabehere & Iyengar 1995, Finkel 1993). Both candidate visits and television advertisements certainly have an important impact on votes, but the relative impacts are difficult to gauge. There is no clear causal arrow running from visits to votes or from TV ads to votes. Indeed, voters need to be in some sense predisposed to a candidate for a visit to have an impact (Vavreck, Spiliotes & Fowler 2002) just as television ads have an impact that depends largely on a viewer's ideology and party identification (Joslyn & Ceccoli 1996).

Candidate visits have direct and indirect effects on voters. Some are personally persuaded by a candidate (the direct effect). Many more voters in an area that has been recently been visited by a candidate, however, are moved by the local media coverage of candidate visits. Campaign visits can have very large multiplier effects through local media outlets. Television, especially, reaches voters, but the free local media generated by candidate visits are especially valuable and are likely to have been underappreciated by campaigns.

Local Media

In July 2000 the Gore campaign began discussions on campaign tactics and how to best generate energy and positive press coverage leading into and out of the Democratic Convention. Previous Democratic presidential campaigns had used thematic trips with creative modes of transportation to great effect in generating positive local and national press coverage and energizing the base. For example, in 1992 the Clinton/Gore campaign left New York, site of the 1992 Democratic Convention, in a bus caravan across New York, Pennsylvania, and West Virginia. They subsequently had bus trips in the Lake Erie region, Texas, Georgia, and North Carolina. These were designed to go through battleground states and hit both small towns and large media markets while conveying a sense of connectedness with everyday Americans. The rolling bus trips became a campaign metaphor for the Clinton campaign and were credited with playing a pivotal role in Clinton's upset win over the incumbent George Bush.

Local newspapers and television stations are eager to cover campaign events, and they tend to approach politics with less cynicism than one finds among the national press corps. Candidates covered by local media outlets generate sustained stories, often crossing several news cycles. Furthermore, voters pay closer attention to local television news than they do to national news coverage of campaigns.

A Pew Research Center survey, conducted in the wake of the 2002 off-year elections, reported on 2,745 respondents who were asked: "Did you get most of your news about the election campaigns from network TV news, from local TV news, or from cable news networks such as CNN or MSNBC?" Local television news came in first with 35%, followed by newspapers, cable television, and radio at 33%, 21%, and 13%, respectively. Just 7% reported getting most of their campaign news from network television stations (Pew 2003).

Local media coverage, one should hasten to add, is free. And while many viewers now channel surf during political commercials, viewers are more likely to stay tuned while local television news stories—replete with video of the high school marching band—are running. And a candidate's interview with a trusted local columnist or news anchor is often more compelling than an Associated Press story by a remote reporter in Texas or Tennessee.

In 1996, the Clinton/Gore campaign, trying to replicate some of the campaign magic from the 1992 campaign, decided to use a train instead of a bus to travel to Chicago for the convention. The train started in Huntington, West Virginia, and traveled on a whistle-stop tour through Ohio, Kentucky, and Illinois on its way to the convention. This trip also managed to create energy, mobilize supporters, generate positive local press coverage, and provide a novelty for the national media.

Part of the geographic strategy of both of these trips was not only to travel through targeted states, but to stop in second- and third-tier cities and towns that were within reasonable proximity to larger media market hubs, and preferably multimedia markets. This strategy allowed the campaign to go into crucial swing areas that do not normally get many presidential candidate visits. These towns often provided a more Americana-oriented backdrop for the candidate and a friendlier audience.

Consider President Clinton's February 19, 1993, stop in Chillicothe, Ohio, a town of 23,000 located an hour and a half south of Columbus. The local media covered an event at which more than half of the town showed up, and television stations from Columbus and Dayton sent news crews to cover the visit. President Clinton returned to Chillicothe on August 25, 1996, for a campaign appearance that generated tremendous local news coverage. As Chaz Osburn, managing editor for the *Chillicothe Gazette,* explained to other editors in the Gannet Newspaper chain (News Watch, 2000):

> President Clinton's stop in Chillicothe was significant for two reasons. First, he *is* the president. But even more interesting was that Clinton had come to Chillicothe 42 months earlier, in February 1993, to conduct his first town meeting as president. So his 90-minute stop here on Aug. 25 was, in a way, a homecoming of sorts.

We were tipped off by Bob Gabordi, whose staff was well into covering plans for the whistlestop, to the possibility of a visit. The dog days of summer came crashing to a halt with that call: every available reporter was reassigned to nail down the story.

As it turned out, Clinton's visit was lead story material for nine days. Once the stop was confirmed, we ran a box asking people what question they would ask Clinton if they had the opportunity and forwarded those to Clinton's staff the day before he arrived. We also tried to include plenty of coping information—where to call for tickets, what could be brought to the site, etc.

For our main story the day before Clinton's arrival, we contacted some of the people who had asked Clinton questions during his '93 visit—a visit in which he talked about accountability—to find out what they thought of the job the president has been doing since then. Because of the timeliness (Clinton arrived in Chillicothe at 8:05 P.M.) and newsworthiness of the visit, we published a morning edition rather than an afternoon edition for that Monday.

During the general election in 2000 the Gore campaign spent $10.7 million on candidate travel, yet they did not base this expenditure on any quantifiable data. They, like other campaigns before and after, simply know that candidate visits to targeted areas have a positive effect on voters. Why?

Candidate visits serve to motivate the base, recruit volunteers, generate enthusiasm, and produce sustained positive local press coverage. They also allow the candidate to connect with voters, raise money, and communicate their message.

At the campaign managers conference, sponsored by the Institute of Politics and held at Harvard's Kennedy School of Government in 2001, Karl Rove, the Bush strategist, made two observations about campaign stops (Institute of Politics, 2002). Asked if he could have done anything different in 2000, what would it would have been, Rove answered that he would have gotten a faster plane—a metaphor for making more campaign stops. Second, when asked what he thought was the best tactical move the Gore campaign made, he responded that he thought it was the Mississippi River trip after the Democratic Convention. He went on to say that it was good because it got the candidate "glowing news coverage in some relatively inaccessible areas of eastern Iowa, and other key battle ground states." He did not say that ad buys in this or that place should have been increased or decreased. He did not say that message could have been tweaked. He talked about the Mississippi River trip and the importance of other local campaign events.

In the last six weeks of the 2000 campaign, Al Gore spent a total of 4 nights out of 34 at his home near the Naval Observatory in Washington, DC. For 3 of the 4 nights at home, he had day trips to Wisconsin, Iowa, and Michigan. Why this tremendous investment in time campaigning? While researchers have spent a considerable amount of time and effort on focus groups and the effects of advertising, mail drops, door knocking, parental preferences, and phone banks, the effects of candidate appearances and their impact on local media need to be better understood.

Moving Voters along the Mississippi River

Local visits move poll numbers for candidates, though the evidence on this is often difficult to disentangle because television advertisements are typically bought for the same period. Table 12.1 shows state visits by Vice President Gore and Governor Bush from October 18, 2000, through election day, November 7. State-level polling data can be especially useful in the closing days of a campaign when only a few swing states are in play (Franklin 2002). Using state-level polling data provided by Charles Franklin we calculated, whenever possible, the Bush and Gore advantages in polls one week prior to a state visit and one week after a state visit. The boost

Table 12.1 Presidential Candidate Visits, October 18 through November 7, 2000.

	October 2000														November 2000						
	18	19	20	21	22	23	24	25	26	27	28	29	30	31	1	2	3	4	5	6	7
Bush	WI MI	MI NY	NH ME			IA WI	IL TN FL	FL	PA OH	MI IN	WI MO		NM CA	CA OR WA	MN IA	MO IL WI	MI WV	MI PA NJ	FL	TN WI IA AR	TX
Cheney	PA NJ	WV IL	MN WI MI	MI			WA OR NV	NM LA	TN OH	WV PA	WI IA		IA IL	MO AR LA	FL	TX IL PA	PA NH ME	MI WI NM	CA NV	NV OR WA	WY
Gore	MO IA MI	NY	NY MO LA	PA	TX NM OR	WA	AR LA TN	TN MO	IA WI	WV PA	PA MN	MI	MI WI	OR CA	FL PA	PA IL NM	MO TN	TN WV PA	PA MI WI	IA MO MI	FL TN
Lieberman	WI MD NY NJ	NY NJ	PA			FL	TN IN	TN	NM NV	WA		MI	WI	ME NH FL	FL AR	MO WI MN PA	FL	FL AR	NM NV OR WA	MN WI ME NH PA	FL

Source: Compiled by the authors from candidates' daily schedules.

from these visits averaged 1.56 percentage points for Bush and 1.40 percentages points for Gore.

The state-level results from the last few weeks of the campaign are instructive, and small percentage point swings in key states may well have made all the difference in the campaign. However, state-level analysis fails to capture the kind of boost in visibility that candidates can get from local visits and friendly small-market media outlets. President Clinton's visits to places like Chillicothe, Ohio, were very much on the minds of Vice President Gore's campaign staff.

With the 1992 and 1996 successes as the backdrop, the 2000 Gore campaign held a series of meetings to discuss what could be done to break out double-digit losses to George Bush in early August public opinion polls. The campaign was looking for something that would have a serious electoral effect. Media consultants, Bob Shrum and Carter Eskew joined a campaign leadership team consisting of Tad Devine, Chris Lehane, Mark Fabiani, David Morehouse, Jim Loftus, and Sam Myers. They gathered to decide what "bold strike" the campaign could unleash.

Tad Devine was, among other things, in charge of allocating resources to the various competing entities within the campaign (administration, advertising, travel, field operations, grassroots organizing, etc.). Knowing that the Bush campaign had a significant money advantage made any strategic or tactical decision involving money that much more important. For the Gore campaign, there was not much room for error. In budgeting, Devine said, "No one got everything they wanted as far as money is concerned, but each ultimately got what they needed."

During the discussion, Morehouse, Loftus, and Myers made a case for a Mississippi River boat trip. They laid out the plan that would, in effect, be the bold plan the campaign was looking for. The plan called for Al Gore, Tipper Gore, and the newly named vice presidential nominee, Senator Joseph Lieberman and his wife Hadassah, to embark on a riverboat trip immediately after the convention. The trip would take place on what was described as the "spine of America," the Mississippi River.

The trip was designed as a means of generating the visual images that the campaign was looking for and creating enthusiasm and positive press coverage in several targeted states. As part of the message development and targeting strategy, it was agreed that the trip would start in La Crosse, Wisconsin and travel through eastern Iowa, western Illinois, and Missouri, picking up small-town local media coverage as well as coverage from the Milwaukee, Des Moines, Chicago, and St. Louis media markets.

As Karl Rove stated, the trip generated glowing local press coverage and allowed Gore and Lieberman to travel to relatively remote but important stops in key states. Stops along the way were planned for La Crosse and Prairie Du Chien, Wisconsin, on August 18, 2000; Dubuque, Bellevue, and Clinton, Iowa, on August 19; Moline, Illinois, on August 20 as well as Muscatine, Burlington, and Keokuk, Iowa, on the same day. The trip concluded with stops in Quincy, Illinois, and Hannibal, Missouri, on August 21.

The cost of the entire trip was roughly $600,000. Paid media penetration would have cost several million dollars for the same level of media exposure within those same markets. The trip also facilitated paid media for weeks after the trip ended. By using the trip as a stage from which to shoot campaign ads, the Gore campaign was able to prolong the sense of enthusiasm the convention produced more than three weeks after it happened, rather than the two days Gore spent at the convention.

The reaction of local media in Prairie Du Chien, Wisconsin, was much like that generated by President Clinton's visit to Chillicothe, Ohio, four years earlier. The *Courier Press* began blanket coverage of the visit from the moment it was announced. "If all goes well," reported the *Courier Press* on August 14, 2000, "and the timing is right, the Mississippi Blackhawk Water Ski Show Team will be leading the Mark Twain Riverboat with Al and Tipper Gore on board as they approach Lawler Park Friday night." As described in the August 21, 2000, *Courier Press*, "Thousands enthusiastically gathered at Lawler Park Friday evening to greet Al and Tipper Gore. The Mark Twain Riverboat docked at 7:50 P.M. to the cheers of the crowd while 'Take Me to the River' sounded from large speakers. Al and Tipper Gore stepped onto stage while 'Hometown' by John Cougar Mellencamp played. The Gores followed short speeches by Attorney General James Doyle and Congressman Ron Kind. . . . Following the 15-minute speech, Gore spent more than a half hour shaking hands with the crowd. He also met the ski team, and received a Mississippi Blackhawk windbreaker."

One would expect such enthusiastic and sustained local media attention to move voters closer to Gore, but the impact of local visits has traditionally been difficult to gauge. Internal Gore campaign polling, kindly provided here by campaign strategist Harrison Hickman, maps the impact of the Mississippi River Trip in several local media markets. (The data for Illinois are based on regions, not media markets per se.) Polls were taken in late July 2000, during the river trip in August, and again in September. Polls in areas that were visited during the trip are highlighted in bold in Table 12.2.

Table 12.2 Gore Campaign Internal Polling around the Mississippi River Trip

	Gore	Bush	Other/Und.	Net Gore	Gore	Bush	Other/Und.	Net Gore	Gore	Bush	Other/Und.	Net Gore
Iowa Media Markets	July 22–25				August 19–23				September 5–8			
Des Moines	45	40	14	5	46	46	8	0	49	41	10	8
Cedar Rapids	45	36	19	9	51	40	9	11	49	36	15	13
Quad Cities	31	44	25	-13	41	47	12	-6	41	43	16	-2
Sioux City	37	43	20	-6	35	52	14	-17	37	44	19	-7
Other	42	43	15	-1	47	40	13	7	39	49	12	-10
Illinois Regions	July 27–30				August 19–23				September 10–12			
Chicago	60	32	9	28	63	30	7	33	59	27	13	32
Other Cook Co	50	44	6	6	48	40	11	8	51	39	10	12
Chicago Suburbs	39	51	10	-12	40	46	15	-6	38	51	11	-13
Downstate No.	41	45	14	-4	51	39	10	12	60	31	9	29
Downstate So.	47	40	13	7	43	45	13	-2	48	45	7	3
Wisconsin Media Markets	July 22–25				August 21–24				September 5–8			
Milwaukee	36	46	18	-10	43	45	12	-2	46	42	12	4
Green Bay	36	46	19	-10	44	51	6	-7	45	42	14	3
Wausau	46	41	13	5	47	51	1	-4	46	42	11	4
La Crosse	34	41	24	-7	50	37	13	13	46	39	15	7
Madison	50	37	13	13	49	36	15	13	45	38	17	7
Other	54	25	20	29	58	33	9	25	35	47	18	-12

Note: Media Markets and Regions highlighted in bold were visited during the Mississippi River Trip.
Source: Compiled by the authors with Gore 2000 presidential campaign internal polling, provided by Harrison Hickman, Global Strategy Group.

Contrasted with state-level polls, the results in Table 12.2 give us a much clearer look at the impact of campaign visits. The La Crosse and Eau Clair, Wisconsin, media market is fairly well encapsulated, separate from the Madison and Wausau markets. In 2000 there were 153,630 Wisconsin homes and 23,860 Minnesota homes in the La Crosse market. Polls there in late July had Gore trailing Bush 41% to 34%, with 24% of the voters undecided. In the wake of the Mississippi River trip, Gore led Bush by 13 percentage points, and the number of undecided voters was nearly cut in half. Prairie Du Chien is in Crawford County, Wisconsin, and in November Gore won the 57% of the vote. Four years earlier, with Ross Perot also in the race, President Clinton received just under 52% in the county. In the cities of La Crosse and Prairie Du Chien, Gore handily won every ward.

The impact on Gore's support found in the La Crosse media market was repeated all the way down the river. Within the four locally polled areas visited during the trip, Gore's net gain was 11.25 percentage points. Notably, the undecided voters fell 9.5 percentage points. That kind of a drop in undecideds over less than a month is virtually unknown in modern presidential campaigns. Elsewhere in the same states, Gore's net support dropped slightly (by a half of a percentage point), and the undecideds fell just 3.3 percent. The Mississippi River trip played well locally, but it also made news nationally. Every network covered the trip, and the tone of the coverage was captured by a *Christian Science Monitor* article on August 21, 2000, headlined "For Gore, Finally, Momentum Arrives."

In the areas visited by Vice President Gore, the effects of the river trip lingered well into September. His net gain over Bush in those media markets rose 11.25% in August to 16.5% by September. There appears to have been a strong friends-and-neighbors effect that was not counteracted by heavy Bush campaign spending on television advertisements in those same markets.

While the polling discussed above was commissioned by the Gore campaign, the numbers were not reviewed until well after the November elections. There was casual talk that the Mississippi River trip helped win Wisconsin and Iowa, but, as shown in Table 12.1, Governor Bush and Vice President Gore made several trips, and according to Goldstein (2004) spent a lot of money on television in those two states in the closing days of the campaign. Gore bought more advertising in Wisconsin than Bush did in those closing days, but the two were about even in Iowa.

The polling numbers in Iowa and Wisconsin, combined with the numbers of households in the various media markets, suggest that the Mississippi River trip was, indeed, crucial to Gore's successes in both states. Consider

Table 12.3, which shows the number of households in the Iowa media markets as of 2000.

Assume for simplicity that one person voted for either Bush or Gore from each household. Then multiply the increase from July to September in the Gore polls in each area following the Mississippi River trip. (The Quincy market is tracked in Table 12.2 under the Downstate North polls.) To be conservative in our estimates, we also assume that once election day came, the effect of the Mississippi River Trip was just half of that found in the September polls. Under these conditions, the trip generated 6,004 votes in the Cedar Rapids media market, 7,859 in the Quad Cities area, and 2,468 in the Quincy market. That is a total of 16,331 votes or about four times the actual vote difference of 4,114 on election day. Gore won in Iowa 638,517 to 634,373. A similar analysis of media markets in Wisconsin, which Gore won by 5,708 votes, also suggests the pivotal importance of those mid-August local visits.

After the success of the Mississippi River trip, the campaign explored three other potential river excursions. One, along the Ohio River going through Pennsylvania, Ohio, West Virginia, and Kentucky; another along the lower Mississippi River through Tennessee, Arkansas, and Louisiana; and finally one along the intercoastal waterway in southeastern Florida. Again, the idea was to travel through targeted battleground states generating sustained positive local news coverage and providing a metaphoric backdrop of campaigning along the nation's waterways stopping in river towns along the way.

Table 12.3 Iowa Media Markets by Number of Households, 2000.

Market	Households (1,091,700 total)	Percentage
Cedar Rapids-Waterloo & Dubuque	300,200	27.50%
Davenport - Rock Island - Moline	130,990	12.00%
Des Moines-Ames	371,960	34.07%
Mankato	4,240	0.39%
Omaha	74,460	6.82%
Ottumwa-Kirksville	27,510	2.52%
Quincy-Hannibal-Keokuk	14,960	1.37%
Rochester-Mason City-Austin	53,600	4.91%
Sioux City	106,880	9.79%
Sioux Falls (Mitchell)	6,900	0.63%

Source: Compiled by the authors with data available through LUC Media, Inc.
http://www.lucmedia.com/mkst.html

The Ohio River trip was not pursued mainly because the campaign made a strategic decision not to continue to pour resources into Ohio and to take Ohio off of its list of states to target (however, even without Ohio, the trip still would have gone through western Pennsylvania and West Virginia, two very important regions for the campaign). In Florida, the campaign sent Jim Loftus, director of advance, to scout possible routes along the waterways there. He came back with a plan to travel through West Palm Beach County, Broward County, and Dade County.

Ultimately a decision was made not to do any additional river trips. The relatively high travel cost, combined with the amount of time spent meandering along the rivers between stops, were two of the reasons the campaign did not pursue these tactics, but the main reason was resource allocation. The general consensus at the time was simply that money was better spent on paid advertising. That general consensus, however, was not informed by any close look at the polling numbers nor clear sense for how many news cycles could be dominated by local coverage.

Given the money disadvantage the Gore campaign had in comparison with the Bush campaign, there was no room to maneuver when trying to match ad buys, dollar for dollar, in the targeted markets. Despite the near unanimous anecdotal evidence that the boat trip generated both the positive press coverage and the energy the campaign was looking for, the collective mind set of the campaign defaulted to the accepted means for moving voters—paid advertising.

Looking back, in a race as close as 2000 proved to be, there are any number of individual strategic and tactical decisions that in retrospect, could have tilted the outcome in Vice President Gore's favor. Would another river trip through Tennessee, Louisiana, or Kentucky have moved enough voters to give those states to Gore? Probably not. Would another trip through Ohio, Arkansas, or West Virginia have given Gore an advantage? Maybe. Would a trip in Florida, through three of the four counties that ultimately became recount counties, have given Gore the additional 537 votes he needed to win the state? Most likely so.

Discussion

In the wake of the 2000 presidential elections, Karl Rove resolved to build the Republican Party's grassroots get-out-the-vote efforts. The key to that strategy involved local presidential visits timed to bring out the party faithful and attract local media coverage. To that end, President Bush campaigned on behalf of members of Congress in the months leading up to the 2002 off-year elections. In one year he made six low-visibility campaign trips to Georgia on behalf of senatorial hopeful Saxby Chambliss. By flying into Georgia after dinner and leaving by midnight, President Bush avoided the national media and gathered local press coverage (Carney & Dickerson 2002). Even his daytime visits to Georgia, however, such as an October 17, 2002, luncheon for Chambliss, were covered exclusively by the local press.

In his first 14 months in office, President Bush made more local campaign trips on behalf of congressional candidates than President Clinton had during his full first term. Flying out of Washington, DC, after the national media had compiled the nightly television news, President Bush tended to get strong local news coverage for his visits without generating much national interest in his activities. In those first 14 months, President Bush attended fundraisers that netted Republican congressional candidates $66.8 million. Doug Sosnick, who served as political director in Clinton's White House said of the Bush organization, "They're far more organized, far more disciplined and far more political than we were. And they're smart enough not to talk about it." (Keen 2002)

Of course, it is much easier to travel among local media markets when one is on Air Force One than when one is struggling for attention in a presidential campaign. As campaigns move into general election mode, television—not local visits and local media—has been king. Recall that the ratio of money spent on television ads versus travel in the 2000 Gore general election campaign was 4.14 to 1. We suspect that would be far too high for any primary campaign. Candidates in general elections may be too quick to abandon the kinds of vote-getting techniques they used during the caucuses and primaries. The Iowa caucuses and the New Hampshire primaries are all about local visits and local media. Money is spent on television advertisements, but these campaigns are won and lost by the strength of "troops on the ground." Yet after the party conventions, candidates tend to run national campaigns largely through television ads.

Presidential campaigns are not truly national events though. In 2004, perhaps no more than 15 states will be up for grabs, including: Arizona, Florida, Iowa, Maine, Michigan, Minnesota, Missouri, Nevada, New Hampshire, New Mexico, Ohio, Oregon, Pennsylvania, West Virginia, and Wisconsin (Seelye 2003). Soon after the 2000 election, President Bush began focusing his trips on those states. In his first two years in office, President Bush visited Ohio, for example, every nine weeks on average (Riechmann 2003). On December 4, 2003, when President Bush announced an end to U.S. steel tariffs, he did so while making his twenty-third visit to Pennsylvania—the most visits to any state in which the president did not also have a home (DeCoursey 2003).

As the 2004 presidential campaign heats up in the wake of the Democratic and Republican conventions, television advertisements will again seem pervasive—especially in those few states that will actually be up for grabs. With that air war, well funded on both sides, filling networks, we expect to see both candidates moving voters, not just reaching voters though sustained small-market campaign visits in key states. For far less than the costs of a national advertising, Vice President Gore moved voters to his side with the August 2002 Mississippi River trip. Those voters in Hannibal and La Crosse and Muscatine were critical voters in key states. The lessons of Mississippi River journey have not been lost on campaign operatives in either political party.

REFERENCES

"3,500-plus Attend Gore Rally in PdC." 2000. *Courier Press* (Prairie Du Chien, Wisconsin), August 21, 2002, A1.

Ansolabehere, Stephen, & Shanto Iyengar. 1995. *Going Negative: How Political Ads Shrink and Polarize the Electorate.* New York: Free Press.

Campbell, James. 2000. *The American Campaign.* College Station: Texas A&M Press.

Carney, James, & John F. Dickerson. 2002. "W. and the 'Boy Genius.'" *Time,* November 9, 2002.

"City Prepares for Gore 2000." 2000. *Courier Press* (Prairie Du Chien, Wisconsin), August 14, 2002, A1.

DeCoursey, Peter L. "Tariff's End Will Hit State Hard." *Patriot News,* December 5, 2003.

Finkel, Steven. 1993. "Re-examining the Minimal Effects Model in Recent Presidential Campaigns." *Journal of Politics* 55, 1–21.

Franklin, Charles H. 2002. "Pre-Election Polls in Nation and State: A Dynamic Bayesian Hierarchical Model." Typescript. University of Wisconsin.

Freedman, Paul, & Ken Goldstein. 1999. "Measuring Media Exposure and the Effects of Negative Campaign Ads." *American Journal of Political Science* 43 (4), 1189–1208.

Friedrichs, Ryan. 2003. "Mobilizing 18–35 Year Old Voters: An Analysis of the Michigan Democratic Party's 2002 Youth Coordinated Campaign." Typescript, Harvard University.

Gerber, Alan S., and Donald P. Green. 2000a. "The Effect of a Nonpartisan Get-out-the-Vote Drive: An Experimental Study of Leafleting." *The Journal of Politics* 62:3 (August), 846–857.

Gerber, Alan S., and Donald P. Green. 2000b. "The Effects of Canvassing, Telephone Calls, and Direct Mail on Voter Turnout: A Field Experiment." *American Political Science Review* 94:3 (September 2000) 653–63.

Gerber, Alan S., and Donald P. Green. 2001a. "Do Phone Calls Increase Voter Turnout? A Field Experiment." *Public Opinion Quarterly* 65, 75–85.

Gerber, Alan S., and Donald P. Green. 2001b. "Getting out the Youth Vote: Results from Randomized Field Experiments." Unpublished report to the Pew Charitable Trusts and Yale University's Institute for Social and Policy Studies, December 29.

Gerber, Alan S., and Donald P. Green. 2003. "Mobilizing African Americans Using Mail and Commercial Phone Banks: A Field Experiment." Unpublished report, Institute for Social and Political Studies, Yale University, January 2.

Gerber, Alan S., Donald P. Green, and David W. Nickerson. 2003. "Getting out the Youth Vote in Local Elections: Results from Six Door-to-Door Canvassing Experiments." *Journal of Politics*. 64(4), 1083–1096.

Goldstein, Ken. 2004. "What Did They See and When Did They See It?" in *The Medium and the Message*, Ken Goldstein and Patty Strach, eds. Upper Saddle River, NJ: Prentice Hall.

Holbrook, Thomas M. 1996. *Do Campaigns Matter?* Thousand Oaks, CA: Sage Publications.

Holbrook, Thomas M. 2002. "Did the Whistle-Stop Matter?" *PS: Political Science* (March 2002): 59–66.

Institute of Politics. 2002. *Campaign for President: The Managers Look at 2000.* Hollis, NH: Hollis Publishing.

Jones, Jeffrey M. 1998. "Does Bringing out the Candidate Bring out the Votes?" *American Politics Quarterly* 26 (4), 395–419.

Joslyn, Mark R., & Steve Ceccoli. 1996. "Attentiveness to Television News and Opinion Change in the Fall 1992 Presidential Campaign. *Political Behavior* 18(2),141–170.

Just, Marion R., Ann N. Crigler, Dean E. Alger, Timothy E. Cook, Montague Kern, and Darrell M. West. 1996. *Crosstalk: Citizens, Candidates and the Media in a Presidential Campaign.* Chicago: University of Chicago Press.

Keen, Judy. 2002. "Bush Isn't on the Ballot, but His Influence Is." *USA Today,* April 28.

News Watch. 2000. Gannet News Service. Comments on the Internet at http://update.usato-day.com/go/newswatch/96/nw0908-3.htm

Pew Research Center for the People and the Press. 2003. "November 2002 Campaign and Internet (Poll), October 30–November 24, 2002. Released January 5, 2003.

Riechmann, Deb. 2003. "Between Fund-raisers, Bush Visits Ohio Factory." Associated Press National Wire, October 30.

Seelye, Katharine Q. 2003. "Shifts in States May Give Bush Electoral Edge." *New York Times,* December 2.

Shaw, Daron. 1999a. "The Effect of TV Ads and Candidate Appearances on Statewide Presidential Votes, 1988–1996." *American Political Science Review.* 93, 345–961.

Shaw, Daron. 199b. "A Study of Presidential Campaign Event Effects from 1952 to 1992." *Journal of Politics* 61(2), 387–422.

Vavreck, Lynn, Constantine J. Spiliotes, & Linda L. Fowler. 2002. "The Effects of Retail Politics in the New Hampshire Primary." *American Journal of Political Science* 46(3), 595–610.

Contributors

MELISSA CULLY ANDERSON is a doctoral candidate in political science at the University of California, Berkeley, focusing on American politics and public law. Her dissertation examines variation in state-level electoral reform during the Progressive era and the post-WWII period.

CHRISTOPHER A. COOPER (Ph.D. University of Tennessee) is Assistant Professor of Political Science and Social Science Analyst at the Center for Regional Development at Western Carolina University. His research on state politics, political communication, political behavior, and interest groups has appeared in *American Politics Research, Political Research Quarterly, Social Science Quarterly, State Politics and Policy Quarterly*, and other journals.

BRENDAN DOHERTY is a doctoral candidate in political science at the University of California, Berkeley. He is currently working on a dissertation that investigates the geographic distribution of presidential action to assess the extent to which U.S. presidents behave as if they were single-minded seekers of reelection.

CHRIS J. DOLAN (Ph.D. University of South Carolina) is Assistant Professor of Political Science at the University of Central Florida. Professor Dolan's teaching and research focuses on the Presidency, Congress, and the mass media and appears in *International Politics, Policy Studies Journal, Congress and the Presidency, White House Studies, Politics and Policy, American Diplomacy,* and in several upcoming edited volumes, such as *Debating the Presidency, Debating the Issues, George W. Bush: A Political and Ethical Assessment at the Midterm, Contemporary Presidential Studies: A Reader,* and *American National Security and Civil Liberties in an Age of Terrorism.* His co-edited volume *Striking First* will appear in November 2004, and his book *President Bush and the Morality of Offensive War* will be published in 2005.

AMY E. JASPERSON (Ph.D. University of Minnesota) has been Assistant Professor of Political Science at the University of Texas at San Antonio since 1999. She also serves as Director of the Media & Elections Studio, which she helped to establish in 2002 as a center for data collection and research in political communication. She has published in a variety of edited books and journals including, *Political Communication, Polity, the Journal of Advertising,* and the *American University Journal of Gender, Social Policy and the Law* and has appeared locally on San Antonio television and served as a commentator on campaigns and elections for media sources in the United States, Spain, and Mexico.

DAVID C. KING is Associate Professor of Public Policy at Harvard University's John F. Kennedy School of Government, where he also serves as the Research Director for the Institute of Politics. He teaches about the U.S. Congress and runs Harvard's program for Newly Elected Members of Congress. He is the author of three books and numerous articles.

H. GIBBS KNOTTS (Ph.D. Emory University) is Assistant Professor and MPA Director in the Department of Political Science and Public Affairs at Western Carolina University. His research has been published in such academic journals as *The Journal of Politics, The American Review of Politics,* and *PS: Political Science & Politics* and cited in mainstream publications including *The Washington Post* and *The National Journal.*

STEPHEN K. MEDVIC is Assistant Professor of government at Franklin & Marshall College. In addition to numerous academic articles and book chapters, he is the author of *Political Consultants in U.S. Congressional Elections* and co-editor of *Shades of Gray: Perspectives on Campaign Ethics.*

DAVID MOREHOUSE is a veteran of four presidential campaigns. He served as Communications Director in Senator John Kerry's 2004 presidential bid, and in during the 2000 campaign, he was Vice President Gore's Senior Counselor and Trip Director. Morehouse joined the Kerry campaign upon leaving Harvard University's John F. Kennedy School of Government, where he was Deputy Director of Executive Education. He held several positions in the Clinton administration including Director of Strategic Planning and Communications at the White House Office of Drug Control Policy (ONDCP), Deputy Director of Presidential Advance at the White House, and Special Assistant to the Secretary of Defense.

PAUL NESBITT-LARKING is Associate Professor and Chair of Political Science at Huron University College in Canada. Recently elected to the international governing council of the International Society of Political Psychology, Nesbitt-Larking is currently a participant in two cross-national research projects in the fields of distributive justice and globalization, racism and xenophobia. His recent publications include *Politics, Society and the Media: Canadian Perspectives* and articles in *Political Psychology, The London Review of Canadian Studies, The Interamerican Journal of Psychology* and *The Canadian Journal of Political Science*.

GEOFFREY D. PETERSON is Assistant Professor of Political Science at the University of Wisconsin-Eau Claire and director of the University of Wisconsin-Eau Claire Political Research Institute. His work has appeared in *Political Behavior, Congress & the Presidency, American Indian Quarterly,* and *The Journal of Political Marketing,* and he is currently working on a textbook on the politics of film.

JONATHAN ROSE is Associate Professor of Political Studies at Queen's University in Kingston, Ontario, where he teaches courses in political communication, the mass media and an introduction to politics. He has taught at Queen's and St. Lawrence University in New York and Kwansei Gakuin University in Japan. He is the author of *Making Pictures in our Heads, Government Advertising in Canada* published the co-editor of *Canada: The State of the Federation* (1998) and is the lead author of *First Ministers' Conference, the Art of Negotiation.*

ARTHUR SANDERS is Professor of Politics and Director of the Honors Program at Drake University in Des Moines, Iowa. He is author of three books, most recently *Prime Time Politics* (2002), an exploration of the impact of television on American politics. His other books and articles examine various aspects of American politics including public opinion, political parties, elections and campaign finance. He is currently working on a book on the changing nature of the Presidential election process.

DAVID L. SCHECTER (Ph.D. University of Florida) is Assistant Professor of Political Science at California State University, Fresno and Director of the Graduate MPA Program. His recent publications have appeared in *Legislative Studies Quarterly, Women and Politics* and *Public Integrity*. During the 2003 California recall campaign Schecter was frequently called on by the print and television media for commentary.

DAVID SCHULTZ is Professor in the Graduate School of Public Administration and Management at Hamline University. Professor Schultz also holds appointments in the Hamline University Department of Criminal Justice and Forensic Science, as well as at the law schools of Hamline University, University of Minnesota, and University of St. Thomas. He is the author of 16 books and over 40 articles on American politics, with his most recent publications including *Encyclopedia of Public Administration and Public Policy* (2003); *Social Capital: Critical Perspectives on Community and Bowling Alone* (2002); *Money, Politics, and Campaign Finance Reform Law in the States* (2002); and *It's Show Time! Media, Politics, and Popular Culture* (2000).

TIMOTHY VERCELLOTTI (Ph.D. University of North Carolina-Chapel Hill) is an assistant professor in the Department of Political Science at Elon University in Elon, NC. He also directs the Elon University Poll, a statewide survey of North Carolinians that is conducted six times per year. He teaches courses in American politics, political behavior, public opinion polling, and state and local government.

**Popular Politics
& Governance
In America**

Steven E. Schier, General Editor

Popular Politics and Governance in America, a new series of books on contemporary political science, seeks to publish scholarly and teaching materials about the processes of popular politics and the operations of governmental institutions at both the national and state levels. Although many titles in this series will appeal to graduate and professional audiences, they will employ qualitative and quantitative analysis in fashions primarily appropriate for undergraduate classrooms. Topics will include studies of parties, interest groups, elections, public opinion, chief executives, legislatures, and the bureaucracy. Peter Lang views this new series as a flagship among their several on-going series that have published numerous well-received and useful volumes in political science.

For additional information about this series or for the submission of manuscripts, please contact:

Peter Lang Publishing, Inc.
275 Seventh Avenue, 28th floor
New York, New York 10001

To order other books in this series, please contact our Customer Service Department:

(800) 770-LANG (within the U.S.)
(212) 647-7706 (outside the U.S.)
(212) 647-7707 FAX

Or browse online by series:

www.peterlangusa.com